T0298457

Industry Automation:
The Technologies, Platforms and Use Cases

RIVER PUBLISHERS SERIES IN AUTOMATION, CONTROL AND ROBOTICS

Series Editors:

ISHWAR K. SETHI
Oakland University, USA

TAREK SOBH
University of Bridgeport, USA

FENG QIAO
Shenyang JianZhu University, China

The "River Publishers Series in Automation, Control and Robotics" is a series of comprehensive academic and professional books which focus on the theory and applications of automation, control and robotics. The series focuses on topics ranging from the theory and use of control systems, automation engineering, robotics and intelligent machines.

Books published in the series include research monographs, edited volumes, handbooks and textbooks. The books provide professionals, researchers, educators, and advanced students in the field with an invaluable insight into the latest research and developments.

Topics covered in the series include, but are by no means restricted to the following:

- Robots and Intelligent Machines
- Robotics
- Control Systems
- Control Theory
- Automation Engineering

For a list of other books in this series, visit www.riverpublishers.com

Industry Automation: The Technologies, Platforms and Use Cases

Editors

Pethuru Raj

Edge AI Division, Reliance Jio Platforms Ltd, Bangalore, India

Abhishek Kumar

Chandigarh University, Punjab, India

Ananth Kumar

IFET College of Engineering, Tamil Nadu, India

Neha Singhal

Christ University, Central Campus, Bangalore, India

Routledge
Taylor & Francis Group

NEW YORK AND LONDON

Published 2024 by River Publishers
River Publishers
Alsbjergvej 10, 9260 Gistrup, Denmark
www.riverpublishers.com

Distributed exclusively by Routledge
605 Third Avenue, New York, NY 10017, USA
4 Park Square, Milton Park, Abingdon, Oxon OX14 4RN

Industry Automation: The Technologies, Platforms and Use Cases / by
Pethuru Raj, Abhishek Kumar, Ananth Kumar, Neha Singhal.

Routledge is an imprint of the Taylor & Francis Group, an informa
business

ISBN 978-87-7004-039-6 (hardback)
ISBN 978-87-7004-189-8 (paperback)
ISBN 978-10-4012-363-8 (online)
ISBN 978-10-0351-666-8 (master ebook)

While every effort is made to provide dependable information, the
publisher, authors, and editors cannot be held responsible for any errors
or omissions.

Contents

**3 Industry Automation: The Contributions of Artificial
Intelligence** **57**

B. Akoramurthy, K. Dhivya, and Kassian T. T. Amesho

*P. Dharanyadevi, C. Krishnakoumar, K. Revathy, J. Karkavelraja,
K. Venkatalakshmi, and G. Zayaraz*

7   Waste Management 4.0: An Industry Automation Approach to the Future Waste Management System   **163**

M. Julie Therese, P. Dharanyadevi, A. Devi, and Christo Ananth

Preface

With the faster maturity and stability of digital technologies and tools, all kinds of industrial houses across the globe are journeying through delectable and decisive advancements. Industry verticals are experiencing a dazzling array of evolutions and revolutions in their offerings, operations, and outputs. Industrial processes are continuously optimized with the strategic aim of accelerating and automating industrial activities. Business behemoths and start-ups meticulously leverage all noteworthy improvisations occurring in the digital technology ecosystem. There are plentiful digitization and edge technologies such as sensors, actuators, stickers, codes, chips and controllers, beacons, RFID tags, LED lights, etc., for empowering all kinds of physical, mechanical, and electrical systems in our midst to be methodically digitized. With the adoption of powerful communication technologies and network topologies, digitized entities in our everyday environments (homes, hotels, hospitals, industrial floors, airports, etc.) become connected. These are being termed as networked embedded systems. Further on, digitized elements increasingly are getting integrated with the web-based software applications and data sources in order to be smartly enabled in their actions and reactions. The dynamic network of Internet-enabled digitized entities is being pronounced as the Internet of Things (IoT). When the Internet-attached sensors and devices interact with one another in the vicinity and with the software libraries and packages running in the Internet servers, there is a possibility for the realization of a massive amount of multi-structured digital data. Thus, the aspect of digitization is becoming penetrative and pervasive these days.

Another concept capturing the imagination of technocrats and academic professors is the cyber–physical system (CPS) paradigm. All kinds of physical systems on the ground are formally hooked into web-based software services and datastores (cyber systems) and thereby empowered physical systems can exhibit an adaptive behavior in their assignments and obligations. Thus, software-enabled devices, equipment, appliances, instruments, robots, and drones are all set to enthuse the total human society. There will be people-centric, event-driven, service-oriented, knowledge-filled, process-aware, business-critical, context-sensitive, and real-world cyber applications that can be elegantly designed and deployed in order to succulently delight employees, end-users, and executives.

The digital twins is another popular subject of study and research across information and communication technologies (ICT) organizations and academic institutions. With the Internet-enabled physical systems, a wider variety of automation and acceleration activities are being unearthed and unleashed. For designing, developing, and deploying mission-critical systems such as satellites, rockets, humanoid robots, drones, manufacturing machineries, defense equipment, medical instruments, etc., the role and responsibility of AI-inspired and blockchain-supported digital twins are on the higher side. We have explained these technological paradigms in the book chapters for enlightening our esteemed readers. Highly reliable and high-bandwidth communication technologies such as 5G are being widely put in place to ensure low-latency applications. Cloud-native, edge, and server-less computing paradigms are also acquiring a surging popularity as the next-generation phenomenon for enabling the much-talked digital transformation targets.

Next in line is the arrival of competent digitalization technologies. The tremendous amount of digital data has to be subjected to a variety of deeper investigations to extract actionable insights. That is, the challenges of transitioning raw data into information and into knowledge are heavily minimized through the careful application of digitalization technologies such as the data analytics methods and platforms, artificial intelligence (AI) algorithms and models, etc. Thus, digital data and making sense out of digital data are the twin requirements for bringing forth a galaxy of state-of-the-art systems for real business transformation. The blending of the IoT, artificial intelligence, and blockchain is being proclaimed as the technology cluster for the future.

With the continued advancements in the digital technology space, there are mesmerizing innovations and disruptions happening in the industry front. Today we extensively talk about Industry 4.0 and 5.0 applications. Smart manufacturing will see the light, whereas factory automation initiatives and implementations will be speeded up so that the industry of the future will be agile, adaptive, affordable, and adroit. This book is designed and developed with the serious goal of putting forward the details of the significance of industry automation and how various digital technologies individually and collaboratively contribute for simplifying and speeding up the complex process of industry automation. Also, the book chapters will illustrate how digital technologies assist and aid in envisaging and implementing intelligent industry applications. This book explains how people, industrial assets and machineries, ICT infrastructures, and optimized processes gel well in order to establish and sustain digitally transformed factories, which are rewarding, risk-free, resilient, and versatile.

List of Figures

List of Tables

List of Contributors

Ajagbe, Sunday Adeola, *Department of Computer Engineering, Ladoke Akintola University of Technology, LAUTECH, Nigeria*

Akoramurthy, B., *School of Computing & Information Technology, REVA University, India*

Alkali, Yusuf Jibrin, *Federal Inland Revenue Service, Nigeria*

Amesho, Kassian T. T., *Tshwane School for Business and Society, Tshwane University of Technology, South Africa*

Ananth, Christo, *Samarkand State University, Uzbekistan*

Chalishajar, Dimplekumar N., *Department of Applied Mathematics, Virginia Military Institute (VMI), USA*

Das, Santosh, *SWAN Lab, Indian Institute of Technology, Kharagpur; Department of Computer Science & Engineering, OmDayal Group of Institutions, India*

Devi, A., *Department of ECE, IFET College of Engineering, India*

Dharanyadevi, P., *Department of CSE, Puducherry Technological University, India*

Dharishini, P. Padma Priya, *Department of CSE, Faculty of Engineering and Technology, Ramaiah University of Applied Sciences, India*

Dhivya, K., *Department of Computer Science & Engineering, India*

Ezhilkumar, Marimuthu Rajendran, *Department of Civil Engineering, Sri Krishna College of Engineering and Technology, India*

Gowthaman, Naveenbalaji, *Electronic Engineering, University of KwaZulu-Natal, South Africa*

Hedabou, Mustapha, *School of Computer Science, University Mohammed VI Polytechnic, Morocco*

Jyothi, A. P., *Department of CSE, Faculty of Engineering and Technology, Ramaiah University of Applied Sciences, India*

Kalaiselvi, K., *Department of ECE, Hindusthan College of Engineering and Technology, India*

Karkavelraja, J., *Department of CSE, Puducherry Technological University, India*

Karthikeyan, Singaram, *Centre for Environmental Studies, Anna University, India*

Khadidos, Alaa O., *Department of Information Technology, Faculty of Computing and Information Technology, King Abdulaziz University, Saudi Arabia*

Kiruthika, R., *Electronics and Communication Engineering, SNS College of Technology, India*

Krishnakoumar, C., *Department of CSE, Puducherry Technological University, India*

Lincy, S. S. Blessy Trencia, *School of Mathematics and Data Science, Emirates Aviation University, Dubai, The United Arab Emirates*

Mohammed, Gouse Baig, *Department of Computer Science & Engineering, Vardhaman College of Engineering, India*

Moses, M. Leeban, *Department of ECE, Bannari Amman Institute of Technology, India*

Nadikattu, Rahul Reddy, *Department of IT, University of Cumbersome, USA*

Nalini, M., *Department of Electronics and Instrumentation Engineering, Sri Sairam Engineering*

Pauliah Nadar, Kannan, *Department of Electrical and Computer Engineering, Institute of Technology, Jigjiga University, Ethiopia*

Pon Bharathi, A., *Department of ECE, Amrita College of Engineering and Technology, India*

Prabhu, T., *Electronics and Communication Engineering, Presidency University, India*

Raam, R. Bharath, *Loyola-ICAM College of Engineering and Technology, India*

Raj, Pethuru, *Edge AI Division, Reliance Jio Platforms Ltd., India*

Rajalingam, Prithiviraj, *SRM University, India*

Ramesh, Rajappa, *Department of Science & Humanities, Sri Krishna College of Engineering and Technology, India*

Ravi Kumar, A., *Department of Computer Science & Engineering, Sridevi Women's Engineering College, India*

Revathy, K., *Department of CSE, Puducherry Technological University, India*

Samuel, Dinesh Jackson, *Biomedical Engineering, University of California, USA*

Sangeetha, K., *Department of Computer Science & Engineering, Kebri Dehar University, Ethiopia*

Senthil, P., *Department of ECE, SRM Institute of Science & Technology Ramapuram Campus, India*

Shitharth, S., *Department of Computer Science & Engineering, Kebri Dehar University, Ethiopia*

Shivaprasad, D., *School of Science and Technology, International University of East Africa, Uganda*

Sirajudeen, *School of Computer Science and Engineering, VIT University, India*

Srinivasan, Balaji, *Loyola-ICAM College of Engineering and Technology, India*

Sudharsan, S., *Department of ECE, Rajalakshmi Engineering College, India*

Sundaresan, S., *Department of Electronics & Communication, NIT Karaikal, India*

Surender, R., *Department of ECE, SRM Institute of Science & Technology Ramapuram Campus, India*

Surianarayanan, Chellammal, *Centre for Distance and Online Education, Bharathidasan University, India*

Therese, M. Julie, *Department of ECE, Sri Manakula Vinayagar Engineering College, India*

Vatchala, S., *School of Computer Science and Engineering, VIT Chennai Campus, India*

Velu, Arun, *Equifax, USA*

Venkatalakshmi, K., *Department of ECE, University College of Engineering Tindivanam, India*

Vinodha, D. Vedha, *Department of ECE, JCT College of Engineering and Technology, India*

Whig, Pawan, *Vivekananda Institute of Professional Studies, India*

Wilson, Allan J., *Department of ECE, Amrita College of Engineering and Technology, India*

Yogesh, C. K., *School of Computer Science and Engineering, VIT Chennai Campus*

Zayaraz, G., *Department of CSE, Puducherry Technological University, India*

List of Abbreviations

3GPP	3G partnership project
ABAI	Automation based on AI
ABHS	Alcohol-based hand sanitizer
ABS	Anti-lock braking system/anti-skid breaking system
AC	Automated coding
ADAS	Advanced driver aid system
ADC	Analog to digital conversion
ADS	Automated driving system
AFDS	Ambient fine dust samplers
AGC	Automatic gain control
AGI	Artificial general intelligence
AI	Artificial intelligence
AIoT	Artificial intelligence of things
AL	Algorithmic learning
ANFIS	Adopted neuro-fuzzy inference system
ANN	Artificial neural network
ANPR	Automatic number plate recognition
AP	Automatic hypothesis proving
API	Application programming interface
AR	Augmented reality
ASC	Asymmetrical street canyon
AWS	Amazon web services
BDA	Big data analytics
BDMA	Beam division multiple access
BPNN	Back-propagation neural network
BS	Base station
CAGR	Compound annual growth rate
CAP	Constrained application protocol
CH	Cluster head
CHF	Congestive heart failure
CMMS	Computerized maintenance management system

CNN	Convolutional neural network
CoAP	Constrained application protocol
CP	Collapse prevention
CPS	Cyber−physical system
CPU	Central processing unit
CRE	Circular economy
CRM	Customer relationship management
CSI	Channel state information
CV	Computer vision
CVS	Concurrent versions system
DBM	Deep Boltzmann machine
DBMS	Database management system
DCNN	Deep convolutional neural network
DDoS	Distributed denial-of-service
DEM	Digital elevation model
DL	Deep learning
DPC	Dirty paper coding
DR-PSLTE	Dual-resolution polarimetric synthetic aperture radar time-frequency domain data
DSP	Digital signal processing
DTC	Decision tree classifier
DYN	Dynamic
ECC	Elliptic curve cryptography
ECG	Electrocardiography
ED-CNN	Edge-deployed convolution neural network
ECNN	Enhanced convolutional neural network
EC-OU	Energy consumption optimization using
EDA	Event-driven architecture
EDRLEACH	Enhanced distributed energy-efficient LEACH
EEG	Electroencephalography
EFFRA	European factories of the future research association
eMBB	Enhanced mobile broadband
EMG	Electromyogram
ENISA	European union agency for cybersecurity
ERP	Enterprise resource planning
ES-MAC	Energy-saving medium access control
ESODR	Earth system observing data and information retrieval

EWS	Early warning system
FDC	Fault detection and classification
FEM	Finite element model
FERA 2015	Facial expression recognition and analysis
FFNN	Feedforward neural network
FL	Federated learning
FN	False negative
FP	False positive
FUSE	Framework for understanding structural errors
GCP	Ground control point
GDP	Gross domestic product
GIS	Geographic information system
GPU	Graphics processing unit
GSD	Ground sampling distance
GSI	Global standards initiative
GSR	Galvanic skin response
HCI	Human-computer interaction
HEC-RAS	Hydrologic engineering center's river analysis system
HHL	Harrow, Hassidim, and Lloyd
HOG	Histogram of oriented gradient
HRM	Human resource management
I4.0	Fourth industrial revolution
I4.0	Industry 4.0
I-A	Industrial automation and artificial intelligence
ICS	Industrial control systems
ICT	Information and communication technologies
ITS	Intelligent transportation systems
IDS	Intrusion detection system
IDT	Intrusion detection technique
IEC	International electrotechnical commission
IERC	Industrial internet consortium
IHSS	Intelligent healthcare systems
IIC	Industrial internet consortium
IIoT	Industrial internet of things
IIRA	Industrial internet reference architecture
IIS	Internet information services
InTraSafEd5G	INcreasing TRAffic SAFety with EDge and 5G
IO	Immediate occupancy

IoD	Internet of data
IoE	Internet of everything
IoP	Internet of people
IoS	Internet of services
IoT	Internet of things
IoU	Intersection over union
IP	Internet protocol
IPA	Intelligent process automation
IPD	Innovative product development
IPv6	Internet protocol version 6
IQ	Intelligence quotient
IR	Infrared
ISP	Intelligent power system
ISWA	International solid waste association
IT	Information technology
ITS	Intelligent mobility system
JAFFE	Japanese female facial expression
KF-MAC	Kalman filter-based medium access control
KNN	K-neighbor classifier
KPI	Key performance indicator
LDA	Linear discriminant analysis
LEACH	Low energy adaptive clustering hierarchy
LIVE	Layered information viewing environment
LR	Logistic regression
LS	Life safety
LSTM	Long short-term memory
LTE	Long-term evolution
LTE-A	Long-term evolution advanced
LWC	Lightweight cipher
M2M	Machine-to-machine
MaaS	Manufacturing as a service
MAE	Mean absolute error
MANET	Mobile Ad hoc network
MCP	Mobile controlled production
MCS	Monte Carlo simulation
MEC	Multi-access edge computing
MF	Matched filter
MIMO	Multiple input multiple output
ML	Machine learning

MLP	Multilayer perceptron
MMF	Max-min fairness
mMIMO	Massive multiple input multiple output
MMSE	Minimum mean square error
mMTC	Massive machine type communication
MQTT	Messaging queue telemetry transport
MRC	Maximal ratio combining
MRF	Materials recovery facility
MRT	Multiple-input multiple-output radio transmission
MSA	Microservices architecture
MTCNN	Multi-task cascaded convolutional network
NAN	Neighborhood area network
NB	Naive Bayes
NFC	Near field communication
NFV	Network function virtualization
NLP	Natural language processing
NPU	Neural processing unit
NSC	Non-street canyon
OCAP	Out of control action plan
OCP	Order-controlled production
OCR	Optical character recognition
OEE	Overall equipment effectiveness
ORLEACH	Optimized Re-clustering LEACH
OS	Operating system
OT	Operational technology
PaaS	Platform as a service
PC	Pre-stressed concrete
PCA	Principal component analysis
PdM	Predictive maintenance
PI4.0	Industry 4.0 platform
PLC	Power line communication
PM	Particulate matter
POS	Point of sales
P-ZF	Pilot zero-forcing
QE	Quantitative easing
QHCR	Qualified and heterogeneous cluster routing
QML	Quantum machine learning
QoE	Quality of everything

QoS	Quality of service
QRAM	Quantum random access memory
Q-SVM	Quantum support vector
RAMI4.0	Reference architectural model industry 4.0
RAN	Radio access network
RBAC	Role-based access control
RBF	Radial basis function
RC	Remote control
RES	Renewable energy sources
RFID	Radio-frequency identification
RMSE	Root mean square error
ROI	Region of interest
RP	Regular pilot
RPA	Robotic process automation
RR	Respiration rate
RS	Robotic systems
RSA	Rivest-Shamir-Adleman (encryption algorithm)
RSU	Road side unit
RTK	Real-time kinematic
RTU	Remote telemetry unit
RZF	Regularized zero-forcing
SaaS	Software as a service
SAE	Society of automotive engineers
SC	Street canyon
SCA	Small cell access
SCADA	Supervisory control and data acquisition
SDMA	Space division multiple access
SDN	Software-defined networking
SDP	Seamless and dynamic engineering of plants
SHM	Structural health monitoring
SI	Self-interference
SINR	Signal-to-interference noise ratio
SLR	Single lens reflex
SNR	Signal-to-noise ratio
SoF	State of function
SoH	State of health
SRE	Site reliability engineering
SSCV	Symmetrical street canyon with viaduct
SSI	Soil structure interaction

SSP	Social signal processing
SVM	Support vector machine
TanDEM-X	TerraSAR-X add-on for digital elevation measurement
TCP	Transmission control protocol
TCS	Traction control system
TN	True negative
TP	True positive
TPU	Tensor processing unit
TSN	Time-sensitive networking
UAV	Unmanned aerial vehicle
UI	Urban intelligence
UMTS	Universal mobile telecommunication system
UPF	User plane function
URLLC	Ultra-reliable low latency communication
VM	Virtual machine
VPU	Vision processing unit
VQE	Variational quantum eigensolver
VSM	Value stream management
WEVA	Wireless evolution for automation
WoT	Web of things
WSN	Wireless sensor network
ZF	Zero-forcing

1

An Analytical Framework for the Industrial Internet of Things (IIoT): Importance, Recent Challenges, and Enabling Technologies

Gouse Baig Mohammed[1], Shitharth Selvarajan[2], A. Ravi Kumar[3], K. Sangeetha[4], Alaa O. Khadidos[5], and S. Vatchala[6]

[1]Department of Computer Science & Engineering, Vardhaman College of Engineering, India
[2]School of Built Environment, Engineering and Computing, Leeds Beckett University, LS1 3HE Leeds, U.K.
[3]Department of Computer Science & Engineering, Sridevi Women's Engineering College, India
[4]Department of Computer Science & Engineering, Kebri Dehar University, Ethiopia
[5]Department of Information Technology, Faculty of Computing and Information Technology, King Abdulaziz University, Saudi Arabia
[6]School of Computer Science and Engineering, VIT Chennai Campus, India
E-mail: gousebaig@vardhaman.org; Shitharth.it@gmail.com; aravikumar007@gmail.com; sangeethak@kdu.edu.et; aokhadidos@kau.edu.sa; vatchala.s@vit.ac.in

Abstract

The Internet of Things (IoT) is a novel idea that can benefit any manufacturing company that adopts it. IoT is still in its early stages in industrial operations, leading to higher prices, slower development in data management, and fewer deployments. The proliferation of Internet of Things (IoT) applications and the adoption of cutting-edge technology trends in industrial systems are driving the development of industrial IoT (IIoT). A novel vision of the Internet of Things applied to the manufacturing sector is realized when smart things are used to automatically detect, gather, process, and communicate real-time events in industrial processes. By creating smart monitoring of production floor shops and machine health applications and for predictive and preventative maintenance of industrial equipment, the industrial Internet of Things (IIoT) seeks to enhance operational efficiency, productivity, and the management of industrial assets. Due to the proliferation of IoT (Internet of Things) applications that gather information from real and virtual sensors, massive amounts of digital data are becoming increasingly important. However, without the right tools, such information is useless. This research provides a novel and concise definition of IIoT that can aid readers in their understanding of this emerging field. Current research trends in the II T have been outlined. We conclude by outlining the current issues and enabling technologies for the IIoT.

Keywords: Industrial Internet of Things, cyber-physical systems, cloud computing, machine to machine (M2M) communication

1.1 Introduction

The Internet of Things (IoT) continues to be one of the currently available options that are the most comprehensive, productive, and cost-effective choice. Physical data is augmented with computer systems, which are then deployed to give sensors the impression that they are more powerful, trustworthy, and in control of their environments [1]. The objective of the subset of the IoT known as the industrial Internet of Things (IIoT) is to improve the safety, security, and reliability of industrial processes while simultaneously maintaining the capability for real-time data exchange. The industrial Internet of Things (IIoT) allows businesses to improve their asset and operation management and reduce downtime through predictive maintenance. The Internet of Things (IoT) primarily seeks to improve workplace security and operational effectiveness in manufacturing (IIoT). In the next generation of industrial networks, it is anticipated that large-scale applications of the industrial Internet of Things (IIoT) will be implemented. The industrial Internet of Things (IIOT) will help break down barriers between humans and robots, which is necessary to realize the vast personalization potential of Industry 6.0 systems. As a result, we will discuss the industrial Internet of Things and how it relates to the final objective of the Industry 4.0 initiative. According to the most recent forecasts [2], seventy billion devices will be connected to the Internet by 2025 . The global market share of the IIoT is anticipated to reach $14.2 trillion by 2023.

As a result, the Internet of Things will be able to provide interconnectivity between a variety of sensors and PLCs (in addition to other smart devices) for the more advanced cyber systems that surround the significant technologies, "such as a smart grid and intelligent vehicle systems," in addition to city intelligence and other advanced cyber systems. Machine-to-machine communications, also known as M2M communications, are on the verge of becoming a reality, thanks to the widespread adoption of real-time protocols, networks, and system software and hardware based on M2M. The Internet of Things (IoT) is a network that connects and manages various devices, such as automobiles, buildings, and other physical infrastructure [2]. The Internet of Things Global Standards Initiative (IoT-GSI) referred to it as "infrastructure for the information society by the Global Standards Initiative on the Internet of Things" in its official description in 2013. This description was published in 2013. By utilizing the Internet of Things, the physical integration of computer-based applications can be improved, and monitoring and managing artifacts can be carried out by utilizing pre-existing network infrastructures. The Internet of Things, which includes sensors and drives, is only a subset of the more comprehensive cyber-physical networks.

Every object incorporates a computer system capable of connecting to the pre-existing network infrastructure of the Internet and transmitting data. It is anticipated that almost 50 billion devices will be connected to the Internet of Things by 2020 [3, 4]. The Internet of Things (IoT) refers to a diverse collection of devices connected to the web through various sensors and network connections, including wired and wireless. A device that can do additional research will accept data from embedded sensors connected to the Internet of Things, humans, and any inanimate item (IoT). Thanks to the Internet of Things, we can soon link industrial networks, smart medical telephone monitoring systems, smart transportation systems, and information-sharing equipment. With the rapid growth of IoT devices and networks in industrial manufacturing, several sensors result in a large volume of data. The inspection of production, which detects defects in the goods, is one of the most common examples. In this chapter, we suggest a profound learning-based classification model and introduce a rigorous inspection scheme with greater precision to find potential faulty goods. As a factory may be equipped with several assembly lines, the real-time processing of such big data is a significant challenge in this case [4]. That is why we build our device using the fog computing principle. The machine can handle extensive data by downloading the calculation workload from the central server to the fog node. In our scheme, there are two clear benefits. The first is that the CNN paradigm is adapted to the fog computing environment and increases its computing

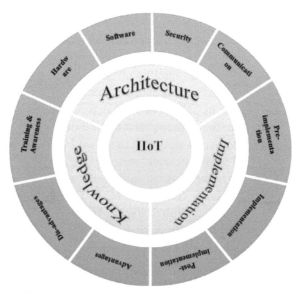

Figure 1.1   Industrial Internet of Things framework.

performance considerably. The other is that we develop an inspection model to denote the form and degree of the defect simultaneously. The trials have shown that the approach proposed is stable and efficient. The analytical framework of IIoT is given in Fig 1.1

1.1.1 Industrial automation with IoT

Manufacturing is critical to economic growth in the globalization period [1] and continues to play a vital role in economic development. It has a good effect on both industrialized and developing countries growth. The manufacturing industry is using emerging technology to boost individual enterprises' economic competitiveness and the sustainability of the whole industrial field. In the manufacture of ICTs, a transfer from traditional to modern production techniques has been possible [2]. As a part of the ICT application, monitoring systems play a significant role in the supervision and control of manufacturing processes. Recent improvements in IT allow the integration of one complicated system for the supply chain of multiple monitoring applications. Usually, a monitoring system is essential in illness prediction, improved production, cost reduction, and early warning system [4]. Applying and integrating contemporary technology monitoring systems, such as the Internet of Things (IoT) based sensors, is feasible. Industrial studies showed significant benefits from IoT-based monitors, including improved working conditions, defect avoidance, quality prediction, and support for better decision-making by managers [6].

The Internet of Things (IoT) will be able to link increasingly sophisticated cyber systems based on essential technologies such as intelligent power systems (ISPs), intelligent transportation systems (ICTs), intelligent healthcare systems (IHSS), urban intelligence (UI), and other intelligent systems (IIS). It is essential for the Internet of Things to be able to provide advanced and intelligent communications to future electronic and intelligent machines and computers that various standard and actual protocol implementations, network realms, and machine-to-machine IoT software and hardware systems be implemented. The Internet of Things (IoT) refers to interconnected electronic devices that collect data from other devices, such as automobiles. These devices include sensors, actuators, and communication systems (IoT). Infrastructure for the information society was how the Internet of Things Global Standards Initiative (IoT-GSI) referred to it back in 2013. Implementing Internet of Things based monitoring and control of artifacts over pre-existing-existing network infrastructure can increase efficiencies, precision, and cost-effectiveness [6]. This can be accomplished by connecting the artifacts in question to the Internet. Examples include the more extensive cyber-physical networks that employ IoT enhancements such as sensors and drives. These networks are also an example. Each is outfitted with a computer system capable of communicating with the Internet [56]. By 2020, it is anticipated that there will be approximately 50 billion devices connected to the Internet of Things.

Sensing devices can now create large volumes of data, thanks to the Internet of Things (IoT), raising the challenge of making this data useful. A networked system can be optimized or interacted more often via the Internet of Things to improve people's quality of life [7]. While your ability to acquire, analyze, and act on data depends on your background knowledge, this does not guarantee your success. Big data analytics' current state is therefore clouded with doubt. Analyses can range from basic correlations between outdoor temperature and grid loading to more complicated causative relationships, such as roads causing a gradual delay in energy use owing to electric vehicles or warmer days leading to more air conditioner usage and higher system loads.

The industry is a term reflecting the latest phase in the production revolution or, in other words, the smart industry. Automation and data are two major topics in this era of the smart industry. The first is one of our key goals, and the other is one of our most valuable instruments. Some techniques of artificial intelligence (AI), deep learning, and machine learning, for example, will process and learn data and make computers and manipulators capable of becoming human-like. IoT-enabled devices are increasingly used in smart factories to gather more data, which is essential for AI approaches. With the help of these data, several new methods have been found for automating and efficient manufacturing processes.

1.1.2 Objective

a. To make the smart industrial environment, which allows users to monitor and control industrial parameters on a mobile device in real-time.
b. To preserve the workstation's energy by completing the cutter tools blade aging system on the website.

For this research, the term "industrial IoT" refers to a framework for investigating how Internet of Things (IoT) technologies are implemented in industrial settings. During this study, our goal was to develop a framework for analyzing the nature and applications of IoT devices and their vulnerabilities and threats, which would be used as part of this process. For example, we hope to discover cross-cutting risks and vulnerabilities by methodically characterizing the devices rather than focusing on technological or sector-specific difficulties.

The following is how the chapter is organized. Literature survey is detailed in Section 1.3, which is framed within the context of Industry 4.0. It is in Section 1.5 that we provide enabling technologies for IIoT. We lay the framework and case studies in Section 1.6. Section 1.7 gives details about challenges in IIoT, Section 1.8 details the application for IIoT framework, and Section 1.9 concludes by pointing out areas of research that still need to be carried out.

1.2 Literature Survey

Data from IoT devices and industrial data sources flows through layers 1 and 2 of the stack. Edge servers and cloud computing systems are used at layer 3 to run IIoT applications. The Industrial Internet Consortium [8] examined this general design for IIoT systems. Enterprise applications are illustrated in Layer-4. As shown in Figure 1.2, data and information are being orchestrated for resource management, operational purposes, and the flow of data and information between the various layers.

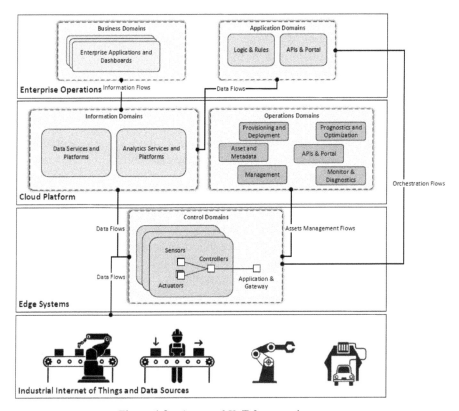

Figure 1.2 A general IIoT framework system.

Researchers have a new perspective on these designs because of the numerous changes in location awareness and communication paradigms, computational assignments and execution paradigms, and resource management systems. These architectures are described in depth in the following paragraphs: It was built by [9] and used open-source software and IoT communication protocols to create the wireless evolution for automation (WEVA) system. Everything from operating systems to protocols to access gateways to services is part of the system's infrastructure. In addition, the network is monitored and controlled by WEVA using easy WSN, a graphical administration application. According to the authors, IPv6 is vital for the IIoT in terms of adaptability. However, achieving a high-performance IIoT in terms of networks is not an easy process (latency, security, etc.). Many academics, on the other hand, have failed to take into account the critical role played by WSNs in industrial applications.

Katsikeas et al. [10] have proposed an IoT suite that addresses several issues, including identifying real-time object locations throughout manufacturing processes, establishing a network system that allows objects to communicate between the network and other objects in real time, and so forth. A cloud platform and a smart hub are essential for the IIoT suite design. Managing IoT devices is done through the smart hub, which acts as both a gateway and a management platform.

In [11], the phrase "Internet of Things" was coined to represent the growing number of smart and connected objects and highlight the new opportunities they can create. Because of their dynamic character, smart and connected products stand out from the crowd. I believe it is their increased skills and the data they can collect. For example, "Internet" and "Thing" are derived from two words and two conceptions. Internet is defined as TCP/IP, a standard communication protocol that connects computer networks worldwide. An "unidentifiable" entity is implied by it.

After being coined in 1999 by Kevin Ashton of Auto-ID Center, the phrase "Intemet of Things" has been used. Computers can interpret, identify, and monitor the world, thanks to RFID (radio frequency identification) and sensor technologies presented by Ashton, who argued that we should empower computers to acquire information independently without limits of human-centered data to keep an accurate count and track of everything. This would allow us to cut costs, eliminate wasteful spending, and determine whether anything is needed to be repaired or replaced (Ashton 2009). As well as being quoted in Forbes Magazine in 2002, Ashton prophesied that RFID would lead to a 100% automation of data collection. According to his statement, "We need an intemet for things so that computers can grasp the real world," which may be the first reported use of this word [13].

The Intemet of Things (IoT) envisions a scenario in which the Intemet extends into the real world, connecting everyday things and physical products to the virtual world. Access points for Intemet services are built-in, and remote control and monitoring are possible [14]. People, media, and content will not be the only things on the Intemet in the following years. It will be a comprehensive system if it includes all real-world assets that develop knowledge, share information, interact with people, and support business activities.

We believe that the developments in information technology, communications, and microelectronics will continue for a long time in the Internet of Things (IoT). As the size of communication modules, processors, and other electronic components shrinks, energy usage decreases, and the price of these components continues to fall; they can already be integrated into our everyday products. As a result of embedded ICT, smart things play a vital part in this IoT vision. They can see their surroundings by using sensors. They can also communicate with each other and engage with people by using networking systems that are built into their devices [15].

Most importantly, the IoT vision will have a significant impact on a variety of daily activities. As shown in Figure 1.3, the Internet of Things is a network of interconnected gadgets affecting many aspects of our daily lives. For private users, IoT's impact will be seen in the home and at work. As for business users, the most noticeable consequences will be in industrial manufacturing and automation, business and process management, logistics, and smart transportation of products and people [16].

According to the company, the industrial internet is a network of sensors and software that integrates complicated physical machines. Machine data may be collected and analyzed with machine-to-machine connectivity and the Internet of Things (IoT). By connecting smart devices, machines, and people at work, the Industrial Internet Consortium claims that it will improve decision-making through advanced analytics, leading to revolutionary economic results. IoT in industrial contexts is a non-consumer application of IoT [17].

Figure 1.3 shows the three major components of the industrial internet. First and foremost, there are intelligent machines. To do this, modern controls, sensors, and software applications must be used to connect the world's machines as well as fleets, facilities, and networks. The strength of physics-based analytics is combined with domain expertise, automation, and prediction algorithms when doing advanced analytics to better understand how machines and systems operate. Linked personnel at all times are included as a

Figure 1.3   Critical elements of industrial internet.

third component, which encourages smarter operational design, maintenance, and excellent service quality.

1.2.1 Industry 4.0

Factory automation, electricity, and mass labor fueled the first three industrial revolutions (water and steam power, mass labor, and electrical energy). In 2011, the German government adopted "Industry 4.0" as a strategy to increase the country's gross domestic product [18]. With the ability to communicate and make autonomous, decentralized decisions, CPS is crucial to this revolution, which aims to increase industrial efficiency, productivity, safety, and transparency. The American Industrial Internet and the German idea of Industry 4.0 have a lot in common. To put it another way, the term "industrial intemet" refers to a network of interconnected devices, computers, and people that enables advanced data analytics to revolutionize industrial operations and, in turn, the landscape for enterprises and individuals alike [5]. The rise of the industrial intemet impacts businesses and individuals alike.

Value chain management is the context in which the various technologies and ideas that make up "Industry 4.0 " are discussed. In the modular smart factories of Industry 4.0, CPS keeps tabs on the workings of the factory floor, builds a digital twin of the real world, and makes decisions without a command center. Through the IoT, CPS can have two-way conversations in real time with one another and with humans (IoT). Intemet-based access is provided for the provision of collaborative as well as collaboration services (IoS). Research demonstrates that the standards for the industry are still being developed, even though both the Intemet of Things and the industrial Internet of Things are relatively new concepts. The market is fragmented, and the range of applications is vast. Even within a single application, the number of distinct technical solutions is staggering.

Perhaps 5-10 years will pass before standards are adequately developed. Research in the manufacturing industry has shown that IoT sensors can improve working conditions, avoid erroneous designs, provide fault diagnosis and quality prediction, and assist managers in making better decisions. To measure the air quality inside a facility, Moon et al. created an Intemet of Things-based sensor [19]. Infrared sensors were used to capture data such as temperature, humidity, CO_2 level, dust, and odors. Since this technology is incredibly reliable, it should be able to help managers maintain a healthy working environment for everyone in production. A low-cost IoT sensor system was developed by [20] in order to avoid errors during the design process of additive manufacturing. Researchers were able to obtain data on temperature and humidity using the sensors. According to the study, knowing the environmental factors during the design phase of additive manufacturing could help reduce errors in the production process. According to the study's findings, IoT sensors can help give complete diagnostic data and improve diagnostic results. IoT and machine learning were combined in a framework [14]. Real-world implementation of the technology was done using metal casting. We were able to forecast the quality of castings using this technology and increase the operation control with it. Securing the fourth industrial revolution framework was developed by [15] by integrating sensors and SCADA systems. It was found that the proposed system is feasible and will aid managers in migrating old systems to Industry 4.0.

The introduction of IoT has enabled this shift from traditional to modern digitalized production possible. It is possible to manage huge volumes of sensor data input using big data technology since the number of sensors in production is being multiplied. Ge et al. have used big data technologies in IoT to build a conceptual paradigm for critical decision-making [21]. Managers can make better judgments when provided with a wealth of data gathered from a number of sources (sensor devices).

A framework for simultaneous temperature monitoring on at least two fishing vessels was examined experimentally by [22]. The fishing vessel became a remote sensor arrangement when distant temperature data were circulated over an associated platform and base station. As a result of the presence of this remote sensor arrangement, the temperature was constantly monitored, and the temperature data was sent over the Internet.

One of the components of emotional support network was an overview of a remote monitoring structure. The remote monitoring framework could aid the unmanned evening shifts of extended manufacturing, which are common in medium-sized Japanese enterprises. 3D layered information viewing environment (LIVE) and an array adjusting framework based on remote monitoring were developed using open-source technologies, tested, and debated [23].

Centralized database management system (DBMS) collected real-time meteorological data as well as numerous recurrent functional measurements in international RES factories (DBMS). In order to calculate each plant and govern database activities, a properly created graphic representation of statistical and functional parameters was used.

According to Shitharth et al. [24], wireless sensor networks (WSNs) needed to have stronger signals in order to get near-ideal answers for the location of sensors in terms of limiting the number of jumps between each hub of the objective district and the sink hub while covering as much of the intrigue zone as could reasonably be anticipated (2005). By reducing the number of jumps, the energy saving was also advanced. In the end, this work demonstrated the adaptability of this system to focus on the impact of many aspects of enthusiasm at the planning phase of the system, prior to the actual organization of wireless sensor network hubs.

In the first phase, this comprehensive research process encompasses various stages, including the formulation of inquiries, the development of study designs, the collection of data, and the interpretation of findings [25]. During the second phase, the decline continued. By selecting the working conditions between segments, it was possible to construct minuscule decreased subsets of parts, which provided comprehensive information about the status of the overall framework. To maintain the framework's regular by and large graphic structure, the second step decided how to present the links between sections in a reduced context.

Sensors, processors (MSP430), wireless radio interfaces (CC2650), and multisource power support are the fundamental components of I3Mote, an open industrial hardware platform suggested by Rehman et al. [16] (battery, solar, thermoelectric, etc.). I3Mote supplies all of the sensors and connectivity components necessary for the IIoT, ultimately leading to the finished product. The I3Mote platform also provides a set of software packages for the quick creation of industrial applications.

The use of software tools can help rapid application development. Because it has two distinct CPUs for communication and apps, I3Mote provides a unique potential for simple app creation (CC2650; MSP432). If you are looking for an industrial automation solution, I3Mote has you covered.

Mitchell and Jones [26] have presented an LTE-based DR-PSLTE (a threelayer architecture). Unmanned aerial vehicles such as cloudlets, software-defined networks, and radio access networks are only a few of the new technologies included in the proposed design to improve disaster resilience and minimize communication delays. The three strata of the proposed architecture are network synchronization and control signals, as well as resources, which are managed by the SDN controller in the first layer. Using a UAV, the second layer serves as a cloudlet. In disaster or emergency scenarios, these unmanned aerial vehicles (UAVs) perform two essential services: data processing and data communication.

1.3 Enabling Technologies for IIoT

The Internet of Things (IoT) facilitates real-time data collection and the initiation of actions in the context of a connected factory. These gadgets are the backbone of IIoT's global factory asset tracking. Internet of Things devices monitor the entire production process, from the raw materials to the finished goods, to reduce labor costs and increase the efficiency of manual system management. An industrial Internet of Things (IIoT) system that uses Internet of Things devices is integrated into every facet of a manufacturing facility, from warehouses to assembly lines to distribution centers. In order to set up, deploy, monitor, and maintain these devices, you will need a team of highly skilled technicians.

1.3.1 Blockchain technology

When realizing the IIoT vision, one of the most critical technologies is the blockchain [2]. Blockchain technology is the subject of extensive academic and industrial investigation in various domains, including banking, healthcare, supply chain management, and automobile insurance. The smart industry's use of IoTenabled devices generates massive amounts of data. These Internet of Things devices have a wide variety of applications, including but not limited to performance monitoring, anomaly detection and diagnosis, predictive maintenance, asset monitoring, and tracking the entire product lifecycle from raw materials to finished goods. Other possible applications include: It is a challenging task, however, to communicate this information securely with all of the participants in the IIoT. For IIoT, blockchain technology has many advantages, including distributed nature, data provenance, tamper-resistance, trust, and trustworthiness. IoT device firmware upgrades and access control have recently been implemented using blockchain technology.

1.3.2 Cloud computing

Massive amounts of data generated by IIoT require distributed high-performance computing systems across a wide area for management, processing, analysis, and storage. These systems must be able to handle high volumes of data. The capabilities of storage, computing, and networking are made available to all participating facilities in an IIOT system through the utilization of cloud computing technologies. Backend clouds and linked devices communicate directly with one another without the use of any intermediaries. Depending on the organization's requirements, the Internet of Things can be implemented using private, public, or hybrid cloud service models (whereby a mix of both service models is used). Private cloud service models are out of reach for new entrants and small- and medium-sized businesses due to the significant costs associated with setting up data centers and hiring technical employees. As a result, major and well-established international corporations choose the construction of a private cloud in order to protect their data from industrial espionage.

1.3.3 Big data analytics

Data streams generated by IoT devices and systems are so large that high-end, high-performance computing platforms are needed to handle them. Due to latency and real-time considerations, big data processing and analysis in IIoT systems may be troublesome. Big data collection, storage, management, and processing, as well as the capacity to analyze and act on that data, are all supported by IIoT systems. Onboard data collectors, web-enabled data sources, and humane machine movements are ways data can be collected in an industrial Internet of Things (IIoT) system. Similar to how big data storage can benefit from on-premises, networked, and remote cloud storage, a cloud environment can reap benefits from all three types of cloud storage. New data management and processing methods have been developed to cope with the massive amounts of data that must be dealt with. At various levels within an IIoT system, various data mining, machine learning, deep learning, and statistical data analysis methods can be utilized. Actuation technology allows devices that are part of an IIoT network to communicate with the environments in which they are located. Despite the complexity of these systems, the next generation of IIoT systems places a significant emphasis on the processing and analysis of large amounts of data.

1.3.4 Artificial intelligence and cyber-physical systems

Humane interventions are minimized, and system efficiency is increased by using AI technology to ensure that IIoT systems operate autonomously and intelligently on their own. The IIoT is self-aware, thanks to AI technologies like multi-agent systems and conversational artificial intelligence. IoT systems use a wide range of search and optimization algorithms, from sensors to devices to edge servers and cloud data centers. Various industrial robots and manufacturing systems can benefit from IoT technology by reducing the need for human intervention and effort. In order for sensors and actuators to be used in industrial settings, CPS relies on embedded Internet of Things devices. These onboard integrated IoT devices also allow autonomous operations and better efficiency in IIoT systems. For example, in CPS and IIoT, efficiencies might range from operational to overall system efficiency.

1.3.5 Augmented and virtual reality

Workers in the industrial sector can benefit from augmented reality (AR) technology, which assists them in doing complex tasks, including assembling and dismantling machinery, sophisticated industrial products, and mission-critical systems. While working, people and machines can be monitored using AR technology to make changes or notifications quickly to avoid mishaps. Visualizing an industrial function and module configurations and re-configurations using VR technologies is possible before they are implemented in IIoT systems. Virtual reality can shorten the time it takes to reconfigure and shut down industrial machinery and plants. Open standards are used to construct VR simulations for CPS and IoT systems with heterogeneity.

1.4 Framework and Case Studies

BDA processes increasingly serve as the primary engine for delivering value for customers and businesses [8]. Similarities can be drawn between this new technology and the Internet of Things (IoT). BDA processes make combining consumer and company data feasible for highly customized production with zero faults. The Internet of Things is all about integrating historical and real-time data at various levels (IoT). This multi-source data integration can help design new business models more successfully. In addition to developing product offerings and value capture methods, value networks, and value communication strategies for internal and external stakeholders, businesses address a wide range of industrywide value creation processes [18]. In an ideal world, BDA processes would make it easier for companies to create value at the corporate level by enhancing internal operations. Outbound intelligence, on the other hand, leads to consumer value development. Despite these possibilities, realizing the full potential of BDA technologies is difficult. Few frameworks and use cases like this can be found in the existing literature.

1.4.1 SnappyData

Apache Spark and GemFire are integrated with SnappyData, an open-source BDA framework. Data processing with Apache Spark is used for large datasets, while GemFire handles transactional data storage. SnappyData's unified BDA engine is unmatched in the industry when it comes to online transaction processing, analytical processing, and operational data streaming analytics. Because of this, SnappyData's real-time interactive visualization speed suffers when dealing with large amounts of streaming data.

1.4.2 Fault detection classification

Industrial cyber manufacturing systems are built on a foundation of numerous geographically dispersed yet interconnected production facilities [6, 7]. The framework for fault detection and classification, also known as FDC, is what is responsible for finding flaws in the product during the manufacturing process. The foundation of the FDC architecture is the integration of IoT devices into CPS and cloud computing. Io T devices in manufacturing plants continuously gather and analyze data streams to detect various signals. This information is then transmitted to cloud servers. These cloud servers use deep belief networks and deep learning algorithms to discover and classify defective products [87, 88]. An automobile headlight manufacturing facility tested FDC, and the results were trustworthy.

1.5 Challenges in IIoT

Interoperability, privacy, scalability, heterogeneity, reliability, and resource management are just some of the technical concerns that have been brought to light as a result of the varied and complex structure of the IIoT system. However, there are a number of significant challenges that need to be addressed. In the following chapter, we will talk about the challenges that we faced.

1.5.1 Schemes for efficient data storage

Data volume has skyrocketed as a result of the widespread adoption of heterogeneous IoT devices. There is a high transmission rate of data generated by sensors and actuators built into industrial devices. A wide variety of IIoT devices, gateway/edge servers, and cloud servers are used to collect and store the data that is generated by these heterogeneous devices. Processing and storing sensor data is a time-consuming and challenging task. Data management models that are effective in dealing with these problems are required. These models should be able to deal effectively with the vast volume of raw data created by heterogeneous IoT devices. These models should be able to provide fast, dependable, and secure data processing, storage, retrieval, and flow for data management services.

1.5.2 IoT systems from different vendors working together

The IIoT system suite is made up of a variety of components, including industrial machines, robotics, Internet of Things devices, sensors, actuators, gateways, edge nodes, edge/cloud data servers (data centers), wired/wireless communication networks, and cellular networks (Wi-Fi, 5G, etc.). One of the most significant challenges posed by IIoT is figuring out how to effectively integrate a diverse array of technologies and vendors and collaborate with them. Integration and collaboration are made more challenging by problems such as synchronization, sharing of resources and data, interoperability, and data privacy. Research and development efforts still need to be expanded to produce methods of interoperability and collaboration that are both flexible and effective.

1.5.3 Adaptable and resilient technologies for analyzing large datasets

To achieve the goal of the IIoT and get the most out of the massive amount of data produced by the devices that make up the IIoT, there is a significant need for dependable and flexible big data analytics solutions. Unfortunately, massive datasets cannot be processed and analyzed using state-of-the-art database management tools. Real-time processing of this data is required because it is pivotal for a wide range of real-time industrial automation activities, including fault prediction, predictive maintenance, output improvement, downtime reduction, and anomaly detection. Because of the volume of data produced by IIoT devices, real-time big data analytics solutions are essential for satisfying the various needs of IIoT applications (in terms of, for example, data rates, latency, dependability, and so on). An enterprise-wide perspective can be gained from processing and visualizing data gathered throughout the entire product lifecycle (including the stages of development and production, testing, customer feedback, and post-sale services, for example).

1.5.4 Trust in IIoT systems

The success of any technology is strongly linked to consumer acceptance and adaptation, which is heavily impacted by consumer trust in these technologies. The commercial clients' (e.g., industry owners) trust in these IIoT systems has an impact on the effective adoption of these systems. Security and privacy have been a prominent focus of recent research on IIOT systems, which are still in their infancy. Poor IIoT security and privacy will deter customers from using these systems, harming IIoT adoptions in the long run. As a result, for IIoT systems to be successfully deployed and adapted in the industry, client trust must be appropriately dealt with. As a result, further study into customer trust models is needed if IIoT solutions are to gain widespread acceptance.

1.5.5 Integration of wireless technologies and protocols in the Internet of Things (IIoT)

The Internet of Things (IoT) is receiving an ever-increasing amount of attention from businesses and academic institutions. Communication is necessary for the functioning of the industrial Internet of Things. Consequently, communication in the IIoT needs to be able to link a large number of different types of devices, have an adequate capacity for the transfer of data, and behave in a deterministic manner while having a low amount of delay. On the other hand, the requirements for reliability, availability, and security in specific industrial applications are significantly more stringent than those in others. IIoT uses a wide range of communication technologies, protocols, and standards. With wireless systems (WLAN, IEEE 802.15) and wireless devices (WSN) becoming more popular, cable communication has been losing its luster. There are also other difficulties associated with using wireless communication. Some numerous wireless systems and protocols must work together in the IIoT. There are a plethora of communication protocols and technologies available. There is no single wireless technology or protocol that can meet all of the needs of the IIoT. As a result, deciding on communication technology and protocol might be difficult.

1.5.6 The edge of decentralization

Network, storage, and storage services must be computed at the Internet's edge to accommodate the variety of data sources and the vast output of continuous data streams. Centralized cloud controllers fully choreograph edge services and data management at their edges, allowing end nodes to benefit from edge computing. Not only does this raise the need for highly accessible communication lines, it also leads to industrial systems having a solitary point of failure. This can be addressed by utilizing edge-cloud services that are decentralized. Using blockchain technology, end-point devices, and app resource requirements can be permanently recorded on edge servers. Servers can also enable decentralized resource provisioning and service orchestration without central control mechanisms being in place first.

1.5.7 New operating systems for the Internet of Things

An operating system (OS) for the Internet of Things is developed to function properly despite the constraints imposed by IoT devices, which can include restrictions on memory, size, power consumption, and processor capability. In [3], popular Internet of Things operating systems are broken down regarding memory use, programming language support, scheduler, and architectural design. Researchers utilize TinvOS and Contiki as the two primary Internet of Things operating systems because they satisfy most of their requirements. It is essential for an operating system designed for the Internet of Things to have a low memory footprint, the ability to perform real-time operations, high energy efficiency, and independence from the underlying hardware. The quality of service $(Q_0 S)$ standards for IIoT applications are noticeably more stringent than those for IoT applications. Some examples of IIoT applications include the "Smart Home," "Smart Grid," "Smart Traffic," and "Smart Health." The most critical concerns regarding the Internet of Things are data protection and security, dependable network connections (such as cellular and Wi-Fi), low power consumption, interoperability, support for various devices, and adequate bandwidth (IoT). All of the IoT OS implementations, issues, and case studies brought up during their conversation took place within the context of the communication technologies they had already implemented.

1.5.8 Public safety in IIoT

When dealing with an incident involving Internet of Things technology, the general public's safety must be the top priority. In an emergency, the fire department, ambulance service, disaster management team, traffic police, and other law enforcement agencies are crucial to the safety of industrial workers and equipment. Nevertheless, one of the most significant challenges in disaster zones is the inability of communication systems to function correctly or entirely. Interoperability between the IIRI's disparate components and older forms of electronic networking is also a significant issue. Unmanned aerial vehicles (UAVs), software-defined networks (SDNs), edge computing, and other cuttingedge communication technologies like LTE, 4G/5G, etc., were all recommended in a recent study on the Internet of Things and possible future intelligent cities that prioritized public safety communications. Even yet, disaster-resilient, selfsufficient architectures that enable high-efficiency communication under normal circumstances would necessitate development. As a result, these architectures are viewed as providing public safety with disaster recovery methods in an emergency.

1.6 Application for IIoT Framework

Industrial businesses may take full advantage of the IIoT's potential by utilizing the framework, which outlines how the IIoT can be used to inform product, technical, and business choices. To get a better idea of what is needed in terms of technical and business decisions on different tiers of the IIoT, we can follow these steps:

1. First, it is essential to establish a clear business case or need for the benefits that the IIoT might bring to industrial processes before implementing it.
2. Second, an evaluation of the necessary infrastructure (hardware and software) for any IIoT implementation follows the business.
3. As soon as an IIoT solution has been assessed and understood, the user would consider the before, during, and post-implementation considerations in the industrial contexts.

1.7 Conclusion and Future Scope

With the help of the IIoT, businesses are able to collect and analyze vast amounts of data, which can then be used, monetized, and improved upon to offer customers brand-new services. This chapter discusses new findings in the study of IIoT in industry. The primary concerns of this study are the frameworks and architecture of the IIoT, the communication protocols and data management mechanisms that are currently in use, and their potential future development. For instance, the Internet of Things can use many enabling technologies (IoT). Problems related to IIoT implementation, such as an extensive list of research questions, have also been uncovered. Let us assume that the IoT in the industry will catch on and become commonplace.

If this is the case, the IIoT will have to overcome several obstacles, such as the need for trustworthy systems and the coexistence of wireless technology and protocol standards. Other difficulties include the requirement for effective data management schemes and collaborations between heterogeneous IIoT systems and robust and flexible technologies for big data analytics. The correct responses to these issues are not out of reach at all. Some of IIoT's outstanding issues can be addressed with the help of this research. Personalized manufacturing in IIoT systems will be a focus of our future study.

References

[1] Muntjir, M., Rahul, M., Alhumyani, H. A.: An Internet of Things (IoT) analysis: novel architectures, modern applications, security aspects and future scope with latest case studies. Int. J. Eng. Res. Technol. 2017; 6(2), 422-427.

[2] C. K. M. Lee, S. Z. Zhang, K. K. H. Ng, Development of an industrial internet of things suite for smart factory towards re-industrialization, Advances in Manufacturing. 2017; 5 (4):335-343. doi:10.1007/s40436-017-0197-2.

[3] W. Z. Khan, M. Y. Aalsalem, M. K. Khan, M. S. Hossain, M. Atiquzzaman, A reliable internet of things-based architecture for oil and gas industry, in Advanced Communication Technology (ICACT), 2017 19th International Conference on, IEEE, 2017;705-710.

[4] Kumar, Abhishek, SwarnAvinash Kumar, Vishal Dutt, Ashutosh Kumar Dubey, and Vicente García-Díaz. "IoT-based ECG monitoring for arrhythmia classification using Coyote Grey Wolf optimization-based deep learning CNN classifier." Biomedical Signal Processing and Control 76 (2022): 103638.

[5] B. Martinez, X. Vilajosana, I. Kim, J. Zhou, P. Tuset-Peiro, A. Xhafa, D. Poissonnier, X. Lu, I3mote: An open development platform for the intelligent industrial internet, Sensors. 2017; 17 (5): 986. doi:10.3390/s17050986.

[6] Pavithra, M., R. Rajmohan, T. Ananth Kumar, S. Usharani, and P. Manju Bala. "Investigation of Energy Optimization for Spectrum Sensing in Distributed Cooperative IoT Network Using Deep Learning Techniques." Hybrid Intelligent Approaches for Smart Energy: Practical Applications (2022): 107-127.

[7] Z. Meng, Z.Wu, C. Muvianto, J. Gray, A data-oriented m2 m messaging mechanism for industrial IoT applications, IEEE Internet of Things Journal 4 (1) (2017) 236{246 (2017).

[8] M. Padmaja, S. Shithart, K. Prasuna, Abhay Chaturvedi, Pravin R. Kshirsagar, A. Vani, 'Growth of Artificial Intelligence to Challenge Security in IoT Application,' Wireless Personal Communications, Springer, 2021, DOI: https://doi.org/10.1007/s11277-021-08725-4.

[9] T. Qiu, Y. Zhang, D. Qiao, X. Zhang, M. L. Wymore, A. K. Sangaiah, A robust time synchronization scheme for industrial internet of things, IEEE Transactions on Industrial Informatics. 2017; 14 (8): 3570-3580.

[10] S. Katsikeas, K. Fysarakis, A. Miaoudakis, A. Van Bemten, I. Askoxylakis, I. Papaefstathiou, A. Plemenos, Lightweight & secure industrial iot communications via the mq telemetry transport protocol, in Computers and Communications (ISCC), 2017 IEEE Symposium on, IEEE. 2017;1193-1200.

[11] P. Ferrari, E. Sisinni, D. Brand -ao, M. Rocha, Evaluation of communication latency in industrial IoT applications, Measurement and Networking (M&N), 2017 IEEE International Workshop on, IEEE, 2017;1-6.

[12] Shitharth, D.Prince Winston, "A New Probabilistic Relevancy Classification (PRC) based Intrusion Detection System (IDS) for SCADA network," Journal of Electrical Engineering, Vol.16, No.3, 2016, pp. 278-288.

[13] T. P. Raptis, A. Passarella, A distributed data management scheme for industrial iot environments, in Wireless and Mobile Computing, Networking and Communications (WiMob), IEEE, 2017;196-203.

[14] S. Rao, R. Shorey, Efficient device-to-device association and data aggregation in industrial IoT systems, in Communication Systems and Networks (COMSNETS), 2017 9th International Conference on, IEEE, 2017;314-321.

[15] T. P. Raptis, A. Passarella, M. Conti, Maximizing industrial iot network lifetime under latency constraints through edge data distribution, in 1st IEEE International Conference on Industrial Cyber-Physical Systems, (ICPS) (May 2018), available at http://cnd. iit. cnr. it/traptis/2018-raptis-icps. pdf.

[16] M. H. ur Rehman, I. Yagoob, K. Salah, M. Imran, P. P. Jayaraman, C. Perera, The role of big data analytics in industrial internet of things, Future Generation Computer Systems. 2019; 99:247-259. Doi:10.1016/j.future.2019.04.020.

[17] D. Miller, Blockchain and the Internet of Things in the industrial sector, IT Professional. 2018; 20 (3):15-18.

[18] F. Javed, M. K. Afzal, M. Sharif, B.-S. Kim, internet of things (IoT) operating systems support, networking technologies, applications, and challenges: A comparative review, IEEE Communications Surveys & Tutorials. 2018; 20 (3): 2062-2100.

[19] M. Padmaja, S. Shitharth, K. Prasuna, Abhay Chaturvedi, Pravin R. Kshirsagar, A. Vani, 'Grow of Artificial Intelligence to Challenge Security in IoT Application,' wireless personal communication, Springer, https://doi.org/10.1007/s11277-021-08725-4

[20] Dawson, C.: Introduction to Research Methods: A Practical Guide for Anyone Undertaking a Research Project, 4th ed. How to Books, London (2009).

[21] S. Shitharth, N. Satheesh, B. Praveen Kumar, K. Sangeetha, "IDS Detection Based on Optimization Based on WI-CS and GNN Algorithm in SCADA Network', Architectural Wireless Networks Solutions and Security Issues, Lecture notes in network and systems, Springer, vol. 196, Issue 1, 2021, pp. 247-266.

[22] Schultze, U., Orlikowski, W. J.: A practice perspective on technologymediated network relations: the use of internet-based self-serve technologies. Inf. Syst. Res. 2004 ; 15(1): 89-106.

[23] Yin, R. K.: Case Study Research: Design and Methods. Applied Social Research Methods, 5th ed. Sage, Beverly Hills (1984).

[24] S. Shitharth, Masood Shaik, Sirajudeen, Sangeetha, 'Mining of intrusion attack in SCADA network using clustering and genetically seeded flora based optimal classification algorithm', Information Security, IET, vol. 14, Issue 1, 2019, pp. 1-11

[25] Creswell, J., Plano Clark, V. L.: Designing and Conducting Mixed Method Research, 2nd edition. Sage, Thousand Oaks (2011).

[26] Mitchell, T., Jones, S.: Leading and coordinating a multi-nurse researcher project. Nurse Res. 2004; 12(2): 42-55.

2

Industry Automation: The Contributions of Artificial Intelligence (AI)

M. Nalini

Department of Electronics and Instrumentation Engineering,
Sri Sairam Engineering College, India
E-mail: nalini.ei@sairam.edu.

Abstract

Artificial intelligence (AI) refers to a computer's or a robot's capability to execute jobs that intelligent people ordinarily achieve. Artificial intelligence permits machines to learn from their mistakes, adapt and react to new inputs, and accomplish human-like tasks. It is used in a wide range of industries, including gambling, banking, retail, commercial, and government, to name a few. AI is used in industrial automation since it is extensively used and is steadily becoming more common in manufacturing. AI-driven robots are leading the road to the future by offering a host of advantages, such as new opportunities, high manufacturing efficiency, and a good fit between machine and human engagement. Knowledge-based, automated labor is a hallmark of the Fourth Industrial Revolution. Many internal industrial difficulties, ranging from a lack of expertise to sophistication in decision-making, integration of problems, and information overload, may be solved using AI. By incorporating AI into manufacturing plants, businesses can radically transform their operations. The importance of artificial intelligence in industrial automation is explained in this chapter, which begins with a brief introduction, then application landscape and production-related scenarios, and then moves on to a classification scheme with real-time examples. This chapter also covers the impact of artificial intelligence in industrial automation, followed by applications of artificial intelligence examples in different industry sectors, and ends with future scope.

Keywords: artificial intelligence, industrial automation, Industry 4.0, smart production, robotic process automation

2.1 Introduction

"Industry 4.0" has been called "a name for the current trend of automation and data exchange in manufacturing technologies." For this trend to reach its full potential, it needs cyber–physical systems, the Internet of Things, cloud computing, cognitive computing, and the creation of "smart factories." When people talk about Industry 4.0, they usually mean "the current trend of automation and data exchange in manufacturing technologies," which is what this page says it is. By developing new ways using the latest technologies to automate jobs, we can renovate how people and machines live, engage, and cooperate, resulting in a superior, healthier, and more robust digital economy. For a long time, computer visualizing has been used to uncover product flaws in real time for quality assurance. On the other hand, manufacturing now demands more info than ever before, as well as the fact that management does not want to pay employees to enter data. Data collection may be rationalized using AI and computer vision. A factory employee would be able to remove raw materials from a rack and then have the stock transaction conducted automatically, depending on the activity being monitored with a camera. It will be the primary user-friendly interface, with the user concentrating on the job instead of typing or scanning data into a computer. Second, artificial intelligence will impact the Internet of Things (IoT). The IoT will allow businesses to distribute products and services to customers who may not realize they require them. IoT may also provide extensive data to producers and retailers, allowing them to assess quality and identify variables that could create difficulties [1]. In a word, the IoT is an incoming data stream that artificial intelligence (AI) may use to reason and grow. This will make the enhanced generative design process much easier, allowing for the more evolutionary reimagining of products.

From 2021 to 2028, the global market for AI is projected to expand at a CAGR of 40.2%, from USD 62.35 billion in 2021 to USD 62.35 billion in 2028 (Figure 2.1). Industry after industry, from healthcare to automotive to retail to finance to manufacturing, is adopting cutting-edge technology, thanks to the relentless efforts of the tech giants in this field. On the other

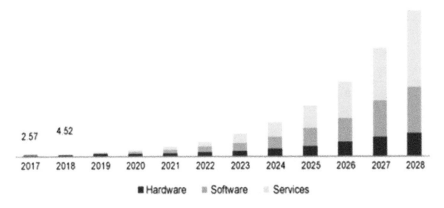

Figure 2.1 Market value of AI.

hand, technology has continuously played a vital role in these organizations, although AI technology has transported it to the fore. Artificial intelligence is now being integrated into nearly every tool and program, from self-driving cars to medical devices that save lives. Artificial intelligence has proven to be a massive game-changer in the past, and it will only get bigger and better in the coming digital age.

Artificial intelligence technology usage is increasing in the manufacturing sector to provide new possibilities and improve functional competencies by utilizing innovative technologies, speeding up methods, and creating businesses more adaptive to future changes. The impact of AI in industries will make the following changes [2].

- Formal assertions are inferred from logical statements, and systems to verify the correctness of hardware and software are built using deductive methods and machine-based proofs.
- Knowledge-based systems include approaches for modeling and gathering knowledge and software that can mimic human competency and assist specialists.
- Inductive computational methods, in general, and machine learning, in particular, are used to recognize and analyze patterns.
- Robotics: the uncontrolled operation of robotic equipment, such as self-driving cars.
- Intelligent multimodal human−machine interaction: words (in combination with linguistics), visuals, gestures, and other human contact are analyzed and "understood."

Important Industry Use cases	
Products and services	Autonomous vehicles
Manufacturing operations	AI - enchanced predicted maintenance collaborative and content aware robots
	Yield enhancement in manufactturing
	Automated quality testing
Business Processes	AI enabled supply chain management
	High performance R&D projects
	Business support function automation

Figure 2.2   Impacts of AI on the industry.

Machine learning is the most widely utilized AI technique across sectors. This is unquestionably owing to its broad application, which makes it applicable to many use cases across the value chain represented in Figure 2.2. While companies have typically depended on internal information for supervised machine learning, many more are increasingly looking at the possibility of combining internal and external datasets, as well as internal and external data science skills, to provide even more insightful findings.

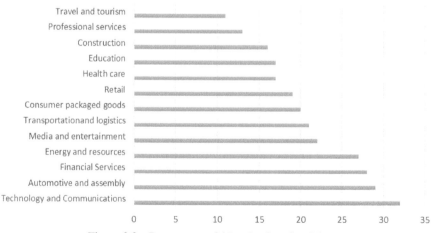

Figure 2.3   Percentages of AI technology breakdown.

Knowledge-based representations, communication via natural languages, the deployment of tactics, the appraisal of irregularities, and action are all characteristics of artificial intelligence. AI systems can detect and react to threats, as well as support decision-making, math-oriented intelligence, and cognitive research. The most popular sort of machine learning is supervised learning, which involves feeding software with organized data to detect patterns and comprehend and understand new findings. Machine learning and smart robotics have been determined to be the most beneficial in using AI in businesses. The McKinsey Global Institute surveyed 3000 executives of various firms in 2017; based on this survey, the technological breakdown between various industries illustrates in Figure 2.3.

2.2 Automation Systems Potential

Bulk production is the way of producing many identical things using manufacturing lines or automation technologies. Mass manufacturing allows for the efficient fabrication of many comparable things. Client-centric production, in which the customer is a co-designer of the product, has supplanted the traditional mass production approach [4]. This can be enabled using artificial intelligence technologies, as shown in Figure 2.4.

Figure 2.4, left side, shows the automation and manufacturing plan designed to service mass manufacturing at the lowest possible cost. The production process is stiff after it has been created and does not allow for flexibility. A paradigm shift towards personalization is shown in the middle, with the consumer becoming a co-designer of his product. Digital twins, machines, and services are illustrated on the right side, allowing new service-oriented cost models. Artificial intelligence, which integrates current infrastructures, digital twins, and more data resources, enables computers to independently

Figure 2.4 Customer-driven production.

create sophisticated goods, manufacturing processes, and lines. Digital twins refer to both existing and non-existing (historical) materials. This strategy defies existing assumptions and creates incredible opportunities for innovative ideas to be accepted in industries around the world [4].

2.3 Application Landscape and Production-related Scenarios

The AI Map (Platform Learned System, 2021), created by the Federal Ministries of Education and Research (BMBF) and Economic Affairs and Energy (BMWi), provides a snapshot of AI application areas, research institutes, and transfer initiatives in Germany. The properties of AI applications may be mapped into the "orange dotted box," as shown in Figure 2.5; it covers the functioning of machines and systems if we use the Reference Architectural Model Industry4.0 (RAMI4.0) model, which is the reference shown in Figure 2.5. RAMI4.0 is a three-dimensional plan that depicts the key elements of Industry 4.0 (I4.0). Processes are optimized using data. This comes after the initial wave of digitizing industries by integrating sensors into existing machinery, often known as "brownfield" optimization [5]. The function of AI in the RAMI4.0 model's left half has yet to be researched, but the concurrent growth of digital duplication and wireless communication will power it. The "blue dotted box" in Figure 2.5 concentrates on the technical side of AI to allow new use cases in networked manufacturing and the association of AI services based on trustworthy infrastructures. RAMI4.0 model consists of three axes [7], which are explained here.

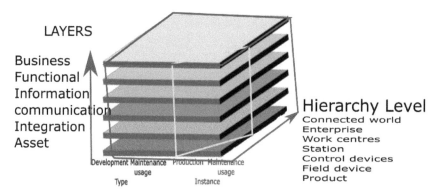

Figure 2.5   RAMI4.0 model.

"Hierarchy levels" axis

The hierarchical levels from IEC 62264, the worldwide regulations on integrating enterprise IT, and control systems are shown on the right horizontal axis. These hierarchy stages represent the different functionalities inside the factory or plant.

"Life cycle and value stream" axis

The lifespan of plants and goods is represented on a left horizontal axis. The IEC 62890 standard on monitoring and management serves as the foundation for this. There is also a difference made between type and instance. Whenever the development and prototype production phases are completed, and the actual product is built in the production department, a "type" becomes an "instance."

"Layers" axis

The IT representation, i.e., the digital picture of a machine, is defined in an organized method layer by layer using the six layers on the y-axis of the model. The characterization in layers arrives from information and communication technology. It is typical practice in this industry to stack sophisticated items.

The three axes reflect all of the critical elements of Industry 4.0. They categorize an item in the model, such as a machine. RAMI 4.0 may therefore be used to express and implement highly flexible Industry 4.0 principles. The Reference Architecture Model enables a gradual transition from the current state to the world of Industry 4.0 [6].

2.3.1 Autonomy-level classification of industrial AI applications

In 2018, the Society of Automotive Engineers (SAE) investigated and issued an autonomy for self-driving cars. According to that standard, the acceptable phrases are driving automation or driving automation systems. The employment of electrical or mechanical equipment to replace human work is known as automation. The amount of human effort required is significant. As a result, automation is being pushed. The SAE standard is particularly important since it defines the SAE levels or levels of driving automation. Figure 2.6 illustrates these five stages and shows the role of artificial intelligence in achieving self-driving cars.

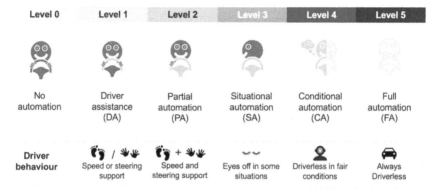

Figure 2.6   SAE standard level of automation for autonomous car.

Level 1: Assistance to the driver

A cruise controller, anti-lock braking system or anti-skid breaking system (ABS), traction control system (TCS), and electronic stability control are all parts of the ADAS (advanced driver aid system). The driver must maintain complete control when receiving help from the ADAS.

Level 2: Partially automated

The driver must remain engaged while driving, but the ADAS provides even more help, such as simultaneously regulating accelerating, decelerating, and turning. A backup camera is an example of this. Tesla's complete self-driving is also an example of this level.

Level 3: Automation based on condition

The ADS (automated driving system) includes environmental detecting features such as pedestrian safety, lane-changing aid, and junction assistance, allowing the automobile to respond to its surroundings independently. On the other hand, the human driver must be alert and ready to interfere and take control if necessary. Autopilot is yet another instance of a Level 3 automation categorization.

Level 4: High-level automation

In some conditions, such as within a geo-fenced region, the ADS can operate and perform all driving operations on its own, including monitoring its environment. The human driver may turn their focus away from the functions, but they retain the power to override if necessary.

Level 5: Totally automated

Full automation drives the future and has been promised for decades in futuristic blockbusters like Minority Report, Knight Rider, and Time Cop. These cars will not require a driver; drivers may become passengers since they can do business, work on their newest hobby, or snooze while being transported using a Level 5 autonomous vehicle.

2.4 Impact of Artificial Intelligence in Industry4.0 (I4.0)

The German Industry 4.0 Platform (PI4.0) has released 11+ key industry 4.0 implementation and technology scenarios for several industrial value streams. Expert groups from DIN/DKE-SVCI4.0 and IEC-TC65 examined over 50 AI use cases in about various parts of the industrial internet reference architecture (IIRA). According to the data, there is a shortage in engineering.

The AI capability in particular situations is presented below, using autonomy levels as a reference (AL). Six different application situations and a novel technological scenario will be covered.

2.4.1 Order-controlled production (OCP)

At its core, the "order-controlled production" scenario is concerned with how a company could automatically order the integration of other firms' assets and capabilities into its own manufacturing to generate customized items across manufacturing lines. This scenario is depicted in Figure 2.7. The contributions of artificial intelligence, in this case, are as follows:

- The investigation and selection of possible suppliers as well as their roles in the supply chain to determine the much more cost-effective offer that fits the requirements.
- Automated discovery and negotiation with potential manufacturing-skilled suppliers.

Manufacturers can include external manufacturing modules mostly automated with order-controlled production. They extend their manufacturing capabilities and capacities in response to demand on a case-by-case basis. This procedure does not necessitate any financial investment. This allows businesses to respond quickly to changing market conditions and client needs. On the other hand, companies that put their skills and capacities on the market can maximize the use of their production capacity. When adopting flexible order-controlled manufacturing, new business models are also feasible. This

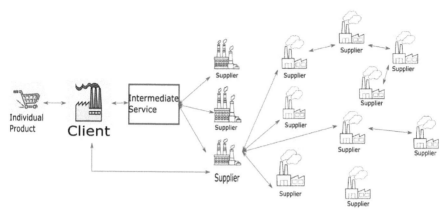

Figure 2.7   The scenario of order-controlled production.

is strongly tied to the transition to the so-called platform economy, where services are supplied via digital platforms in the B2B sector, as stated in the "value-based services" scenario.

2.4.2 Smart production (SP2)

Using smart production, smart products can be developed. Future product digital twins, also with sensor-equipped mechanisms, offer innovative types of engineering cooperation as well as the automation of engineering tasks. During the production process, digital twins, as well as sensor information, are given. The digital twin will be customized for each process stage. Different digital clones may exist for the same product, each reacting to client needs. This scenario is depicted in Figure 2.8. Smart goods are one of the most important parts of the next industry transformation, which will impact both products and processes. This section examines the recent developments in the industrial environment as well as the improvements in product creation procedures. Furthermore, with the introduction of novel technology that includes powerful computer platforms, Industry 4.0 (I4.0) is creating new options for SP2 [7].

The contributions of artificial intelligence, in this case, are as follows:

- Artificial intelligence provides a complete platform for its full lifespan.
- Simulation and modeling tools with artificial intelligence.

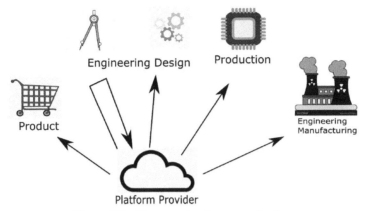

Figure 2.8 The scenario of smart production.

2.4.3 Innovative product development (IPD)

Methods for creative product creation based on intelligent networking and collaboration amongst various players are at the heart of this application scenario. This is made feasible through Internet-based cooperation, which allows people to exchange tools, services, and information. Figure 2.9 depicts this situation, in which innovative product development, by speeding up the digital product development process, reduces the product development lifespan from discovery to launch. The product development process allows for speedy prototyping and regular feedback when joined with perfectly matched digital tools. Customer data and feedback are regularly examined as part of the innovation generation process. Rather than segregating development and user experience design, a multi-discipline team works to address problems with the current products depending on customer input or problem statements.

IPD has several advantages:

1. Increase the speed with which digital things are created.
2. Rapid prototyping helps you to test your business concepts quickly.
3. Use APIs and low-code environments to try out different features or services easily.
4. Examine existing products for ways to improve them.
5. Product development innovation could also be used to enhance an existing product line.
6. To fulfill the expectations of its consumers, a successful product should evolve over time.

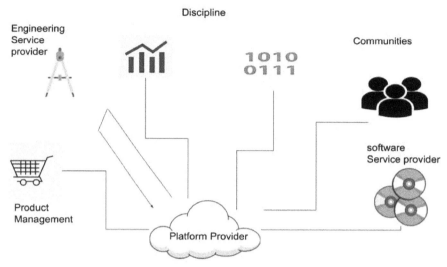

Figure 2.9 The scenario of innovative product development.

7. With such a shorter development cycle, such as that utilized in the innovative product development process, it is feasible to adapt quickly to client requests.

Streamline product/service development to save money. Reduce service and product development costs by merging interdisciplinary collaboration into a more practical approach to creative product creation.

The contributions of artificial intelligence, in this case, are as follows:

- In the value chain, the entire life cycle is covered.
- In the virtual world, customer centric product design is covered.

2.4.4 Seamless and dynamic engineering of plants (SDP)

This setup explains in what way such an integrating plant model is formed and utilized, starting with an early engineering procedure for establishing a system, and how it is sustained and maintained constantly during the entire life cycle of the realized plant interconnected processes, starting from engineering, process, and service. Boundary circumstances, background information, feasible plant variations, believable and actual engineering conclusions, as well as the prospective and real impacts of such decisions are all included in this model [8] (Technical Committee 6.12, VDI-GMA, 2018). IPD and SP2 are concerned with the product, whereas SDP is concerned with the plant,

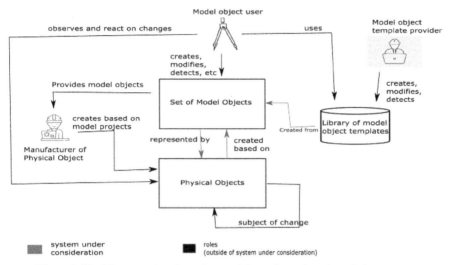

Figure 2.10   The scenario of seamless and dynamic engineering of plants usage.

which is usually associated with a specific location. This scenario is shown in Figure 2.10. The following positions generally stand out.

- The model object template provider is in charge of building a model object template library.
- The model object user is in charge of the entire collection of model objects.
- A physical object maker can make a physical thing from one or more model objects.

The contributions of artificial intelligence, in this case, are:

- assisting with the system engineering and model generation processes;
- monitoring the data with additional context data to make the perfect engineering choices throughout the entire life cycle of the plant.

2.4.5 Circular economy (CRE)

One of the three pillars upon which the circular economy rests is that process design should be prioritized. Waste and effluent must be eliminated, and recycling products and materials must be a top priority (at their highest value). The world's natural environments would be revitalized. The "circular economy" application scenario shows how industrial procedures can take cues from biological processes to make better use of a given resource's capacity and produce less waste, thereby enabling the "cradle-to-grave" reusing, repurposing, and recycling of items. Figure 2.11 illustrates this situation. They are reducing environmental impact while considering life cycle analysis. Instead of discarding things and relying on the discovery of new resources, a circular economy will have marketplaces that encourage people to repurpose existing items. Used items such as clothing, metal scraps, and outdated gadgets can all find new homes in this system or at least find new uses. It is possible that this will aid in environmental protection as well as the management of natural resources, the development of innovative economic ventures, the fostering of fresh talent, and the provision of new job opportunities. To facilitate this, we must shift to using renewable sources of power and building supplies. In a circular economy, the production and consumption of goods and services are no longer intrinsically linked. It is a trusted method that helps businesses, people, and the planet.

The contribution of artificial intelligence, in this case, is:

- Life cycle assessment preparation and validation: Designing goods and systems such that components may be reused, hence reducing the production's "green footprint."
- Assisting in the categorization procedure: AI aids in the prediction of the state of function (SoF) and state of health (SoH).

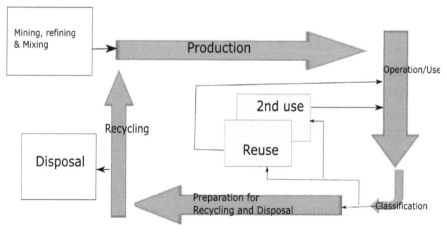

Figure 2.11   The scenario of circular economy.

2.4.6 5G for digital factories — mobile controlled production (MCP)

It was the first technological scenario of 2019 that has been released. By preventing the need for cables using smart technologies like cloud-based services and wireless communication, innovative novel design solutions are developed for the manufacturing and logistics industry. Five use case families have been identified by the EFFRA (European Factories of the Future Research Association) research and white paper [1] on 5G, each representing a different subset of rigorous needs within the supply chain and industrial networks, as shown in Figure 2.12.

UC1: Optimizing time-critical processes inside the factory to achieve zero-defect production, increased efficiency, worker satisfaction, and safety through 3D scanning, wearables, and collaborative robots in closed-loop control systems. This set of use cases necessitates a latency of less than 1 ms.

Different sorts of network characteristics (quality of service criteria) and solutions may be required by various players in the value chain.

The contributions of artificial intelligence, in this case, are:

- Finding the best network-slicing technique to assist the manufacturing process and system engineering.
- Private data connection with high processing speed.
- Home and business broadband.

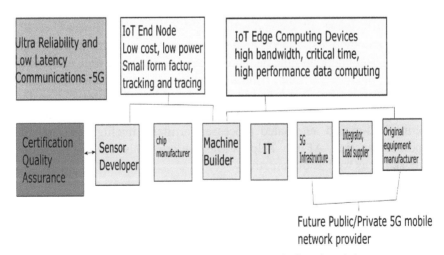

Figure 2.12 The scenario of different actors in the value chain.

- Smart antenna design and activation for internal application optimization (ETSI, 2020).
- Self-healing as well as forecasting.
- Network resource allocation and management.
- Internet Protocol version 6 (IPv6) has intelligent security, and so on.

2.5 Industry Use Cases for AI-enabled Collaboration

Artificial intelligence can take industrial automation to the next new level of automation by allowing for automated combined engineering with many stakeholders across the value chain in various sectors. New service-based business models, including the value chain and manufacturing ecosystem partners, are emerging. Even though a significant number of companies have implemented AI to automate mundane tasks, those companies that use AI to supplant human workers will, at best, see only temporary increases in output. Humans and artificial intelligence can improve upon each other's strengths by combining their respective intelligence. These strengths include leadership, teamwork, creativity, social skills, scalability, and quantitative abilities. What comes naturally to humans, such as telling a story, may be impossible for machines to imitate. On the other hand, what machines do automatically, such as analyzing gigabytes of data, may be impossible for humans. Both of these abilities are necessary for sustained success in the business world.

Artificial intelligence's effect is becoming more prominent with each advancement. Almost all the industries, like banking and finance, retail, healthcare, automobiles, telecommunications, manufacturing, defense and military, entertainment and media, and education, are being transformed by technology. Machine learning, natural language processing, data analytics, and image analytics are just a few of the artificial intelligence sub-domains that are proving to be successful in various industries. Furthermore, by exploiting end-to-end automated processes, artificial intelligence serves a commercial function. AI may help us improve our analytical and decision-making skills, as well as our creativity.

2.5.1 Artificial intelligence in healthcare industry

2.5.1.1 The use of predictive analytics to confirm the need for surgery

Healthcare has been given a gift in the form of predictive analytics. We occasionally encounter patients who claim they had unneeded surgery due

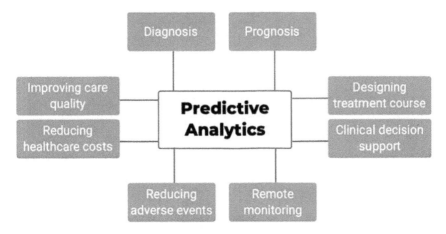

Figure 2.13 Predictive analytics in healthcare: use cases.

to a lack of forewarning about what was to follow. Artificial intelligence, thankfully, is altering the fate of such hefty risks and unnecessary operations. Healthcare providers may determine whether or not a patient requires surgery using artificial intelligence and predictive analytics. The technology will aid doctors in determining whether the procedure is indeed essential or whether there is a less risky option [9].

In the ICU and general ward, predictive analytics may assist in noticing early indicators of patient weakening and identifying at-risk patients at home to lessen hospital readmission rates and avoid downtime for healthcare equipment. Some of the notable areas of healthcare predictive analytics at different stages of the patient journey utilize AI, as shown in Figure 2.13.

Diagnosis: Patients who are diagnosed early can begin treatment immediately, boosting their chances of survival; this prediction is a valuable tool. For example, diagnoses of malignant mesothelioma were predicted using a patient group's predictive analytics.

Prognosis: The researchers employed predictive analytics to find which patients, for example, suffering from congestive heart failure (CHF), had the maximum chances of being readmitted after a hospital stay based on physiological data. Doctors may utilize this knowledge to undertake therapies early to avoid the expected readmissions.

Therapy: To identify the most successful treatment method for patients with prolonged pain, clinicians used machine-learning-based predictive analytic models.

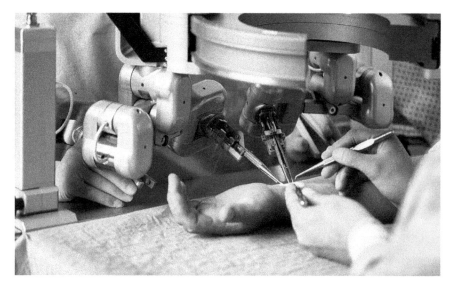

Figure 2.14   Example of surgical robot.

2.5.1.2 Intelligent surgical robots

Robot surgeons are necessary in the twenty-first century due to the growing worldwide population and need for doctors. Aside from standing in for human surgeons, robot surgeons may often outperform them. Surgery operations need extreme patience and accuracy, and medical surgeons' abilities do not decrease even when they operate nonstop for hours on end [8]. As a result, robotic assistance in operations can assist surgeons in achieving a new degree of precision, even for the tiniest movements.

Surgical robots can regulate their movements' direction, depth, and speed with extreme precision. Because they do not grow weary, they are especially well-suited to activities that need the same repetitive movements. Robots can also stay in one place for a long time and go places while traditional tools cannot do this.

2.5.2 Artificial intelligence in manufacturing and factories

2.5.2.1 Analytical services for advanced data

The industrial industry has had great success using AI for sophisticated data analytics. Digital transformation has resulted in an abundance of large-scale real-time datasets that may be leveraged to get in-depth insights and forecast current market trends. The mix of data and sophisticated analytics has aided risk management, data visualization, supply chain management, and the efficient and effective decision-making.

2.5.2.2 Predictive maintenance

Maintenance planned ahead of time is called predictive maintenance, or PdM, and uses real-time data to identify critical faults in the manufacturing process so that remedial measures may be taken quickly. It assists in data analysis by examining differences in nature and frequency, and it notifies the system to lessen the chance of failure. Predictive maintenance extends a product's life, as shown in the graph in Figure 2.15. While unplanned maintenance and preventive maintenance have a tradeoff, predictive maintenance (PdM) is an auspicious method that can break the exchange by optimizing component useful life and uptime simultaneously. Its purpose is to keep track of the status of in-service equipment and anticipate when it may break [10].

It is a sign that the plant's equipment's future behavior and condition can be predicted, allowing for more effective maintenance (e.g., predictive health monitoring). This allows for the minimum downtime and maintenance costs for machines possible [15].

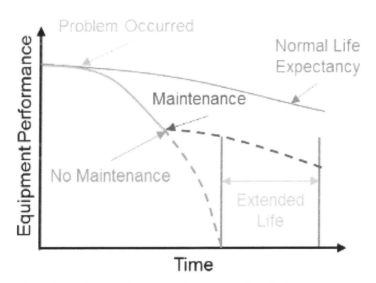

Figure 2.15   Graphical representation – effect of predictive maintenance.

2.5.2.3 Automation of robotic processes

RPA software, or robotic process automation, can successfully handle the organization's backend functions without the need for human interaction. It allows employees to concentrate on other tasks, resulting in increased productivity. RPA automates high-volume, repetitive processes requiring complicated computations and maintains correct records. RPA software may be implemented in various production processes to assist in cutting time and enhance workflow compared to rivals, as shown in Figure 2.16. By adopting RPA, businesses will increase their profits, agility, and responsiveness. The software can remove time-consuming tasks from their daily routine to improve employee happiness, engagement, and productivity. Unlike other digital transformation methods, RPA does not have to slow down day-to-day operations to speed up the process. Working with antiquated systems that lack modern conveniences like application programming interfaces, virtual desktop infrastructures, and database access is also helpful in automating tasks.

The advantages of RPA

- RPA does not always require developer setup; less coding is required. Drag-and-drop features in user interfaces make it easier for people without technical knowledge to get started.
- RPA's ability to reduce team effort results in immediate cost savings. Because of this, personnel can be reallocated to perform other, more critical tasks that call for human judgment, boosting output and ROI.
- Increased happiness among the company's clientele: Customers are more likely to be satisfied with a company after using a bot or chatbot because they do not have to wait much long for help to become available.
- Increased happiness among workers: By automating routine, high-volume tasks, robots like RPA allow workers to put their minds to more

Figure 2.16   The scenario of robotic process automation.

strategic, creative problems. As a result, morale among workers rises. Workers are happier now due to the shift in the workplace.

- Robotic process automation (RPA) bots can be set up to follow a set of predetermined rules and procedures. Therefore, the possibility of human error is eliminated entirely, which is especially helpful in areas like regulatory compliance, where accuracy and conformity are fundamental. An audit trail can be generated by RPA software, making it easier to track development and easing the way for quicker problem-solving.
- The regular operation of preexisting systems will be preserved, as the software used in robotic process automation has no effect on the underlying infrastructure. This is because bots function at the presentation layer of the currently deployed applications. If you lack an API or the personnel to create complicated integrations, you may want to think about using bots instead.

2.5.3 Artificial intelligence in automobile

2.5.3.1 The use of artificial intelligence to improve design

Artificial intelligence (AI), programmable shading, and real-time ray tracing are all employed extensively to modify the product's traditional design process. The disruption of advanced AI has resulted in an advanced ecosystem that speeds up new design workflows and increases team communication. It is stated that AI algorithms will be the future of automotive design, as they can develop infinite viable techniques by specifying product concepts and the problem [15].

2.5.3.2 AI application in manufacturing

Companies employ AI-based robots and a human workforce to complete industrial and supply chain operations. In manufacturing, AI-powered robots have demonstrated outcomes in material handling, test performance, and packaging final goods. Machine learning, automation, advanced and predictive analytics, and the Internet of Things (IoT) are all important Fourth Industrial Revolution (I4.0) technologies that manufacturers may use to monitor their facilities in real time (Internet of Things).

This supports to accumulate enormous quantities of operational data to:

- preserve track of vital performance measures like overall equipment effectiveness (OEE), production, and scrap rates;
- predict date of delivery and pickup accurately to prevent missing deadlines;

Figure 2.17   Benefits of AI in manufacturing industries.

- predict future supply chain interruptions;
- troubleshoot any bottlenecks in the production process;
- identify and regulate equipment inefficiencies whenever they arise.

2.5.3.3 Examples of AI in manufacturing – inspiring changes

AI is revolutionizing the production process in ground-breaking ways. Machine learning is being utilized by the Danone Group, a French food company, to improve its demand forecasting accuracy. As a result, we now have the following:

- Errors in forecasting have decreased by 20%.
- Lost sales have decreased by 30%.
- Demand planners' workload has been reduced by 50%.

- Predictive maintenance (PdM) has decreased unplanned downtime of equipment.
- Using advanced manufacturing technologies (3D printers, robots, etc.) has reduced labor costs and flexibility in the face of supply chain inferences.
- The finest, AI-enabled generative design has been created to ensure efficiency and reduce waste.

Fanuc, a Japanese company specializing in automation, uses robot labor to keep its operations going (24 × 7) around the clock every day of the week. Robots can construct risky components for CNCs and motors, run all factory floor gear continuously, and monitor all processes nonstop. BMW Group uses automatic image recognition for quality control, inspections, and eliminating false problems (deviations from target despite no actual faults). As a result, they have attained exceptional stages of production accuracy [11].

2.5.4 Application of artificial intelligence in quality control

Quality control, which includes checking painted automobile bodywork, is aided by artificial intelligence. When done by humans, such delicate detections are prone to mistakes. Artificial-intelligence-enabled computers can spot flaws more quickly and precisely than people. Machine learning (ML) quality inspection is expected to replace present optical crack detection. Manufacturers are benefitting from the arrangement of smart cameras with AI-enabled software to achieve higher quality checks at speeds, latency, and prices that are beyond the capability of human supervisors. And, considering an example of COVID-19's social distance criteria, the emergence of such AI-enabled smart camera technology is fortunate. Machine vision has, of course, been used in quality governor applications for many years. However, incorporating quality control software powered by deep learning is a change from earlier machine vision technology [12]. The adoption of AI in conjunction with test automation allows for a better understanding of the current status of QE and aids in the actions shown in Figure 2.18.

Test cases can be used again

AI-based test automation solutions simplify the complex process of creating and reusing well-written test cases in the future. An AI-based testing tool inspects the application and captures critical data through images to evaluate load time, assess fundamental UI aspects, and create appealing test case suites.

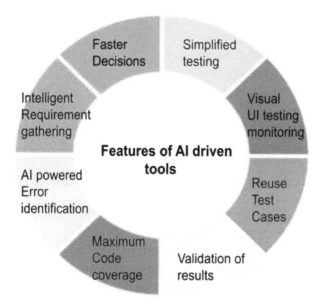

Figure 2.18   Features of AI-powered quality assurance.

Gathering intelligent requirements

Several manual operations, including reporting, controlling the effect of change, and tracking approvals, influence project deliverables during requirements collecting. Artificial-intelligence-assisted requirement collecting recognizes the constraints of complex systems and maintains critical indicators and KPIs that may be used to identify quality and performance concerns ahead of time.

Exploratory testing made simple

Using an AI-engineered technique, testing may be made more successful with fewer resources and codes while maximizing device coverage in the shortest amount of time. Through intelligent assistants that gather test data and user performances while navigating through an application or system and recording default test cases, AI readily discovers possibilities.

Error detection assisted by artificial intelligence

Utilize AI-driven QA to uncover problems ahead of time, improve testing, and forecast failure spots, lowering total costs and increasing customer satisfaction. AI-enabled performance analysis ensures an application's or system's security by detecting any possible attempts at unwanted access.

Visual UI testing and monitoring with AI

Artificial intelligence enhances the test platform's visual testing capabilities to help development teams deliver aesthetically flawless web apps at unbeatable speed and quality. Analyzing regression testing results is straightforward, effective, and painless using AI-powered monitoring tools.

Maximum code coverage in a short amount of time

Maximum test coverage may be achieved when the test plan, test strategy, test cases, and other elements are well-planned. Real-time engagements, user flows, keyword interactions, and data-driven techniques might all be used in the tests. Businesses may attain 100% code coverage using AI-based solutions to measure test coverage.

AI-assisted decision-making

AI can go deep into data to find the source of problems affecting corporate performance. It allows for analyzing consumer data for maximum efficiency, more excellent inventive capabilities, fine-tuning of products and services, or better possibilities. It so contributes considerably to the streamlining of decisions for better processes.

2.5.5 Manufacturing industry trends with emerging AI

AI will impact manufacturing in ways we have not considered. Nonetheless, we may look at some more notable cases right now.

For a long time, computer visualization has been used for quality management, discovering product flaws in real time. However, because manufacturing now demands more data than ever, and plant managers are unwilling to pay humans to input data, AI and machine vision can help rationalize data collection [14]. An employee in a manufacturing facility may take raw materials from a shelf and then have the stock operation carried out automatically based on the activity being monitored with the assistance of a camera. It will evolve into a natural user interface, allowing users to focus on the task rather than manually entering data into a computer by typing it in or scanning it in.

Second, artificial intelligence will impact the Internet of Things (IoT). The IoT will allow businesses to distribute products and services to customers who may not realize they require them. IoT may also provide extensive data to manufacturers and distributors, allowing them to assess quality and identify variables that could create difficulties.

Some key AI statistics in different industries are shown in Figure 2.19.

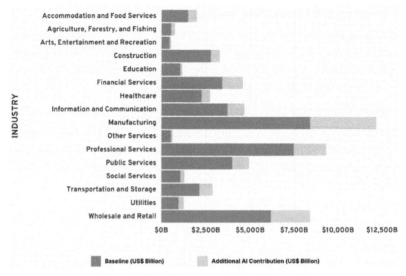

Figure 2.19   AI effect on industrial growth.

- By 2035, AI technology growth is estimated to increase production by 40%.
- By 2035, AI technologies will improve economic growth by an average 1.7% across 16 industries, as shown in Figure 2.19.

The bar chart shown in Figure 2.20 depicts the expected expansion of AI as a new component of production.

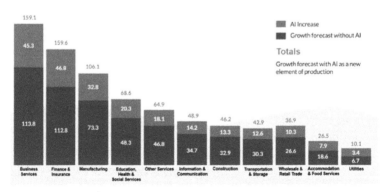

Figure 2.20   The effect of AI on the growth of different industries.
Survey Sources: MarketWatch Accenture, Accenture, Markets and Markets, Gartner, Servion, Microsoft, and Demandbase.

2.5.6 The Internet of Things is emerging as Industry 4.0's future

Two of the most significant recent advancements in information technology are the Internet of Things (IoT) and artificial intelligence (AI). Nevertheless, when placed in the context of the industrial revolution, these two technologies are much more than just buzzwords or current debate topics. The convergence of AI and IoT has reimagined what the future of industrial automation will look like. It is anticipated to play a leading role in the Fourth Industrial Revolution. These are two different technologies that have a significant impact on a wide range of other business sectors. While the Internet of Things (IoT) is the digital nervous system, AI is the brain that makes choices that manage the whole system. AIoT (artificial intelligence of things) is a deadly mix of AI and IoT that produces an intelligent and linked system that is capable of self-correcting and self-healing; this scenario is shown in Figure 2.21.

By acting on the telemetry data's patterns and correlations, AI goes beyond visualizations. It closes the critical gap by adopting suitable data-driven actions. Instead of simply delivering data to people so that they may act, artificial intelligence finishes the loop by taking action on its own. It effectively serves as the central nervous system for all related systems.

Artificial intelligence (AI) will boost industrial IoT on two levels. To begin with, it influences telemetry data by adding intelligence to the sensors. Second, in real-time or batch mode, AI will be employed to evaluate the inbound telemetry data stream. It connects the beginning to the end, i.e., devices, to the analysis of the IoT spectrum.

For example, a camera, which functions as an image sensor, will send a transmission to the IoT system for each frame it captures to perform an

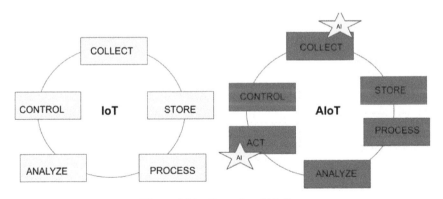

Figure 2.21   Scenario of AIoT.

analysis of the feed looking for specific things. The camera accessory uses artificial intelligence to hold off on delivering the frame until a particular object has been identified. This expedites the process by reducing the time the central processing unit (CPU) spends processing each frame.

Other forms of telemetry data, such as speech or natural language processing, can also be processed in a manner analogous to that described above. In the not-too-distant future, sensors enabled by AI technology will dominate IoT systems. Soon, intelligent cameras equipped with AI accelerators from Intel, NVIDIA, and Qualcomm will be the standard image sensors used across industries.

Deep learning models based on neural networks will be applied to the incoming sensor telemetry data by advanced Internet of Things (IoT) systems, allowing these systems to detect anomalies in real time. When the neural network detects a potentially catastrophic error, the faulty machinery might be shut down to avoid a potentially fatal accident or incident. The primary difference between engines based on traditional Internet of Things (IoT) rules and engines based on artificial intelligence Internet of Things (IoT) rules is that AIoT rules are proactive rather than reactive.

AIoT systems can identify faults and events in advance, unlike IoT systems, which are designed to react after an event. Incorporating AI into the Internet of Things systems holds the promise of predictive maintenance, which will save businesses millions of dollars in support and maintenance costs for their equipment.

The integration of AI and IoT is the key to the future of industrial automation. Artificial intelligence of things (IoT) will influence nearly every business sector, for example, automobile, aviation, economics, healthcare, manufacturing, and supply chain management.

2.5.7 Future scope of research

Processes in industries will become more effective and ultimately more straightforward as a result of AI or AGI, but they will require considerably more complicated systems to support them. To reach the automated-AI future-designed phase, a lot of design, analysis, testing, and implementation is required, as well as a study on top of deep industrial process and AI expertise. AGI will manage the matching, bidding, and execution, as shown in Figure 2.22, on a distributed network in the future.

The question of whether consumers and society will embrace the solutions is dependent on proof that the keys have shown to be safe, trustworthy,

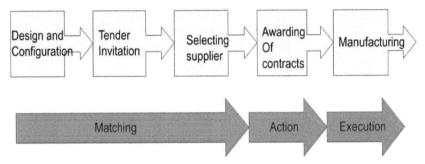

Figure 2.22 The trend of next industry automation.

and valuable to humans. There is still more study to be done, both in terms of technological and sociological factors, particularly regarding the importance of acceptability. The impact of AGI is heavily influenced by the aim utilized during the creation process. AGI research is also looking into how intention may be managed. We must begin designing this future today, using our shared European principles of human-centered AI.

2.6 Conclusion

This chapter starts with the role of artificial intelligence in industrial automation and then explains the potential of automated systems. Application landscape and production-related scenarios were explained with a real-time model. Autonomy-level classification of industrial AI applications was explained using one particular example. The impact of artificial intelligence in Industry 4.0 was explained for different production scenarios and finally ended with industry use cases for AI-enabled collaboration in various industry sectors. It also explained the future scope in the area of industrial automation. Artificial intelligence blends communication, computation, and control processes to satisfy industrial objectives. The emergence of artificial intelligence unquestionably made significant advances in all human endeavors.

References

[1] Tomohiko Sakao, Peter Funk, Johannes Matschewsky, Marcus Bengtsson, Mobyen Uddin Ahmed, AI-LCE: Adaptive and Intelligent Life Cycle Engineering by applying digitalization and A.I. methods – An emerging paradigm shift in Life Cycle Engineering, Procedia CIRP, Volume 98, 2021, Pages 571-576, ISSN 2212-8271.

[2] Baicun Wang, Fei Tao, Xudong Fang, Chao Liu, Yufei Liu, Theodor Freiheit, Smart Manufacturing and Intelligent Manufacturing: A Comparative Review, Engineering, Volume 7, Issue 6, 2021, Pages 738-757, ISSN 2095-8099.

[3] Kumar, T. Ananth, S. Arunmozhi Selvi, R. S. Rajesh, and G. Glorindal. "Safety wing for industry (SWI 2020)–an advanced unmanned aerial vehicle design for safety and security facility management in industries." In Industry 4.0 Interoperability, Analytics, Security, and Case Studies, pp. 181-198. CRC Press, 2021.

[4] Berry, W. L., Hill, T. J. and Klompmaker, J. E. (1995), "Customer-driven manufacturing," International Journal of Operations & Production Management, Vol. 15 No. 3, pp. 4-15.

[5] Raj, Pethuru, Jyotir Moy Chatterjee, Abhishek Kumar, and B. Balamurugan, eds. Internet of Things uses cases for the healthcare industry. Springer, 2020.

[6] Erwin Rauch, Patrick Dallasega, Dominik T. Matt, The Way from Lean Product Development (LPD) to Smart Product Development (SPD), Procedia CIRP, Volume 50, 2016, Pages 26-31, ISSN 2212-8271.

[7] M. Lopes Nunes, A. C. Pereira, A. C. Alves, Smart products development approaches for Industry 4.0, Procedia Manufacturing, Volume 13, 2017, Pages 1215-1222, ISSN 2351-9789.

[8] Kumar, T. Ananth, S. Arunmozhi Selvi, R. S. Rajesh, and G. Glorindal. "Safety wing for industry (SWI 2020)–an advanced unmanned aerial vehicle design for safety and security facility management in industries." In Industry 4.0 Interoperability, Analytics, Security, and Case Studies, pp. 181-198. CRC Press, 2021.

[9] Gudin J, Mavroudi S, Korfiati A, Theofilatos K, Dietze D, Hurwitz P. Reducing Opioid Prescriptions by Identifying Responders on Topical Analgesic Treatment Using an Individualized Medicine and Predictive Analytics Approach. J Pain Res. 2020;13:1255-1266.

[10] Wo Jae Lee, Haiyue Wu, Huitaek Yun, Hanjun Kim, Martin B. G. Jun, John W. Sutherland, Predictive Maintenance of Machine Tool Systems Using Artificial Intelligence Techniques Applied to Machine Condition Data, Procedia CIRP, Volume 80, 2019, Pages 506-511, ISSN 2212-8271.

[11] Jay Lee, Hossein Davari, Jaskaran Singh, Vibhor Pandhare, Industrial Artificial Intelligence for industry 4.0-based manufacturing systems, Manufacturing Letters, Volume 18, 2018, Pages 20-23, ISSN 2213-8463.

[12] B. Chen, J. Wan, L. Shu, P. Li, M. Mukherjee, and B. Yin, "Smart Factory of Industry 4.0: Key Technologies, Application Case, and Challenges," in IEEE Access, vol. 6, pp. 6505-6519, 2018, doi: 10.1109/ACCESS.2017.2783682.

[13] Alejandro Germán Frank, Lucas Santos Dalenogare, Néstor Fabián Ayala, Industry 4.0 technologies: Implementation patterns in manufacturing companies, International Journal of Production Economics, Volume 210, 2019, Pages 15-26, ISSN 0925-5273.

[14] ozdić, E. (2015). Smart factory for industry 4.0: A review. International Journal of Modern Manufacturing Technologies, 7(1), 28-35.

[15] orge Ribeiro, Rui Lima, Tiago Eckhardt, Sara Paiva, Robotic Process Automation and Artificial Intelligence in Industry 4.0 – A Literature review, Procedia Computer Science, Volume 181, 2021, Pages 51-58, ISSN 1877-0509.

[16] onepudi, P. K. (2018). Application of Artificial Intelligence in the automation industry. Asian Journal of Applied Science and Engineering, 7(1), 7-20.

3

Industry Automation: The Contributions of Artificial Intelligence

B. Akoramurthy[1], K. Dhivya[2], and Kassian T. T. Amesho[3]

[1]School of Computing & Information Technology, REVA University, India
[2]Department of Computer Science & Engineering, India
[3]Tshwane School for Business and Society, Tshwane University of Technology, South Africa
E-mail: akor.theanchor@gmail.com; dhivyaakoramurthy@gmail.com; kassian.amesho@gmail.com

Abstract

In the last decade, there has been a tremendous technological breakthrough in almost any industry, like healthcare, the military, education, and manufacturing industries, which includes new gadgets, discoveries, and refinements in the existing system. The current implementation of 5G technology tells us that Industry 5.0 has stormed into the market, where people are working with smart machines and robots. This also addresses the automated information exchange mechanism and other various technologies. So, in order to create smart factories and industries, it connects the ideas of the Internet of Things, cloud technology, and cognitive computing. Industry 5.0 ties together physical and digital advancements to build such intelligent businesses. Furthermore, it simplifies and maintains the actual needs as well as the supply chain in businesses. Companies and organizations profit from it because of its efficiency and capacity for quick judgments. Artificial intelligence is the core of this technology and a crucial factor in Industry 5.0. AI manages every technological item we use nowadays. The environment significantly impacts AI since every piece of data is linked to the Internet. A range of enterprises, such as those associated with manufacturing, e-commerce, sports, security, and defense, have shown the efficacy of AI due to its malleability. Thanks to the combination of Industry 5.0 and AI, almost all applications can access various options and services. Even though Industry 5.0 has demonstrated great success across all domains, it is still in the early stages of its extension, adoption, and hiring. We researched AI and Industry 5.0 in this work and explored their difficulties, significance, methods, and results. The relevance of innovation in the context of industry and everyday life has also been examined, along with its impacts and advantages.

Keywords: Industry 5.0, artificial intelligence, energy efficient metrics, datacenter carbon footprint computation

3.1 Introduction

In order to increase production, businesses and initiatives are investing more money daily. The Internet of Things, artificial intelligence, cloud computing, and other cutting-edge technologies are currently driving the production world forward. Adopting these technologies significantly impacts the advancement of physical resources and robots.

Businesses are motivated by their advancement, that is, by incorporating technologies that boost our country's economic growth to a better level [1]. The data is exchanged among these intelligent robots with this technology, and these computers use artificial intelligence to act like humans and make choices about every issue. Currently, artificial intelligence is a growing field of study. According to the market assessment, a 170 billion-dollar growth is anticipated by year's end. The manufacturing rate will increase with this new technology, and labor costs will drop by 80 billion dollars. On the other hand, the Internet of Things, which connects all electronic gadgets and has a target of 95 billion US dollars to expand to around 200+ ZB bytes by the year 2030, has had a significant influence in addition to AI. Likewise, AI systems can be anticipated to develop into a gadget with swift and grassed-up outcomes in the foreseeable future in order to acquire this large volume of facts and advance significant ideas from them. The business environment is shifting due to rapid breakthroughs in AI technology, and its use is replacing human-held tasks. Also, it fosters various application-based concepts and boosts company efficiency. Some of the most advanced nations are embracing this innovation in all its application-based situations and enhancing their economies. Natural language processing and perceptual computing have found new ways and are being altered by the rapid development of deep neural networks and machine learning technologies. Sales, human resource management, personal finance, ads, corporate plans, source and supply chains, commerce, retailing, systems engineering, etc., are only a few characteristics that make up artificial intelligence. The deployment-oriented categories of AI are depicted in Figure 3.1 precisely. AI aims to bring technology and machines together so that they can brilliantly use human intelligence. One of the fastest-growing industries today is AI, and jobs in this industry are also increasing.

The use of AI in numerous industries, including education, transportation, industry, banking, construction, recreation, governance, and healthcare, is explained in this section. The administration, individuals, or any organization can meet the changing market and industry demands for technical solutions to economic problems. Various forums for administration, financial plans, and company endeavors must be built using an agglomeration of data from various sources, including digital networking, channels, adverts, etc. Every company's economic progress is negatively impacted by the barriers that arise in business [6]. Businesses of any size may use artificial intelligence in emerging nations to aid with supply chain and delivery system problems and provide a variety of service availability. The use of automated corporate processes increased productivity, investment firms' and governments' support, and other technologies connected to AI, advanced analytics, and IoT may all contribute to the growth of possibilities in various fields [7]. AI systems are a technology that has been trained to replicate human behavior. Its various areas set it apart from other software packages, thanks to its unique attributes of quick efficiency, numerical simulations, and methods, and it is the most widely used data source. AI researchers use various algorithms to link highly relevant data and deliver high-quality software competence services. Our study will also offer a framework for using AI in business to address diverse technical problems.

Objectives

1. To review research and analysis on the role of AI in the development of Industry 5.0.
2. To determine the relationship between AI and Industry 5.0 and to design necessary technologies' future.

3.2 Literature Review

AI and its many tools are essential in modern production plants. Many organizations are heavily exploiting it and changing their manufacturing and functioning methods. Most gadgets and equipment use a variety of sensors and a digital storage system and are intelligent enough to carry out tasks. Along with operations, they are also preserving real-time data. Due to this, productivity and healthy competition have also improved. Real-time data collection has increased the analytical capacity of the system, and since the system makes decisions depending on the analysis of the information, the industry as a whole is more efficient. Industries use various AI- and ML-related technologies to expand operations, find new growth opportunities, build high-quality architecture, and more. There is the participation of Fortune 500 corporations in it as well. The majority of offices now have AI capabilities, which boosts productivity. Industry 5.0 is closely tied to IT-based solutions, software, and applications like AI, IoT, deep learning, etc. These cutting-edge technical advancements are providing tremendous assistance to organizations making progress to keep up with the times [10]. Virtual and practical perspectives are integrated into Industry 5.0, and big data analysis is a critical component of this. 3D printing and robotic systems are excellent supporters of Industry 5.0.

3.3 Industry 5.0 and AI

In the past, the concept of AI was compartmentalized into various business sectors. Natural language processing (NLP), automated coding (AC), robotic systems (RS), computer vision (CV), automatic hypothesis proving (AP), and intelligent data extraction are a few examples of these types of technologies (IDT). Because these fields of application have grown to such a large extent, each one can stand on its own as an independent academic specialization. Currently, the most accurate definition of artificial intelligence (AI) is a set of guiding principles underpinning many of these applications [9].

Robots' application of artificial intelligence (AI) to complete previously impossible tasks, reduce costs, and improve product quality is essential to smart manufacturing and Industry 5.0 [10]. Cyber–physical systems make incorporating artificial intelligence technologies into the manufacturing sector easier. This contributes to the ongoing convergence of the physical and digital worlds. The application of AI has a revolutionary impact on the manufacturing sector, allowing it to meet modern demands such as increased reliance on sensors, increased personalization of products, and faster product development cycles [11]. Various goods can be produced thanks to artificial intelligence (AI) and flexible robot technology efficiently. When sorting

Figure 3.1 Bibliographic analysis of Industry 5.0.

through mountains of raw datasets [12] collected by various sensors, information retrieval and other forms of artificial intelligence can be utilized as valuable tools.

There have been three significant shifts in the approaches taken by technological practitioners. According to the vast majority of available data sources, we are currently in the fourth one, or at least we should be. Figure 3.2 depicts the times that these uprisings took place in the form of a clock face. Take note of the shorter gaps in time that now exist between rotations. There was a 100-year gap between the three earliest revolutions in history. Approximately 40 years was all it took to get from the third to the fourth one. There is a possibility that we will reach the fifth one in fewer than 40 years from now.

The German government recently initiated a brand new initiative that they are referring to as "Industry 4.0." The overarching goal of Industry 4.0 is to facilitate "Smart Manufacturing for the Future." Its purpose is straightforward and in line with previous revolutions: to use cutting-edge technology to increase output and make it possible to produce on a large scale. Industry 4.0 is making progress, thanks to the contributions of many well-established technologies. The Internet of Things, robots, artificial intelligence (AI), big data, and cloud computing are some of the most prominent technologies currently trending. Industry 4.0 is made possible by many other technological

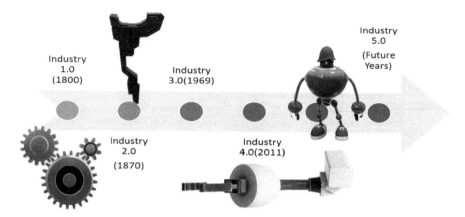

Figure 3.2   From Industry 1.0 to Future Industry 5.0.

advancements as well. This encompasses ambient intelligence and 3D printing technologies, augmented and virtual reality, smart factories, intelligent
supply chains [6], and other similar innovations. It is essential to keep in
mind that none of these advancements were designed with Industry 4.0 in
mind when they were developed. These recent technological developments
have been brought together under the umbrella term of Industry 4.0 to achieve
"smart production" [7, 13]. This is because it is a government project being
carried out from the highest level down, with the idea already being decided.

Regarding Industry 5.0, there are currently two different schools of
thought. One is the idea of "humans and robots working together." In the
future, humans and robots will work together to accomplish shared goals
whenever and wherever feasible. The remainder of the work will be completed by machines, freeing up more time for people to devote to creative
endeavors. The blue economy is not the same thing as Industry 5.0; it is its
own distinct concept [7]. It is possible that the requirements of industry, the
environment, and the economy can all be satisfied through the strategic use
of biological resources in industrial settings. This is a distinct possibility. The
European Commission refers to developing sustainable natural resources and
transforming these consumption and waste processes into value-added goods
as a "low-carbon economy." The term "low-carbon economy" was coined
by the European Commission. Products with additional value include, but
are not limited to, food, vitamins, biofuels, and biogas. The same holds for
other examples. Biogas is yet another example of this. Agriculture, forestry,

fishing, farming, pulp, and paper production are all included as segments of the chemical, biotechnology, and energy sectors.

Microbiology, nanotechnology, information and communication technologies (ICT), engineering, and local and tacit expertise all play essential roles in their respective fields, making them fertile ground for innovation [14]. The concept of colonization is the driving force behind the economy, and it has the potential to cause revolutionary shifts in many different sectors [15]. Because of this, the blue economy may play a role in the subsequent industrialization, or it may even be its primary focus. The perspectives of Industry 4.0 and Industry 5.0 are contrasted and compared in Table 3.1. If you want a thorough evaluation of these predictions, refer to [7]. Remember that the blue economy may not be the sole focus of Industry 5.0 but rather the collaboration of humans and robots.

Further, topics like the space industry, space farming, and space habitation may either usher in the next generation or be a part of it. Space is a finite resource, and scientists have warned us to use it sparingly [16]. As with the "mining boom" of the past, space farming could be the next economic upswing.

Table 3.1 A comparison of different industrial revolutions' visions.

	Industry 4.0	*Industry 5(a)*	*Industry 5(b)*
Modus operandi	Smart manufacturing	Robots working along with humans	Blue economy
Inspiration	Mass manufacturing	A connected society	Resilience
Energy source	Electric and solar	Renewable sources	Sustainable ad bionics
Related technologies	AI, IoT, cloud computing, robotics, and big data	Robot–human collaboration	Cognitive computing, quantum computing, and robot–human interactions
Research areas	Organizational research, process improvement, and product manufacturing	Smart cities Innovation and business management	Agriculture, smart environment, biology, and finance sectors

3.4 Problems with Human–Robot Collaboration

Incorporating robots into companies was covered in a previous paper [2]. The problems found point to the potential for considerable organizational adjustments. Changes in organizational behavior, structure, workflow, ethics, and work environment are among the problems. Other significant challenges include the adoption of machines in the workplace, bias against humans or robots, confidentiality and confidence in a human–robot workplace, redesigning environments for cyborgs, teaching, and orientation. The concerns are listed in Table 3.2.

Bagdasarov and her associates looked at the organizational aspects of using robots at work [11]. Three variables were discussed: interpersonal, organizational, and robotic agents. The experts advise taking into account numerous criteria for each collection. Individual aspects include the employee's age, gender, educational degree, technological knowledge and experience, expectations, social perception, and social competence. The organizational aspects include the procedure, external conditions, psychological and social context, orientation, and synchronization of worker and machine goals. The robotic agent elements include the robot's look, behavior, interactivity, and safety.

In the remaining section, we concentrate on human–robot co-working challenges not covered in [2]. Be aware that some of the problems affect the organization and its stakeholders. It might be challenging to distinguish between a business and an emotional problem.

Table 3.2   Impacts associated with robot integration in industries.

Impacts of Robot Integration on Organizations
Genesis of organizational behavior
Employment acceptance of robots
Changes in workflows and organizational structures
Changes in ethical behavior
Discriminatory policies directed at humans or machines
Confidentiality and trust are essential in a human–robot workplace
Constructing and disseminating information
Reorganizing the factory floor with robots

3.4.1 Issues with law and regulation

According to one definition [5], robots are machines that have the ability to detect, reason, and act. This definition is straightforward yet troublesome. *What do a robot's thoughts and behavior mean?* The Oxford Dictionary defines a robot as a device capable of automatically performing a complicated sequence of tasks, particularly one that a computer can program. The robot is a device that resembles a person and can carry out various complicated human functions, including walking and talking, according to the Merriam-Webster dictionary. A robot is a device that resembles a person. These definitions contain their own set of errors as well. One resorts to an abstract concept, such as acting out a complicated series of behaviors in a habitual manner. The other individual thinks that a robot can pass for a human. These hazy explanations demonstrate that we have not yet developed a successful solution.

The many complications that would arise without the right legislation make collaborative labor with robots impossible. An official legal definition of a robot is needed first. Although "robot" has a scientific meaning, only the legal meaning is enforceable by businesses and other organizations. The range of possible automated machines is quite broad. A robot is an example of an automated machine. Different degrees of machine automation have been identified [4]. Any regulation governing the collaboration of humans and robots must make it abundantly clear that an automatic system is not the same as a robot. There is also a strong connection between drones and robots. The legislation should spell out the similarities between robots, drones, and cobots. It is essential for the legislation to clearly define the categories of robots, aircraft, and cobots.

Whether or not robot software is required to adhere to stringent and complex rules or is allowed some leeway in the event of system failures should all be addressed in the legislation and any other relevant regulations governing the use of robots in the workplace. The rules governing robot creation, production, and licensing will be the subject of several controversies. Are we going to permit any individual, business, or organization to create a robot and integrate it into our residences, businesses, and everyday lives? Most nations are presently ineffective in controlling the use of drones in the air. With the accomplished things of autonomous robots, we must be prepared. A large number of research investigations will concentrate on the legal and ethical challenges related to the usage of bots, aircraft, and cobots.

3.4.2 Subjective opinion for using robots at work

Everyone has a distinct taste for utilizing or refraining from a specific technology. Some people are keen to work with machines and will be vehemently opposed to the concept.

Companies interested in utilizing human—robot collaboration in the workplace should be conscious of these individual inclinations. It will not be simple or even practicable for firms to convert to human—robot co-working settings if the majority of their workers have a hostile perception of robots. Although human—robot co-working is not a reality, representations of collaborating with robots rather than actual experiences significantly influence people's preferences. Numerous well-known films and television programs have portrayed the futuristic idea of robots destroying humanity or ruling over the earth. These unfavorable media reports have an impact on people's preferences for dealing with robots.

3.4.3 Psychosocial problems caused by human–robot collaboration

Modern technology has a particular psychological impact on people. Video game addiction is seen as a psychological condition that is receiving more attention. Some people are really devoted to their cell phones. Even a phobia known as "nomophobia" or "fear of not being able to use mobile phones" exists. Nomophobia, as described by the Collins dictionary, is a stressful condition brought on by not having access to or being unable to use a mobile phone. At this time, whether there will be a "robophobia" or a "nomophobia" is unknown. Nevertheless, it is very possible that a robot will have a number of psychological consequences for many workers that have never been seen before. Corporate robotics will be a study area for the mental disorders associated with using robots at work and their impact on organizational environments.

3.4.4 Changes that result from human—robot collaboration

Humans are hardwired to interact with others. They engage with people like them in all aspects of their lives, including their careers. Many workplaces engage in the practice of organizing social activities to increase productivity. As the number of robots working alongside humans rises, the number of humans may fall. A consequence of this could be diminished social interaction between individuals. The introduction of robots into the workplace is likely to have unintended consequences for human interaction, even if the total number of employees remains unchanged. Some humans may even prefer interacting with sociable robots. Some people may assume that robots' social behavior is merely a result of clever programming, but this is not necessarily the case. Workers will have different ideas about interacting with robots in the workplace. The situation deteriorates rapidly when robots are elevated to managerial or executive roles. Employees are appreciative of their superiors and employers in general. Treating others with deference is a hallmark of sociability. People might wonder if they would like a robot manager or not. This sort of issue may seem strange, confusing, or even frustrating to some people because a robot will not have any concept of respect. Findings from the study [18] show that young people can develop strong emotional attachments to robots in the same way they do to real pets. In the not-too-distant future, humans may interact with robots in a way that is similar to how today's youth interacts with and views their cell phones. The study of how humans can work together with robots appears to require a substantial contribution from the social sciences.

3.4.5 The shifting functions of human resources divisions

One of the key duties of HR departments is to carry out employment assessments, create position descriptions, and fill open positions with qualified candidates. Except for those sectors that use industrial robots, most businesses now employ people. Human resource departments will encounter new difficulties as robots become integral to enterprises. Workers will be expected to determine the jobs that robots will take over in addition to their existing duties. In essence, they will choose which occupations to assign to robots. Divisions in charge of HR will become more significant and have more duties. HRM divisions will inevitably change, and they could even have new names.

Many organizations and enterprises nowadays promote themselves as "eco-friendly." They assert that they are environmentally conscious. Whether these activities increase prices, "eco-friendly" firms and organizations aim to behave appropriately toward the ecosystem. There may even be companies in the future calling themselves "human." Even if it costs more to be a "human" company, some businesses will only hire people, even if using robots would be less expensive. These "human" organizations will assert that they treat people with social responsibility and provide jobs.

3.5 Wafer Fabrication Automation

The wafer fabrication sector has changed tremendously in recent times. An assortment of technological improvements, including both equipment and software, are fuelling this growth, permitting the manufacturing of electronic chipsets to automate their processes and work at their full potential. Several aspects of production are automated, ranging from supply monitoring to regulatory oversight, supply chain management, and sophisticated control systems. Regardless of the process, automation has been assumed to provide a critical platform for increasing production efficiency and improving quality for the customer industry. The method in which the items are kept, handled, and distributed throughout manufacturing is an evident example of how automation has enhanced chip production processes, as shown in Figure 3.3. Previously, clean room professionals performed all of these tasks mechanically. Thanks to automated technology, processing and delivering clean room chips hardly require extensive human interaction. This in itself improves pollution control, and that also enables much better product changes across the fabrication using path optimization systems.

Another case in point is process control automation. Experts were once obliged to physically enter input variables and make assessments to check for operational irregularities. Once errors are found, instrument measures must

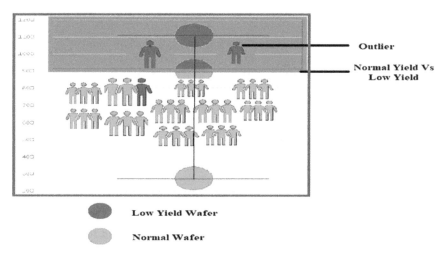

Figure 3.3 Wafer fabric automation.

be explicitly performed to prevent further yield losses. Such a long-time process and error-prone procedure is tedious. Automation has gradually replaced this traditional approach with contemporary practices (i.e., automatic error detection systems, profit/output management systems, etc.). In some circumstances, OCAP (out of control action plan) may respond proactively to reduce the loss drastically. Data generated can now be automatically gathered and evaluated in real time. These robotic architectural solutions give businesses unprecedented insight into their operations, allowing managers to discover and resolve issues with minimal human interaction.

3.6 AI as a Vital Technology in Industry 5.0

Around 2032, artificial intelligence (AI) technologies are expected to have increased the global GDP by US$17 trillion.

Between 2019 and 2024, the market for AI will increase by $79 billion. Due to the consistent acceleration of month-over-month growth, the market's expansion pace will pick up throughout the projection period.

Businesses are quickly implementing AI-based products and solutions to transform their processes and boost revenue. In order to take advantage of technological advances, streamline operations, and make companies more flexible for planned increases, AI-powered technologies are increasingly being adopted in the industrial sector.

3.6.1 Impact of AI on different industries

The following are the areas where the AI technology has been mostly used, as shown in Figure 3.4.

1. Algorithms for deducing formalized assertions from logical formulations and providing machine-based proofs, as well as for demonstrating the accuracy of hardware and software.
2. Knowledge-based systems include techniques for simulating and gathering expertise; software that supports experts and simulates human competence (formerly referred to as "expert systems").
3. Pattern recognition and analysis: general intuitive methodological approaches, and ML in specific.
4. Robotics: unsupervised networks, or the control of robots without human intervention.

5. Intelligent multimodal human—machine interaction involves linguistic analysis and "understanding" of words, pictures, actions, and other social interactional modalities.

The application of the AI technique known as machine learning can be found across many different industries. The fact that it has such a wide range of applications, making it suitable for various use cases along the value stream depicted in Figure 3.4, is indisputable evidence.

Although in the past, most companies have relied on their internal data for supervised machine learning, recently, several companies have begun investigating the possibility of combining their own internal and external datasets as well as their own internal and external data-science-related capabilities in order to provide even more in-depth insights.

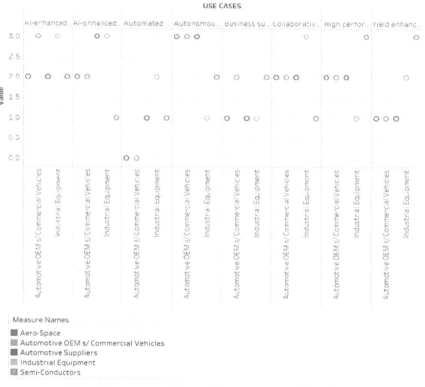

Figure 3.4   Impact of AI on different use cases (industries).

3.7 Artificial General Intelligence (AGI)

However, concentrating on current actions involving poor or narrow artificial intelligence, this chapter will also outline a future scenario in which AI no longer merely reacts but acts proactively, smartly, and adaptable. Along with offering the answer, it is important to comprehend the overall structure, see connections on your own, and make new deductions. This type of AI, often known as artificial general intelligence, is equivalent to human cognitive abilities.

Knowledge-based presentations, linguistic interactions in natural settings, the application of tactics, the detection of anomalies, and acting are only a few examples of the characteristics of artificial general intelligence. AGI systems assist cognitive research, math-focused intelligence, and decision-making, as well as notice and respond to risks. There are currently no commercially available solutions except ROSS Intelligence, Expert System, Self-driving Cars, IBM's Project Debater, etc.

Research is being done on systems with cognitive synergies that enable the generation of AGI by combining several types of memory and their associated learning techniques. CogPrime is a promising initiative. Work on self-reflecting systems is still ongoing in the ability to form original and unique judgments, which is discussed in the context of AGI. Kurt Gödel's self-referential formulations served as inspiration for several useful examples, including the Gödel machine, which, besides resolving issues, searches for self-rewrites for which it can provide evidence of their benefits.

3.8 The Scenario of AI in the Focus of Manufacturing

The most popular kind of machine learning is supervised machine learning, in which software applications are given organized data in order to identify trends and comprehend and analyze breakthroughs. The applications of Machine Learning and Intelligent Robots that have been a scenario of AI Implementation in businesses. In Figure 3.5, a technological breakdown is shown.

Possibilities for Information systems and automation throughout its life cycle

Within the organization, services are powered by data challenge traditional value chains. The new "manufacturing as a service (MaaS)" model makes the consumer a stakeholder of any new product developed, which is made

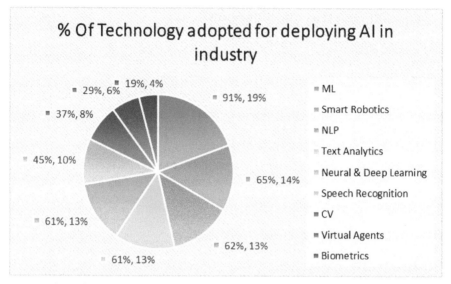

Figure 3.5 Percentage of technology adopted for deploying AI in Industry.

possible via interconnected production. Figure 3.4 shows that this results in the design, manufacture, and consumption of items in local areas.

3.9 Automation based on AI (ABAI)

Automation benefits companies by streamlining tasks that were previously handled by humans while adhering to a set of criteria. This saves time and effort, ensures reproducible outcomes, and considerably improves productivity. When mankind reaches the epoch of Industrial Automation 5.0, powered by technology such as artificial intelligence, automated processes are poised to grow further. Industries anticipate technology that can give some operational flexibility rather than merely regulated automation. AI-powered automation allows machines to make decisions like people, responding to new things in real time. This enables jobs to be completed more wisely and efficiently, allowing firms to enhance output quality, minimize response time to challenges, and boost productivity and sustainability.

In this chapter, we shall review the major industrial automation application cases to demonstrate the value of AI-driven "smart automation" in device fabrication.

3.9.1 Computerized root cause analysis using AI

Another vital engineering activity in the semiconductor industry is root cause analysis. Conventional RCA methods rely significantly on manual coordination between tools and software solutions. For instance, when a productivity problem arises in fabrication, a product engineer may perform the first analysis stage by reviewing silicon output maps to hunt for any failure anomalies. The corresponding process expert will then be contacted, and they will work together to collect and analyze pertinent data input and search for connections. An instrument specialist will also be required if the malfunction indicator is specific to a particular processing instrument in order to help determine the underlying reason. The RCA procedure requires many resources, is laborious, and often takes days to weeks to complete. Latency to the root cause may take longer for complicated problems, delaying the effect on productivity. This procedure can be considerably enhanced by automation. Sophisticated analytic solutions offer a variety of mechanized capabilities, from data collection to thorough trace analysis, to assist in reducing the work required for RCA and accelerating time-to-RCA. Like CM in the semiconductor industry, modern analytical tools give professionals a basis for automated data collection that enables them to combine quality and process data from many data sources into a unified, integrated solution. An instrument designer, for instance, may swiftly perform drill-down analytics and quickly investigate a problem from several viewpoints when all pertinent information is immediately accessible.

Additionally, cutting-edge technologies like complete trace insights, information retrieval, and semiconductor mapping predictive analysis are combined into one coherent system, enabling a more straightforward and automated process. This makes having different domain assets and software packages unnecessary, considerably streamlining the RCA procedure. Let us examine the automated components of this streamlined approach in more detail. The system can evaluate a collection of silicon yield maps to track, identify, and sort typical failure trends, providing a technician with unique strategic priorities for further assessment. This is possible because all pertinent quality and process data have been collected into the platform of the solution.

The next step is to specify the decision-making process, which may be done either explicitly by an expert, depending on the domain, or automatically by employing the system's AI-driven anomaly identification functionality. With the help of this automated characteristic, the option can accurately set the assessment cutoff point for data comparison and intelligently identify data that falls outside of the typically performing groups. For illustration, in Figure 3.6, chips with yield levels above a certain percentage can be equated to chips with yield levels below, or chips with a critical failure sequence can be, especially compared to chips without a typical failure trend. The same analysis mentioned above in RCA platform includes similarity functions and data harvesting, which are carried out automatically on all relevant information in order to learn and locate the alleged process tool (study of commonalities). Once more, utilize AI to gather data from the suspicious tool statistics and smartly examine them to rapidly and precisely identify the sources of problems to the ingredient and ingredient stage level. An architect could use this autonomous data analysis platform to determine the origin of any output or hiccup using a single technology platform without involving other subject matter experts. A streamlined methodology like this could reduce RCA time from days to hours.

Consequently, an architect may conduct appropriate measures more rapidly and reduce the effect of problems. As indicated in the preceding section, another illustration of automation that might boost training and knowledge is the capacity to launch data analysis via a project timescale automatically. Recurrent studies might be performed automatically, and summaries containing the root of the issue with its results can be delivered to experts, allowing them to become more successful in controlling process performance and productivity. Daily productivity reports, for instance, including

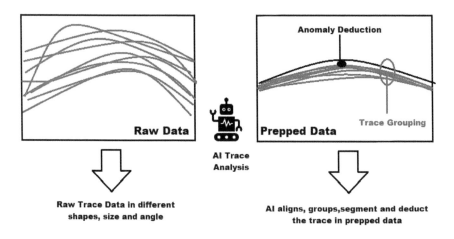

Figure 3.6 Automated trace analysis.

RC results, enable an analyst to fix output effect concerns while physically conducting a study, thus eliminating operational effects. Likewise, a model of data containing linear measuring data, including RCA results, enables an expert to track failure events and take remedial steps as needed.

3.9.2 Intelligent computing in product matching

In production, product matching is a critical technical activity. Engineers may more efficiently maintain high customer satisfaction and production output by maintaining quality tool effectiveness across the device fleet within a processing region. The conventional way of product matching involves an expert collecting device information and contrasting the overall stats of the information on each sensor, two compartments at a time. In some instances, an expert may need to visually analyze the data collected from the suspicious sensor to search for anomalies. This compartment analysis method is laborious and might take a long time if completed over a whole array of devices. Product matching has been dramatically enhanced by mechanization in product comparison analysis. The very first benefit is the removal of the requirement for experts to constantly collect information by providing an interface to combine sensor readings from all operational instruments automatically. Asset/inventory assessment may be completed much more quickly since the information from all pieces of equipment is compiled onto a unified platform, allowing for real-time data comparison between several compartments, as shown in Figure 3.7.

A system can plan product assessment events using automation as well. Now, periodic tank condition data may be created electronically and sent to an engineer daily, monthly, or on other schedules. This makes it possible for them to efficiently monitor device operation trends and quickly respond to any emerging problems. Technical performance has significantly increased due to the elimination of mechanical examinations.

The analysis of product data is automated through the use of computer intelligence. An AI-driven platform may easily execute trail analysis by automatically and frequently aligning, segmenting, and comparing all trail data, even with thousands of variables in each cell to be studied. This enables the model to identify every anomaly in great detail, regardless of how obscure the problem may be. With AI, the system can automatically do trail analysis on all track data, unlike product analysis, which uses aggregate data and might cause delicate signals to be missed in the computations of the overall statistics. Designers benefit from the greatest insight into possible

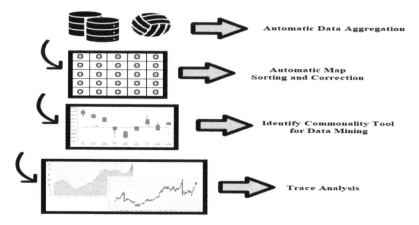

Figure 3.7   Aggregated product matching and trace analysis.

process problems as well as the most precise outcomes. Additionally, AI-driven automation enables a system to correctly and intelligently select the compartment with the best reliable behavior and designate it as the benchmark product or compartment. While choosing the benchmark product, an expert can additionally make modifications to test against relevant quality data to strengthen the benchmark's validity. It is represented in Figure 3.7. A time-consuming and tedious task for an expert to physically choose the benchmark data for each study is eliminated by this automated capability. The functionality guarantees that the optimal cell is consistently used as the benchmark and significantly lowers the work needed to build up newer analyses.

3.10 Robotic Process Automation

Robotic process automation (RPA) is when computers do jobs that were used to be done by people in the service industry. Software robots or AI workers that can do simple tasks are used to automate the process. The designer will probably take a screenshot and use variables to set up the task parameters. These tasks include opening emails, filling out forms, copying and pasting data, signing into programs, and so on [4]. Logging into programs and copying and pasting data are also tasks that need to be done. Van der Aalst et al. [3] say that RPA is an umbrella term for software that interacts with the user interface of different computer systems. This is what researchers said about RPA. RPA's main function is based on component identifiers instead of screen coordinates or XPath options. This is different from traditional models of process automation, such as screen capturing, scraping, and macros, which rely heavily on the graphical interface of the workstation. Robotic Process Automation refers to the automation of service that mimic human labor[3]. Software robots or AI employees who can efficiently do basic activities are used to automate the process. The designer sets the job instructions using some type of screen capture and create variables. These operations range from signing into programmes,copying data, pasting it , opening emails and filling out forms among others [4]. According to Vander der Aalst et.al [3] RPA is an umbrella term encompassing This makes it more likely that the user will remember the GUI for a long time. Since 2015, sales at RPA software companies have increased [3, 4]. These technologies have also been used to automate business processes, inspections, and digital forensics [4, 5]. The fifth industrial revolution, also called Industry 5.0, opens up new ways to automate mundane, standard business processes using robotic process automation (RPA) technologies and data from connected devices [6]. RPA is the automation of low-level business processes that are done repeatedly (in which the operations are done swiftly and very financially beneficial). The plan is to slowly replace human labor with systems that do the work for us. RPA differs from other methods because it does not depend on digital information. Because of this, there is not much violence [7] and a chance to save money. It is expected that using RPA technology will cut the costs of running transactional tasks in shared services by up to 60% [8].

3.11 The Digital Solutions Entangled in Industry 5.0

The economic and industrial outlook has rapidly changed in recent years. In the past 10 years, this technology has improved extraordinarily. Applications for Industry 5.0 are diverse and numerous [13]. It needs linked gadgets that are actively functioning. One may describe Industry 5.0 as a highly automated, united, and effective transformation. Industry 5.0 was characterized as "the digitalization of the industrial sector, with embedded sensors in almost all individual elements and production equipment, omnipresent cyber-physical systems, and analysis of all pertinent data" [14] by Wee et al. in 2015. Additionally, Industry 5.0 incorporates HCI, data, networking, data and analytics, and business intelligence. Schmidt outlines a blend of traditional industrial methods and contemporary innovations that leads to clever commercial product creation. Irrespective of geography, this method fosters collaboration across many areas [15]. According to researchers, Industry 5.0 aspires to integrate all current industrial technology and digitalize data generation and processing methods. The definition of the data varies. Assimilation is used in both the vertical and horizontal aspects of the product lifecycle [16]. The results of modern techniques can also be divided into product and service categories. The business model includes both the services and advanced applications offered by all of these sectors, which power Industry 5.0 [17].

3.12 AMS for Industry 5.0: Advanced Manufacturing System

The economics and well-being of a nation are significantly impacted by the industrial sector [18]. It also possesses connections to the industry's numerous other divisions, including transportation, management, IT operations, etc. The Internet of Things (IoT) offers several services, including real-time data monitoring and processing and various others [19]. Industrial IoT is now considered to be the most revolutionary technique for Industry 5.0. Therefore, the Internet of Things (IoT) offers a solution to many of the maintenance and growth problems in today's businesses [20]. Consequently, smart technology in production is seen as a new paradigm that makes use of all the advantages of contemporary technology and methodologies to address manufacturing concerns that are largely addressed by Industry 5.0. It turns core businesses into intelligent industries that are able to meet consumer expectations [21].

3.13 Methods, Data, and Results

By adding up the intelligent machine motions, the suggested work in this chapter has provided the outcome of progress and frequency change. There exists a significant need for AI across a wide range of applications, and these needs are met by expanding to international functional hubs [22]. There are approximately more than 300 new AI job openings from various firms that are implementing AI algorithms in nearly 15–25 start-ups. The Mosaic algorithm (6), which is based on factors like forensic cases, quality of information, and technological considerations, is used to choose the list of various AI casts from a pool of over 1500 enterprises. The annual growth rate and the investment sum for various AI castings throughout India are displayed in Table 3.3b [23]. According to a survey by AIM Research, start-ups in the fields of artificial intelligence and data analytics earned $1108 million in investment in 2021, the most in seven years and with a 32.5-yearly growth rate. Three months into 2023, there have already been significant investments

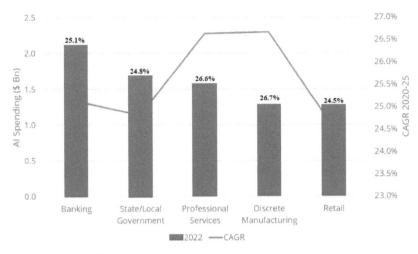

Figure 3.8   AI spending on various sectors of India.

Table 3.3a   Amount invested in Indian start-ups in 2022.

S. No	Indian start-ups	Amount invested
1	Fractal	$360 M
2	DataSutram	$2.07 M
3	Atlan	$50 M
4	Actyv.ai	$5 M
5	Locofy.ai	$3 M
6	Scribble data	$2.2 M

Table 3.3b   Amount invested in the last seven years in Indian start-ups.

S. No	Year	Amount invested
1	2016	$260 M
2	2017	$3.89 B
3	2018	$112.8 M
4	2019	$ 529.52 M
5	2020	$762.5 M
6	2021	$ 283 M
7	2022	$ 654 M***

*** Expecting to increase

made in the intelligence and AI fields. Let us examine some of the significant investments for 2022 in the form of Table 3.3a, and Table 3.3b exhibits the last seven years of AI expenditure. Figure 3.8 displays the AI spending on various sectors in India with respect to CAGR 2020−25.

3.14 Conclusion

The advancement of numerous mathematical equations bolstered with technology that link up AI with actual data interpretation in Industry 5.0 systems is urgently needed because AI is becoming a mandate and aiding sectors in growing in accordance with Industry 5.0 parameters with the help of their cutting-edge technology. In this chapter, we provide a summary of the manufacturing industry's AI ecological system, which is the foundation for industry progress. In our effort, we have aimed to develop certain tactics that will function with industry-based AI systems. Research articles highlight how AI has dramatically impacted the industrial landscape in crucial domains such as production loss reduction, process automation, and security enhancement.

Industry automation is now the largest issue, yet the application of AI has enabled companies to develop exponentially. We have observed a six-fold increase in investment in AI and other related technologies over the past several years, and we are certain that this trend will continue. Many AI-based sectors have recently developed in startup companies as well. AI has demonstrated a vital role in many different industries. Our upcoming study will focus on the impact of AI on Industry 5.0 and potential development opportunities.

Regardless of whether or not Industry 5.0 places a greater emphasis on the collaboration of humans and robots, it will still have a significant impact on the business world. In fact, it is highly probable that significant changes for humanity will occur as a consequence of the integration of robots into normal human activities. We are doing everything in our power to develop machines that are remarkably similar to us in important respects. This will invigorate and motivate certain individuals to a greater degree. Some people will find it humorous, while others will find it annoying or even potentially hazardous. The media actively disseminate this anti-robot sentiment across a variety of different platforms.

The responses to our polls and surveys about how people feel about robots in society will be skewed as a result of this criticism. A pessimistic point of view was considered when developing one of the very first surveys that looked into how people feel about robots. We cannot speculate on how the general public will react to robots until they become a standard fixture in the homes and workplaces of everyday people. People's perceptions of robots may shift as they gain more experience interacting with them. Children of today will be exposed to this technology or one very similar to it at an earlier age than we were, and their reactions may be different from those of us who grew up with it. The descendants of these robots will one day become members of a society that is highly technologically advanced. We must consider the differences between the generations if we are going to build a society in which people can enjoy the benefits of technology while minimizing the potential drawbacks it may bring and if we are going to avoid becoming a society dominated by robots. In this chapter, we took a look at some of the difficulties that might arise from the collaboration of humans and robots in the workplace. Concerns pertaining to law and order, social psychology, and morality are among the most urgent of these issues.

References

[1] 5G-ACIA. (2021, 03 04). 5G-ACIA. Retrieved from 5G Alliance for Connected Industries and Automation: www.5g-acia.org

[2] Aguirre, Santiago & Rodriguez, Alejandro. (2017). Automation of a Business Process Using Robotic Process Automation (RPA): A Case Study. 65-71. DOI: 10.1007/978-3-319-66963-2_7. Available from:

[3] Enríquez, J. G., Jiménez-Ramírez, A., Domínguez-Mayo, F. J., & García García, J. A. (2020). Robotic Process Automation: A Scientific and Industrial Systematic Mapping Study. IEEE Access, 8, 39113-39129.

[4] Bahrin, M. A. K., Othman, M. F., Azli, N. N., & Talib, M. F. (2016). Industry 4.0: A review on industrial automation and robotics. Jurnal Teknologi, 78(6-13), pp:137-143.

[5] Tripathi, A. (2018). Learning robotic process automation: Create software robots and automate business processes with the leading RPA tool, UiPath. Packt Publishing Book Series.

[6] E. Gökalp, U. S, ener, and P. E. Eren, "Development of an assessment model for industry 4.0: industry 4.0-mm,;" in International Conference on Software Process Improvement and Capability Determination. Springer, 2017, pp. 128-142.

[7] Akoramurthy, B., and T. Ananth Kumar. "10 Digital Linked." Blockchain Technology: Fundamentals, Applications, and Case Studies (2020): 155.

[8] Delloite (2019). Automation with intelligence Reimagining the organization in the 'Age of With.' Available from: https://www2.deloitte.com/content/dam/Deloitte/tw/Documents/strategy/tw-Automation-with-intelligence.pdf

[9] Y. Qi, Z. Mao, M. Zhang, and H. Guo, "Manufacturing practices and servitization: The role of mass customization and product innovation capabilities," International Journal of Production Economics, vol. 228, p. 107747, 2020.

[10] Chatterjee, Jyotir Moy, P. Srinivas Kumar, Abhishek Kumar, and B. Balamurugan. "Blockchain, Bitcoin, and the Internet of Things: Overview." Blockchain Technology and the Internet of Things (2020): 47-67.

[11] P. Chaturvedi, S. Dahiya and S. Agrawal, "Technological innovation: A necessity for sustainable MSME sector in India," 2015 International Conference on Futuristic Trends on Computational Analysis and Knowledge Management (ABLAZE), 2015, pp. 206-211, doi: 10.1109/ABLAZE.2015.7154993. Authorized

[12] Demir, Kadir Alpaslan, Ebru Caymaz, and Meral Elci (2017) "Issues in Integrating Robots into Organizations.", The 12th International Scientific Conference on Defense Resources Management in the 21st Century, November 09-10, 2017, Brasov, Romania.

[13] G Bhardwaj, SV Singh, V Kumar . "An empirical study of artificial intelligence and its impact on human resource functions," International Conference on Computation . . . , 2020

[14] Kadir Alpaslan Demir, Halil Cicibaş "Industry 5.0 and a Critique of Industry 4.0." 4th International Management Information Systems Conference Istanbul, Turkey, 2017 (2017), pp. 17-20

[15] Haenlein, Michael & Kaplan, Andreas. (2019). A Brief History of Artificial Intelligence: On the Past, Present, and Future of Artificial Intelligence. California Management Review.

[16] Cormier, Derek, Gem Newman, Nakane, Masayuki, James E. Young, and Stephane Durocher (2013) "Would you do as a robot commands? An obedience study for human–robot interaction" International Conference on Human-Agent Interaction.

[17] Moffitt, K. C., Rozario, A. M., & Vasarhelyi, M. A. (2018). Robotic process automation for auditing. Journal of Emerging Technologies in Accounting, 15(1), 1-10.

[18] Peter Sachsenmeier "Industry 5.0—The Relevance and Implications of Bionics and Synthetic Biology." Engineering., 2 (2016), pp. 225-229

[19] E. Marilungo, A. Papetti, M. Germani, M. Peruzzini, From PSS to CPS design: a real industrial use case toward Industry 4.0, The 9th CIRP IPSS Conference: Circular Perspectives on Product/Service-Systems, Procedia CIRP 64 (2017) 357 – 362.

[20] S. Hjorth, D. Chrysostomou Human–robot collaboration in industrial environments: a literature review on non-destructive disassembly Robot. Comput. Integrated Manuf., 73 (2022), p. 102208, 10.1016/j.rcim.2021.102208

[21] Haidegger, T. (2019). Autonomy for surgical robots: Concepts and paradigms. IEEE Transactions on Medical Robotics and Bionics, 1(2), 65-76.

[22] A. Al-Yacoub, Y. C. Zhao, W. Eaton, Y. M. Goh, N. Lohse Improving human–robot collaboration through Force/Torque based learning for object manipulation Robot. Comput. Integrated Manuf., 69 (Jun. 2021), p. 102111, 10.1016/j.rcim.2020.102111

[23] Dmytro Romanov, Olga Korostynska, Odd Ivar Lekang, Alex Mason, Towards human–robot collaboration in meat processing: Challenges and possibilities, Journal of Food Engineering, Volume 331,2022,111117, ISSN 0260-8774, https://doi.org/10.1016/j.jfoodeng.2022.111117.

[24] Laurent, H., Boer, E. D., "Fourth Industrial Revolution Beacons of Technology and Innovation in Manufacturing" White Paper, January 10, 2019. https://www.weforum.org/whitepapers/fourth-industrialrevolution- beacons-of-technology-and innovation-in-manufacturing

[25] R. Cioffi, M. Travaglioni, G. Piscitelli, A. Petrillo, and F. De Felice, "Artificial intelligence and machine learning applications in smart production: Progress, trends, and directions," Sustainability, vol. 12, no. 2, p. 492, 2020.

[26] Gordon Briggs, Matthias Scheutz "How Robots Can Affect Human Behavior: Investigating The Effects of Robotic Displays of Protest and Distress." International Journal of Social Robotics., 6 (3) (2014), pp. 343-355 2014.

[27] Kadir Alpaslan Demir, Halil Cicibaş "The Next Industrial Revolution: Industry 5.0 and Discussions on Industry 4.0." Industry 4.0 From the Management Information Systems Perspectives, Peter Lang Publishing House (2018)

[28] Rupa CD, Hasan MK, Alhumyani H, Saeed RA (2021) Industry 5.0: Ethereum blockchain technology-based DApp smart contract. Math Biosci Eng 18(5):7010–7027

[29] Chowdhury MZ, Shahjalal M, Ahmed S, Jang YM (2020) 6G wireless communication systems: applications, requirements, technologies, challenges, and research directions. IEEE Open J Commun Soc 1:957–975

[30] Phuyal S, Bista D, Bista R (2020) Challenges, opportunities and future directions of smart manufacturing: a state of the art review. Sustain Futures 2:100023.

[31] Briggs, Gordon, and Matthias Scheutz.(2014) "How Robots Can Affect Human Behavior: Investigating The Effects of Robotic Displays of Protest and Distress." International Journal of Social Robotics 6 (3), 2014: 343-355.

[32] Demir, Kadir Alpaslan, Ebru Caymaz, and Meral Elci (2017) "Issues in Integrating Robots into Organizations.", The 12th International Scientific Conference on Defense Resources Management in the 21st Century, November 09-10, 2017, Brasov, Romania.

[33] Bartlett, Brendan, Vladimir Estivill-Castro, and Stuart Seymon. (2004) "Dogs or robots: why do children see them as robotic pets rather than canine machines?" In Proceedings of the fifth conference on Australasian user interface-Volume 28, pp. 7-14. Australian Computer Society.

[34] Cormier, Derek, Gem Newman, Nakane, Masayuki, James E. Young, and Stephane Durocher (2013) "Would you do as a robot commands? An obedience study for human–robot interaction" International Conference on Human-Agent Interaction.

[35] Briggs, Gordon, and Matthias Scheutz.(2014) "How Robots Can Affect Human Behavior: Investigating The Effects of Robotic Displays of Protest and Distress." International Journal of Social Robotics 6 (3), 2014: 343-355.

[36] Demir, Kadir Alpaslan, and Halil Cicibaş (2018) "The Next Industrial Revolution: Industry 5.0 and Discussions on Industry 4.0." Industry 4.0 From the Management Information Systems Perspectives. Peter Lang Publishing House.

[37] Cormier, Derek, Gem Newman, Nakane, Masayuki, James E. Young, and Stephane Durocher (2013) "Would you do as a robot commands? An obedience study for human–robot interaction" International Conference on Human-Agent Interaction.

4

Artificial Intelligence (AI) Driven Industrial Automation

S. S. Blessy Trencia Lincy

Faculty of Mathematics and Data Science, Emirates Aviation University, Dubai, The United Arab Emirates
E-mail: blessy.shepherd@eau.ac.ae

Abstract

Artificial Intelligence (AI) driven industrial automation outspreads the contemporary use of control technologies and robotics at much greater levels. Industrial automation is the concept of using control systems, which include computers, robots, and other information technologies, to manage diverse processes and machinery in the industrial world to replace human beings. This process involves integrating smart tools and computers into numerous operations. Artificial intelligence is the capability of the machine to learn from practice and experience, tune and acclimate to new ideas or inputs without manual human intervention, or perform human-like tasks. AI has played a vital role in research for over three decades. Hence, industrial automation and AI are transmuting businesses and will subsidize economic growth by contributing to productivity. AI-driven automation helps overcome the inherent challenges and demands that have been afflicting industries. This might include the scarcity of domain expertise, complexity in decision-making, integration issues, and the overloaded information that needs to be processed. The progress and advancement in machine learning technologies, the ever-growing computing power, and advances in sensors have contributed to creating a new generation of robots. AI aids and assists the machines in collecting and extracting knowledge, identifying or recognizing patterns, learning, and familiarizing with new situations through machine intelligence, adaptive learning, and speech recognition. Thus, AI helps manufacturers make faster and data-driven decision support, enhance the production outcome, increase the efficiency of the processes involved, reduce the costs involved in the operations, and support the innovation of the products.

Keywords: artificial intelligence, computer vision, industry automation

4.1 Introduction

In today's ever-growing digitized economy, researchers and experts should concentrate on creating and adapting the right solutions and platforms that revise and enhance business outcomes and strive toward success. The influence of AI might be remarkable, with businesses extending from retail, healthcare, product sales involving supply chain, finance, engineering and manufacturing, and services, all projects potentially varying and radically changing by the inception of AI technologies [1].

Industrial automation with artificial intelligence can be shown based on seven dimensions: objects, specific domain area, stages of application, requirements of the application, intelligent technologies, intelligent functions, roles, and solutions of industrial automation and artificial intelligence (I-A). When integrated with the business aspects, these dimensions are considered a breakthrough in artificial intelligence technologies [2].

Nevertheless, deploying AI strategies and solutions for industrial automation has been difficult and is a more significant challenge. While comparing the traditional computer vision (CV), AI and ML practices are still new in industrial automation. The automation engineers and experts in the manufacturing field do not yet have the skills or expertise to develop effective algorithms for AI. Numerous AI technology establishments are eradicating these hurdles by providing a complete inference strategy in a small form, i.e., high-performing and low-power hardware with trained, ready-to-deploy, tuned AI algorithms to improve efficiency and workplace safety.

Developments in the-AI processing have highlighted the means for today's AI technologies and will open new opportunities and prospects for techniques in the future. The automated systems have to process an implausible amount of information and will make decisions in real time; so it is much more competent for these machines to process information at the individual end instead of sending them to the cloud and so forth. The need for automation grows drastically daily, and as a result, industries continue to cultivate AI-powered techniques to enhance the productivity and performance of business activity. This has led to even more innovative techniques and applications in today's industrial world, from smart anomaly detection systems to autonomous robotics. This chapter discusses and analyzes various technologies and platforms that contribute to industrial automation and artificial intelligence's impact on industrial automation.

4.2 Evolution of Artificial Intelligence

Artificial intelligence can be characterized into three elementary stages based on the growth and progress of the technologies [3].

- Basic AI: The basic AI involves a system with only one functional area. AlphaGo, a board game computer program, is an example.
- Advanced AI: It involves a system with additional fields, such as the influence of abstract rational thinking, reasoning, or solving problems with human beings.
- Autonomous AI: It involves systems across all fields, which is the last stage of AI. This phase of AI is not likely to be established entirely for several decades.

4.3 Industry 4.0 Technologies

Industrial development utilizing stability, reliability, growth, dynamic response, technical advancement, selection, and strengthening, irrespective of the diverse organizations, is indispensable. Various organizations and governmental bodies are investing billions of dollars in the technologies that contribute to these factors to harvest, to meet the changing demand and supply patterns, rising demand, efficiency, optimization, and planning of their resources.

Table 4.1 shows the evolution of the industry technologies [4]: (1) the first revolution with the technologies for waterpower, steam power, mechanical manufacturing, etc., evolved in the year 1784, referred to as Industry 1.0; (2) the second revolution with the assembly line manufacturing, electrical energy, mass production technologies, etc., progressed around the year 1870, called Industry 2.0;

(3) the third revolution evolved in 1969 with technologies that include computers, electronics, robotics, industrial automation, etc.; (4) the fourth revolution refers to the current and emerging technologies, including information exchange, cloud computing, IoT, digitization, etc.

Table 4.1 Industry revolution.

Industry	Year	Revolution	Description
Industry 1.0	1784	First revolution	Waterpower, steam power, and mechanical manufacturing
Industry 2.0	1870	Second revolution	Assembly line manufacturing, electrical energy, and mass production
Industry 3.0	1969	Third revolution	Computers, electronics, robotics, and industrial automation
Industry 4.0	Present	Fourth revolution	Information exchange, cloud computing, IoT, and digitization

In this situation, AI is thriving to play a significant role in the current market. Distinguishing and identifying the importance of AI, with diverse technologies, schemes, and their different applications, the chief drivers are the four required methods used in contemporary AI methodologies, including (a) artificial neural networks, (b) fuzzy logic systems, (c) expert systems, and (d) genetic algorithms. Various industries in developed countries have begun using AI to connect with smart grids, meters, and IoT devices. Therefore, these techniques in AI will prime the practical usage and management of resources, improvement of efficiency, and many more factors. In recent years, emerging technologies in AI have advanced system devices and communications mean within the systems in unprecedented ways [4].

4.4 Development in AI

The unceasing evolution of intelligent smart cities, medical systems care, intelligent transport carriage units, intelligent robots, self-driving automated vehicles, intelligent toys, intelligent logistics, smart economies, smartphones, and smart communities, to tag but a few, affords a total market demand and lashing force in terms of innovative development of both AI technologies and applications [5].

Intelligent industrial manufacturing is a novel manufacturing model and the methodological means where many technologies are being integrated, which includes intelligent science and technology, systems engineering techniques, information and communication technology, massive manufacturing technologies (from the various phases of design, production/development, maintenance/management, testing, and integration), and associated product technologies throughout the entire lifecycle of the product development. The process involved in the manufacturing/industrial lifecycle uses self-directed sensing devices, autonomous collaboration, interconnection, perception, investigation, knowledge, control, and decision-making based on the learning and the implementation of human, material, machines mechanism, and ecological information to support and aid the optimization and integration of diverse characteristics of industrial, manufacturing or engineering organizations, other groups, and enterprises. This includes the people, management involving the operations, equipment, or technologies, and the various flows concerning the information, capital, logistics, knowledge, and service. This shortens the manufacture and provides a high-quality, high-efficiency, and profitable rewarding system, and better setting approachable facility and provision for operators. It consequently progresses the market affordability and competitiveness of the industrial initiative or group, irrespective of the product involved. The role of AI tools and technologies in smart manufacturing is an emerging topic. The revolution of AI is in its infancy, and numerous companies have noteworthy activities on-going. Currently, both small and big devices deployed in the industries are equipped/provided with sensors that can collect and share huge volumes of data and capture a multitude of activities. Manufacturers have started identifying the tactical importance of big data analytics, and, therefore, to enhance manufacturing competitiveness, the data is becoming a key enabler [6].

Visualizing automation as a batch of equipment/machines/robots implementing predefined processes and operations can be rendered to a fixed set of constraints and rules in a limited number of situations. Nevertheless, AI-based techniques and machines do not just follow the rules; they perceptively and intelligently comprehend and identify patterns within the data; they learn from previous experiences and advance imminent future performance.

Table 4.2 describes the different machine learning and artificial intelligence techniques that can be applied to different tasks like classification, regression, clustering, dimensionality reduction, decision-making, and other miscellaneous tasks with respect to the application [6]. Consequently,

Table 4.2 ML and AI techniques.

ML and AI techniques	Tasks	Approaches
Supervised learning	Classification, Regression	Support vector machine, logistic regression
Unsupervised learning	Clustering, dimensionality reduction	k-Means
Reinforcement learning	Decision-making	Q-learning
Miscellaneous	Miscellaneous	Backpropagation

AI empowers the same machinery, equipment, and techniques to solve multifaceted issues within a specified solution space.

Figure 4.1 involves the most frequently used algorithms in machine learning and artificial intelligence in industrial applications.

While this idea is all-encompassing, business leaders, scientists, and engineers worldwide are facing a few issues deterring the real-time deployment of AI, especially in the manufacturing industries. This may be due to the below-mentioned reasons [6].

1) there is no adequate evidence that the industry will succeed in embracing technologies in AI;
2) deficiency of a systematic approach for its deployment for a variety of industrial applications;

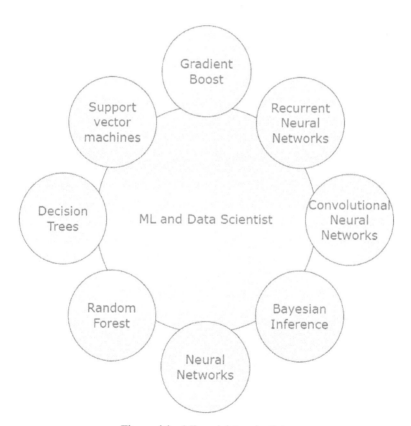

Figure 4.1   ML and data scientists.

3) absence of consistent and structured data from equipment and machines as the data is collected and loaded in different formats;
4) absence of data related to machine failure since the industries hardly tolerate running their failed machines;
5) involvement and intervention of the humans in working the dynamic application contexts to augment common sense to validate and verify the results.

4.5 AI Future Perception

Until recently, automation has primarily affected low-skilled routine workers and tasks. Furthermore, AI may automate non-routine, intellectual, and cognitive tasks involving highly skilled workers. An advantage of this perception is that it lets us use previous historical knowledge and outcome to enlighten us about the probable future effects of AI. The several benefits of AI, including direct automation, improved forecasting of the demand [7], a better workplace, smarter workforce, sophisticated root cause event analysis, easier 24/7 delivery of service/manufacture, enhanced profit, amplified workplace safety, reduced costs involved in operations, enhanced identification of defects, automation of quality control, advanced and efficient supply chain, improved product design or equipment design, rapid decision-making, predictive maintenance, quality optimization, testing, etc.

4.6 Digital Transformation

To successfully adapt to digital transformation, businesses must recognize the abilities and competencies of these AI methods and technologies and how they can influence the existing environment and ecosystem. Nevertheless, many establishments do not have an inclusive expertise roadmap and background about these technologies and how they could entrench AI in their tactics and businesses. Henceforth, they are yet to see evocative bottom-line profits from its implementation, and thereby most of its economic impression is yet to come. They appear to be trapped in "pilot purgatory" and cannot thrive in developing systematic capabilities. To speculate how AI can impact digital transformation based on economic growth, the following research queries discuss these aspects [8].

- How will AI impact economic growth if they enhance automation in producing goods and services?

- Can we relate, narrate, and understand AI's progression and the observed business growth over the twentieth century?
- Can we assume this growth to be persistent in the twentieth century?
- Whether applying AI and automation to production contribute to new ideas?
- Whether AI leads to a rapid increase in economic growth as data scientists and researchers predicted, and under what circumstances? Are these circumstances reasonable?
- How is the interconnection between the organization's growth and AI modulated?
- Whether AI affects internal industries or organizations, and with what inferences?

These queries proximately suggest essential economic issues. For example, what will happen if AI technologies allow a forever-growing number of tasks formerly performed by human labor to become automated? The AI may be organized and deployed in making or manufacturing goods and services, possibly affecting the financial development and the organization's income stocks. Nonetheless, AI may also revolutionize the process and procedure by which we produce new novel ideas, designs, notions, and technologies, unraveling complex, intricate problems and scaling creative, inventive efforts. This also suggests that the definition of AI, i.e., the machine's ability to perform tasks in a wide range of environments [8].

4.7 Components of AI in Automation

- Machine vision: Machine vision denotes any program's competence to understand the pictorial input. The machine exploits the training data as a type of groundwork for the classification or the mechanism for identification. For example, iPhone's face recognition system uses machine vision technology.
- Natural language processing (NLP): As the machine language depends on the illustrations and visuals, the NLP does the same to understand the input texts and the human voice. It is now probable for technologies to understand the background behind the message being passed out and then take action depending on the kind of data prebuilt and related variables that are vital. A few examples of this include Amazon's Alexa, Apple's Siri, etc.
- Machine learning: It refers to the ability of a machine to learn using the data provided to it. This encompasses the consequences of

environmental attributes/variables and decisions to advance itself. It will be possible to progress the total competence of existing solutions using machine learning approaches and techniques. Consider the example of an intelligent automation system to resolve an issue without human intervention. The intelligent system will vary automatically and follow the set of procedures or measures that a human uses. Consequently, over time, the effort of humans will be reduced, and the system's competence will improve [9].

4.8 Artificial Intelligence Applications in Automation

Figure 4.2 shows the various applications or domains where artificial intelligence technologies can be adapted in numerous ways in automation. From drones to self-driving automated cars, inventory management, sales and marketing, planning and decision-making services, asset forecast and maintenance, digital development, quality control, customer relationship management (CRM), optimization of machines, and software tools, all are using intelligent automation.

Smart retail business: AI empowers the retail and industrial/manufacturing industries in making appropriate decisions/choices with precise and real-time prediction, refining management of the supply chain, defining impactful upgrades, and improving the pricing strategy. AI is also making the operation of the organization and processing more competent because of the automated robotics technologies and optimization of processes, which advances production and decreases the labor-intensive physical costs. The usage of interacting custom robots in the warehouse and stores are well recognized. More prevailing computers, novel or hybrid algorithmic models, and hefty training datasets empower the development of heightened vision. Privileged within-object recognition, computer vision, and semantic segmentation, which is the capability to classify object types, such as differentiating a device from an element or module, have lately progressed suggestively in their performance.

Enhanced satisfactory customer service: A good example of this is chatbots, which became prevalent and widespread in a very short period. It started with Apple's Siri and then has been implemented by most brands now. The chatbots can understand the context-based user's input and then retort to those queries appropriately. Automating sales, customer-friendly services, and marketing message communications make use of these bots. The customer help desk services can be replaced with bots, which can feel human and reduce manual physical burdens.

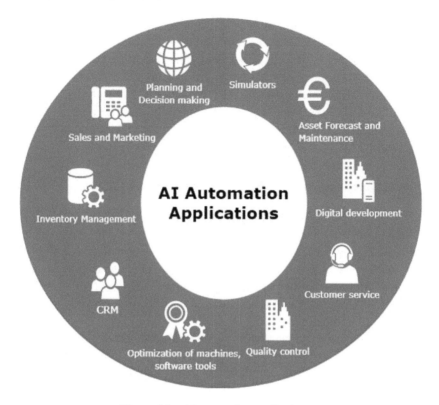

Figure 4.2   AI automation applications.

Market brand management: The brand management process and tasks can be made a lot easier with the aid of automation. In order to completely understand the consumer's opinion, brand marketers struggle a lot, even with their brand. Consequently, they will be capable of automating the analysis of the content across the Internet with the aid of automation. In addition, they can help in recognizing critical issues daily. Watson Analytics for Social Media is an appropriate example of such automation. The user will define a set of words and their context and try to understand what the online users relate to in a specific duration.

Software development and testing: Automated software testing is an emerging field in this current era. With a wide variety of tools that are evolving today, the testing process can likely be fully automated in the future. SauceLabs and ReTest are examples of a few prevalent testing tools available. By using these tools, testers and developers can concentrate on performing core testing and ignore the worries of fixing bugs in intelligent systems. Development automation is a long way to go, but these tools can surely aid developers in performing tedious tasks.

Thwarting fraud: The face of the perpetrator can be connected directly to the theft using AI. The POS system with a camera attached will record and save all types of transactions and then can be directly linked to the face with the base details already saved within the system. For example, if someone commits credit card fraud, it will be much easier to put them behind bars. Furthermore, using an intelligent system will be capable of averting cyberattacks by quickly recognizing abnormal or irregular behavior from the user. In such particular situations, the system can automatically cease taking any further requests and fire off an alert to the administrator.

Improving efficiency: People make mistakes irrespective of their experience level or job type. However, with automation, errors and mistakes can be reduced greatly. Furthermore, with time, the machines can learn from the outcome of the processes and improve the system's efficiency in the future.

Human resource management: The recruitment team struggles a lot in arranging and sorting the candidate resumes they receive. With the advancement in automation, it will be easy to shortlist potential candidates based on the data previously collected. Usually, automated applicant tracking systems are used to receive the CVS. The automation solution is provided using these collected materials when the users apply for different roles, which will be stored in the database.

Reducing cost: The cost involved in training a human for a particular task will be recurring. This includes the employee turnover rate, the time needed for the individual to learn the task gradually, experience, and develop the skill may vary greatly. However, a machine can be trained only once and, over time, might improve its performance without incurring more cost and repeated training.

Smart manufacturing: The usage of AI technologies has altered the manufacturing business sectors, from employing virtual assistants to unconventional automated robotics, which has empowered engineering businesses to produce more products or services with reduced faults to meet claims. Using AI, which facilitated swift progress as they can condense the growth processes and cycles, the efficiency of progress engineering, thwart faults, upsurge security by systematizing hazardous actions and events, decrease inventory expenses with improved supply and forecasting of demand, and upsurge the revenue with improved identification of sales lead and optimization of price, etc. This new concept is intelligent manufacturing, a clever method of manufacturing where machines are associated with humans, i.e., both humans and machines work together with negligible supervision.

Moreover, we are starting to see autonomous systems that can accomplish tasks without human participation, as the system can train itself and fine-tune to new training data. Consider the automated financial trading application. Since it depends utterly on algorithms, businesses can complete business transactions much quicker with autonomous technologies than with systems relying on humans. Similarly, robots are accomplishing narrow tasks and responsibilities autonomously in industrial settings [10].

Some organizations/businesses, such as Google and Amazon, have endeavored to produce highly determined applications of AI, including unattended checkout counters, drone delivery, autonomous vehicles, etc. Some of these applications have been effective, but some highly determined projects, like cancer treatment, have been mostly unsuccessful despite substantial expenditures and outlays. Less determined projects have been more successful in most organizations and are perhaps more reliable and dependable with the narrow intelligence influenced by AI systems at the moment. Similarly, most autonomous AI applications endure limited to low-risk extents where the cost of catastrophe is limited. Even though many AI techniques can do few things better than humans, the workers' faith in AI technology is still inadequate due to the matters involving such technology, which might increase the algorithmic biases, unexplainable consequences, conquered privacy discretion, and/or lack of credibility or accountability. Customers are also skeptical about AI, and reviews suggest that utmost or many would not need autonomous vehicles, do not involve dealing with chatbots, and so forth.

There is a growing need for high-quality and trustworthy AI schemes since they work meticulously with human beings. It is consequently vital to deliver a vibrant path for understanding and handling the complications intrinsic to highly eminent AI systems [11]. The datasets gathered from heterogeneous resources and information technology (IT) systems can be used in the data-driven analytics actions to provision additional well-versed business intelligence support and decisions. Nevertheless, these outcomes are presently used in remote and discrete portions of the manufacturing or manufacture process. Meanwhile, at the same time, a complete combination of artificial intelligence in all facets of industrial systems is presently deficient [12].

4.9 Automation and AI

When robotic method automation relates to elements of AI like machine learning, the outcome is recognized as intelligent process automation (IPA). An IPA technique is powerful since it consensuses us to get both the benefits of automation, which include amplified speed, time savings, efficiency, and capability to measure along with the AI's elasticity, visions, and processing power. Vendors who use IPA can expand their support and skills while off-loading uninteresting operating management errands to the machine. This is unlike pure robotic automation in that the AI techniques can begin, halt, or even transform whatever it undertakes depending on the situation in which it functions. Moreover, since the finest AI systems permit the vendors to set railings, there is no chance of unanticipated actions taking consequences too far awry. For vendors, this means preferably sooner, more improved imple-mentation and processes, greater use and exactness in data, and enhancements in overall client experience and satisfaction. Marketers move from unsettling over-bid alterations or changes and budget deliveries to sophisticated higher value-added, human-centric contributions like, "How do we raise our value intent to initiate more business and production?" As of these clear profits, Forrester stated that in 2021, 25% of Fortune 510 establishments reported hundreds of illustrations of IPA use cases. Conceivably up to 2050, we entirely hinge on automation and AI since it makes life easier and more precise [13].

Automation and artificial intelligence is the invention of science. The impression that the diverse types of machinery could anticipate and accom-plish tasks and processes just as humans or individuals do is thousands of years old. The knowledgeable truths articulated in AI and automation systems and technologies are not new moreover. It may be better to interpret these skills as the operation or procedures of powerful and long-recognized knowledgeable values through engineering. The practice of automation and intelligence upsurges day by day almost all over the world. Currently, people rely entirely upon them. These technologies and methods are time-saving and can perform numerous tasks with more correctness at a time that humans cannot perform or do [13].

Innovation and adaptation are enormously imperative to the engineering industry. This advancement should prime to supportable engineering using novel technologies. To endorse smart delivery, sustainability, and production necessitates global perceptions of smart application manufacturing technol-ogy. In this respect, thanks to rigorous study and analysis efforts in the arena of AI, a wide range of AI-based methods and techniques, including machine learning, have already been familiar in the business industry to accomplish sustainable engineering. Thus, AI subfields, including image processing, machine learning, data mining, and natural language processing, have also become a significant matter for today's tech titans. The focus on AI creates substantial attention and curiosity in the scientific community, featuring assets of the unceasing progression of the technologies presented today. The variety of AI techniques has grown immensely; meanwhile, the intelligence of machines with machine learning competencies has fashioned deep impacts on corporate businesses, civilization, and governments. They also impact the greater trends in worldwide sustainability. AI can be beneficial in unraveling perilous issues for sustainable business (e.g., logistics, waste management, optimization of resources involving energy, management of supply chain, etc.). With this background, in smart manufacturing, there is an inclination to integrate AI into green industrial manufacturing processes for firmer conservational policies [14]. The hasty progress and fusion of new AI methods/technologies with the Internet, energy, materials, new-generation information technologies, and biotechnology is a crucial part of this new epoch, which in turn will empower the game-changing revolution of models and environments in relation to their application.

4.10 Conclusion

AI technology is presently empowering substantial digital transformations that are redefining what an organization does and even obscuring the industry's limitations and boundaries. Various traditional manufacturing and industrial organizations are taking advantage of machine learning technologies to transform their emphasis from manufacturing goods to delivering services. Different human skills will be rendered obsolete with the AI significantly influencing diverse occupations by automating mundane tasks. The effect of AI-enabled automated technologies varies from the prior technologies, given that they can accomplish tasks that previously mandated human judgment, as they get to distress the knowledge workers for the first time. Most of the professionals, like architects, consultants, lawyers, and doctors, whose creativity, judgment, and expertise have thus been exceedingly valued and considered inimitable, appear threatened now. The changing nature and way of their work is already a realism.

Acknowledgments

I thank the Emirates Aviation University for supporting me in performing this analysis and study.

References

[1] Dwivedi, Y. K., Hughes, L., Ismagilova, E., Aarts, G., Coombs, C., Crick, T., & Williams, M. D. (2021). Artificial Intelligence (AI): Multidisciplinary perspectives on emerging challenges, opportunities, and agenda for research, practice and policy. *International Journal of Information Management*, *57*, 101994.

[2] Zhang, X., Ming, X., Liu, Z., Yin, D., Chen, Z., & Chang, Y. (2019). A reference framework and overall industrial artificial intelligence (I-AI) planning for new application scenarios. *The International Journal of Advanced Manufacturing Technology*, *101*(9), 2367-2389.

[3] Mou, X. (2019). Artificial intelligence: investment trends and selected industry uses. *International Finance Corporation*, *8*.

[4] Ahmad, T., Zhu, H., Zhang, D., Tariq, R., Bassam, A., Ullah, F., & Alshamrani, S. S. (2022). Energetics Systems and artificial intelligence: Applications of Industry 4.0. *Energy Reports*, *8*, 334-361.

[5] Li, B. H., Hou, B. C., Yu, W. T., Lu, X. B., & Yang, C. W. (2017). Applications of artificial intelligence in intelligent manufacturing: a review. *Frontiers of Information Technology & Electronic Engineering*, *18*(1), 86-96.

[6] Lee, J., Singh, J., & Azamfar, M. (2019). Industrial artificial intelligence. *arXiv preprint arXiv:1908.02150*.

[7] Bedi, J., & Toshniwal, D. (2019). Deep learning framework to forecast electricity demand. *Applied energy*, *238*, 1312-1326.

[8] Aghion, P., Jones, B. F., & Jones, C. I. (2018). Artificial intelligence and economic growth. In *The economics of artificial intelligence: An agenda* (pp. 237-282). University of Chicago Press.

[9] Shekhar, S. S. (2019). Artificial intelligence in automation. *Artificial Intelligence*, *3085*(06), 14-17.

[10] Benbya, H., Davenport, T. H., & Pachidi, S. (2020). Artificial intelligence in organizations: current state and future opportunities. *MIS Quarterly Executive*, *19*(4).

[11] Hamada, K., Ishikawa, F., Masuda, S., Myojin, T., Nishi, Y., Ogawa, H., & Matsuya, M. (2020, July). Guidelines for Quality Assurance of Machine Learning-based Artificial Intelligence. In *SEKE* (pp. 335-341).

[12] Trakadas, P., Simoens, P., Gkonis, P., Sarakis, L., Angelopoulos, A., Ramallo-González, A. P., ... & Karkazis, P. (2020). An artificial intelligence-based collaboration approach in industrial iot manufacturing: Key concepts, architectural extensions and potential applications. *Sensors*, *20*(19), 5480.

[13] Donepudi, P. K. (2018). Application of artificial intelligence in the automation industry. *Asian Journal of Applied Science and Engineering*, *7*(1), 7-20.

[14] Cioffi, R., Travaglioni, M., Piscitelli, G., Petrillo, A., & De Felice, F. (2020). Artificial intelligence and machine learning applications in smart production: Progress, trends, and directions. *Sustainability*, *12*(2), 492.

5

Quantum Machine and Deep Learning Models for Industry Automation

Pawan Whig[1], Arun Velu[2], Rahul Reddy Nadikattu[3], and Yusuf Jibrin Alkali[4]

[1]Vivekananda Institute of Professional Studies-TC, India
[2]Equifax, USA
[3]Department of IT, University of Cumbersome, USA
[4]Federal Inland Revenue Service, Nigeria

Abstract

Quantum machine learning unites two of the most contentious subfields in science: quantum computing and classical machine learning. Quantum machine learning is the study of how to solve machine learning problems using insights from quantum mechanics. As more and more information accumulates, the capacity of existing computing machines to successfully train it onto a conventional computation model is stretched to its limits. Quantum computing could be helpful for continuous training with large datasets. When developing learning algorithms, quantum machine learning aims to do so much more quickly than traditional methods. Finding patterns in data and using those patterns to predict the future is at the heart of traditional machine learning. The data can be mined for insights like these. Quantum systems, on either extreme, generate unusual patterns those conventional systems cannot, implying that quantum computers might be able to outpace traditional CPUs in ML tasks. This chapter discusses the past research on quantum machine learning and an update on its current state.

Keywords: Quantum, machine learning, conventional system

5.1 Introduction

Understanding which uses for these technologies may use their potential is crucial as quantum technologies develop quickly. Likewise, machine learning on traditional computers has advanced significantly, revolutionizing tasks like picture identification, language translation, and even physics applications (Whig et al., 2022). This is because additional processing power enables ever-improving performance. Therefore, the potential for effect is immense if quantum computers could speed up machine learning (Hussein, 2019).

The quantum improvement of machine learning has at least two potential directions. Quantum applications first inspired them in optimization; quantum computing's capabilities might theoretically be utilized to speed up the training of current classical models or improve inference in graphical models, as shown in Figure 5.1. This can entail locating better optima in a training environment or locating optima using fewer queries. The benefit of these appearances may only be limited to modest multifaceted accelerations without a deeper understanding of the issue's underlying structure (Anand et al., 2022).

Quantum computing employs devices that use quantum physical science features to stock data and execute calculations. This may benefit some jobs where they can considerably beat even our most powerful supercomputers. In Montiel-Ross (2020), the authors analyzed which subatomic inhabitants metaheuristics may be converted to be employed in current quantum computers based on the circuit model programming paradigm. Montiel-Ross et al., (2019) also proposed the quantum-inspired acronymic evolutionary algorithm as an optimal optimization algorithm for complicated systems.

Employing quantum replicas to produce associations between variable quantities impractical to describe using traditional computing is of particular interest. The recent theoretical and practical advancements in achieving quantum multiplications beyond classical controllability could be construed as evidence that quantum computers are capable of transitioning from delivering examples from increasingly difficult prospects to examples from more typical ones. If these provisions matched real-world distributions, it would indicate the possibility of a significant benefit (Jiwani et al., 2021).

In current research on quantum neural networks, which aim to characterize an allocation through a set of tunable parameters, as well as quantum kernel methods, which employ quantum mechanics to describe extracted features that map conventional information into the quantum Hilbert space, this type of advantage is frequently sought after (Alkali et al., 2022). The rationale

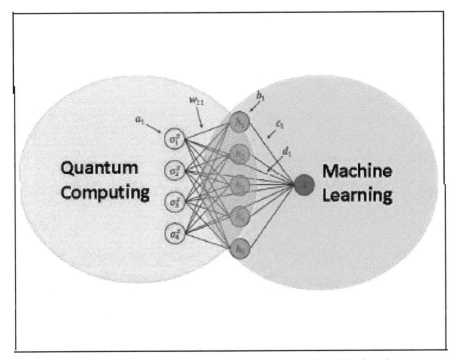

Figure 5.1 Relation between quantum computing and machine learning.

for these techniques' ability to outperform classical models frequently uses the same arguments as or outcomes from quantum simulations. For instance, there may be a quantum benefit if the model uses a quantum circuitry that is challenging to sample data conventionally (George et al., 2021).

The distinction between a conventional computer and a quantum computer was explained at a conference in 2017 by Microsoft CEO Satya Nadella using the example of a corn maze. A traditional computer would start along a path, run into an obstacle, and then turn around. It would then start again, run into another obstacle, and so on until it ran out of alternatives. Although a solution can be reached, this method could take a long time (Bhargav & Whig, 2021).

Quantum computers, however, unlock remarkable parallelism. They simultaneously travel every route through the cornfield. Consequently, the number of steps needed to solve an issue is exponentially reduced (Khera et al., 2021).

5.2 Difference Between Classical and Quantum Data

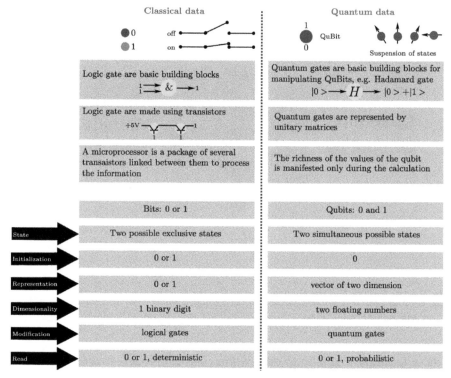

Figure 5.2   Classical data vs. quantum data.

5.3 Quantum Computing

The tiniest conceivable unit of any physical substance, such as energy or mass, is called a quantum. Max Planck hypothesized in 1900 that a body's energy is stored in discrete packets known as quanta at the atomic and subatomic levels. Quantic atoms have pulse dualism, which causes them to behave occasionally like waves and occasionally like particles, depending on the circumstances (Velu & Whig, 2021a). A key aspect of quantum theory is finding a particle's likelihood at a particular point x in space rather than its precise position.

5.3.1 Qubit

A computer conducts operations using traditional "bits," which are either 0 or 1. Nevertheless, a quantum computer operates on bits, often called "qubits."

Qubits can be modeled as follows:

While $|1\rangle$ and $|0\rangle$ are the exciton and grounded phase of electrons circling a nuclei, correspondingly.

A photon: The polarizing filters are $|1\rangle$ and $|0\rangle$, as shown in Figure 5.3.

5.3.2 Superposition

Qubits are simultaneously both 0 AND 1. The term "superposition" refers to this phenomenon.

However, particles can exist in numerous quantum states; when their energies or location are measured, the combination is gone, and the atom only exists inside one state.

5.3.3 Entanglement

The phenomenon known as "quantum entanglement" occurs when quantum particles interact and are characterized in terms of one another rather than separately, even though the particles are spaced far apart (Whig & Ahmad, 2019).

During the measurement of a pair of entangled particles, if one of the particles is set to the lowest energy state (the spin state of "down" when the electron is aligned with its magnetic field), the other correlated particles will

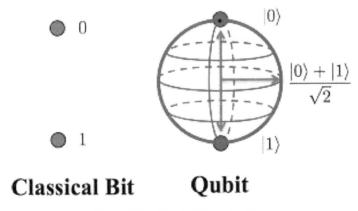

Classical Bit   **Qubit**

Figure 5.3   Classical bit and qubit.

take on the opposite spin state (the spin state of "up") in response. This will happen if the other particle is set to the lowest energy state. When two or more particles interact with one another in a way that causes them to become entangled, the properties of those particles become inextricably intertwined, making it impossible to measure each of them separately. Through the process of quantum entanglement, it is possible to have instant communication between physically separated qubits.

5.4 Quantum Machine Learning (QML)

Recently, a theoretical field known as quantum machine learning has started to show signs of taking shape. It can be found at the intersection of deep learning and particle physics. Quantum machine learning's primary goal is to accelerate processes by integrating. Come again; we distinguish quantum computation from ML. Aspects of standard ML theory are included in the theory of quantum machine learning, which approaches quantum computing through that framework.

Suppose the straightforward problem of identifying whether a quantity is uniform or abnormal in order to contrast traditional program design, traditional ML, and quantum ML, as shown in Figure 5.4.

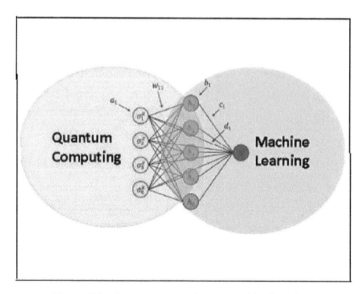

Figure 5.4   Quantum computing vs. machine learning.

The answer is straightforward: you need to ask the user for a number, and then split it in half. The number is odd if you receive a remainder. The number is even if there is not any leftover (Rupani & Sujediya, 2016).

A similar concept underlies quantum computing. Data is processed at the bit level in a traditional computer. Quantum physics, in the context of quantum computers, is the specific behavior that controls the system. The interaction between several atoms may be described using several methods from the field of quantum physics. Such atoms are known as "qubits" in the context of quantum computers. A qubit functions as both a wave and a particle. A wave dispersion may hold a lot more information (or bit) relative to a particle.

Algorithms are used to monitor a machine learning optimizer's accuracy. We frequently notice that not all of the predictions by a machine learning model are accurate when building it. The output of the mathematical expression used to describe the loss function reveals how much the program has exceeded the desired outcome (Nadikattu et al., 2020).

The loss function is another goal of a quantum computer. It contains a technology called quantum tunneling that scans the whole loss function space in search of the value with the smallest loss, which determines where the method will operate most effectively and quickly.

5.5 Classical Machine Learning vs. Quantum Computing

Quantum computers employ several approaches to handle machine learning challenges now that you are familiar with the fundamental ideas of quantum computing, as shown in Figure 5.5. The following is a list of the approaches we will examine:

- Algebraic problems solved via quantum computer vision
- Confirmatory factor analysis in quantum
- Kernel techniques and quantum support vector machines
- Precision optimization
- Quantum thinking in depth

5.5.1 Linear algebra problems have been solved via quantum machine learning

Matrix operations on variables in an ample vector space can be used to solve a wide range of issues arising in data analysis and machine learning. An interplanetary trajectory within a complex sequence of dimensions, denoted

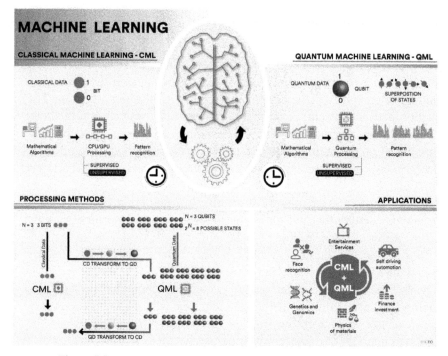

Figure 5.5   Classical machine learning vs. quantum machine learning.

as 2a, symbolizes the classical state of a quantum system in a quantum computer. A planetary orbit trajectory describes this pattern. Several matrices undergo different transformations inside this domain. The Fourier transform, eigenvector and eigenvalue identification, and the solution of linear systems of equations over two-dimensional trajectory places are all examples of problems that could be solved in polynomial time by quantum systems. One example is the Harrow, Hassidim, and Lloyd (HHL) method.

5.6 Quantum Thinking in Depth

The dimensions of large datasets can be simplified with the help of a technique known as principal component analysis. Whenever we process data, we have to decide which factors to keep and which to eliminate, and in doing so, we sacrifice accuracy. Working with a dataset can become noticeably less complicated when correctly carried out, making the machine learning process significantly less taxing.

5.6.1 Principal component analysis in quantum

For instance, when given a dataset with 10 input values, a standard system can perform principal component analysis (PCA) in a reasonable amount of time. However, if the input dataset has a million characteristics, traditional principal component analysis methods will not work because of the difficulty in displaying the relative value of each feature. Principal component analysis's tried-and-true methods break down when dealing with input datasets with more than a million characteristics.

Computing eigenvectors and eigenvalues presents another difficulty when using classical computers. The larger the input, the larger the set of eigenvectors and associated eigenvalues. The use of QRAM (quantum random access memory), which allows quantum computers to pick a path through the data in a completely random fashion, allows quantum computers to solve this problem quickly and efficiently. As shown in Figure 5.6, the vector is transformed into a quantum state by employing qubits.

When performing quantum principal component analysis, the resulting summary vector contains logarithmic qubits. A dense matrix is produced when the provided random vector is used as the generator. Designers can generate the basic version of any random course and deconstruct it into its primary mechanisms by repeatedly sampling the data, using a density matrix

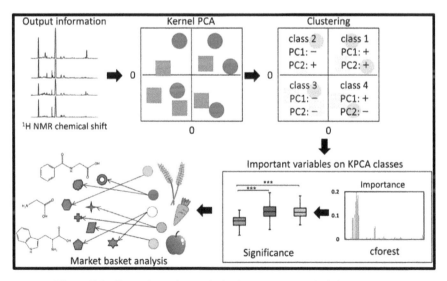

Figure 5.6   Example to show principal component analysis in quantum.

exponentiation method, and employing the quantum phase estimation algorithm (Velu & Whig, n.d.). Consequently, both the computational complexity and the time complexity are drastically reduced by an exponential factor.

5.6.2 Support vector quantum machines

When it comes to machine learning, one of the most well-known methods is called the support vector machine, and we use that to carry out both regression and classification. Its primary function in classification tasks is to organize low-dimensional datasets into the appropriate categories. Imagine that the data sizes are increased to the point where they can be linearly separated, as demonstrated in Figure 5.7.

On desktop computers, the SVM will only make use of a selected number of dimensions. It will become challenging after a certain point because these machines do not possess adequate computing control (Asopa et al., 2021)..

The support vector algorithm can be executed exponentially more quickly on quantum systems. It operates effectively and produces results more quickly thanks to the overlap and entangled principles.

5.6.3 Optimization

Optimizing means getting something done with as little work and as few resources as possible. Machine learning models can be made more capable of making good and accurate predictions by optimizing the learning process.

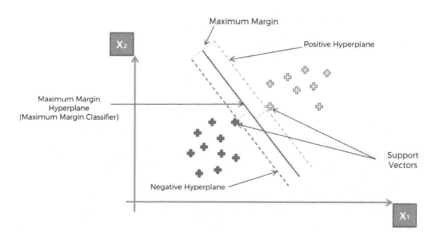

Figure 5.7   Support vector quantum machines.

Optimization focuses on reducing the loss function as much as possible. However, increasing the loss function can be costly and result in less precise estimates because it reduces the outputs' accuracy and consistency. The success of the vast majority of machine learning strategies requires iterative performance optimization. Quantum algorithms may be the key to solving the optimization problems plaguing machine learning. Because of the quantum entanglement property, a quantum government can pre-program infinite copies of the currently applicable explanation. In order to improve the final results of machine learning, they are incorporated at every stage of the process (Velu & Whig, 2021b).

5.7 Quantum Learning in Depth

Teaching neural networks can go faster when deep learning and quantum computing are used together. Using this method, we might be able to make a new framework for deep learning and optimize the core. Scientists can copy the results of traditional deep learning methods if they have access to a real, physical quantum computer.

For multi-layer perceptron topologies, the amount of work that needs to be done on the computer is proportional to the number of network neurons. By using dedicated GPU clusters to improve performance, training time may be able to be cut down by a lot. Unlike what was thought, it will grow compared to quantum computers (Pawan Whig et al., 2017). Instead of the traditional software used by regular computers, quantum computers use neural networks to model their hardware. In particular, a qubit replaces a neuron, the basic building block of any neural network. So, a quantum system with qubits might be able to imitate a neuronic net and be used for deep learning applications much faster than more traditional machine learning techniques.

5.7.1 Why is quantum machine learning so exciting?

Leading businesses worldwide are vying for the most practical quantum computer. By doing so, it will be possible to handle highly complicated problems, such as cracking encryptions, advancing the development of new medicines, revolutionizing communications networks, or advancing artificial intelligence (AI) solutions.

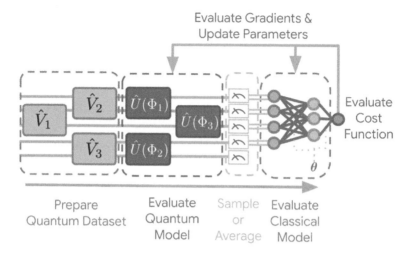

Figure 5.8   Quantum machine learning model.

More than three billion online users are feeding massive data banks, testing the capabilities of contemporary PCs. When Moore's law was initially proposed in 1965, it foretold that the number of integrated circuits would double every two years. At the time, however, conditions were far from stable. Quantum machine learning model is shown in Figure 5.8. Today's top businesses are vying for the most practical quantum machine available; so let us fast forward to today. By doing so, it will be possible to access a tenfold quicker machine and use it to tackle complex problems like cracking encryptions, advancing drug discovery, transforming communications networks, or advancing artificial intelligence (AI) solutions.

Consider Google as an example. With a 54-qubit Sycamore processor that can compute in under 200 seconds, as opposed to the best supercomputer's 10,000 years, it claims to have attained quantum supremacy today. That is important because, when processing a huge quantity of data to solve complex issues, things are sure to change dramatically. Therefore, it is crucial to understand all real-world problems exclusively regarding quantum theory. Even though Google's assertion drew criticism, it nevertheless represents a turning point for technology when looking into the future.

In research, Google examined the quantum advantage theory for machine learning to better understand its applicability. The study showed how a moderately complicated problem may alter when the appropriate datasets are available, and it also showed how quantum algorithms can provide you with a competitive advantage. It also showed how to create a valuable technique for screening for data embeddings, notably by applying kernel approaches. Thus, a relatively innovative approach to a few properties of a quantum machine was offered thanks to the learning constraints and the insights from the screening process. In essence, it aids in illustrating the greatest possible empirical separation – a key benefit of quantum computing – and helps to support quantum techniques using ideas drawn from classical learning.

5.8 The Essence of Quantum Computing

Some very important concepts which everyone should know about quantum computing are as follows.

5.8.1 Taking the initiative to manage uncertainty

You have two choices when trying to solve a puzzle or navigate a maze: you may call a quantum computer for assistance or a contemporary PC.

What distinguishes quantum computers is the difference in how the issue is solved. A quantum machine will evaluate all feasible pathways at once instead of a typical computer, which will consider all options and rule out each one until it finds the best one.

In other words, quantum computers are well ahead of the game when coping with ambiguity. One can only speculate about how quantum machines will be able to address the most severe challenges ever when you apply that viewpoint to more significant topics like AI or healthcare.

5.8.2 Welcoming a new AI era

There is no denying that AI has profoundly influenced our lives. Everything that makes life simpler, from smartphones to smart homes, to education, healthcare, and transportation, is made possible by AI.

While this is all wonderful, AI is still regarded as a relatively new technology, particularly when it comes to thinking like humans. Things might take a fascinating turn with quantum computing, turning AI systems into more robots by giving them what is commonly called "thinking power." As a result, we are striving to improve goods' durability and dependability.

5.8.3 Cybersecurity advancement

Cybersecurity derives its guiding concept by factoring a considerable number into its primes. This is one area in which quantum computers are naturally advantageous, and as they become more widely used, things like encryption will soon be history. Having said that, if quantum computers get into the wrong hands, our data might be utilized against us in unfathomable ways.

5.8.4 Accuracy of weather predictions

Weather forecasting is far more complicated than just telling you to bring an umbrella because it will rain today. It directly affects a country's economics, development, and general functionality, especially considering food crops.

5.8.5 A signal to develop better life-saving drugs

In order to determine the effectiveness of a medical condition, available drug research examines several interactions between proteins, molecules, and other substances. The exercise is supported by several combinations that demand careful thought and investigation.

Chemists can significantly benefit from quantum computing by using it to find the most practical medication choices. It can also drastically reduce the time it takes for medications to be discovered before they are used for a variety of individualized therapies. Threats to some cutting-edge technologies are shown in Figure 5.9.

5.9 A Portal to Exciting Future Technology

In the future, quantum computing will be the hub of operations for the research and development division of the world's top universities. For instance, businesses are currently investing billions in enhancing the software used in autonomous vehicles or in enhancing chemistry.

5.9.1 How AI will change thanks to quantum computing

When the terms "quantum" and "computer" are used, it is simple to picture science fiction programs like Star Trek. When you discover that quantum computing uses the combined features of superposition, interference, and entanglement to run computations exceedingly rapidly, it does not make the idea seem any less complicated. Fortunately, most do not need to worry about the minute details. We must be aware that quicker data access and more secure networking are two benefits of quantum computing.

This vast data collection is the foundation for machine learning techniques employed by AI; the more data an algorithm can take in, the better its predictions or choices. Sadly, the speed and stability provided by quantum

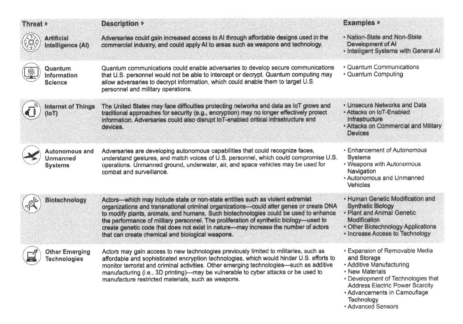

Threat »	Description »	Examples »
Artificial Intelligence (AI)	Adversaries could gain increased access to AI through affordable designs used in the commercial industry, and could apply AI to areas such as weapons and technology.	• Nation-State and Non-State Development of AI • Intelligent Systems with General AI
Quantum Information Science	Quantum communications could enable adversaries to develop secure communications that U.S. personnel would not be able to intercept or decrypt. Quantum computing may allow adversaries to decrypt information, which could enable them to target U.S. personnel and military operations.	• Quantum Communications • Quantum Computing
Internet of Things (IoT)	The United States may face difficulties protecting networks and data as IoT grows and traditional approaches for security (e.g., encryption) may no longer effectively protect information. Adversaries could also disrupt IoT-enabled critical infrastructure and devices.	• Unsecure Networks and Data • Attacks on IoT-Enabled Infrastructure • Attacks on Commercial and Military Devices
Autonomous and Unmanned Systems	Adversaries are developing autonomous capabilities that could recognize faces, understand gestures, and match voices of U.S. personnel, which could compromise U.S. operations. Unmanned ground, underwater, air, and space vehicles may be used for combat and surveillance.	• Enhancement of Autonomous Systems • Weapons with Autonomous Navigation • Autonomous and Unmanned Vehicles
Biotechnology	Actors—which may include state or non-state entities such as violent extremist organizations and transnational criminal organizations—could alter genes or create DNA to modify plants, animals, and humans. Such biotechnologies could be used to enhance the performance of military personnel. The proliferation of synthetic biology—used to create genetic code that does not exist in nature—may increase the number of actors that can create chemical and biological weapons.	• Human Genetic Modification and Synthetic Biology • Plant and Animal Genetic Modification • Other Biotechnology Applications • Increase Access to Technology
Other Emerging Technologies	Actors may gain access to new technologies previously limited to militaries, such as affordable and sophisticated encryption technologies, which would hinder U.S. efforts to monitor terrorist and criminal activities. Other emerging technologies—such as additive manufacturing (i.e., 3D printing)—may be vulnerable to cyber attacks or be used to manufacture restricted materials, such as weapons.	• Expansion of Removable Media and Storage • Additive Manufacturing • New Materials • Development of Technologies that Address Electric Power Scarcity • Advancements in Camouflage Technology • Advanced Sensors

Figure 5.9   Threats to some cutting-edge technologies.

computing are necessary due to exponential development and the more complex nature of inquiries.

Big data is the foundation of AI, a multipurpose technology. AI can find trends and forecast events by studying databases – the price of gathering and storing data formerly acted as a barrier to AI advancement. Nowadays, the difficulty is in promptly consuming, finding, and presenting useful information.

5.9.2 Processes for making better business decisions

Productivity gains and quicker decision-making will be key as we move toward a quantum computing future. Reaching specific audiences, analyzing data, and forecasting trends are significant benefits.

5.9.3 Quantum security and artificial intelligence

It has always been difficult to keep up with the development of security risks and assaults. Enterprises may more accurately forecast potential security concerns and fend off prospective assaults by combining the speed of quantum computing with the data analytics capabilities of AI.

Understanding that verifying data is just as crucial as interpreting it is crucial as quantum computing and AI advance. A growing kind of cyberterrorism that should not be disregarded involves weaponizing data, falsifying analytics, and disrupting AI systems' learning experience.

5.9.4 AI and quantum computing complement DevOps

As DevOps teams struggle to establish business targets and objectives, design and create new software solutions, and manage the continuing maintenance and testing of current systems, quantum computing, and AI are formidable partners.

Regression testing, functional testing, and user acceptability testing may all be aided by DevOps teams looking at the data that AI provides. Testing may be consistent and thorough because quantum computing allows AI to swiftly and effectively handle data from different sources.

5.9.5 Where are our IT systems vulnerable?

Using quantum computing and AI to assist ITOps, when should our hardware or software be upgraded? How can we handle situations more quickly? How much time is devoted to managing activities that might be done automatically? Big data analysis is the most effective method for addressing these ITOps problems. These AI queries can provide comprehensive visibility into operational data and real-time information thanks to the speed provided by quantum computing.

It is most thrilling to think about how advancing these technologies might truly benefit society by assisting in developing solutions for diseases, untangling traffic, or securing sensitive data as corporations use quantum computing and AI.

5.9.6 Limitation of quantum machine learning

Users may physically alter factors in quantum computing, such as the intensity of an electromagnetic field or the frequency of a laser pulse, to address issues. Quantum computers can therefore be trained similarly to neural networks. The main benefit of quantum computers is their capacity to generate patterns that classical systems find challenging. Therefore, it is logical to anticipate that quantum computers may perform better on machine learning tasks than conventional computers. As a result, the discipline of quantum machine learning has emerged. Learning algorithms can be improved by quantum technology. This is known as machine learning with a quantum enhancement. Machine learning techniques for analyzing data that cannot be processed by classical computing are the most widely used quantum computers in the area.

Quantum machine learning accelerates computing and can control how algorithms in software store data. Running machine learning algorithms on cutting-edge computing hardware like quantum computers expands the evidence of learning. Compared to computer models, information processing is based on quantum mechanics and its laws.

However, it is fair to say that the discipline of quantum machine learning continues to work in more fantastical areas of physics.

5.9.7 Hardware constraints

Researchers frequently find themselves cut off from others in their industry when conducting their work. Due to quantum decoherence, qubits may lose quantum characteristics such as entanglement, decreasing the amount of data that qubits can store. Quantum decoherence can be caused by exposure to heat or light. Second, changes in the states of qubits require rotations in the logic gates of quantum computers, which are well-known for being particularly prone to errors. Any misalignment can lead to issues with the output. Quantum machine learning also requires longer computer circuit lengths and error correction (with redundancy for every qubit).

5.9.8 Program restrictions

It is crucial to consider the physics of quantum computers when designing algorithms for them. However, while a classical algorithm can be designed in the Turing machine style, a quantum algorithm must be designed in the style of pure physics without using any simple formulae that would link it to logic.

Scalability is always a top priority in a system like this one. We are creating software with more power to process data. Unfortunately, only a tiny fraction of the information required to create such quantum computing algorithms is currently available. Consequently, most progress is made via untrained intuition.

Due to the limitations of particular simulations, creating models that can significantly influence machine learning is complex. Due to these restrictions, most well-known quantum algorithms are not applicable in the real world. As for the third rule of quantum computing, there is a cap on how many qubits can be kept on a quantum circle. Although these restrictions apply to all quantum computing, attracting more attention and guiding research in the right direction is possible by incorporating disciplines like machine learning.

5.10 More on Quantum Computing and Machine Learning Connections

Future advancements in quantum computing should increase our capacity to handle important computational jobs. The way we now utilize computers in research and daily life is changing due to machine learning. It is only logical to look for linkages between these two new computing paradigms to gain several advantages.

5.10.1 Wavefunction

Today, one of the fastest routes to quantum advantage is expected to be the prediction of the electronic structural features of molecules and materials. The wavefunction for electrons is shown in Figure 5.10.

On the other hand, the most cutting-edge machine learning technique, neural networks, has a brand-new application: simulating quantum physics. Neural networks have only recently been utilized to categorize quantum phase transitions or as a variational approach for interacting with many-body systems.

The representation of quantum wavefunctions is a goal shared by quantum computers and neural networks. This area of agreement might serve as

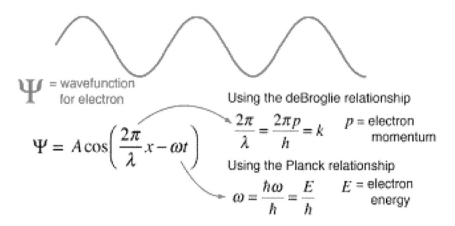

Figure 5.10   Wavefunction for the electrons.

a jumping-off point for investigating potential linkages. Every strategy has strengths and weaknesses.

5.10.2 The significance of accuracy

Along with other low-depth algorithms for electronic structure, the variational quantum eigensolver (VQE), as shown in Figure 5.11, uses quantum state storage and manipulation to recover ground and excited state features of quantum target systems. To achieve that, we must calculate the expected value of Hamiltonian operators, which stand in for molecule energies in the case of molecular systems. Additionally, we must do the measurement exactly since any significant random fluctuations will render the entire quantum procedure useless. It turns out that quantum computers are not particularly effective at this. More peculiarly, it is impractical for existing technology to do enough measurements to obtain sufficient accuracy for applications demonstrating quantum advantage.

We employed neural network methods, as shown in Figure 5.12, on quantum computing for more precise chemical simulations in PRR's "Precise measurement of quantum observables with neural-network estimators," in cooperation with two researchers from the Flatiron Institute, Giacomo Torlai and Giuseppe Carleo. The method relies on measurement data obtained by a

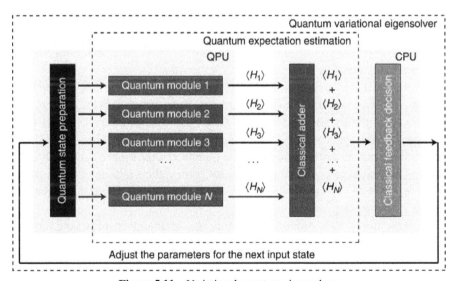

Figure 5.11 Variational quantum eigensolver.

$$U^1 = U_3^1 \, U_2^1 \, U_1^1$$

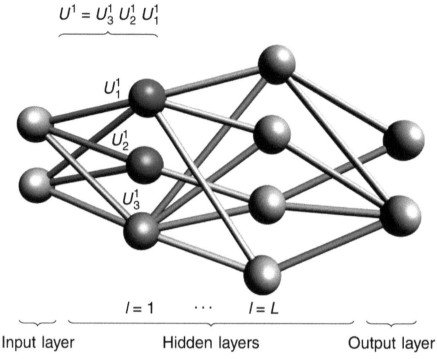

Figure 5.12   Quantum neural network.

quantum computer to train a neural network. After being trained, the neural network encodes a portion of the quantum state, which is accurate enough to retrieve molecule energies.

By integrating a quantum computer with our novel neural-network estimator, we can combine the benefits of the two methods. We use quantum computers' ability to interfere with states throughout an exponentially expanding Hilbert space while a chosen quantum circuit is being run. We get a limited set of measurements once the quantum interference process has finished. The neural network, a classical tool, may then take advantage of this sparse input to effectively represent some aspects of a quantum state, including its simulated energy.

The main query that remains after this data transfer from a quantum processor to a conventional network is:

How well can neural networks capture the quantum correlations of a dataset of limited measurements produced by sampling molecular wavefunctions?

For computer scientists, a toolset for quantum computing encompasses a suite of software, algorithms, hardware frameworks, and specialized languages designed to manipulate and harness the power of quantum systems.

We must consider how neural networks could replicate fermionic matter to respond to this challenge. Spin lattice and continuous-space issue simulation has previously been carried out using neural networks. It is still difficult to solve fermionic models with neural networks. We investigated how molecules are simulated on quantum computers to try to identify a workaround for that.

We employed encodings of fermionic degrees of freedom to qubit ones, precisely the same encodings employed in variational algorithms and molecular simulations on quantum computers. We have created fermionic neural network states using these mappings accessible on Qiskit Aqua. On a traditional computer, we put them to the test against molecular ground states, which are quantum objects.

5.10.3 Data power and quantum machine learning

In recent years, quantum computing has grown quickly in both theory and practice, raising hopes that it may have an influence on actual applications. How quantum computers could impact machine learning is an important topic of research. The ability of quantum computers to naturally handle some problems with intricate input correlations that may be highly challenging to conventional or "classical" computers was recently experimentally shown. In light of this, it is possible that learning models developed on quantum computers, as shown in Figure 5.13, would be significantly more powerful for specific applications, possibly offering quicker processing, greater generalization on fewer datasets, or both. Therefore, it is crucial to comprehend the circumstances in which a "quantum advantage" may be obtained.

In most cases, the notion of quantum advantage is expressed in terms of computing gains. Can a quantum computer, given a task with well-specified inputs and outputs, provide a more accurate result than a conventional machine in the same amount of time? Quantum computers are thought to provide a significant performance advantage for various algorithms, including Shor's factoring method for factoring huge prime products (important for RSA encryption) and the quantum modeling of quantum systems. However, the availability of data can significantly influence a problem's difficulty and, thus, the potential benefit for a quantum computer.

We analyze the issue of the quantum advantage in machine learning to understand better when it would apply in "power of data in quantum

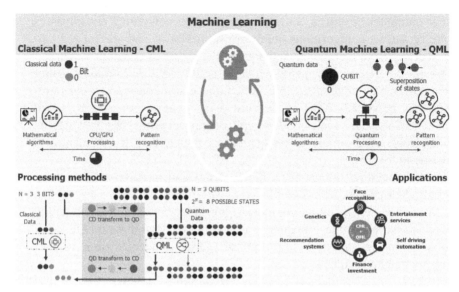

Figure 5.13   Quantum machine learning model.

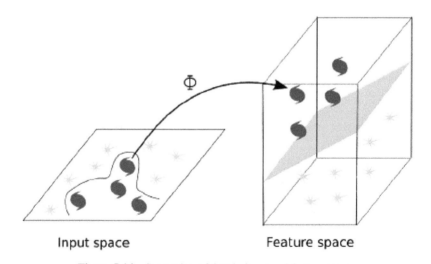

Figure 5.14   Separation of data in input and feature space.

machine learning," which was published in Nature Communications. We demonstrate how a problem's formal complexity changes when more data become available and how this might occasionally make classical learning models competitive with quantum algorithms. We then create a useful technique for determining if a certain collection of data embeddings may have a quantum advantage when used with kernel approaches. We offer a unique approach that projects certain features of feature maps from a quantum computer back into classical space using the learning bounds and insights from the screening method.

5.11 Case Study

5.11.1 Q-SVM (quantum support vector machine algorithm)

Although quantum computers and quantum programming are very new fields, they both arouse curiosity and stage experimental studies to understand what can be done. One of these experimental areas of study is the study of machine learning and testing of deep learning algorithms, even artificial intelligence, on quantum computers. However, even deep learning methods and artificial intelligence studies are at the beginning, while their application in quantum computers continues to be academic and theoretical studies rather than practical uses.

As far as in search, implementing the QSVM algorithm can be accomplished in two different ways. The first of these methods is to run the kernel function only on a quantum computer and to get the data from a conventional computer and conventional feature space by reducing it with conventional methods. The second is to do both the reduction of data in the property space and the labels of the data and the kernel function on quantum computers.

We first need to know how the classic version of SVM classifies the data to understand the difference between these two methods. Assuming we know this, let us remember with an image that shows how data is separated from each other in the property space by increasing size, as shown in Figure 5.10.

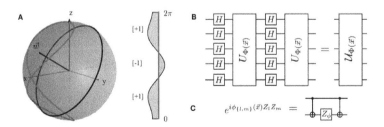

Figure 5.15 Quantum property space.

The difference between the two methods mentioned above is that our feature space is also calculated in quantum circuits in the first one. The quantum property space can also be shown in Figure 5.15.

The common point in both methods is that the kernel function is obtained by quantum calculations rather than the traditional way. However, to increase the success rate, the data labels must be provided in the superposition state. In order to do this, the data must be read from a quantum circuit, but we do not have the opportunity to apply this method of data provision here. However, the results obtained in experimental studies show that 100% predictive success can be achieved with this method. (Of course, this was done by using regular data that can achieve 100% success.)

Although we cannot provide the data from the quantum computer, a function is provided inside the Qiskit library that allows the data to be separated using the quantum property space. We will use this library named feature_map below.

5.11.2 Why did they need Q-SVM?

There is no compelling reason to cling to antiquated strategies for machine learning in an era when quantum computers and algorithms are readily available. The use of properties of quantum physics, such as entanglement and the computational power that is made available by quantum computers, are two approaches that can be taken to answer this question. It is utilized in the SVM algorithm to classify the data by forging support points from clusters of data points that are very similar to one another. The images of feature spaces above demonstrate that a data classification in two or three dimensions is impossible. Images of this caliber contribute significantly to the argument's weight. For this, it may be necessary to increase the size towards an *n*-dimensional space and separate our data from the points representing it. However, as we work in multi-dimensional spaces, our computing power is insufficient in classical computers.

5.11.3 Import the library

First, we will use the SVM algorithm in qiskit.aqua. But other libraries have an alternative to SVM algorithms. The dataset we will use is the iris dataset, which is one of the most frequently used datasets in machine learning studies.

In [2]:
import numpy as np
from sklearn.datasets import load_iris

```
from sklearn.model_selection import train_test_split
import qiskit
from qiskit import BasicAer, Aer
from qiskit.aqua import QuantumInstance
from qiskit.aqua.algorithms import QSVM
from qiskit.aqua.components.multiclass_extensions import one_against
_rest, all_pairs
from qiskit.aqua.components.feature_maps import SecondOrderExpan-
sion
from qiskit.aqua.input import ClassificationInput
from qiskit.aqua import run_algorithm
backend = Aer.get_backend('qasm_simulator')
iris = load_iris()
```

Since it takes too long to run the algorithm on IBM-Q, I run it on qasm_simulator. But nevertheless, it will take time.

5.11.4 Install the dataset

Iris, which is the dataset we will use, consists of three separate classes as the target variable and four feature columns.

In [3]:

```
X, Y = iris.data, iris.target
print(X.shape)
print(len(set(Y)))
train_x, test_x, train_y, test_y = train_test_split(X, Y, test_size=0.2)
num_features = 4
training_size = 120
test_size = 30
feature_map = SecondOrderExpansion(feature_dimension=num_features,
depth=3)
```

 # With feature_map, we have defined the function we will use in the abovementioned quantum property space.

(150, 4)

3

We defined the feature map above but did not need to define it here since we will give it as a parameter below. For the sake of example, both remain for now.

In [4]:

```
params = {
```

```
'problem': {'name': 'classification', 'random_seed': 794},
'algorithm': {
'name': 'QSVM',
},
'backend': {'shots': 1},
'multiclass_extension': {'name': 'OneAgainstRest'},
'feature_map': {'name': 'SecondOrderExpansion', 'depth': 3, 'entan-
gler_map': [[1, 0]]}
#'feature_map': {'name': 'SecondOrderExpansion,' 'depth': 3}
}
training_dataset={'A':train_x[train_y==0],
'B':train_x[train_y==1],
'C':train_x[train_y==2]}
test_dataset={'A':test_x[test_y==0],
'B':test_x[test_y==1],
'C':test_x[test_y==2]} total_arr = np.concatenate((test_dataset['A'],test
_dataset['B'],test_dataset['C']))
alg_input = ClassificationInput(training_dataset, test_dataset, total_arr)
```

In [5]:

```
result = run_algorithm(params, algo_input=alg_input, backend=backend)
```

Let us print the results and see how we got the output.

In [6]:

```
result
```

Out[6]:

```
{'testing_accuracy': 0.7,
'test_success_ratio': 0.7,
'predicted_labels': array([0, 0, 0, 0, 0, 0, 0, 0, 0, 1, 0, 1, 2, 0, 1, 1, 1, 0, 1,
1, 0, 2,
1, 2, 1, 2, 0, 2, 2, 1]),
'predicted_classes': ['A',
'A',
'A',
'A',
'A',
'A',
'A',
'A',
'A',
'B',
```

'A',
'B',
'C',
'A',
'B',
'B',
'B',
'A',
'B',
'B',
'A',
'C',
'B',
'C',
'B',
'C',
'A',
'C',
'C',
'B']}

Our results are relatively good. The fact that we have not run a full QSVM technically in these results also has an impact. Nevertheless, you can see that it is possible to obtain more precise results by examining the case study. With the development of technology and hardware obstacles disappearing one by one in the next 10 years, we will be able to run more advanced algorithms in quantum computers with more precise results.

5.12 Quantum Computing and Machine Learning for Industry Automation

It is expected that quantum computing will aid in developing revolutionary products and services, which will shake up and reshape the manufacturing sector. Benefits in business dealings: Quantum computing is expected to have a significant impact on many areas of manufacturing, including chemical discovery, product development, and process optimization, to name a few. Significant influence: Early adopters will be able to secure advantages that will be extremely tough to overcome.

In this section, we look at prospective manufacturing use cases in four categories: find, design, control, and supply:

5.12.1 Discover

It is a shared secret that even modestly large molecules are difficult to represent with perfect chemical precision using today's traditional computers. With its exponentially huge state space, quantum computing could offer detailed modeling of incredibly complicated molecules, which can significantly improve materials and medication research.

To the best of our knowledge, there are around 15 million defined chemical compounds and around 300,000 materials today. More and more practical chemicals will undoubtedly be uncovered in the future. Nature creates materials with extraordinary properties that conventional industrial manufacturing methods cannot duplicate. For example, spider silk is stronger than steel when measured by its specific weight and can be produced at body temperature rather than in a furnace. Only wastewater from production is discarded. Given that spider silk is a protein derived from DNA, one day, we may be able to create a substance that is comparable to or superior to spider silk that is produced in a manner that is equally as good for the environment thanks to the increased capacity of quantum computing to simulate at the subatomic level.

5.12.2 Design

Many items today are developed and validated using numerical simulations. Individual engineering safety margins are used to 3D-model auto and aerospace components and sub-assemblies. These margins can add up, resulting in goods that are overweight or cost more than required, limiting their profitability.

However, in the future, quantum mechanics will be able to model component interactions within complex hardware systems, allowing for more accurate and comprehensive calculations of system loads, load pathways, noise, and vibration. The potential long-term impact of multiple individual safety margins can be reduced, costs can be reduced, and system performance can be maintained or improved if the system as a whole is analyzed in detail.

5.12.3 Control

Cutting-edge analytics is tested to its limits when new production control methods are implemented, especially when machine learning and many variables are in play. String theory has the potential to enhance traditional computing by aiding in the development of pattern recognition and the advancement of categorization. The following business areas are expected to be significantly impacted by the integration of quantum computers and algorithms and by the optimization opportunities that this integration presents.

Machine learning and standard multi-variate analysis are currently used in semiconductor chip production. However, classical computing has hit a technological wall and cannot accommodate further increases in the parameters required for more complex analysis. Quantum computing's end goal is to improve manufacturing output by allowing for the evaluation of more interactive elements and processes.

Modeling and optimizing the production processes and robotics scheduling for complicated items like automobiles requires much computational power. These products, like automobiles, are well-known for their notoriously high levels of complexity. Quantum computing has the potential to speed up refinement processes and allow for more versatile optimization in practice.

5.12.4 Supply chains

The structure of supply chains is shifting from one that is linear and event-driven, with discontinuous, sequential operations, to one that is more organic and flexible and is based on the evolving needs of the true market and the currently available components. In the context of Industry 4.0, the addition of quantum computing to the toolkit of the digital supply chain has the potential to hasten decision-making, improve risk management, and bring about a reduction in operating costs and sales that were lost as a result of items being discontinued or out of stock. The supply chain may undergo a complete revolution due to quantum computing in the long run. This could involve adapting the supply chain to optimize vendor orders and associated logistics by utilizing dynamic near-real-time decision-making based on shifting market requirements, increasing competitive flexibility.

Quantum computing is poised to become a critical transformational tool for manufacturing. With the predicted influence on product design and development production methods, and supply chain operations, early buyers who embraced the quantum future today may gain a significant advantage.

5.12.5 How does manufacturing begin?

1. Delegate the task of conducting experiments with actual supercomputers and researching the potential applications of quantum mechanics in your sector to individuals within your company who have been designated as

"quantum champions." Allow your quantum champions to report their findings to a quantum steering committee comprising line-of-business leaders and market analysts to assist in concentrating on the most significant challenges.

2. Determine which potential applications of quantum computing should be prioritized based on the extent to which they can deliver a competitive advantage, taking into account the business strategy of your company, the associated consumer value propositions, and the long-term development objectives. Maintain a close eye on developments in quantum application development so that you can stay one step ahead of any potential use cases that could be commercialized sooner rather than later.

3. Contemplate the possibility of working together with a new quantum ecosystem that is currently in the process of developing. This ecosystem is made up of like-minded research laboratories and academic institutions, quantum technology suppliers, quantum application developers and coders, and start-ups with supporting technologies. Involve other companies experiencing the same problems to gain rapid access to an all-encompassing quantum computing stack that can construct and execute quantum algorithms tailored to your specific company's needs. Keep an eye out for developments in quantum technology that might call for a reorganization of partnerships.

5.13 Conclusion and Future Scope

Although the potential of using quantum computing for machine learning is still intriguing, certain nuanced aspects must be carefully considered when measuring quantum benefit. Here, we built a framework for comprehending quantum benefit chances in a learning environment. We demonstrated in the case study how data-driven classical ML algorithms can become exponentially more effective, and we demonstrated that even if the data originate from a dynamic process that is difficult to reproduce separately, a forecast benefit for classical modeling is not assured. This chapter is highly beneficial for researchers in the same field.

References

Alkali, Y., Routray, I., & Whig, P. (2022). Study of various methods for reliable, efficient, and Secured IoT using Artificial Intelligence. Available at SSRN 4020364.

Anand, M., Velu, A., & Whig, P. (2022). Prediction of Loan Behaviour with Machine Learning Models for Secure Banking. Journal of Computer Science and Engineering (JCSE), 3(1), 1–13.

Asopa, P., Purohit, P., Nadikattu, R. R., & Whig, P. (2021). Reducing carbon footprint for sustainable development of smart cities using IoT. 2021 Third International Conference on Intelligent Communication Technologies and Virtual Mobile Networks (ICICV), 361–367.

Bhargav, R., & Whig, P. (2021). More Insight on Data Analysis of Titanic Data Set. International Journal of Sustainable Development in Computing Science, 3(4), 1–10.

Chouhan, S. (2019). Using an Arduino and a temperature, humidity sensor, Automate the fan speed. International Journal of Sustainable Development in Computing Science, 1(2).

George, N., Muiz, K., Whig, P., & Velu, A. (2021). Framework of Perceptive Artificial Intelligence using Natural Language Processing (PAIN). Artificial & Computational Intelligence/Published Online: July.

Hussein, A. H. (2019). Internet of Things (IoT): Research Challenges and Future Applications. In IJACSA) International Journal of Advanced Computer Science and Applications (Vol. 10, Issue 6). www.ijacsa.thesai.org

Jiwani, N., Gupta, K., & Whig, P. (2021). Novel HealthCare Framework for Cardiac Arrest With the Application of AI Using ANN. 2021 5th International Conference on Information Systems and Computer Networks (ISCON), 1–5.

Khera, Y., Whig, P., & Velu, A. (2021). efficient, effective, and secured electronic billing system using AI. Vivekananda Journal of Research, 10, 53–60.

Nadikattu, R. R., Mohammad, S. M., & Whig, P. (2020). Novel economical social distancing smart Device for COVID-19 (SSRN Scholarly Paper ID 3640230). Social Science Research Network. Https://Papers. Ssrn. Com/Abstract, 3640230.

Anupam Priyam et al. (2018). Simulation & performance analysis of various R2R D/A converter using various topologies. International Robotics & Automation Journal, 4(2), 128–131.

Rupani, A., & Sujediya, G. (2016). A Review of FPGA implementation of Internet of Things. International Journal of Innovative Research in Computer and Communication Engineering, 4(9).

Shrivastav, P., Whig, P., & Gupta, K. (n.d.). Bandwidth Enhancement by Slotted Stacked Arrangement and its Comparative Analysis with Conventional Single and Stacked Patch Antenna.

Velu, A., & Whig, P. (2022). Studying the Impact of the COVID Vaccination on the World Using Data Analytics.

Velu, A., & Whig, P. (2021a). Protect Personal Privacy And Wasting Time Using Nlp: A Comparative Approach Using Ai. Vivekananda Journal of Research, 10, 42–52.

Whig, P., & Ahmad, S. N. (2017). Controlling the Output Error for Photo Catalytic Sensor (PCS) Using Fuzzy Logic. Journal of Earth Science and Climate Change, 8(4), 1–6.

Whig, P., & Ahmad, S. N. (2019). Methodology for Calibrating Photocatalytic Sensor Output. International Journal of Sustainable Development in Computing Science, 1(1), 1–10.

Whig, P., Nadikattu, R. R., & Velu, A. (2022). COVID-19 pandemic analysis using application of AI. Healthcare Monitoring and Data Analysis Using IoT: Technologies and Applications, 1.

Jupalle, H., Kouser, S., Bhatia, A. B. et al. Automation of human behaviors and their prediction using machine learning. Microsyst Technol (2022). https://doi.org/10.1007/s00542-022-05326-4

P Whig, A Velu, P Sharma (2022) Demystifying Federated Learning for Blockchain: A Case Study , pp1-22

Alkali, Yusuf, et al. (2022) Strategy for Reliable, Efficient and Secure IoT Using Artificial Intelligence. IUP Journal of Computer Sciences . Apr 2022, Vol. 16 Issue 2, p16-25.

Shama et al. (2022), Fog-IoT-Assisted-Based Smart Agriculture Application, Demystifying Federated Learning for Blockchain: A Case Study, PP-1-20

Schuld, M.; Petruccione, F. Supervised Learning with Quantum Computers; Springer: Berlin/Heidelberg, Germany, 2018; Volume 17.

Montanaro, A. Quantum algorithms: An overview. Npj Quantum Inf. 2016, 2, 15023.

Jordan, S. The Quantum Algorithm Zoo. 2021.

Marais, A.; Adams, B.; Ringsmuth, A. K.; Ferretti, M.; Gruber, J. M.; Hendrikx, R.; Schuld, M.; Smith, S. L.; Sinayskiy, I.; Krüger,

T. P.; et al. The future of quantum biology. J. R. Soc. Interface 2018, 15, 20180640.

Biamonte, J.; Faccin, M.; De Domenico, M. Complex networks from classical to quantum. Commun. Phys. 2019, 2, 53.

McMahon, D. Quantum Mechanics Demystified; McGraw-Hill Education: New York, NY, USA, 2013.

Samuel, A. L. Some studies in machine learning using the game of checkers. IBM J. Res. Dev. 1959, 3, 210–229.

Alzubi, J.; Nayyar, A.; Kumar, A. Machine Learning from Theory to Algorithms: An Overview. J. Phys. Conf. Ser. 2018,

Rivas, P. Deep Learning for Beginners: A Beginner's Guide to Getting Up and Running with Deep Learning from Scratch Using Python; Packt Publishing Ltd.: Birmingham, UK, 2020.

Mehta, P.; Bukov, M.; Wang, C. H.; Day, A. G.; Richardson, C.; Fisher, C. K.; Schwab, D. J. A high-bias, low-variance introduction to machine learning for physicists. Phys. Rep. 2019, 810, 1–124.

Mahesh, B. Machine Learning Algorithms—A Review. Int. J. Sci. Res. (IJSR) 2020, 9, 381–386.

Bonaccorso, G. Machine Learning Algorithms; Packt Publishing Ltd.: Birmingham, UK, 2017.

Wittek, P. Quantum Machine Learning: What Quantum Computing Means to Data Mining; Academic Press: Cambridge, MA, USA, 2014.

Nielsen, M. A.; Chuang, I. L. Quantum computation and quantum information. Phys. Today 2001, 54, 60.

McMahon, D. Quantum Computing Explained; John Wiley & Sons: Hoboken, NJ, USA, 2007.

6

The Contribution of Computer Vision in the Manufacturing Industries and the Scope for Further Excellence

P. Dharanyadevi[1], C. Krishnakoumar[1], K. Revathy[1], J. Karkavelraja[1], K. Venkatalakshmi[2], and G. Zayaraz[1]

[1]Department of CSE, Puducherry Technological University, India
[2]Department of ECE, University College of Engineering Tindivanam, India
E-mail: dharanyadevi@gmail.com; krishnakoumar.c@pec.edu;
karkavelraja.j@pec.edu; revathy.k@pec.edu; venkata_krish@yahoo.com;
gzayaraz@ptuniv.edu.in

Abstract

The most important mission of manufacturing industries worldwide is to achieve high-quality product throughput with their ongoing mass production agenda. "Quality is inversely proportional to Quantity" is a widely well-known notion among business leaders and consumers. Computer vision is revolutionizing industries with its ineffable contribution to the mass production of products and services. Computer vision is a sub-field of artificial intelligence that deals with image recognition and automation. Computer vision is used for automatic inspection and assessment in most industries, but to leverage AI's maximum potential, we must implement computer vision in the appropriate place. Apart from manufacturing, computer vision can be used in other industrial processes like logistics, human resource management, security components, analysis of machinery for its proper functionality, and more. Effectively implementing this technology has drastically reduced running costs in many manufacturing sectors. Unlike other fields of AI, computer vision or machine vision requires minimal hardware initialization cost and a more coherent system layout. AI is a technology, and most of the part is used in industries to increase overall efficiency and to reduce running costs. So, the cruder meaning of "AI" is "increase efficiency" for the most part. If diverse industries incorporate computer vision effectively within their systems, it will lead to better organization of raw materials, supply chain, quality control, human resource management, maintenance of machinery, and so on.

This chapter discusses the workflow of computer vision and its different domains implemented in various industries, such as automation, agriculture, and so on. This chapter also discusses how computer vision can help in achieving sustainable industries. This paper demonstrates the various possible implications of computer vision in manufacturing industries and also discusses how computer vision has been effectively implemented. This chapter will furnish a new dimension for researchers and gives an idea to alleviate the overall production cost and complexity.

Keywords: artificial intelligence, computer vision, automation, use cases, performance metrics

6.1 Introduction

Computers are an integral part of present-day industries. They automate most of the tiring jobs that humans performed in the past. Human laborers have their major drawbacks in performing low-end jobs. In the past, industries have adopted various methods to do specific tasks efficiently through various revolutions. The fifth industrial revolution focuses on connecting every machinery within each industry to be connected and work seamlessly. With the advent of connectivity technologies, we have more information about the machine than ever. We can access all the data we gathered throughout history and feed it into the machines [1].

Humans process information from the external environment through the sensory organs. The sensory organ is a biological system used to gather information from the environment or respond to stimuli [2]. Vision is one of the six senses that humans possess. It is one of the most critical sensory systems that is closely bound to the brain. Computer vision is an area with a huge scope for development and improvement that can replace the places where these systems are where human interventions are least required.

Table 6.1 Comparison between human vision and computer vision.

Human vision	Computer vision
Can identify people and objects	It needs to be explicitly programmed to identify people and objects
Does not care about the accuracy of the world	Differentiates the objects around the world based on probabilistic and statistical interventions
Can understand the mood in the scene	It can understand the mood in the scene when it is explicitly programmed
Ignores many details	Stores and processes every tiny detail
Can imagine stories	I cannot imagine
Suffers from illusions	Illusions are not possible
Ambiguous description of the world	It gives an accurate description of the world
Can navigate through obstacles	Can navigate through the world when it is explicitly programmed

The main objective of computer vision is to automate the information extracted from the image. Here the information can be anything from 3D models, object detection and recognition, searching image content, and camera position [1]. Some tasks involved in computer vision are image processing, cognitive processing, statistical pattern identification, and geometric modeling. Computer vision requires both high-level and low-level capabilities to perform well [3].

Computer vision contribution toward manufacturing industries is already making remarkable progress. Human vision can identify minute nuances within a fraction of a second. We need the best-in-class cameras and algorithms to achieve computers that mimic human intelligence. Computer vision algorithms need to be trained well to achieve high-precision image recognition capabilities.

Table 6.1 illustrates the comparison between human vision and computer vision. At present, computer vision systems are way beyond detecting objects. They are entering the arena competing with human vision. Figure 6.1 depicts the pictorial representation of computer vision in a different milieu. Computer vision systems consist of optics and high-resolution cameras integrated with algorithms to perform a specific task [4]. The number of tasks these computer vision systems handle in today's manufacturing industries is impeccable since it takes care of most often considered organized and repetitive tasks.

Computer vision is hard because we are trying to actively look into the unknown with very sparse data to conclude a solution. To tackle this problem, we use probabilistic models and classical physics for a firm

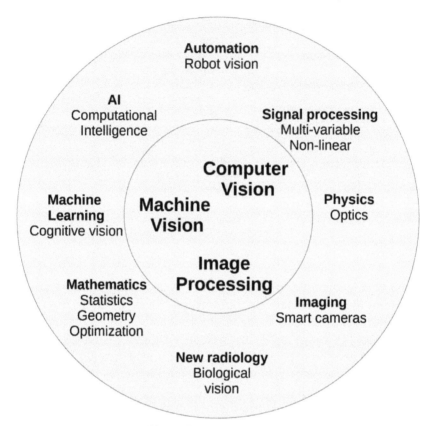

Figure 6.1   Machine vision.

understanding. Researchers are currently developing mathematical models to produce/recover the 3D shape and appearance of objects in images. For example, let us consider optical character recognition (OCR), which is used for recognizing handwritten postal codes on letters and recognizing numbers on a car's number plate using the technology of automatic number plate recognition (ANPR) [5].

6.2 Components of a Machine Vision Systems

Table 6.2 illustrates the various components of a machine vision system. Each component holds a specific task in computer vision.

Figure 6.2 illustrates the image-sensing pipeline. The accuracy of computer vision depends on the configuration of these components along the

Table 6.2 Components of vision systems.

Camera	A camera is an optical instrument that can capture a visual image. Its components can be digital or analog. The shutter speed, sampling pitch, fill factor, chip size, analog gain, sensor noise, and resolution are the factors that cause a delay in the performance of the digital image sensor [6].
Shutter speed	The amount of time the image sensor is exposed to light can either be controlled by the shutter speed or the exposure time, resulting in either an overexposed or underexposed photograph.
Sampling pitch	The amount of space between neighboring cells on the sensor of the imaging chip is referred to as the sampling pitch. The sampling pitch has a relationship that is inversely proportional to the sampling density. A sensor with a small sampling pitch can produce images with a high resolution. A sensor with a more extensive sampling pitch has a smaller sensor area since there is a larger space between the cells. Thus, the sensor can only accumulate smaller photons, thus making it less light sensitive and more toward producing noise in the image.
Fill factor	The fill factor is the ratio between the pixel's light-sensitive area to the pixel's total area on the sensor. A higher fill factor is preferred for a quality image. The high fill factor results in more light capture that, in turn, increases the quality of the image [7].
Chip size	Point-and-shoot cameras and camcorders often use smaller sensors ranging between 0.25 inches and 0.5 inches in size, while single lens reflex (SLR) cameras try to come closer to 1 inch to 1.9 inches. A larger sensor size is directly proportional to a photosensitive image. Hence a larger chip size is always advisable for a better vision system.
Analog gain	A sense amplifier boosts the signals received by the image sensor. In cameras, this is controlled by automatic gain control (AGC) logic. AGC logic automatically adjusts the incoming signal to obtain a good image exposure.
Sensor noise	Noise can be defined as unwanted signals. In images, noises are always in the form of film grains. Senor noise is the random variation noises added from various sources, including amplified noise, fixed pattern noises, quantization noises, shot noises, and dark current noises.
ADC resolution	It is defined as analog to digital conversion resolution, a final step procedure that can elevate the information gain of the image from the sensor. ADC resolution works by a minute incremental voltage that can be recognized by the camera, which changes the digital output.

Table 6.2   (Continued.)

Digital post-processing	This is the final step inside a camera. In this step, the output from the sensor is converted into digital bits. Based on the camera's utility, it performs various digital signal processing (DSP) operations to enhance the images for extracting the most out of every pixel.
Lighting	Lighting is an essential part of image processing. There are different lighting techniques; each serves a particular purpose for computer vision operations.
Directional	This technique is used for picking out surface effects. It is mostly similar to the sun.
Diffused	This is used to better position the objects, providing fewer shadows and reflections.
Polarized light	Polarization is achieved using polarized lenses on the camera. Polarizing backlighting can even render surface tension visibility.
Infrared or ultraviolet	They are most commonly used for observing heat formation and dissipation, fluorescence/phosphorescence, and ionization. And the lighting can be manually arranged for front, back, and ring lighting.

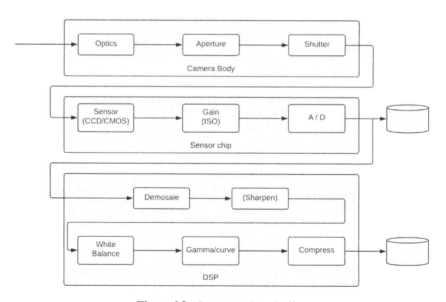

Figure 6.2   Image sensing pipeline.

pipeline. The two key computer vision concepts are image formation and computer vision algorithms. The description is stated below:

6.3 Image Formation

An image is formed when some electromagnetic waves bounce off an object, reaching the observer's eyes or electromagnetic sensing instrument. Computer vision is based on input from electromagnetic radiation. Electromagnetic radiation can be categorized into different ranges of frequencies. Many electromagnetic spectrums can create a visual of an object. Electromagnetic frequencies can be classified into different types within the spectrum range. The following spectrum ranges are not helpful to machine vision; they are

- Radio waves (3 Hz–30 MHz)
- Microwave waves (300 MHz–30 GHz)
- Ionizing radiation (3 PHz–300 EHz)

Infrared, visible light, and ultraviolet spectrums are used based on their specific use cases. While all spectrums have specific use cases, like gamma rays, imaging is most commonly used in space industries to capture images from the gamma rays emitting from distant galaxies. For example, the infrared spectrum is most commonly used for creating a thermal image that uses infrared radiation (IR), similar to a normal camera that uses visible light for taking images.

6.4 Computer vision algorithms

As shown in Figure 6.3, computer vision algorithms have improved tremendously in recent decades. The availability of cheaper computation systems and improved hardware performance leads to the development of more complex vision systems that are accurate in identifying objects.

6.5 Use Case of the Computer Vision in Industries

6.5.1 Product assembly

Machine vision's contributions can be seen throughout product assembly lines of various manufacturing companies across various domains around the world. The most important part of a machine vision's ability is its efficiency

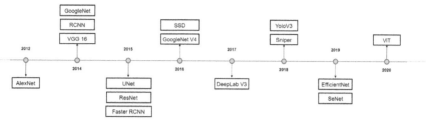

Figure 6.3   Timeline of the latest advancement in computer vision algorithms.

and accuracy in looking out for defects. Incorporating computer vision in industries reduces the overall cost of producing a product. The manufacturing industries are seeing a tremendous increase in the implementation of automated systems into their workflow pipeline to cut down on running costs. Nearly all the manufacturing giants we hear of around the planet have implemented automation in assembly lines to ramp up their production output [8]. Computer vision can provide inspection services like 3D modeling of the products, surface anomaly detection, deformed product elimination, and rupture identification, to name a few. All this happened in a fraction of a second with the best accuracy across various other options. Computer vision's efficacy is not limited to just within the assembly line; they are assisting machines and workers in manual assembly units. Additionally, computer vision can help avoid purchases after returns and product recall situations, thus ensuring customer satisfaction.

Industrial Revolution 4.0 is happening worldwide, and computer vision has become a significant part of this revolution. Almost every industry is trying to incorporate complete automation into its manufacturing pipeline. 3D models designed for the assembly process are designed with the help of computer-aided design software, based on which the machine vision systems guide the assembly process precisely as defined. It also helps employees and various other robot systems work parallelly without interruptions. As shown in Figure 6.4, for example, computer vision is implemented in analyzing the distribution of salami over pizza crust [9].

6.5.2 Defect detection

Manufacturing products with 100 percent accuracy in defect detection is the priority of many manufacturing companies, and they struggle to achieve that at any cost. This is mainly because detecting the defects after delivery or at the end of the production results in a hike in the overall cost of production

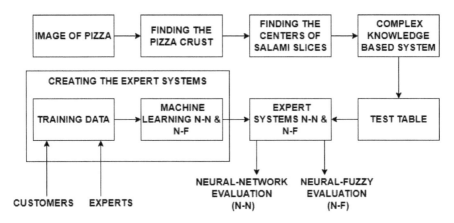

Figure 6.4 Overview of salami placement in pizza.

and decreased customer satisfaction and trust. This often leads to increased customer dissatisfaction and decreased brand value. Ultimately this results in loss to both manufacturers and customers. Moreover, implementing computer vision and automation into the production line decreases the net production cost that can incur when these upgrades are not implemented.

Detecting defects much later than sorting them out in the beginning stage is costlier. Funding the computer vision and automation-based systems for defect detection systems can be the most accessible and cost-effective solution. The computer vision system generally gathers real-time data from the image sensors. With the help of artificial neural networks or machine learning models, it analyzes the data and, based on the predefined quality standards, detects the defects or provides the percentage of deviation of the defects based on the employees can solve the problem [10]. This can help detect the flaw within the production line and approach the problem at a much earlier stage [2].

Another application of computer vision is the detection of surface deformations [11]. Stereo vision technology can be used to evaluate the precise measurement of surface deviation. This method is efficient compared with other methods because it provides high precision output, is rapid to develop, and is easy to operate.

Another method to effectively segment defective products in a lot can be performed using graph-based image segmentation. This method can be effectively used when the background of the products is chaotic and contains several objects of the same type [6].

Achieving 100 percent accuracy in detecting defects is a distant howl, but detection at a much early stage goes a long way compared with detection at the end of the production line. Machine vision deployed in manufacturing units can help prevent this flaw by detecting defects at macro and micro levels of defections in the production line.

6.5.3 3D Vision system

Humans can identify anomalies with any product in a fraction of a second. At a faster pace, humans struggle to identify any anomalies [12]. Computer vision will take this place in these spots where human efficiency decreases. To handle this situation, the system takes high-resolution images to build the 3D model of the components and their connections.

This system works by analyzing the components which run through the manufacturing pipeline; the computer vision system captures the high-resolution image from various angles across various spots to build a 3D model of the product, which is then fed into an artificial intelligence system to find out any defects or anomalies [15]. This technology is used in various industries, particularly automobiles, energy, electronic circuits, and so on.

Advantages in manufacturing industries: 3D vision systems can identify the object's location, environment, and orientation in space. The cameras inside this system take three-dimensional images of the objects, just like how the human eye perceives the environment. Hence, they open up many implications in the manufacturing sector. The cost of setting up 3D cameras and effective installation of cameras at appropriate places depending on the industry domain is still a challenging task. Another well-known complication of setting up 3D vision is that it requires the constant intervention of experts to look after these systems.

6.5.4 Vision-guided robots

Companies adapting to Industrial Revolution 4.0 have already implemented robots guided by computer vision. These robots have the essential ability of a human, such as navigation within the warehouse or mobility of products within the industry [13]. Some applications of these robots currently performing in these industries are to pick and place the objects around the industry, performing complex rotary die and laser cutting with accurate measurement to sculpt into any design.

6.5.5 Predictive maintenance

Most of the time, industries process various manufacturing processes in harsh temperatures and environments. This may often lead to corrosion and degradation of manufacturing equipment [5]. If not maintained properly, this may lead to hefty maintenance costs or even halting production, leading to severe losses. To handle this situation, these industries employ corrosion engineers to tackle this situation. These engineers perform a constant inspection to ensure the equipment's working condition and avoid corrosion to the machine's movable parts [14]. As we can see, the entire investigation process is performed manually; hence it is restricted to human errors and the number of metrics that can be performed. Computer vision can constantly perform equipment maintenance or corrosion monitoring throughout the day. If the computer vision notices any slightest depletion in the provided safety metrics, it will immediately alert the respective departments of employees to perform maintenance activities.

It is critical to predict maintenance emergencies across the organization, which may incorporate heavy machines in the production line, which is crucial for smooth operation. If the industry fails to identify these problems earlier, it may lead to production delays or even fatal accidents. Computer vision can help to prevent these errors because it intimates the respective departments within the industry before it gets too late. Computer vision performs the alert with the provided metrics set by the maintenance engineers. The computer vision system performs these operations by comparing the current high-resolution image with the pre-existing data in the database for any disruption provided by the safety metrics. Machine vision also reduces the manual intervention of maintenance checks. Limiting manual intervention will reduce the wear and tear that may occur during the regular maintenance process.

6.6 Safety and Security Standards

The risk of injury is much higher in manufacturing industries since some spots within the manufacturing pipeline are prone to dangerous conditions. Employees not adhering to safety standards and protocols can be seriously injured or have a fatal accident. This problem majorly arises with the employee's failure to follow protocols.

The risk of getting injured is much higher in the manufacturing industry. Combined with noncompliant working standards will cause serious problems

[16]. The manufacturing industries must follow the safety protocols given by government bodies. Government bodies or safety agencies must adopt penalization for those who fail to meet these standards.

Currently, most manufacturing industries perform this monitoring process with the help of cameras installed at specific locations. Humans manually complete this task, and they also have to keep their gaze on the video stream. This manual process is liable to human error and also the error of negligence. This can be automated using AI-powered systems that can monitor the entire industry from the entrance to the exit. Based on the provided criteria, the system will monitor constantly to check for any violations. If any employee commits a minor violation of the company's safety protocol, the system will inform the concerned manager about the infringement, and they can take the necessary action immediately.

As shown in Figure 6.5. The process of digital image processing consists of various components that work in sequence to recognize the object. Throughout the process, the knowledge base will be enumerated with data

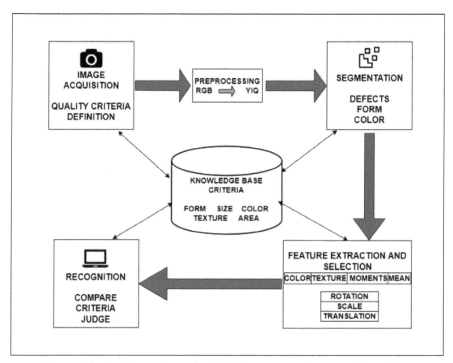

Figure 6.5 Fundamental steps in digital image processing in machine vision.

that will have fewer errors in the recognition of images than in the previous epoch. This process is called learning.

In this way, the manufacturing process becomes secure, and fewer fatal accidents occur, thereby increasing the overall throughput of the company in the long run.

In case of emergencies like an accident, the computer vision technology will immediately alert the managers and staff of the company for their intervention. Also, it can automatically turn off the required machinery to stop further escalation of the situation. This will ensure the safety of other employees, thereby reducing the overall risk of this situation escalating.

The safety of the employees is the most important concern for industries, especially for manufacturing industries worldwide. Vision-based systems powered by AI can aid in reducing the overall chances of any unwanted accidents in the high-risk prone area within the industries [17]. As discussed earlier, implementing computer vision in monitoring events can effectively detect the employees who do not comply with the safety protocol rather than making some employees sit and monitor the employees who are prone to errors.

6.7 Packaging Standards

The most common procedure in almost all manufacturing industries is to tally the items before packing them into a lot. Usually, counting the number of products manufactured is daunting since industries produce the products at a higher rate. Manually counting these products most often leads to errors. This is a severe problem in retailers or pharmaceutical industries. Deployment of computer vision in the packing process helps in making near 100 percent accuracy in counting and packing.

Another use case of vision-based systems in the same product manufacturing line is that after the packages are packed, the system can check for any damage present in the packaging. Damaged packages are diverted into a particular product pipeline, where the items are repacked, thereby increasing the probability of the package reaching the customer safely. They can also be set to check the packing standards of old goods before leaving the warehouse.

Maintaining the package standards is vital in ensuring the product's longevity in the market. Computer vision will ensure that all the products reaching out to the industry will be of top quality. Apart from the stated benefits, it can also constantly collect data related to the level of problems involved with a particular spot and keep track of the colors, measurements, or other tools to effectively keep track of the products over time.

6.8 Barcode Analysis

Another critical application of computer vision is barcode recognition. Barcode provides a visual representation of data which is in the form of a machine-readable configuration. Barcodes represent data by differing the parallel lines' shapes, widths, sizes, and spacing between them. In manufacturing industries, barcodes are used to verify the various attributes of the end product. These may include the date of manufacturing, various information related to models, sorting out spare parts for a particular product, etc. Verifying each bar code by hand takes a lot of man hours, is prone to mistakes due to wrong entries, and is expensive. With the help of computer vision, we can easily verify the barcodes along the product manufacturing pipeline with fewer errors and a convenient operation cost over a long period [18].

The growth of vision-based systems used to read barcodes and QR codes has been increasing in recent years. They are handy in many instances, especially in warehouse management, where the products are quickly sorted out using the barcode. The computer vision system is also deployed at the exit of production lines to check for faulty barcodes, texts, and QR codes present on their products. This may be due to technical faults such as faulty printers, scratches, and smudges that may confuse shop owners or consumers during the billing process. Sorting out these defective products within the production line makes it easier for the manufacturers to sort out the defective products and, simultaneously have more satisfied customers.

6.9 Inventory Management

Currently, computer vision is mainly used in inventory management. Industries that employ computer vision for inventory management need around 5 percent of the original workforce that was required previously. Vision-based systems can aid in keeping track of warehouse stocks [6]. This can also inform the manufacturers about the raw material deficit in advance. The computer vision system also avoids the human errors that can happen when counting the stock [19].

In a large warehouse, it is often difficult to locate the stock of any particular product. This is where the computer vision system shines. We can easily locate the stock with the help of bar codes provided for each product [23].

There are many massive warehouses around the world. These warehouses consist of millions of items in stock and are constantly bombarded with incoming and outgoing stockpiles. With computer vision, companies can do inventory assessments proactively. Moreover, the managers can be intimate in advance of any depletion of product quantity.

6.10 Optimizing Supply Chains

Optimizing the supply chain process periodically is beneficial for any manufacturing industry to maintain the upcoming demands while simultaneously satisfying the consumers by making the product available year-round. While human intervention is required at the exact critical times for most of the process, the computer vision system can handle the situation effectively [21].

Several industries have implemented computer vision in various departments within their manufacturing pipeline. Some of these are managing inventories, warehouse management, and improving the efficiency of overall organizational operations [22].

6.11 Quality Inspection with Computer Vision

Another important implication of machine vision systems in the field manufacturing industry is to inspect the quality of end products. When industries produce hundreds of products within a minute, each product must be inspected for defects and malfunctions. When this process is done manually, it takes a lot of time with high chances of possible human error [16]. As a result, many manufacturers are developing their deep-learning computer vision systems specifically designed for their products to handle their product quality controls [20]. Besides this, computer vision systems are also cost-effective in handling the quality inspection process with much better performance outcomes.

This makes it possible to check all the products for quality verification when produced in large quantities rather than only a small sample size from a large lot in the manual verification process.

For example, a hot sauce maker checks the placement of labels at 1000 per minute. This is impossible for any human being to perform these tasks at that speed and accuracy. Therefore, the computer vision system provides the best performance out of the money spent. Table 6.3 summarizes the object defect detection using computer vision techniques, defect, and accuracy.

Table 6.3   Object defect detection using computer vision.

Author (year)	Country	Object	Technique	Defect	Accuracy
Lerones et al. (2005)	Spain	Brake disk	3D structured light	Circularity, defective grinding, hard masses, feather edges	80
Blasco et al. (2007)	Spain	Citrus	Region oriented segmentation	Peel	95
Peng et al. (2008)	China	Float glass	Texture reverse subtraction	Bubbles, lards, optical distortion, wholesome, diseased	89
Yang et al. (2009)	USA	Electric contacts	Blob analysis and PSO	Deckle edge, back cracks, side cracks, eccentricity	96.7
Mery et al. (2010)	Chile	Corn tortillas	SVM	Size, hedonic scale, production level	96
Gadelmawl et al. (2011)	Saudi Arabia	Spur gears	Tolerances	Outer diameter, diameter pitch, circular pitch	99
Perng et al. (2011)	China	LED	Thresholding	Missing components, incorrect orientations	95
Razmjooy et al. (2012)	Iran	Potato	SVM and ANN	Size, color	96.86
Možina et al. (2013)	Slovenia	Pharmaceutical tablets	PCA	Debossing shallow	84
Lin and Fang (2013)	China	Tile	Corner convergence and clustering	Alignment	90.5

6.12 Computer Vision during the Covid-19 Pandemic

One of the current implications of computer vision is during the Covid-19 pandemic. The pandemic caused many manufacturers to halt production and resume their activities based on the restrictions imposed by the government on their location. Most government authorities provide the general guidelines that have to be followed by all the employees within the company. If the cases start to rise among the employees of a particular company, then government officials can halt the company until the spread of the virus slows down within their employee circle. This can cause disruption in the production process and serious loss.

So, many companies have incorporated computer vision systems in their operational areas, which detect whether the employees are putting the mask on throughout their stay and maintaining a social distance of 6 feet. This system intimates the manager when any of their employees are not following the rule, and they can take further action to prevent such an incident from happening.

Many government and private organizations used optical character recognition (OCR) technology to process and verify applications remotely during the lockdown period.

Apart from mask detection and social distancing monitoring applications, they have also implemented a computer vision system that can identify people with high body temperature with the help of an infrared camera. This system can detect temperatures more accurately and is much more efficient than a manual temperature monitoring system, which is time-consuming.

6.13 Computer Vision in the Automotive Industry

The automotive industry is the de facto example of how efficient computer vision and automation can work together to produce many products with fewer human interventions. For example, it is known that Tesla, an electric car manufacturer, incorporated automation in their production process, which accounts for over 70 percent. The fourth Industrial Revolution, currently in progress, has revolutionized technology such as sensing, processing, and integration technologies between different systems along the production line, making it the best to interrupt less production.

For the most part, the automation process is involved in building the products, while the machine vision is incorporated with quality control, employee management, and warehouse management systems.

Besides these various advancements, most industries have not designed computer vision for horizontal or vertical integration into their existing design as a top priority. Even today, many automotive companies have deployed computer vision to work on individual tasks. To have a near-zero defect in the manufacturing pipeline, computer vision systems can be integrated with the existing systems that work in parallel.

The complexity of the automotive industry comes from its manufacturing procedures and supply chain network around the globe. Some of the activities

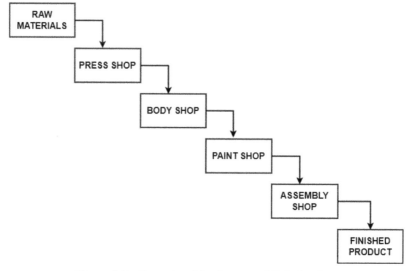

Figure 6.6   Computer vision in automobile industries.

that are required to perform regularly are manufacturing various spare parts for all the car models in use, special components arranged based on the current stock, material shaping, welding operations, and procedures related to final assembly are carried out before the distribution of automobiles into the market all around the world [27].

Machine vision systems can be incorporated into entire automotive manufacturing procedures, including grading quality, welding, positioning and handling of materials, and various other activities. They can reduce completion times, reduce faults at delivery and enhance productivity by approaching zero-fault production.

The automotive industries are the ones that extensively use computer vision in their manufacturing process. Due to the demanding procedures involved in the manufacturing of an automobile, they have implemented computer vision across various shops within their manufacturing pipeline, depicted in Figure 6.6. In the automobile industry, the factory is classified into four stages of production. They are the press shop, the body shop, the paint shop, and the final assembly shop.

6.13.1 Press shop

For each vehicle, the metal components are produced in this phase. The number of metal components produced is about 300. Detecting the defect in these metal components is difficult and consumes huge human effort. But computer vision helps us to automate this difficult defect detection on the metal components. It can also detect various defects. Ferguson et al. proposed faster recurrent CNN (convolutional neural network) or faster R-CNN to detect the defect in the aluminum casting surfaces [28]. Herger et al. proposed the decision tree algorithm (DT-algorithm) to detect door parts' cracks during production time [27]. In detecting cracks in the doors, he used six stages to identify and remove the cracks. He obtained an accuracy of 94 percent.

6.13.2 Body shop

Materials from the press shop are used for the production of chassis. The body shop uses raw materials from various industries or press shops as a source. In this phase, the welding of materials and assembling these materials together. The real success of this welding operation is directly proportional to the quality of the car body. This process of welding and assembling is time-consuming and consumes more manual power. Nevertheless, computer vision technology makes this welding and assembling process more accessible.

Novakovic et al. suggested a 3D vision-based system for inspecting, welding, and assembling the raw materials [27]. He used the 3D vision concept in the autonomous robotics inspection to inspect the weld and automate robotic arms. He obtained an accuracy of approximately 0.15 mm.

For the door panels, the machine vision concept is used in the form of an edge detector to identify the spots to be welded and thereby increasing the accuracy of the welding. The welding spots defect by calculating the distance between the panels and the end-effectors (part of computer vision technology). The entire body part of the car body is tested by considering the accuracy, distance, and collision factor. The hard or rough surface produced during welding is converted into a smooth surface using the grinding end-effectors together with robotic arms.

The replacement of multi-hole abrasives is done manually and requires more accurate alignment. This drawback can be overcome by using computer vision technology by calculating the latent offset of the multi-hole abrasive.

The vision-based defect detection system is used to monitor the welding defect. It uses three layers of CNN (convolutional neural network) to apply filters, LSTM (long short-term memory), and FC (fully connected), which is further connected onto the dense layer with activation functions like SoftMax, Sigmoid, and so on, based on the problem. The CNN layer is used to extract spatial features, the FC layer is used to perform classification, and the LSTM layer is used to perform feature retrieval.

6.13.3 Paint shop

This paint shop workstation produces attractive finesse and body armor, which protects the car body from external weather conditions. Performing this task of painting is very time-consuming and requires more manpower. But, with computer vision, we can automate these processes. In the painting phase, robotic arms are used to deposit colors and perform curing operations of the car body. In some other robotic arms are used to perform painting operations. When we have a small size defect (0.2 mm) in the car body and also for monitoring the painting defects on the lines, edges, and corners, we require more manpower, cost, and time. To overcome this challenge, we use a vision-based system that uses light patterns to detect the defects. QEyeTunnel is a machine vision system that identifies the defect in less than 0.15 s. Sometimes, uncertain vision conditions can affect the lighting. To tackle this problem, SVM (support vector machine) is used to predict the quality of illuminations and thereby ensure suitable conditions for recognizing lighting patterns. In the latter stages, multi-camera vision systems are used to detect the defects on the painting surface and the car body. Irregular lighting is corrected using the TinyDefectRNet method, which in addition identifies abnormalities on the body surfaces and controls the overall painting quality.

6.13.4 Final assembly shop

The final phase of the automation industry is assembling the painted body with the internal and external parts. This phase is also referred to as the final assembling phase. This phase's main activity is verifying the activities done in the entire lifecycle of the automation industry. This verification process by trained and experienced persons takes more time and cost. However, using computer vision technology, we can automate this process and make verifying the correctness of assembled products easier.

A vision-based statistical model is used to find the rare faults in the assembly process. In this method, the rare fault is identified at first, and the recovery steps are carried out to eliminate this fault. But this method cannot identify a fault less than 0.02 mm. To overcome this problem, we use random forest classifier to identify rare faults, provide better accuracy and performance, and improve the classification quality.

To get personalized products, we need to arrange the products before it arrives at the final assembly stage. This process of sorting is done manually by placing wheels. Nevertheless, this manual method takes more time and also more human power. To overcome this problem, we use automated wheels to sort the products with minimum time and manpower consumption.

The glass windows to the car body are one of the external parts that must be fitted. An in-line vision-based system inspects the quality and quantity of glue that fits the glass windows to the car body. Computer vision has made the daunting task of quality checking much more efficient and faster [24].

6.14 Computer Vision Performance Metrics

The accuracy of identifying the object is a crucial task in computer vision systems. Performance metrics serve as a measure of assessment to evaluate the machine's correctness [26]. To observe the metrics, we need to look into the following factors: image object segmentation, object tracking, and object detection. They are intersection over union (IoU), precision, recall, and $F1$ score. The definition is defined below:

6.14.1 Intersection over union (IoU)

As shown in eqn (6.1) and Figure 6.7, it is a principle metric whose value is calculated by dividing the union of the areas of the predicted and ground truth bounding boxes by the area of the overlap between them. The data demonstrate this in practice. It reports both the total number of correctly identified objects and the total number of false positives. When the proportion of objects detected via IoU is more significant than 0.5, we call that true positive (TP) result. When the number of objects detected has an IoU less than 0.5 or has been detected more than once, the result is considered a false positive (FP). A false negative result is obtained if no objects are found or if objects are found but their IoU is less than 0.5. (FN).

$$J\left(B_p,\ B_{gt}\right) = \mathrm{IoU} = \frac{\mathrm{area}(B_p \cap B_{gt})}{\mathrm{area}(B_p \cup B_{gt})} \qquad (6.1)$$

6.14.2 Precision

As shown in eqn (6.2) and Figure 6.8, precision is a performance metric that measures how accurately the outputs are predicted. It returns the percentage

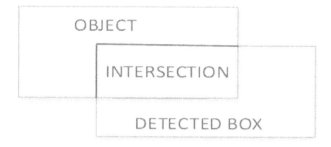

IoU =

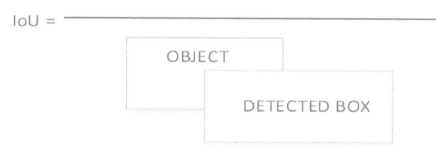

Figure 6.7   Intersection over union (IoU).

of the correct prediction.

$$\text{Precision} = \frac{TP}{TP + FP} = \frac{TP}{\text{all detections}}.$$ (6.2)

6.14.3 Recall

As shown in eqn (6.3) and Figure 6.9, recall returns the percentage of how well the model predicts all the positives.

$$\text{Recall} = \frac{TP}{TP + FN} = \frac{TP}{\text{all ground truths}}.$$ (6.3)

6.14.4 F1 score

As shown in eqn (6.4), the $F1$ score returns the harmonic mean (HM) of precision and recall.

$$F1 \text{ score} = 2 \times \frac{\text{Precision} \times \text{Recall}}{\text{Precision} + \text{Recall}}.$$ (6.4)

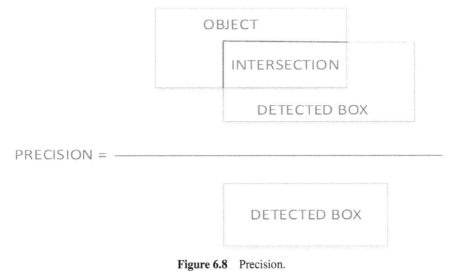

$$PRECISION = \frac{\text{[diagram: INTERSECTION]}}{\text{[diagram: DETECTED BOX]}}$$

Figure 6.8 Precision.

The object perforation of a computer vision model can also be evaluated by calculating erroneous object detection metrics, erroneous object matching metrics, and object correction [27].

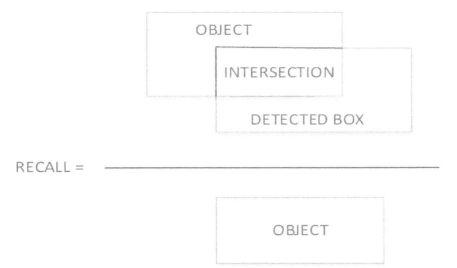

$$RECALL = \frac{\text{[diagram: INTERSECTION]}}{\text{[diagram: OBJECT]}}$$

Figure 6.9 Recall.

6.15 Conclusion

Industries are an essential part of the development of human civilization. Sustainability in industries can increase our longevity and efficiency in developing a product. Computer vision has a long way to go to contribute to different industry domains for maximizing production and reducing the overall carbon footprint. It also transformed the human labor force to focus on imaginative aspects of industries while leaving the intuitive part to computers. Machine vision has enormous implications in various industries. The current implementation of computer vision in manufacturing sectors already provides unparalleled convenience in industrial processes. In the future, the most profitable industry would have leveraged computer vision in their production pipeline to the best of their capability. Automation of industrial processes will also reduce the overall greenhouse gas emission per product, thus guiding the overall technological development sustainably without damaging the environment.

References

[1] S. Dey, A. K. Singh, D. K. Prasad, and K. D. McDonald-Maier, "SoCodeCNN: Program Source Code for Visual CNN Classification Using Computer Vision Methodology," *IEEE Access*, vol. 7, pp. 157158–157172, 2019, doi: 10.1109/ACCESS.2019.2949483.

[2] Y. H. Chen, "Computer vision for general purpose visual inspection: a fuzzy logic approach," *Optics and Lasers in Engineering*, vol. 22, no. 3, pp. 181–192, Jan. 1995, doi: 10.1016/0143-8166(94)00045-C.

[3] W. T. Freeman, K. Tanaka, J. Ohta, and K. Kyuma, "Computer vision for computer games," in *Proceedings of the Second International Conference on Automatic Face and Gesture Recognition*, pp. 100–105. doi: 10.1109/AFGR.1996.557250.

[4] M. Christie, P. Olivier, and J.-M. Normand, "Camera Control in Computer Graphics," *Computer Graphics Forum*, vol. 27, no. 8, pp. 2197–2218, Dec. 2008, doi: 10.1111/j.1467-8659.2008.01181.x.

[5] Shanghai hai yang da Xue and Institute of Electrical and Electronics Engineers, *Proceedings of 2020 IEEE International Conference on Artificial Intelligence and Computer Applicationsă: ICAICA 2020ă: Dalian, China, June 27-29, 2020.*

[6] J. Redmon, S. Divvala, R. Girshick, and A. Farhadi, "You only look once: Unified, real-time object detection," in *Proceedings of the*

IEEE Computer Society Conference on Computer Vision and Pattern Recognition, Dec. 2016, vol. 2016-December, pp. 779–788. doi: 10.1109/CVPR.2016.91.

[7] J. Wright, Y. Ma, J. Mairal, G. Sapiro, T. S. Huang, and S. Yan, "Sparse Representation for Computer Vision and Pattern Recognition," *Proceedings of the IEEE*, vol. 98, no. 6, pp. 1031–1044, Jun. 2010, doi: 10.1109/JPROC.2010.2044470.

[8] Devi, A., Therese, M. J., Devi, P. D., & Kumar, T. A. (2021). IoT-Based Smart Pipeline Leakage Detecting System for Petroleum Industries. In Industry 4.0 Interoperability, Analytics, Security, and Case Studies (pp. 149-168). CRC Press.

[9] Rajmohan, R., Kumar, T. A., Pavithra, M., & Sandhya, S. G. (2020). Blockchain: Next-generation technology for industry 4.0. In Blockchain Technology (pp. 177-198). CRC Press.

[10] X. Zhang and S. Xu, "Research on Image Processing Technology of Computer Vision Algorithm," in *Proceedings - 2020 International Conference on Computer Vision, Image and Deep Learning, CVIDL 2020*, Jul. 2020, pp. 122–124. doi: 10.1109/CVIDL51233.2020.00030.

[11] G. Wang, H. Gao, Q. Li, and C. Fang, "Surface deformations measurement based on computer vision technique," in *2010 International Conference on Machine Vision and Human-Machine Interface, MVHI 2010*, 2010, pp. 191–194. doi: 10.1109/MVHI.2010.130.

[12] K. He, X. Zhang, S. Ren, and J. Sun, "Deep Residual Learning for Image Recognition," Dec. 2015, [Online]. Available: http://arxiv.org/abs/1512.03385

[13] C. S. Sharp, O. Shakernia, and S. S. Sastry, "A vision system for landing an unmanned aerial vehicle," in *Proceedings 2001 ICRA. IEEE International Conference on Robotics and Automation (Cat. No.01CH37164)*, pp. 1720–1727. doi: 10.1109/ROBOT.2001.932859.

[14] S. Xu, J. Wang, W. Shou, T. Ngo, A.-M. Sadick, and X. Wang, "Computer Vision Techniques in Construction: A Critical Review," *Archives of Computational Methods in Engineering*, vol. 28, no. 5, pp. 3383–3397, Aug. 2021, doi: 10.1007/s11831-020-09504-3.

[15] Bo Zhang, "computer_vision_vs_human_vision", 9th IEEE Int. Conf. on Cognitive Informatics.

[16] Agin, "Computer Vision Systems for Industrial Inspection and Assembly," *Computer (Long Beach Calif)*, vol. 13, no. 5, pp. 11–20, May 1980, doi: 10.1109/MC.1980.1653613.

[17] Tai-Hoon Cho and R. W. Conners, "A neural network approach to machine vision systems for automated industrial inspection," in *IJCNN-91-Seattle International Joint Conference on Neural Networks*, pp. 205–210. doi: 10.1109/IJCNN.1991.155177.

[18] Kumar, K. Suresh, T. Ananth Kumar, A. S. Radhamani, and S. Sundaresan. "Blockchain technology: an insight into architecture, use cases, and its application with industrial IoT and big data." In Blockchain Technology, pp. 23-42. CRC Press, 2020.

[19] R. P. Kruger and W. B. Thompson, "A technical and economic assessment of computer vision for industrial inspection and robotic assembly," *Proceedings of the IEEE*, vol. 69, no. 12, pp. 1524–1538, 1981, doi: 10.1109/PROC.1981.12199.

[20] D. Geronimo, J. Serrat, A. M. Lopez, and R. Baldrich, "Traffic sign recognition for computer vision project-based learning," *IEEE Transactions on Education*, vol. 56, no. 3, pp. 364–371, 2013, doi: 10.1109/TE.2013.2239997.

[21] Gonzalez and Safabakhsh, "Computer Vision Techniques for Industrial Applications and Robot Control," *Computer (Long Beach Calif)*, vol. 15, no. 12, pp. 17–32, Dec. 1982, doi: 10.1109/MC.1982.1653913.

[22] E. Murphy-Chutorian and M. M. Trivedi, "Head Pose Estimation in Computer Vision: A Survey," *IEEE Transactions on Pattern Analysis and Machine Intelligence*, vol. 31, no. 4, pp. 607–626, Apr. 2009, doi: 10.1109/TPAMI.2008.106.

[23] J. F. S. Gomes and F. R. Leta, "Applications of computer vision techniques in the agriculture and food industry: a review," *European Food Research and Technology*, vol. 235, no. 6, pp. 989–1000, Dec. 2012, doi: 10.1007/s00217-012-1844-2.

[24] C. Haccius and T. Herfet, "Computer Vision Performance and Image Quality Metricsă: A Reciprocal Relation," Jan. 2017, pp. 27–37. doi: 10.5121/csit.2017.70104.

[25] L. Tychsen-Smith and L. Petersson, "Improving Object Localization with Fitness NMS and Bounded IoU Loss," Oct. 2017, [Online]. Available: http://arxiv.org/abs/1711.00164

[26] R. Padilla, S. L. Netto, E. A. B. da Silva, and S. L. Netto, "A Survey on Performance Metrics for Object-Detection Algorithms Compression of Power Systems Signals View project A Survey on Performance Metrics for Object-Detection Algorithms", doi: 10.1109/IWSSIP48289.2020.

[27] Konstantinidis, Fotios K., Spyridon G. Mouroutsos, and Antonios-Gasteratos. "The Role of Machine Vision in Industry 4.0: an automotive

manufacturing perspective." In *2021 IEEE International Conference on Imaging Systems and Techniques (IST)*, pp. 1-6. IEEE, 2021.

[28] Longsheng Fu, Yali Feng, Yaqoob Majeed, Xin Zhang, Jing Zhang, Manoj Karkee, Qin Zhang,Kiwifruit detection in field images using Faster R-CNN with ZFNet, IFAC-PapersOnLine, Volume 51, Issue 17, 2018, Pages 45-50, ISSN 2405-8963, https://doi.org/10.1016/j.ifacol.2 018.08.059.

7

Waste Management 4.0: An Industry Automation Approach to the Future Waste Management System

M. Julie Therese[1], P. Dharanyadevi[2], A. Devi[3], and Christo Ananth[4]

[1]Department of ECE, Sri Manakula Vinayagar Engineering College, India
[2]Department of CSE, Puducherry Technological University, India
[3]Department of ECE, IFET College of Engineering, India
[4]Samarkand State University, Uzbekistan
E-mail: julietherese88@gmail.com; dharanyadevi@gmail.com;
deviarumugam02@gmail.com; dr.christoananth@gmail.com

Abstract

Industry 4.0 is a trending revolution in the present society, especially in the circular economy system. The latest advances in the domain of data science, artificial intelligence (AI), robotics, the Internet of Things (IoT), big data, augmented reality, and virtual reality have opened the door for smart waste treatment systems. In India, municipal waste generation has increased dramatically during the past several decades, partly due to the country's rapid population expansion. The amount of waste generated in cities across India has risen from 6 million tons in 1947 to 48 million tons by 1997, and it is anticipated to reach 300 million tons per year by 2047. As a result, several substantial efforts must be taken to resolve the waste management problem. The current system arbitrarily collects waste. As a result, some places are occasionally left unattended, resulting in an unpleasant odor and a threat to public health, as the smell of garbage can potentially be harmful to little children and old-aged people. This chapter focuses on overcoming the hazards by adopting a smart waste management system that includes a cyber–physical system (CPS), which makes use of computers

163

to monitor the waste management process, and the Internet of Everything (IoE), which is a type of intelligent computing that connects things, people, services, data, etc., by making use of machine-to-machine communication protocols. These approaches make the waste treatment mechanism smart and could easily enable the waste-the-energy approach, converting energy into electricity, heat, or fuel.

Keywords: circular economy, cyber−physical system, Industry 4.0, Internet of Everything, machine-to-machine communication, waste-to-energy approach

7.1 Introduction

Smart factory is the current trend in Industry 4.0, wherein CPS makes decentralized decisions by monitoring the physical processes of the factory. These cyber−physical systems comprise production facilities, smart machines, and storage systems, which possess the capability of independency in information exchange, triggering activity, and managing each other without human interference. As of this, the physical systems in the Internet of Things interact and coordinate with each other and humans simultaneously through the wireless web. Industry 4.0 is prominently known for its sustainability to support the circular economy.

In order to analyze how the Fourth Industrial Revolution arose, the idea about the previous three industrial revolutions and how evolution has changed the lives of humans and the world should be studied. A brief note on previous industrial revolutions is shown in Figure 7.1.

The First Industrial Revolution occurred in 1784 when a watershed was the first mechanized loom. It also introduced steam power and the factory system, which increased production notably in the inclusion of machines. In 1870, the Second Industrial Revolution laid the foundation for the huge production of electricity [1]. This paved the way for the assembly line; the industrial sector grew exponentially over this century. In 1969, the Third Industrial Revolution came into existence, where the enhancements in computing paved the way for software and programming development, and progressive automation was introduced in this era. Then came the Fourth Industrial Revolution, with a much wider scope for future trends. The combination of the digital, biological, and physical domain interactions makes Industry 4.0 vitally different from previous revolutions. The evolution of Industry 4.0 is visualized above.

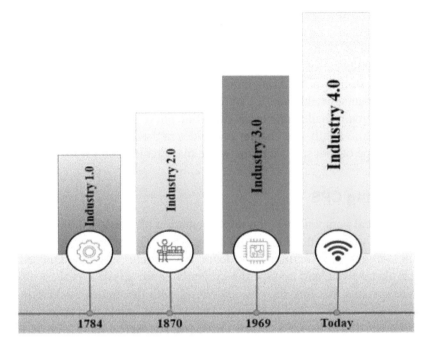

Figure 7.1 Evolution of Industry 4.0.

According to International Solid Waste Association (ISWA), Industry 4.0 comprises AI, automation and big data, IoT, etc., which significantly transfigures waste management [2]. Further, combining technologies creates new chances to accomplish high treatment standards, automate recycling tasks, reduce or prevent and even cut off waste from particular streams and sectors. The automated recycling tasks quoted above are the robotic recycling that will become mainstream in the markets in the next 10 years because of its materials recovery facilities (MRFs), accuracy, flexibility, and market adaptation [3]. More innovations are expected in waste management, which involves the technologies mentioned that ease the development of Industry 4.0.

The first section of this chapter gives an introduction to Industry 4.0. The subsequent section explores the cyber−physical system (CPS) and its advantages and disadvantages. In the third section of this chapter, we will discover the Industry 4.0 environment that is IoE, which is an amalgamation of IoT, industrial Internet of Things (IIoT), Internet of Services (IoS), Internet of Data (IoD), and Internet of People (IoP). Having discussed the Industry

4.0 environment, the next section will highlight the challenges faced by the waste management industry. Applications of CPS in the waste management industry will be dealt with in the next section. Section 6 of this chapter will discuss the influence of Industry 4.0 on the waste management industry. Although the studies prove that there would be a significant development in the waste management industry by implementing Industry 4.0, there are barriers that remain challenging in the execution phase; this is discussed in the next section. And finally, the chapter concludes in the last section discussing the future scope of Industry 4.0 in the waste management industry.

7.2 Exploring CPS

CPS is a critical component in the implementation of Industry 4.0 concepts in supporting the growth of smart manufacturing. The primary purpose of the CPS is to generate continuous feedback in real time, self-adapt and self-optimize themselves, and control the system's entire physical process [4]. CPSs are systems that link the physical world with the digital world using controllers and sensors. The integration of networking, computing power, and physical processes in the CPS creates the digital representation of a physical entity. CPS has its benefits and drawbacks and is discussed below.

7.2.1 CPS

- **Integration:** Integration occurs in a system when the CPS is connected via sensor networks to the cloud. The information delivered to the CPS is tremendous, which is passed to the cloud, a data center for processing [5]. Also, some physical systems are self-decision-making, making them more intelligent.
- **Interaction between human and CPS:** Decentralized logistic choices are formed, which modifies the traditional production process in the plant. This brings forth improvement in the manufacturing process by combining human resources and the accurate information from the plant with a decision-making system that relies on innovative scenarios.
- **Managing uncertainty:** Some physical systems are intelligent. They were created with the ability to self-adapt, self-optimize, and self-configure. Moreover, most importantly, they can grasp how to fit in and adjust to a given circumstance. They can reduce uncertainty to a large amount as the sensor always works, evolves, and learns the environment. Big data analytics is a term used to describe the analysis of large amounts

of data [6]. Thousands of sensors feed that data board, and the physical system comprehends based on this data; this is usually executed by comparing the circumstance to the past or historical data and responding accordingly to the condition.

- **Better system performance:** The CPS is real-time, and they can self-adapt in real time, which gives manufacturers a significant advantage in ensuring business continuity across all manufacturing processes and related activities. Physical systems can gain a comprehensive understanding of how to change themselves in every condition since they interact closely with sensors and other related data.
- **Scalability:** The cloud is connected to the CPS. The cloud provides tremendous stability, and CPSs can scale themselves based on demand or requirement by leveraging the cloud's capacity.
- **Flexibility:** The CPS's cloud marketing and wireless sensor networks add much value to deciding the flexibility in the manufacturing process. Because the CPSs are self-configurable and adaptable, if the equipment fails, the physical system can figure out what went wrong and adjust itself to perform a particular task successfully.
- **Faster response time:** CPS permits proactive breakdown (i.e., predicting when a machine will break down and take the required procedures to prevent it from failure). System failure is possible as the machine's components are erratic or sometimes overloaded. As a result, CPSs can enable early failure prediction and understanding and optimizing resource consumption in production.

7.2.2 Drawbacks of CPS

While the CPS offers numerous advantages, they also have disadvantages.

- Creating CPSs or incorporating CPSs into the manufacturing process is too expensive.
- Small- and medium-sized firms could not afford the considerable financial commitment required. Even huge corporations must audit the production process [7].
- Numerous underlying infrastructures, processes, and business operations must be optimized for CPSs to work as intended.
- Furthermore, in order to provide seamless communication between CPSs, network features like real-time and low-latency networking must be enabled at the factory.

7.3 Industry 4.0 Environment

The concept of a smart factory is essential to the Industry 4.0 environment. Smart buildings, intelligent tools, social web, business web, and smart logistics such as autonomous vehicles, smart grids, and innovative mobility are all part of the Industry 4.0 environment, as shown in Figure 7.2.

As shown in Figure 7.3, the critical elements of the Industry 4.0 environment are the Internet of Things (IoT), Industrial Internet of Things (IIoT), Internet of Services (IoS), Internet of Data (IoD), Internet of People (IoP), and Internet of Everything (IoE). The explanations are given below.

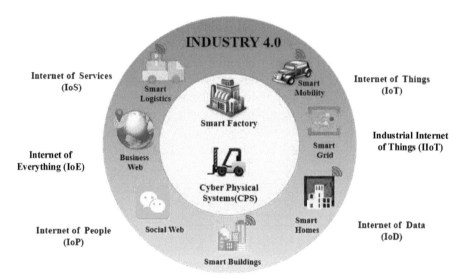

Figure 7.2   Industry 4.0 environment.

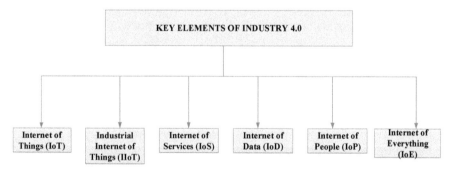

Figure 7.3   Critical elements of Industry 4.0.

IoT: IoT is a computer concept that entails linking everyday physical products, such as television, washing machine, refrigerators, toasters, etc., to the Internet and allowing them to speak with one another [9]. To provide a flawless experience, elements such as high-speed internet connectivity, network infrastructure, and shared communication protocols are taken into account. Machine-to-machine (M2M) communication is the term used in this area to describe the process of ensuring that all devices can understand and communicate with one another.

IIoT: The IIoT refers to a network of interconnected devices or instruments for industrial computing applications to improve industrial and manufacturing processes, such as advanced robotics and machines that can develop and implement a wide range of products and other related processes [10].

IoS: IoS is a global marketplace for web-based software provided as a service. IoS covers benefits such as blockchain, which is regarded as a game changer in supply chain management. IoT enabled by IoS results in disruptive innovation.

IoD: In Industry 4.0, billions of sensors will be connected online, generating vast amounts of data such as distance, wetness, temperature, position, etc. All these data must be processed using a big data analytics tool to obtain useful insights and factors. As a result, IoD is based on the massive amounts of data generated by billions of IoT devices. When big data analytics methods are used to find trends in the data stream, these data streams offer vast potential for industrial applications.

IoP: IoP is a revolutionary new internet concept in which persons and their personal gadgets are treated as active internet elements rather than as end users of applications. IoP is based on a decentralized network like blockchain, where a single body does not hold or control data and information. It aspires to be an internet "for the people, of the people" rather than one that unknowingly compromises people's privacy.

IoE: IoE is the unification and complexity of people, processes, data, and things in a single network system [11]. The IoT, IIoT, IoS, IoP, and IoD are combined to form the IoE. This is the most promising technology for Waste Management 4.0.

7.4 Challenges in the Waste Management Industry

For waste management to be successful, several challenges must first be surmounted. These challenges include but are not limited to a deficiency in sufficient data, the requirement to guarantee the quality of recycled materials, and the recuperation of waste energy. Figure 7.4 presents a graphical representation of the difficulties that must be conquered in the waste management sector.

- **Reusing and recycling waste materials**
  The first and most crucial challenge in waste management is determining whether resources may be reduced, recycled, or reused. The procedure becomes more efficient due to the exact identification of the process.

- **Trash gathering and transportation**
  Biodegradable and non-biodegradable wastes are the two most common types of waste. Food waste, such as banana peels, rotten fruits, and vegetables, is considered biodegradable. Plastics and glasses are examples of non-biodegradable materials. These are the standard categorizations; however, in certain countries, it extends beyond that and separates paper, glass, metal, and plastics that originate from consumer waste from households. However, industrial garbage is a different scenario, including hazardous materials and radioactive waste [13]. Gathering the garbage to be stored, transported, and disposed of needs a great deal of effort, and on a massive scale, people are hesitant to organize; this is one of the most challenging problems in trash management.

- **Garbage removal**
  There are two garbage removal methods; the first is burning it, which releases hazardous gases, ash, and particulates into the atmosphere. The most effective way is to bury the garbage. Each method comes with its own set of difficulties. For example, the atmospheric approach emits many hazardous gases such as carbon monoxide, carbon dioxide, sulfur dioxide, etc. When waste is dumped into the landfill or the ocean, dangerous metals, such as cadmium, barium, etc., are released, harming the ecosystem and affecting human health.

- **Dumping rubbish has a negative influence on the environment**
  Dumping garbage into the environment produces more devastating problems, such as rapid differences in humidity and chemical composition, or alters the number of gases present in a given ecosystem, all of which significantly impact the lifespan of all living species [14]. For example, algae thrives in trash dumps because all the rich nitrogen sources are present.

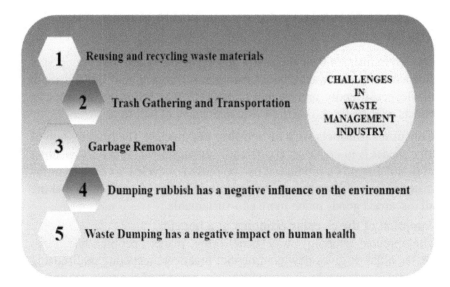

Figure 7.4 Challenges in waste management system.

- **Waste dumping harms human health**
  Many people have had real-life experiences; people who reside near a waste-dumped landfill are exposed to high levels of microorganisms, such as flies, insects, rats, and bugs that survive on trash. These insects come to feed on the garbage and then land on people's bodies, spreading infections quickly. This is a significant problem that Industry 4.0 experts must overcome.

7.5 Applications of CPS in the Waste Management Industry

Industry 4.0 and CPS are two new buzzwords that have earned much interest from researchers and manufacturers. Advanced technologies are made available due to these terms that provide potential solutions and enhancements for future smart waste management systems [15].

- Monitoring the level of toxicity during collection and transport
- Determination of the most environmentally friendly garbage degradation methods
- Recognizing functional components in garbage
- Improving the effectiveness of waste management operations

7.6 Influence of Industry 4.0 on the Waste Management Industry

The goal of Industry 4.0 in the waste management system is to empower its influence to reduce waste, boost resource utilization, and build a more sustainable, eco-friendly, and cleaner planet [16]. The following are some of the impacts of Industry 4.0 on the waste management industry.

- **Consumer products with an eco-first perspective** The primary aim of this impact is to create an eco-friendly environment. When a consumer uses and discards a product, it can be reused, recycled, or used as a raw material for another product. As a result, Industry 4.0 focuses on making all discarded goods much more eco-sustainable.

- **Adoption of the circular economy at a benefit**
  The circular economy will benefit the planet, people, and businesses alike. It gives new commercial practices, recycling and reusing resources, and new business models. As a result of the vast volume of data generated by Industry 4.0, the adoption of the circular economy will be accelerated [17]. It can be created by repurposing materials and extracting valuable components or elements from waste, resulting in a more environmentally friendly and long-lasting product for consumer demand.

- **Greenhouse gas emissions from the waste management industry are being reduced**
  Big data analytics and CPS will monitor every unit or entity in real time. It can also self-adjust, self-optimize, and self-regulate its whole manageable workflow (for example, if CPSs are in charge of a factory, they will constantly monitor and enhance the factory's efficiency, as well as control the waste management sector's greenhouse gas emissions [18]).

- **Large-scale garbage dumping sites are being phased out**
  Many trash heaps are noticeable, especially in underdeveloped countries, where hundreds of trucks arrive and dump their waste, resulting in trash mountains. This is incredibly dangerous because once the trash mountain is formed, all of the highly combustible gases build up, and all it takes is one spark to blow up the entire mountain. This will be overcome by Industry 4.0 and CPS because these waste management systems will autonomously handle waste, as well as self-driving garbage trucks and smart garbage cans; this leads to an antibacterial environment.

- **E-waste is being reduced significantly**
  The CPS will be able to accurately handle and manage e-waste in terms of determining what resources can be extracted, reused, and recycled, and this will undoubtedly result in a far more sustainable e-waste management ecosystem. As a result, people can limit their e-waste, and businesses can focus on incorporating more recycled materials into their products to create an even more sustainable and environmentally friendly supply chain.

- **Increase the use of waste-to-energy technologies**
  In some countries, trash is used to generate energy, which is then used to generate electricity. This drastically reduces the amount of landfill space used for rubbish disposal, and with the advancement of new technologies, one can expect to see things like filters that prevent ashes, dust, and extremely poisonous vapors and gases from reaching the atmosphere. This will also be incredibly sustainable because when waste is burnt, it turns into ashes that can be recycled and turned into bricks, which can then be used to construct houses [19]. As an outcome, a great deal of value-added thinking is required to ensure that waste management is far more sustainable than it is presently.

- **Significant reduction in marine waste**
  CPS can help scientists determine what contaminants are present in the water and how they affect the entire marine ecosystem, from fish to marine mammals and corals. They will also be able to track in real time where these pollutants are leaking into the oceans, and penalties or taxes may be levied to ensure that all of those who contribute to waste are causing offense and that their funds can be used to construct sustainable systems [20]. Ocean cleanup is one of the new business models that can be developed to ensure that the ocean is a healthy ecosystem for marine life.

- **Food waste reduction**
  Food waste is a significant issue, with millions of tons of food thrown away each year. A far more efficient operation in logistics, distribution, storage, and production can be established using Industry 4.0 and developing more imaginative and creative solutions to food waste problems [21].

- **Waste management and treatment facilities on a small scale**
  Industry 4.0 is all about democratizing things; it is about taking something that is used to be done by massive government operations and

breaking it down so that even the average person can do it on a smaller scale; the home may have a micro waste management facility. Perhaps an intelligent robot will constantly be around to clear up the waste and ensure that every garbage is collected and categorized and decides whether the garbage should be recycled, reused, or used as a raw material to manufacture another product.

7.7 Barriers to Implementing Industry 4.0 in the Waste Management Industry

There are insurmountable impediments that have forced us to leave Industry 4.0, some of which are discussed below.

- **Implementation costs are expensive**
  Industry 4.0 appears magnificent and offers many advantages, but it costs a lot of money [22]. A few elements that influence the high implementation costs are a robust internet connection required to build Industry 4.0, a large internet connectivity capacity required, and a large amount of data that will be transferred simultaneously [23]. Billions of gadgets are connected to the Internet worldwide, and many household items such as televisions, refrigerators, computers, and other electronic equipment will be Wi-Fi enabled and capable of connecting online. Also, every workflow must be recorded in real time and fed into an analysis system. As a result, implementing only a small percentage of IoT will not give the actual benefits that it promises.

- **Security problems and concerns**
  Massive amounts of data are generated by Industry 4.0. As a result, this data must be kept secure, recorded, processed, analyzed, and transformed. Consumers would be highly concerned about sharing information with underhanded businesses [24]. To tackle these issues, organizations must establish a strong legal framework for data privacy that ensures consumer data security while holding corporations accountable for the information they collect and share with third parties.

- **A shortage of qualified personnel**
  Industry 4.0 is a relatively new concept; to cope with it, one must ensure that employers are up-skilled to meet the technology's problems. As a result, putting Industry 4.0 solutions in place necessitates specialized knowledge and abilities, and there is a demand for people who are highly experienced and qualified in information technology, as well as people

who have a thorough awareness of how each sector operates, particularly the one to which they cater. As in Industry 4.0, humans and robots work together; humans will focus on creative work while robots perform repetitive tasks. Hence, there are a few roadblocks regarding a lack of qualified personnel.

- **Integration of technology is a problem**
Innovative technologies such as cloud computing, which includes Google Cloud, Amazon Web Services (AWS), etc., are deployed [25]. To run an Industry 4.0-related solution investigation platform is required. Migrating a large amount of data from a local system to the cloud is time-consuming, complicated, and demands huge security protocols.

7.8 Case Study: Machine Learning for Waste Management

Machine learning models can be applied to the present waste management statistical data in order to predict the waste that can be generated in the future; with this knowledge, practical steps can be carried out to monitor, segregate, and thereby significantly reduce the amount of waste.

For this study, the waste dataset was generated from one of Australia's most populated cities. The dataset contains four years of waste management data; the above pie chart shows the visualization of the dataset, i.e., the collection category and subcategory of waste [26]. Figure 7.5 show the types of waste under several collection subcategories; the tons collected subcategory has six types of waste that are split and shown as three categories in Figure 7.5 and three categories in Figure 7.5; Figure 7.5(d) shows the types of waste under bins collected category.

Anaconda prompt software is used for applying machine learning algorithms to the dataset; as a first step, the dataset is imported along with library functions for analyzing and visualizing data [27]. The next step is cleaning the data, removing redundancy, and training and testing the data with machine learning algorithms. In order to determine which machine learning algorithm provides the highest level of accuracy, various machine learning algorithms such as logistic regression (LR), linear discriminant analysis (LDA), K-neighbor classifier (KNN), decision tree classifier (DTC), Gaussian Naive Bayes (NB), and support vector machine (SVM) [28] are applied to the dataset. The algorithms are imported onto the platform using sklearn library files [29]. Accuracy is measured by the ratio of correct predictions to the total number of predictions [30]. Figure 7.5 shows the comparison for accuracy; from the figure, it is clear that the logistic regression algorithm shows an

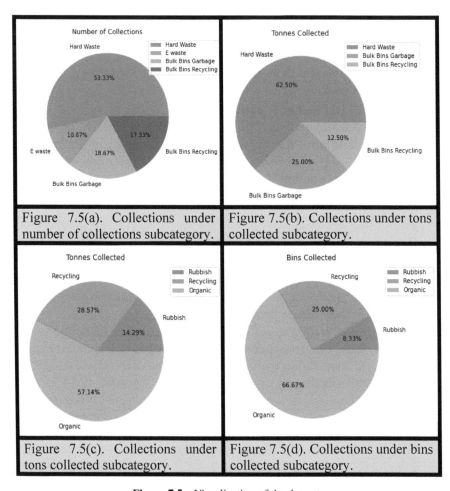

Figure 7.5(a). Collections under number of collections subcategory.	Figure 7.5(b). Collections under tons collected subcategory.
Figure 7.5(c). Collections under tons collected subcategory.	Figure 7.5(d). Collections under bins collected subcategory.

Figure 7.5   Visualization of the dataset.

accuracy of 80% for this dataset, and hence this algorithm can be used to predict the waste generated in the next few years.

Figure 7.6 and Table 7.1 show the performance evaluation of the algorithms based on accuracy; from the table and figure, it is clear that the logistic regression algorithm works well with the dataset and shows 80% accuracy. Hence, this algorithm can be used to predict future waste management data.

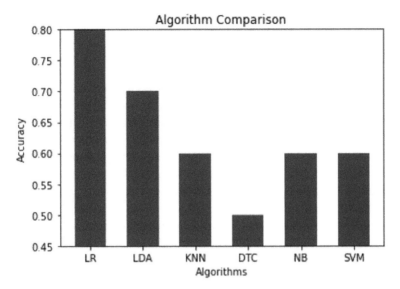

Figure 7.6 Accuracy evaluation of machine learning algorithms.

Table 7.1 Performance evaluation of machine learning algorithms.

Machine Learning Models					
	LR	**LDA**	**KNN**	**DTC**	**NB**	**SVM**
Accuracy	80%	70%	60%	50%	60%	60%

7.9 Conclusion

To summarize, the core of Industry 4.0 is the CPS, which is composed of computers connected over networks to monitor physical processes. This system can exchange data automatically without much human intervention, leading to the exponential increase of profit in engineering sectors, supply chain, and product life cycle management. IoE plays a major role in Industry 4.0 and will also be a key for future industrial revolutions; this is an amalgamation of IoT, IIoT, IoS, IoD, and IoP. This chapter focuses on Waste Management 4.0; as in many countries, door-to-door manual trash collection level is attained only now. The challenges faced by the waste management industry are waste collection, transporting waste safely, disposal of the collected waste, dealing with the environmental impact, health impact, and, most importantly, segregating waste for reuse and recycling; all these require technology in addition to human resources, which leads to the necessity of Industry 4.0. Applying CPS to identify and segregate reusable and unusable waste increases the effectiveness of the waste management process in all its stages and paves the way for sustainable and suitable ways for garbage decomposition. Industry 4.0 has positively impacted the waste processing and treatment system; it has created an eco-friendly approach, thereby significantly reducing e-waste and food waste and increasing in practicing waste-to-energy approach. It has also set a basement for developing reliable small-scale waste management infrastructure, successfully monitors the toxicity of the waste, and protects against health hazards. However, some barriers have to be overcome, and as the system uses sensors and computing resources to automate the waste management system, implementation cost is high since physical devices are connected over the Internet, and privacy issues may also arise.

Additionally, there is a shortage of skilled workers to coordinate the process. In the future, with high-performance computer networks, smart sensors, and professionals with intricate problem-solving and creative skills, human—machine collaboration will pave the way for improving business strategies, boosting the manufacturing domain. It will offer a better environment for work.

References

[1] Yin, Yong, Kathryn E. Stecke, and Dongni Li. "The evolution of production systems from Industry 2.0 through Industry 4.0." *International Journal of Production Research* 56.1-2 (2018): 848-861.

[2] Xu, Li Da, Eric L. Xu, and Ling Li. "Industry 4.0: state of the art and future trends." *International journal of production research* 56.8 (2018): 2941-2962.

[3] Devi, A., et al. "IoT-Based Smart Pipeline Leakage Detecting System for Petroleum Industries." Industry 4.0 Interoperability, Analytics, Security, and Case Studies. CRC Press, 2021. 149-168.

[4] Lee, Jay, Behrad Bagheri, and Hung-An Kao. "A cyber-physical systems architecture for industry 4.0-based manufacturing systems." *Manufacturing Letters* 3 (2015): 18-23.0

[5] Pivoto, Diego GS, et al. "Cyber-physical systems architectures for industrial Internet of things applications in Industry 4.0: A literature review." *Journal of manufacturing systems* 58 (2021): 176-192.

[6] Zhou, Keliang, Taigang Liu, and Ling Liang. "From cyber-physical systems to Industry 4.0: make future manufacturing become possible." *International Journal of Manufacturing Research* 11.2 (2016): 167-188.

[7] Usharani, S., et al. "Smart Energy Management Techniques in Industries 5.0." Hybrid Intelligent Approaches for Smart Energy: Practical Applications (2022): 225-252.

[8] Trstenjak, Maja, and Predrag Cosic. "Process planning in Industry 4.0 environment." *Procedia Manufacturing* 11 (2017): 1744-1750.

[9] Devi, A., et al. "IoT Based Food Grain Wastage Monitoring and Controlling System for Warehouse." 2021 International Conference on System, Computation, Automation and Networking (ICSCAN). IEEE, 2021.

[10] Bagheri, Behrad, et al. "Cyber-physical systems architecture for self-aware machines in industry 4.0 environment." *IFAC-PapersOnLine* 48.3 (2015): 1622-1627.

[11] Hiriyannaiah, Srinidhi, et al. "A Multi-layered Framework for Internet of Everything (IoE) via Wireless Communication and Distributed Computing in Industry 4.0." *Recent Patents on Engineering* 14.4 (2020): 521-529.

[12] Kumar, Sunil, et al. "Challenges and opportunities associated with waste management in India." *Royal Society open science* 4.3 (2017): 160764.

[13] Vaverková, Magdalena Daria, et al. "Municipal solid waste management under COVID-19: challenges and recommendations." *Environmental Geotechnics* 8.3 (2020): 217-232.

[14] Joshi, Rajkumar, and Sirajuddin Ahmed. "Status and challenges of municipal solid waste management in India: A review." *Cogent Environmental Science* 2.1 (2016): 1139434.

[15] Thada, Ayush, et al. "Custom blockchain-based cyber-physical system for solid waste management." *Procedia computer science* 165 (2019): 41-49.

[16] Oláh, Judit, et al. "Impact of Industry 4.0 on environmental sustainability." *Sustainability* 12.11 (2020): 4674.

[17] Rosa, Paolo, et al. "Assessing Relations between Circular Economy and Industry 4.0: a systematic literature review." *International Journal of Production Research* 58.6 (2020): 1662-1687.

[18] de la Barrera, Belen, and Peter S. Hooda. "Greenhouse gas emissions of waste management processes and options: A case study." *Waste Management & Research* 34.7 (2016): 658-665.

[19] Tabasová, Andrea, et al. "Waste-to-energy technologies: Impact on environment." *Energy* 44.1 (2012): 146-155.

[20] Sivadas, Sanitha K., et al. "Litter and plastic monitoring in the Indian marine environment: A review of current research, policies, waste management, and a roadmap for multidisciplinary action." *Marine Pollution Bulletin* 176 (2022): 113424.

[21] Devi, A., et al. "IoT Based Food Grain Wastage Monitoring and Controlling System for Warehouse." *2021 International Conference on System, Computation, Automation and Networking (ICSCAN)*. IEEE, 2021.

[22] Kumar, K. Suresh, et al. "Blockchain technology: an insight into architecture, use cases, and its application with industrial IoT and big data." Blockchain Technology. CRC Press, 2020. 23-42.

[23] Kamble, Sachin S., Angappa Gunasekaran, and Rohit Sharma. "Analysis of the driving and dependence power of barriers to adopt industry 4.0 in Indian manufacturing industry." *Computers in Industry* 101 (2018): 107-119.

[24] Dawson, Maurice. "Cyber security in industry 4.0: The pitfalls of having hyperconnected systems." *Journal of Strategic Management Studies* 10.1 (2018): 19-28.

[25] Therese, M. Julie, P. Dharanyadevi, and K. Harshithaa. "Integrating IoT and Cloud Computing for Wireless Sensor Network Applications." *Cloud and IoT-Based Vehicular Ad Hoc Networks* (2021): 125-143.

[26] Dataset:http://opendata.adelaidecitycouncil.com/Waste_Management/Waste_Management.csv

[27] Dalzochio, Jovani, et al. "Machine learning and reasoning for predictive maintenance in Industry 4.0: Current status and challenges." *Computers in Industry* 123 (2020): 103298.

[28] Candanedo, Inés Sittón, et al. "Machine learning predictive model for industry 4.0." *International Conference on Knowledge Management in Organizations*. Springer, Cham, 2018.

[29] Brik, Bouziane, et al. "Towards predicting system disruption in industry 4.0: machine learning-based approach." *Procedia computer science* 151 (2019): 667-674.

[30] Rai, Rahul, et al. "Machine learning in manufacturing and industry 4.0 applications." *International Journal of Production Research* 59.16 (2021): 4773-4778.

8

Industrial Internet of Things (IIoT) for E-waste Recycling System

A. P. Jyothi and P. Padma Priya Dharishini

Department of CSE, Faculty of Engineering and Technology, Ramaiah University of Applied Sciences, India
E-mail: jyothiarcotprashant@gmail.com; padprishini.paraman@gmail.com

Abstract

Industrial Internet of Things (IIoT) is a word used to portray the framework's organization of genuine things and contraptions with embedded sensors, programming, and correspondence limits. These IoT contraptions can assemble, exchange, and cycle data with each other and with outside structures to additionally foster capability, proficiency, and prosperity, customer relationship management (CRM), or enterprise resource planning (ERP). IIoT is driving one more surge of mechanized change, changing endeavors like collecting, transportation, and energy. By partner contraptions and structures to the web, IIoT engages associations to assemble and analyze data logically, making it possible to smooth out undertakings and further foster execution. A logical examination of circulation place organization using the industrial Internet of Things (IIoT) is inspected comprehensively. As a case study, an E-waste recycling system using IoT is discussed to show the negative impact of e-waste on the environment due to harmful chemicals present in e-waste.

Keywords: IIoT, IoT, CRM, ERP, real-time

8.1 Introduction

The industrial Internet of Things (IIoT) uses technologically advanced sensors and actuators to improve manufacturing and other modern processes.

181

The industrial Internet of Things (IIoT) is the modern web or Industry 4.0. It uses the power of brilliant machines and regular examination to capitalize on the data that "idiotic machines" have been producing in contemporary environments for quite some time. The essential reasoning behind the industrial Internet of Things (IIoT) is that clever machines are not only superior to people in terms of gathering and analyzing data in a more timely manner, but they are also superior in terms of conveying significant data that can be utilized to drive business decisions more expediently precisely [2]. This is the fundamental reasoning behind the IIoT.

Connected sensors and actuators allow businesses to address problems and failures more quickly, thereby saving both time and money while supporting efforts to improve business knowledge. Regarding assembly, more specifically, the IIoT holds enormous potential for quality control, manageable and environmentally friendly practices, production network detectability, and, in general, inventory network proficiency.

8.2 Background Study

The utilization of IoT innovations has expanded quickly inside numerous businesses. Utilizing IoT innovations is likewise expected to work on the data for sharing inside and across different ventures [4]. View of IoT innovations has been practical toward different applications going from home computerization to modern IoT and having the option to impart essential things from any spot through an organization [18].

It tends to be noticed that the number of undertakings that connect with the utilization of the IoT in modern regions has expanded, for example, farming, security reconnaissance, natural observing, food handling, and numerous others [8]. Besides, distributed papers in the IoT regions have extended significantly, crossing various utilizations. Furthermore, numerous different advancements and techniques have been utilized to help the IoT, like Wi-Fi [7].

8.3 IIoT Working

IIoT is an organization of shrewd gadgets associated with structure frameworks that screen, gather, trade, and dissect information. Each modern IoT environment comprises:

- Associated gadgets that can detect, impart, and store data about themselves.
- Public and additionally confidential information correspondences foundation.
- Investigation and applications that create business data from crude information.
- Capacity for the information produced by the IoT gadgets, and individuals. These edge gadgets and canny resources send data straightforwardly to the information correspondence foundation, changing it into important data on how a specific piece of hardware is working. This data can be utilized for prescient support and to enhance business processes.

8.4 IIoT Security

Manufacturers built IoT devices with little consideration for security, which led to the assumption that IoT devices are inherently unsafe. Given the similarities between IoT and IIoT devices, it is important to consider whether using IoT devices is safe.

The device-by-device analysis is required for IIoT devices, just like for any other linked device. It is completely feasible that a device from one manufacturer is secure but not from another. However, device manufacturers now place a higher priority than ever before on security [10].

The Industrial Internet Consortium (IIC) was founded in 2014 by various technological corporations, including AT&T, Cisco, General Electric, IBM, and Intel. Even though this group's primary goal is to hasten the adoption of IIoT and associated technologies, it has prioritized security and even gone so far as to do so.

8.4.1 Risks and challenges of IIoT

Security-related hazards are the ones that concern IIoT use the most [5]. Even after they have been put into production, IIoT devices frequently retain their default passwords. Similarly to this, a lot of IoT devices send data in clear text. Due to these circumstances, it would be pretty simple for a hacker to intercept data flowing from an IoT device. Similar to this, an attacker might seize control of an unsecured IIoT device and use it as a base to attack other network resources [15].

Security is a major concern for people in charge of an organization's IoT devices, but so is device management. Adopting an efficient device management strategy will be crucial as a business deploys more and more IoT devices [11].

8.4.2 Difference between IoT and IIoT

Cloud stages, sensors, networks, machine-to-machine communications, and information examination are only a few of the advancements IoT and IIoT share for all intents and purposes, even though they are used for various things. IoT applications interface gadgets from a few industry areas, for example, rural, medical care, venture, buyer, utilities, government, and metropolitan regions. Brilliant apparatuses, wellness trackers, and other IoT applications commonly do not bring about crisis conditions, assuming something turns out badly.

Then again, IIoT applications connect gear and contraptions in the assembling, oil, gas, and utility areas. In IIoT establishments, framework disappointments and margin time can prompt high-endanger or even hazardous circumstances. Also, contrasted with IoT applications, IoT applications are more centered on upgrading productivity and well-being or security.

8.4.3 IIoT applications and examples

ABB, a power and robotics company, uses linked sensors to monitor its robots' maintenance requirements to suggest repairs before parts break in a real-world IIoT deployment of intelligent robotics [14]. Similarly, Airbus, a manufacturer of commercial jetliners, has started what it calls the factory of the future, a digital manufacturing drive to improve operations and increase output. Airbus has incorporated sensors into equipment and machines on the shop floor to reduce errors and improve worker safety and provided personnel with wearable technology, such as industrial intelligent glasses.

Fanuc, a different robotics manufacturer, uses sensors and cloud-based data analytics to foresee when parts in its robots will break. This allows the plant manager to plan maintenance at reasonable periods, cutting expenses and avoiding unnecessary downtime.

Magna Steyr, an Austrian automaker, uses the IIoT to track its assets, including tools and car parts [6], and purchases more stock automatically when it runs low. In order to track components in its warehouses, the corporation is also experimenting with "smart packaging" supplemented with Bluetooth.

8.5 Industries using IIoT

Processes of industrial automation have many applications. Some of the most important are manufacturing, oil and gas extraction, paper mills, and steel mills. Below are just a few instances where these companies have used this technology.

a. Automated production in the manufacturing industry:
   The manufacturing industry extensively uses industrial automation in many different contexts and purposes. Technology may be used in the manufacturing process, from the design phase through the final inspection, as well as in monitoring upkeep duties and stock levels [17].

b. Oil and gas exploration:
   Since oil and gas drilling often occurs at offshore stations and other distant locations, industrial automation greatly benefits the oil and gas drilling industry. Sensors and other monitoring equipment will reduce the number of complex and potentially dangerous site visits that maintenance workers must make.

c. The paper industry:
   It can be used by paper mills to control instrumentation, plant devices, and equipment and to manage batches of production. Use in this way is also possible. This allows for greater overall system transparency for the production system's operators.

d. Automation in steel mills:
   Hierarchical control is used in other types of industrial automation, such as in steel mills. Because of this technological development, a unified system is now at hand for managing and controlling the entire steel mill [16]. Autopilot controls on commercial jets are one example of the long-standing use of industrial automation in the transportation sector. There is a shift toward autonomous vehicles that can be used for commercial and private purposes, incorporating advances in industrial automation [9].

e. Distribution:
   Once a product has been manufactured and is prepared for shipment, distribution takes over. Worldwide, deadlines are getting shorter and shorter. Because of this, it intends to continue introducing solutions in the distribution field to regulate the shipping and delivery of products at an even quicker pace.

f. Industrial controls and automation for manufacturing process:
   It will be impossible to successfully implement industrial automation controls on your production line without a computerized maintenance

management system (CMMS). This centralized system can gather much data, including stock levels, work order schedules, maintenance records, and data from remote sensors. By combining vital resources, high-quality data, historical data, and real-time alerts or sensor readings, you will be in a solid position to select, refine, and use your industrial automation tools to boost efficiency within your organization. The reason being you will have everything you need in one convenient location.

8.6 Advantages and Disadvantages of IIoT

There are Advantages and disadvantages of IIoT as listed in Table 8.1.

Benefits of IIoT

The first way to see the advantage of robotization is that it removes the requirement for any human intercession. For example, suppose you will robotize your deals pipe. Instead of checking telephone discussions and updating your site physically, you can now have a chatbot accomplish the work for you. This will save time and cash over the long haul − something priceless to many organizations [19]. Different benefits of computerization are as per the following:

   i. Greater rates of production: Robotization is a significant part of the manufacturing industry, making it possible for more excellent rates of production to be achieved while incurring fewer costs and utilizing fewer resources. Because of these benefits, mechanization has become a more common practice in various settings.
   ii. Increased productivity: Mechanization has played a significant role in the labor force and will continue to do so as the industry develops.

Table 8.1   Advantages and disadvantages of IIoT.

Advantages	Disadvantages
Higher production rates	Worker displacement
Expanded productivity	It needs enormous capital consumption
More productive utilization of materials	Can become redundant
Better item quality	Could present new security dangers
Improved safety	It still requires human mediation
Shorter workweeks for labor	
Decreased manufacturing plant lead times	
Consistency	
Saves time	
No labor issues	

Because of this increase in productivity, businesses can now concentrate their efforts on other important tasks, such as product development, while still completing their projects on schedule. These endeavors provide benefits to the organization and pave the way for further accomplishment on their part.

iii. A more effective utilization of the materials: New technology affects how products are manufactured. Mechanization leads to better products because it makes more efficient use of available resources and produces more of them. Because of these benefits, manufacturers can produce better products, resulting in decreased production costs, increased customer satisfaction, and a greater return on investment.

iv. Better item quality: Mechanization is an expense-saving system that organizations have been involved in for a long while. Lately, computerization has been embraced all the more frequently in promoting business since it empowers organizations to deliver their items quicker, less expensive, and with a lot greater. The utilization of mechanization will likely continue developing as advertisers hope to profit from the benefits it offers to increment efficiency.

v. Further developed security: Robotization enjoys many benefits. It can assist with further developing security by restricting human mistakes, lessening expenses, and making the creation cycle more proficient. This is particularly significant in enterprises with a high gamble of injury, like horticulture and mining.

vi. More limited work-filled weeks for work: Mechanization can empower more limited work-filled weeks for work. By involving computerization instead of people, organizations can decrease the number of workers expected to work at a most extreme limit. This will give additional opportunities to workers to zero-in on different undertakings, for example, the executives, preparation, or advancement that require a human connection.

vii. Decreased production line lead times: The advantages of computerization should be visible for the most part in processing plants. Mechanization decreases beginning-to-end manufacturing plant lead times by 60% or more. This not just advantages the assembling result of a plant, yet additionally the quality and proficiency of an item.

viii. Consistency: Mechanization will carry consistency and solidness to the business. It will likewise allow the business an opportunity to adjust to changes in what their clients need. Organizations will believe a more significant amount of this proficiency as they proceed should confront the present changing economic situations and buyers' requests.

xi. Saves time: Making work more accessible by automating it is a huge step forward. The time spent on tasks that a computer program or machine should be able to handle is saved. Tasks like these include: Mechanization has come a long way, and with each passing day comes more discoveries and developments that make the widespread use of computers a reality.

x. No work issues: Mechanization is the way into a work emergency-free future. It will not just cost as much as individuals, yet it will offer quality types of assistance that individuals will pay for.

8.6.1 Hindrances of IIoT

Computerization is a piece of society today. Computerization can be incredible for people and associations when appropriately utilized and executed. It can save time and cash and assist you with finishing work all the more precisely [20]. The cons of mechanization are the expense of supplanting human work with robotized frameworks. Different weaknesses of mechanization are as per the following:

i. Specialist dislodging: The main inconvenience of computerization is the removal of human work. This is because an electronic errand can be executed quicker and with more prominent exactness than can be accomplished by a human. For instance, Disney World has involved self-driving vehicles for quite a long time to ship visitors around the recreation area. Many individuals are anxious about the possibility that this will bring about less employment for people.

ii. Requires significant investment of time and money: Computers have been an integral business component for quite some time. Before switching to computerization, manufacturers must consider several unanticipated consequences. One of these effects is the requirement for a significant amount of financial investment to keep up with and manage computerized systems. These systems are also more vulnerable to digital attacks than manual systems, leaving businesses defenseless if their foundation is not adequately protected. Manual systems would be more effective at fending off physical attacks.

iii. Has the potential to become monotonous: Using computers is a valuable solution to some problems. Nevertheless, this convenience may become inconvenient in certain circumstances, such as when a familiar change necessitates the adjustment of the mechanization. These adjustments will only add to the organization's responsibility, which may cause them to lose valuable time and resources.

iv. Could present new security risks: Mechanization could present new well-being dangers while working circumstances change suddenly. For instance, it is conceivable that a driverless vehicle could be customized to drive independently; however, it can, in any case, cause a mishap when a passerby ventures out into the road under conditions that are not so great (night/low permeability and so on).

v. Still requires human intercession: While the general advantages of mechanization have been demonstrated, there are as yet specific undertakings that require human mediation. We will think about the above illustration of self-driving vehicles – these machines can distinguish most obstructions out and about and can be customized to stop. In any case, a few explicit circumstances can make these machines confound data and produce undesired results – for example, passing through a hindrance that is not obviously noticeable to the vehicle's sensor.

8.7 Case Study - IoT for E-waste Recycling System

The waste generated from electrical or electronic devices, i.e., electronic waste or e-waste, negatively impacts the environment due to the harmful chemicals present in it. Figure 8.1 shows the categorization of e-waste based on its components and composition. The circuit boards and batteries in e-waste can cause damage to ecosystems. New natural resources must be mined to manufacture electronic components that make a massive ecological impact. In order to overcome this, the recovery of materials like copper, gold, aluminum, plastic, and glass from e-waste is needed. To achieve this, e-waste should be recycled.

Figure 8.1 shows the processes in the e-waste recycling system. First, e-waste is collected through recycling bins, collection locations, or through collection services. This mixed e-waste is transported to the e-waste categorization center. In that center, e-waste is categorized into any of the e-waste categories mentioned in Figure 8.2 based on its composition and components. This step is critical because e-waste containing batteries mixed with other waste can be very damaging. Next, the categorized e-waste is loaded into appropriate pallets. The RFID tags are printed on each pallet with information like the e-waste category and its storage location. The dock door of the storage center is mounted with an RFID reader and an antenna. The pallets

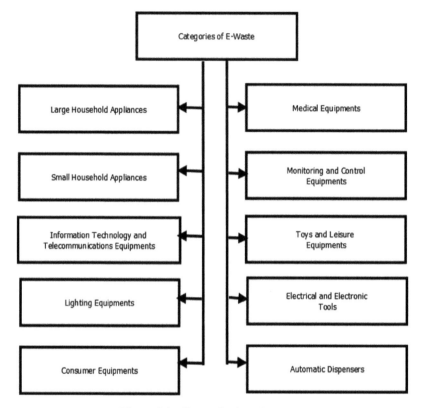

Figure 8.1   Categorization of e-waste.

are loaded into the forklift, and while the forklift passes through the entry dock door, the RFID reader reads the RFID tag pasted on all the pallets. The acquired data is passed to the cloud immediately and stored there for further analysis. The pallets are stored in appropriate locations based on e-waste categorization. When the pallets are dispatched for e-waste recycling, the reader in the exit door dock reads the tag in the pallets when the forklift passes through the exit door and sends the data to the cloud. In the cloud, the received data is compared with the stored data at the time of storing pallets in appropriate locations, and if the match is found, e-waste is dispatched for recycling.

IoT-based e-waste recycling system is developed using NodeMCU and Adafruit IO platform. All e-waste is loaded into proper pallets after e-waste categorization. Based on the category of e-waste, appropriate RFID tags are printed on each pallet. The RFID scanner in the dock doors of the storage

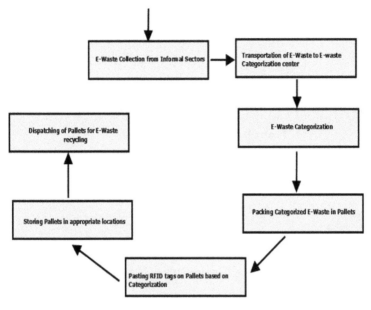

Figure 8.2 Process in e-waste recycling.

center scans the RFID tags in the pallets and stores the information in the Adafruit IO cloud with the help of the ESP8266 Wi-Fi module. This information is displayed in the Adafruit IO dashboard that can be used for analysis. Figure 8.3 shows the hardware setup of the dock door in the storage center.

While forklift pallets pass through the entry dock door of the storage center, the tags in the pallets are getting scanned, and information about e-waste (like storage location and categorization of e-waste) is uploaded to

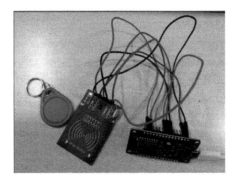

Figure 8.3 Hardware setup in dock door of the storage center.

Figure 8.4   RFID tag information.

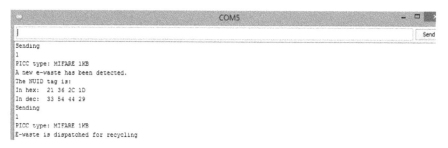

Figure 8.5   E-waste dispatched for recycling.

feeds in the Adafruit cloud as well as printed in serial monitor as shown in Figure 8.4. Based on this information, e-waste is stored in appropriate locations in the storage center.

Similarly, when the pallets are getting dispatched for e-waste recycling, the reader in the exit door dock reads the tag in the pallets when the forklift passes through the exit door and sends the data to the cloud, and e-waste is dispatched, as shown in Figure 8.5.

8.8 Future Trends of IIoT

The eventual fate of IIoT is firmly combined with a pattern known as Industry 4.0 [1]. Industry 4.0 is, basically, the fourth Modern Transformation [3]. Industry 4.0 is where we are today. Industry 4.0 depends on the utilization of associated electronic gadgets – especially IoT gadgets. IoT gadgets will assume a significant part in computerized changes, particularly as associations endeavor to digitize their creation lines and supply chains. Moreover, enormous information investigation will develop to consolidate IIoT information. This will make it workable for associations to recognize changing circumstances progressively and answer in like manner. Even though IIoT gadgets have been around for quite a long time, actual reception is still in its earliest stages. This makes certain to change as 5G turns out to be progressively standard, and the sky is the limit from there, and more associations start to acknowledge how IIoT can help them. Various assets are accessible online for associations that need to find a workable pace on IoT and IIoT. IoT innovations and the Modern Web of Things (WoT) are changing assembling, transportation, and energy. The network permits organizations to create new plans of action and further develop execution through better information-driven bits of knowledge. Get a brief look at 10 patterns you can expect for the eventual fate of IIoT.

More connected devices

The quantity of IIoT-associated gadgets is supposed to be twofold by 2022. The following pages of IoT gadgets are intended to help current arising advances, for example, computerized reasoning, the cloud, AI, portability, augmented reality, and increased reality. These "more astute" gadgets are additionally zeroing in on expanded interoperability to help telemetry information trade among the Web of Things (WoT).

IIoT manufacturing as a service

Modern IoT assembling as a help is another way to deal with assembling in light of a pay-more-only-as-costs-arise model, in which all parts are conveyed or obtained from outsiders. In this course of action, makers consent to keep up with specific norms and particulars yet have the opportunity to pick the particular advancements utilized for execution. Many accept that this pattern will, to some degree, shape the eventual fate of IIoT by 2022.

Cloud and edge computing

The utilization of cloud and edge registering will develop rapidly, with the capacity to gather information from far-off gadgets on the edge of an organization. The most recent age of IIoT gadgets can impart and convey important data and guidelines through neighborhood passages that interface them straightforwardly with the cloud for close quick access by an application or administration. With this sort of execution, inertness is diminished, and reaction time moves along.

Predictive maintenance

One more Modern Web of Things pattern expected in 2022 is proactive upkeep. As IIoT advances keep on propelling, makers can foresee possible disappointments in the functional cycle while a gadget or framework is as of yet on the web and inside its guarantee period. This sort of investigation permits organizations to limit unscheduled free time while further developing general gear execution, lessening costs, and expanding uptime.

Process data management

To remove meaningful experiences from IIoT information, producers need to convey progressed examinations that can rapidly deal with enormous measures of data. This will permit them to gather and dissect immense information from their tasks and individual cycles while safeguarding it against digital assaults. Makers will likewise require many associated gadgets to help the shrewd association of data, examination, and interpretation of information across frameworks.

Digital twins

Computerized twins are a fresher idea in the Modern Web of Things, where they give a virtual portrayal of actual items and empower these items to connect with outside clients. With this innovation, IIoT gadgets can be observed on the web, with the ultimate objective of improving execution, anticipating shortcomings, and diminishing free time. By 2022, advanced twins (virtual imitations) will be utilized as a significant IIoT pattern for checking and overseeing far-off hardware and resources. Producers can likewise utilize computerized twins to unite information from different gadgets and sensors to make a composite perspective on the framework for compelling navigation.

Location tracking

The area following is an IIoT application that empowers organizations to screen the area and state of resources, hardware, and workforce continuously. The area following devices can further develop productivity in assembling tasks by guaranteeing that materials are accessible when required. It likewise empowers makers to comprehend where their items are in the store network, making distinguishing possible issues and deferrals simpler.

Since this innovation utilizes continuous information streams, it will be a significant concentration for IIoT execution in 2022. By gathering data about area and development, this innovation offers knowledge into the whereabouts of resources and merchandise. Coming soon for IIoT, the area following will significantly affect ventures like transportation and strategies.

Blockchain IIoT for supply chain

Makers are expected to satisfy client needs for straightforwardness in their stockpile chains, which can incorporate affirmations and reviews. Blockchain innovation is a successful way that makers can arrive at this objective of straightforwardness by 2022. Blockchain-controlled store network arrangements will likewise assist with keeping up with item trustworthiness throughout the production network process, even after it leaves the industrial facility floor. Blockchain IIoT arrangements will be embraced by producers as a method for giving more prominent perceivability into their stock chains, making it simpler to fulfill client needs for straightforwardness and item quality.

Smart manufacturing

In 2022, shrewd assembling will be a significant IIoT pattern that gives a solitary perspective on all processing plant exercises and assists organizations with working on functional effectiveness. Shrewd assembling can assist makers with distinguishing peculiarities in their work processes to forestall likely issues before they become an issue. With this innovation, makers approach continuous data about the situation with machines and creation processes. This remembers information for engines, siphons, and other gear on the production line floor.

Machine learning

Producers should arrive at savvy conclusions about their items and how they deal with their resources to stay serious. AI can help producers by recognizing designs in cycles and work processes that can prompt more prominent proficiency. Likewise, AI can foresee issues inside an interaction before they end up decreasing free time and work on the plant's general well-being.

In the future, IIoT reception increments to associate more gadgets together, and AI will assume an undeniably significant part in assembling to give ongoing examination. It can likewise assist makers with gaining from their information to find significant experiences that change business results.

8.9 Conclusion

Modern mechanization is a developing pattern that indicates that things are not pulling back. Proceeded with robotization, innovation will drive associations to a consistently more prominent degree of effectiveness and execution. To remain cutthroat in your specific market, you must be one of the leaders.

Organizations should embrace robotization through brilliant gadgets across all endpoints to prevail from here on out. As well as clearing the way for the up-and-coming age of modern computerization, a developing interest in complex mechanical technology and robotization stages is expanding plant proficiency and efficiency. Perpetually, a huge volume of information exists, and the IoT gives the course to smoothing out it in a solid yet noticeable manner. Perceiving new roads and forming innovation to integrate into your organization's tasks straightaway can go quite far toward getting the upper hand.

References

[1] Tan, L.; Wang, N. Future Internet: The Internet of Things. In Proceedings of the 3rd International Conference on Advanced Computer Theory and Engineering, ICACTE 2010, Chengdu, China, 20–22 August 2010; pp. V5-376–V5-380.

[2] Ashton, K. Internet of Things. Page 1—RFID Journal. Available online: https://www.rfidjournal.com/articles/view?4986 (accessed on 2 March 2020).

[3] Okano, M. T. IOT and Industry 4.0: The Industrial new revolution. In Proceedings of the International Conference on Management and Information Systems, ICMIS 2017, Bangkok, Thailand, 25–26 September 2017. Available online:https://www.researchgate.net/publication/31988 1057_IOT_and_Industry_40_The_Industrial_New_Revolution(access edon17September2021).

[4] Rahim, M. A.; Rahman, M. A.; Rahman, M. M.; Asyhari, A. T.; Bhuiyan, M. Z.; Ramasamy, D. Evolution of IOT-enabled connectivity and applications in Automotive Industry: A Review. Veh. Commun. 2021, 27, 100285. [CrossRef]

[5] Rajmohan, R., Kumar, T. A., Pavithra, M., & Sandhya, S. G. (2020). Blockchain: Next-generation technology for industry 4.0. In Blockchain Technology (pp. 177-198). CRC Press. [CrossRef]

[6] Silva, C.; Silva, F.; Sarubbi, J.; Oliveira, T.; Meira, W.; Nogueira, J. Designing mobile content delivery networks for the internet of vehicles. Veh. Commun. 2017, 8, 45–55. [CrossRef]

[7] Lei, T.; Wang, S.; Li, J.; Yang, F. A cooperative route choice approach via virtual vehicle in iov. Veh. Commun. 2017, 9, 281–282. [CrossRef]

[8] Bajaj, R.; Rao, M.; Agrawal, H. Internet of things (IoT) in the smart automotive sector: A review. IOSR J. Comput. Eng. 2018, 9, 36–44.

[9] Fantian, Z.; Chunxiao, L.; Anran, Z.; Xuelong, H. Review of the key technologies and applications in internet of vehicle. In Proceedings of the 2017 13th IEEE International Conference on Electronic Measurement & Instruments (ICEMI), Yangzhou, China, 20–22 October 2017; pp. 228–232.

[10] Adil, M.; Khan, M. K. Emerging IOT applications in Sustainable Smart Cities for COVID-19: Network security and data preservation challenges with future directions. Sustain. Cities Soc. 2021, 75, 103311. [CrossRef] [PubMed]

[11] Mbunge, E. Integrating emerging technologies into COVID-19 contact tracing: Opportunities, challenges and Pitfalls. Diabetes Metab. Syndr. Clin. Res. Rev. 2020, 14, 1631–1636. [CrossRef] [PubMed]

[12] Otoom, M.; Otoum, N.; Alzubaidi, M. A.; Etoom, Y.; Banihani, R. An IOT-based framework for early identification and monitoring of COVID-19 cases. Biomed. Signal Process. Control 2020, 62, 102149. [CrossRef] [PubMed]

[13] Vedaei, S. S.; Fotovvat, A.; Mohebbian, M. R.; Rahman, G. M.; Wahid, K. A.; Babyn, P.; Marateb, H. R.; Mansourian, M.; Sami, R. COVID-safe: An IOT-based system for Automated Health Monitoring and surveillance in post-pandemic life. IEEE Access 2020, 8, 188538–188551. [CrossRef]

[14] Gillis, S. A. What Is Internet of Things (IoT)? Available online: https://internetofthingsagenda.techtarget.com/definition/Internetof-Things-IoT (accessed on 28 December 2021)

[15] Sundmaeker, H.; Guillemin, P.; Friess, P.; Woelfflé, S. Vision and Challenges for Realising the Internet of Things; European Commission Information Society and Media: Brussels, Belgium, 2010. Available online: http://www.internet-of-things-research.eu/pdf/IoT_ Clusterbook_March_2010.pdf (accessed on 7 November 2021).

[16] Perera, C.; Liu, C. H.; Jayawardena, S.; Chen, A. M. A Survey on Internet of Things from Industrial Market Perspective. IEEE Access 2014, 2, 1660–1679. [CrossRef]

[17] Lampropoulos, G.; Siakas, K. V.; Anastasiadis, T. Internet of Things (IoT) in Industry: Contemporary Application Domains, Innovative Technologies and Intelligent Manufacturing. Int. J. Adv. Sci. Res. Eng. 2018, 4, 109–118. [CrossRef]

[18] Atzori, L.; Iera, A.; Morabito, G. The Internet of Things: A survey. Comput. Netw. 2010, 54, 2787–2805. [CrossRef]

[19] ITU Internet Reports 2005: The Internet of Things. Available online: https://www.itu.int/osg/spu/publications/internetofthings/ (accessed on 10 March 2021).

[20] Weber, R. H. Internet of Things–New security and privacy challenges. Comput. Law Secur. Rev. 2020, 26, 23–30. [CrossRef]

9

A Multi-hazard Industry Assessment System Based on Unmanned Aerial Vehicles (UAVs) for Bridges Crossing Seasonal Rivers

Allan J. Wilson[1], A. Pon Bharathi[1], M. Leeban Moses[2], D. Vedha Vinodha[3], K. Kalaiselvi[4], and Kannan Pauliah Nadar[5]

[1]Department of ECE, Amrita College of Engineering and Technology, India
[2]Department of ECE, Bannari Amman Institute of Technology, India
[3]Department of ECE, JCT College of Engineering and Technology, India
[4]Department of ECE, Hindusthan College of Engineering and Technology, India
[5]Department of Electrical and Computer Engineering, Institute of Technology, Jigjiga University, Ethiopia

Abstract

Digital Elevation Models automated multi-hazard performance assessment system based on unmanned aerial vehicles (UAVs) was developed to meet the demand for quick performance evaluation and performance prediction of river crossing RC bridges. In the first stage of the process, the newly developed system obtained the measurements from the UAVs to generate three-dimensional DEMs of the river bed. These DEMs were used to analyze the river bed. The hydraulic model was validated using the Q50 flood event as the basis for the validation. The HEC-RAS software, in conjunction with the flood simulation, provided an estimate of Q5 for the scour depths that a probable flood would cause. After that, the scoured piles were added to the bridge's three-dimensional finite element model (FEM), which was generated automatically using the written code. We were able to determine the flood loads that would be placed on the virtual bridge with the assistance of the

HEC-RAS flood inundation map and the estimated water depths that would be present close to the bridge piers. To conduct the seismic evaluation, nonlinear time history analyses (THAs) were utilized. In addition, multiple-scaled earthquake acceleration records were discovered to act in both principal axes of the bridge simultaneously, which aligns with the surrounding area's seismicity. The Boaçay-II Bridge in Antalya, Turkey, was the case to examine. According to the findings of the analyses, the lateral displacements and the pile internal forces increased as the scour depth increased. Still, the pier column internal forces remained relatively constant throughout the process. Consequently, the seismic displacement and load demands were tracked. They are shifted from the pier columns to the piles in response to the growing scour. As a direct consequence of this, the research report bridge was put to use to verify that the proposed system is applicable.

Keywords: hazard, flood, piles, hydrodynamic, explore, earthquake

9.1 Introduction

Floods are the world's deadliest natural calamity, claiming more lives and causing more casualties than any other natural disaster. Every year, around 1700 people are killed by floods in India, and 39 lakh people are impacted [1]. As a result of climate change and global warming, the frequency of major floods has risen. Recurrent floods have resulted in many deaths and a significant economic loss for the country. Floods are projected to have cost the economy close to 1.5% of GDP [2]. Floods in rural areas are more severe since most people live near rivers. In rural locations, disaster management has been complicated by a lack of infrastructure and a remote location. Because of its ability to collect data more precisely with fewer human interactions, WSNs have gained a lot of interest as a disaster management tool. Recovery efforts will be better coordinated, and data from the field will be collected via the WSN. Unlike their wired counterparts, there are no downtimes for wireless networks in the event of a natural catastrophe.

Additionally, they may be easily scaled and customized to meet specific needs. Using unmanned aerial vehicle (UAVs) to increase surveillance has been the subject of previous studies on WSNs in disaster management [3, 4]. Understanding the fundamental issues WSNs face is necessary before realizing their full potential for disaster management.

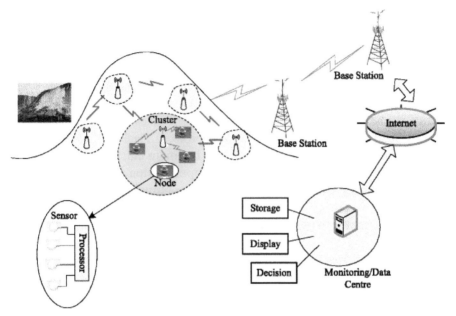

Figure 9.1 Structure of warning system.

UAV-WSN systems for monitoring, exploring, and monitoring large areas of interest are gaining favor. There will be a mix of data coming from the ground, the air, and the Internet with this type of system. To improve the speed of emergency response by making it easier to get to, moving about, and reacting faster [2]. These collaborative methods have been praised as a consequence.

Sensor networks may be utilized in indoor and outdoor areas and in various disciplines to gather data [7]. There have been considerable technological advances due to the advancement of sensor networks and the incorporation of data processing for onboard information. Many publications in the last few years have examined the processing and data transmission capacity, focusing on accessibility and production costs, dependability and scalability, networking protocols, and specific physical limits like autonomy, communication range, and energy consumption.

Environment monitoring, pre-disaster forecast and prevention, early warning system (EWS), emergency preparedness, post-disaster response (such as search and rescue), and structural health monitoring (SHM) have all been successful uses of WSNs when dealing with disasters. We consider SHM an example of disaster monitoring in this work because of its relevance in preventing life loss due to natural catastrophes such as landslides, earth-quakes, and tornadoes. Several approaches and techniques in conjunction with the WSN have been presented to meet the demands of catastrophe moni-toring, including network organizations and architectures, routing algorithms, and sensor node structure. An energy-saving medium access control (ES-MAC) protocol is used in the WSN power consumption process. There was a downside to these methods: the amount of time it takes for many packets to join the network increased. All network protocol stack levels must be addressed to overcome these challenges. The optimum clustering technique and routing protocol are usually formulated as optimization concerns. Recov-ering sensor network management and attaining optimal QoS routing with the least amount of energy consumption and the best path selection for data transmission across the WSN may be achieved with bio-inspired intelligence approaches.

Wireless sensor networks (WSNs) have found energy-efficient routing algorithms to conserve resources while also increasing the network's lifespan. Protocols for detecting paths for transferring observed events help extend the network's lifespan despite sensor node limitations and the complex environments in which they must operate. Health, medical, and agricultural applications began to take hold of WSN as intelligent sensors spread across a wide range of industries and sectors. Achieving energy efficiency and QoS requirements for multiple application domains is a challenging task; however, given the wide variety of traffic flows, changeable network settings, and the ability to regulate network resources of the SNs QoS routing solutions at the energy awareness network layer have attracted a lot of attention since they are well-established. There has been a lot of focus on WSN energy usage due to wireless communication.

This research is aimed to create an automated multi-hazard assessment technique for river-crossing bridges using UAVs. The suggested UAV-based approach may be easily and quickly deployed in areas where several bridges span the same river, with modeling, assessment, and analysis taking up a lim-ited time. Under both seismic excitations and flood loading, the present multi-hazard performance under existing scour circumstances and the anticipated performance under expected scour depths were calculated. The analyses were carried out by the sub-objectives of: (a) examining the effect of scour on the bridge's seismic behavior, (b) using nonlinear explore time history analyses (ETHAs) to observe the effect of scour on pile load and shear capacity, and (c) evaluating the performance of a scoured bridge under flood loading with expected to scour. Section 9.2 introduces similar research in the following sections, including WSN, domain adaption, and flood sensor techniques. In Section 9.3, we go over our framework in further depth. Sections 9.4 and 9.5 discuss the implementation process and undertake extensive experiments. Finally, Section VI brings this work to a conclusion.

9.2 Literature Survey

Wireless sensor networks and remote sensing have played essential roles in this investigation. However, early warning systems and remote sensing have gained more attention in recent years. For early warning systems, Marek et al. [4] utilized WSNs for real-time remote sensing and provided a framework to aid in operating these systems. Pradhan et al. propose using an ensemble to generate flood probability indices. These scientists used geographic information systems (GIS) and remote sensing data (RSD). These models rely on satellite data, which produces a large amount of data, so they demand a sizable amount of resources to operate. Supercomputers can be used to organize and process the massive amounts of data necessary for flood forecasting. Countries with weak economies or low living standards do not have the means to access these materials.

Naji et al. proposed an energy-efficient, decentralized, hierarchical, cluster-based routing strategy for WSNs. To lessen the load on the power supply from sending and receiving control messages, they employ techniques like clustering and multichip routing [6]. Based on the results of the research by Kumar et al., several improvements to the LEACH routing protocol for WSN have been proposed [7]. Based on the LEACH protocol, Aravapalli et al. [8] proposed a hierarchical protocol with enhanced power efficiency and lifetime for the network. The team led by Dr. Aravapalli and colleagues developed this method. A node's energy level is irrelevant in LEACH; the cluster head (CH) is randomly selected so that any node can become CH regardless of its starting state. This affects the network's resilience or ability to function normally despite disruption and repair. Avi et al. proposed a tracking method for identifying and following people in thermal infrared images, which relied on a particle filter in conjunction with background reduction [9]. A group of researchers led by Daanoune et al. formulated an algorithm for tracking people has been proposed to assess the efficacy of region-based passive infrared motion sensors and their applicability in security systems [10]. These algorithms' numerous advantages necessitate a sizable investment of computational resources for their deployment on individual sensor nodes. To accomplish data hiding, WSNs employ EC-OU, which results in more communication overhead. Girao et al. carried out this study [11]. There was a hit to network performance due to the SLEACH algorithm methodology, but Sec Leach Oliveira et al. [12] used symmetric essential cryptography techniques to make the network more secure. Both fundamental methods have been demonstrated to be safe and efficient for transmitting data. After generating a symmetric key, Hu et al. [13] hashed it using the ESODR algorithm. But when image transmission is added, the size of the rudimentary microscopes shrinks dramatically. The EDRLEACH approach is one of many that rely on the SLEACH method. ORLEACH, proposed by Raj [14], increases the time limit and the ratio of utilized energy while providing a practical means of avoiding the need for energy consumption. A proposal for a chaotic map and an ECC encryption scheme was presented by Shankar and Elhoseny [15]. Using elliptic curve cryptography, Sumalatha and Nandalal [16] created the attribute-based encryption method. We used the user's private keys and ciphertext annotated with various metadata tags. The proposed method has been shown to outperform the state-of-the-art alternatives. Chen et al. [17] ciphered the image using lightweight ciphers (LWCs). The proposed security model offers a method to select the best possible key. In addition, the proposed method requires the least time to produce the key for image decryption. The existing algorithms regarding security accuracy regarding input images are Horse, Baboon, Barbara, and Lena. Farouk et al. [18] proposed a fuzzy-based cross-layer security approach to identify malicious nodes that disrupt packet delivery. Installing false monitoring is aided by the enhanced convolutional neural network (ECNN). Jiang et al. [19] favored the elliptic curve Hill cipher method to ensure security in WSNs. The permutation of keys aids in improving their size for the selection of image matrix size. Because of a novel framework that uses clusters and the ECC method, as well as a cluster-based encrypting routing algorithm, the authors achieved increased security, decreased setback, and improved packet release percentage. Yavari et al. present a remote user validation strategy for WSNs based on active ID and temporal credentials [20]. The authors preferred Burrows–Abadi–Needham (BAN) logic for scheme validation. The proposed techniques are superior regarding low-energy usage and computational cost for authentication. Rao et al. [21] showed that a hierarchical K-means cluster formation with knowledge QoS may be used to choose firefly heads for efficient energy use. QoS parameters are reduced when data is sent between the node and its destination. Using the protocol, KF-MAC was used to assess QoS factors like bandwidth, latency, and jitter. Even with minimal power consumption, the KF-MAC protocol could not transport data without encountering collisions.

Quality of service (QoS) and energy efficiency routing based on data categorization was presented by Zhang et al. [22] for industrial WSNs. Quality of service and energy-efficient methods were used to transmit data from industrial sensors (QoS). The research shows that data from events can be sent in real-time with high reliability. The QoS parameter, however, did not improve results regarding either network life or latency. A qualified and heterogeneous cluster routing protocol (QHCR) has been developed, as stated by Amjad et al. [23]. In addition to reducing network energy consumption, this protocol offers the fastest path for time-critical programs. Variable-power WSNs reduced latency in time-critical applications and increased system stability. Actuators and WSNs can benefit from latency- and power-aware QoS-aware routing protocol as stated by Yahiaoui et al. [24]. Each cluster within the network is reported to a chief who oversaw the entire system (CHs). Because of this, the network's dependability is improved, and communication delays are cut down significantly. Both communication latency and energy consumption were found to have decreased noticeably.

Attributable to the work of Gao et al. [25], Mobile Ad Hoc Networks (MANETs) now have distributed trust measures that can adjust to their surroundings. Counting the number of data packets exchanged between nodes, forecasting trust based on the path that such value took, and scaling total trust by comparing its historical significance to its projected value are all parts of the proposed method for increasing trust in communication. Direct trust can be calculated by comparing the requested and extended trust. Trust between nodes was calculated using a combination of direct trust and propagation distance. The results of the studies reveal that the suggested technique effectively prevented malicious node attacks. For mobile education, Gao et al. [25], have presented an energy-balanced uneven clustering routing technique, considering network splits. It has been recommended that data from each network node be sent to the base station via nodes closer to it, such that nodes near the base station form a circle around it and split the network region based on how far away they are from one another. They also created unequal clusters by generating a variety of viable radii, which helps to balance the network's energy consumption. The protocol's testing results show that it can minimize node mortality rates, extend network life, and offset each node's power loss.

The technique of intelligent environment monitoring based on WSNs is examined in this study, as well as the need for such a sensor monitoring system and the hurdles we must overcome to achieve it.

9.3 Methodology

As shown in Figure 9.2, the system depicts the approach for using the suggested method for analyzing hazard bridges. As shown, four main procedures were defined: (a) UAV-derived DEM generation for seasonal flights via 3D reconstruction using the Structure from Motion algorithm (SM), (b) hydraulic analyses using flood-induced scour analyses and flood load/scour depth estimation by HEC-RAS 2D hydraulic modeling, (c) automated 3D FEM generation for the inspected bridge by SAP2000, and (d) multi-hazard assessment methods using flood loading as well as earthquake excitation. The diagram outlined the sub-procedures for getting the DEM, 3D FEM, conducting hydraulic studies, and assessing the bridge's multi-hazard performance.

9.3.1 UAV-derived DEM generation by 3D style

The methodology utilized to build a high-resolution DEM incorporated the point cloud production process using UAV-derived aerial pictures and the SM technique rather than standard survey methods. One hundred and fifty-two ground control points (GCPs) were taken along the river region, stream channel area of approximately 18 km and along the inspected bridge during the UAV flights with real-time kinematic (RTK) GPS measurements in the field via a 28 mm focal length lens with a 78.8° field of view at f/2.2 via

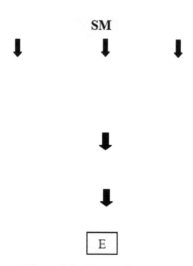

Figure 9.2 Proposed system.

152 GCPs were taken along the river region. The average flight altitude was set at 70 m, the overlapping ratios for both the frontal and lateral directions optimized at 85% and a middle ground sampling distance (GSD) of 12 cm per pixel was ensured in order to obtain the 3D surfaces in the riverbed and bridge regions with high accuracy. After camera alignment and reference, the resulting accuracy in the created point cloud is evaluated during model creation. Planimetric and altimetric accuracies of 0.050 and 0.080 m, respectively, were achieved.

Furthermore, the scour depth under bridge piers was calculated using manual flight height designations with camera angles ranging from 45 to 55 degrees nadir-off angles. The DEM of the riverbed was created after the dense point cloud was created and before the mesh model was created. Change detection analyses were performed using the ESRI ArcGIS AddIn-Geomorphic Change Detection Tool GCD v7.2 and point cloud comparison to trace changes in riverbed morphology.

To put the SM method into action, the photogrammetric software Pix4D was utilized. Clusters of motion-integrated two-dimensional images were used to construct three-dimensional (3D) structural models of terrain, buildings, and landforms, and their corresponding geometry, camera position, and orientation data were simultaneously solved. This allowed the models to be constructed quickly and accurately. Following the edges and corners of remotely sensed objects from one image to the next helped establish a connection between the pictures, and feature trajectories provided evidence for the object's location in three dimensions. Using the high-resolution orthophotos and dense point clouds collected from the riverbed, we could estimate the scour depths that were present close to the piers and piles of the examined bridge. The explore depths measured at the ports were used as input data in developing a 3D FEM of the bridge's substructure. The aforementioned UAV-based measuring methodologies are only applicable and helpful for shallow river systems with dry riverbeds for most of the year. This is the only type of river system in which these methodologies can be used. As a result, measurements of bridges located on deep-water rivers are outside the scope of this research.

9.3.2 Hydrodynamic analyses

The river basin DEM was immediately imported into the HEC-RAS program, designed for 2D hydrodynamic assessments of rivers with multi-way and non-prismatic cross sections to estimate flood water depth, flood velocity, flood load, and appropriate scour depth. The maximum discharge for the region was calculated using the Hydrologic Engineering Center's Hydrodynamic Modeling System (HEC-HMS) rainfall–runoff model. Tropical Rainfall Monitoring Mission (TRMM) satellite, which was developed to provide real-time and high-resolution rainfall data in the tropics and sub-tropics, can be used to track rainfall–runoff changes in rivers where the stream gauge network is insufficient and the intervals of temporal records are inconsistent.

9.3.3 3D FEM generation

The SAP2000 programmer was used to create the 3D FEM for the RC bridge, which included substructure components such as UAV scour depth observations and HEC-RAS scour depth estimates for the bridge piles. Nonlinear 3D beam elements were created to describe RC components like piers and piles and linear springs for elastomeric bearings. Regarding the project designs, the composite deck was treated as a linear element. As a result, instead of manually specifying the bridge members and soil spring characteristics in SAP2000 software (Figure 9.2), an input file was prepared using MATLAB.

9.3.4 Tectonic evaluation

Nonlinear ETHA was carried out in the seismic evaluation utilizing the 3D FEM of the bridge, which directly integrated the nonlinear and inelastic load-deformation characteristics of the bridge elements. The bridge was subjected to 11 lateral earthquake excitations, represented by ground motion acceleration histories chosen from the Pacific Earthquake Resistant Research Center ground motion database as compatible with the bridge's location concerning nearby faults, fault mechanisms, and site-specific geotechnical characteristics. As a result, the recordings were amplitude scaled so that the average of the suite's maximum direction spectra did not fall below 90% of the target elastic design spectrum for the 0.2L1–2L1 time range. According to the Turkish Earthquake Code, the target spectrum was established as the 5% damped adaptable design spectrum for the location. L1 denotes the first basic period of the bridge. Simultaneously in the longitudinal and transverse directions of the bridge, scaled acceleration data were enforced.

9.3.5 Soil modeling

The number, thickness, kind, distinctive features, and number of segments of each soil layer were utilized as the critical parameters in the created code for the input file. The soil deposits around the substructure components (i.e., pier columns, abutments, and piles) were described by lateral and vertical bidirectional nonlinear spring elements using *py* and *tz* curves, respectively, to integrate soil structure interaction (SSI). The preliminary factors used to define the curve features for sand and limestone layers at a given depth are the water table height, soil type, and relative height of the soil layer to the ground surface. Each soil layer was separated into numerous soil segments for multilayer soil deposition, with the nonlinear soil spring characteristics presumed constant along the way. Because the soil spring properties were described in terms of the difference between the mid-height of the soil segment and the ground surface, the new ground level after scouring was used to determine the soil spring properties. The substructure's piles and other underground portions were designed to have the same number of segments as the soil layers to ensure compatibility and direct assignment of soil spring characteristics to the bridge components.

The ordinates of the *py* curves (i.e., *p* values) at the mid-height of each soil segment were computed by multiplying the height of the pile segment under consideration by the ordinates of the *py* curves (i.e., *p* values). After multiplying the prescribed vertical unit resistances by the surface area of the pile segment, curve characteristics were assigned to the mid-height of the pile segments. The lateral and vertical resistance supplied by each soil segment was given to the appropriate pile segment using bidirectional and nonlinear spring elements. A similar procedure was used on bridge piers and abutments that were wholly or partially immersed in the soil. The impact of passive or active earth pressures was neglected since the *py* curves for the abutments were derived in both longitudinal and transverse orientations. To organize the soil spring assignments along the piles, the input file employed the outputs of seasonally observed scour depths or predicted flood-induced scour depths. The soil spring assignments (*py* and *tz* curves) were not considered for the scoured sections of the piles.

As a result of the altered ground level, soil type, and relative height to ground level after scouring, the soil spring characteristics were computed and allocated to the pile segments below the scour depth. Furthermore, the negative impact of regularly aligned piles on pile groups' lateral resistance was recorded using *p*-multipliers, which represented the worsening of lateral soil resistance when shadowing was considered.

Figure 9.3 illustrates the modeling stages used to convert meteorological data into flood inundation data that is important to the effects on various sectors of society. Figure 9.4 is an example of output from the modeling chain

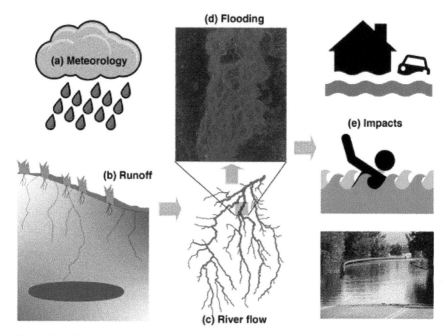

Figure 9.3   Modeling procedures to access flood consequences from meterological effects.

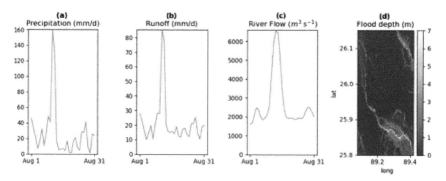

Figure 9.4   Model data visualization: (a) precipitation (input), (b) runoff, (c) mizuRoute river flow, and (d) flood depth.

for a flood event in a small watershed. The following are the modeling phases in this framework.

- preparation of meteorological input;
- rainfall–runoff modeling: we use the modular modeling framework FUSE (Framework for Understanding Structural Errors).

To develop an ensemble of conceptual hydrological models:

- river routing: we utilize a stand-alone river routing programmer to predict flow along river channels;
- flood inundation modeling: we utilize a 2D flood inundation model to evaluate flood danger.

9.3.6 Bridge modeling

The created code described all bridge members, including the deck (slab and supporting girders), elastomeric bearings, pier caps, piers, abutments, pile caps, and piles. 3D beam components were used to simulate the piles, pier columns, pier caps, and supported girders that sat on elastomeric bearings. Elastomeric bearings were also conceptualized as link members that provided axial and shear stiffness. The existence of the RC shear keys between the rafters, however, precluded lateral motions. The RC bridge deck, which consisted of an RC slab and evenly spaced pre-stressed concrete (PC) girders, was represented as a linear 3D beam element with the same cross-section area, the moment of inertia, weight, and mass as the composite superstructure.

Furthermore, at abutments and piers, longitudinally oriented gap components designated at the end of each girder reflected the spacing between two successive rafters. Due to girder hammering, very high rigidity was expected after closing the stipulated gap length. Firm beam components were used to simulate the pile caps, guaranteeing a rigid connection between the piers and the piles.

The pile cap connection was viewed as one of the plastic hinge points for heaps. Sequential pushover investigations in longitudinal and transverse directions and the continuous recording of the maximum bending moment region throughout the pile's length were used to determine the likely locations of all additional hinges. It was determined that the effective stiffness of most of the structural components was half of their gross stiffness during pushover tests. Plastic hinges' lateral and curvature capacities were determined using standard section studies, considering the bridge's position along it and its axial forces during pushover analyses. Additionally, each axial stress level and orientation angle of the member were bi-linearized, allowing it to be included in plastic hinge requirements. These plastic hinge lengths were assumed to match the depth of cross-sectional area for ease of calculation.

Federal highway administration (FHWA) computed the flood loads operating on the submerged bridge deck using the primary parameters of free stream velocity (v), inundation ratio (h), water density (*), and deck

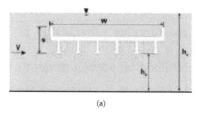
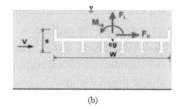

(a)   (b)

Figure 9.5   (a) Parameters that have been set; (b) the pressures and moments acting on the flooded bridge deck.

dimensions (U, T, and s for deck width, length, and height, respectively) as shown in Figure 9.5 (a).

The inundation ratio eqn (9.1) was calculated by dividing the height difference between the free surface during a flood (h_u) and the lowest chord of the bridge deck (h_b) by the deck height (s), including the battlements.

$$h^* = \frac{h_u - h_b}{s}. \tag{9.1}$$

Higher inundation ratios indicate that the bridge will be submerged more. Following the hydrodynamic analyses, the stream velocity and estimated water level following a flood event were determined.

$$C_T = F_T \left(0.5\rho r^2 TU\right) \tag{9.2}$$

$$N_{gc} = F_N \left(0.5\rho r^2 TU^2\right). \tag{9.3}$$

After the hydraulic analyses, the computed parameters of floodwater depth and floodwater velocity were utilized to determine the flood loads in the created input file. The flood loads were computed by multiplying the surface area of the bridge deck and the scoured sections with the expected inverted triangle pressure distribution along the depth while considering flooding.

Nonlinear ETHA was carried out in the seismic evaluation utilizing the 3D FEM of the bridge, which directly integrated the nonlinear and inelastic load-deformation characteristics of the bridge elements. The bridge was subjected to 11 lateral earthquake excitations, which were represented by ground motion acceleration histories chosen from the Pacific Earthquake Engineering Research Center ground motion database as being compatible with the bridge's location in relation to nearby faults, fault mechanisms, and site-specific geotechnical characteristics.

As a result, the recordings were amplitude scaled so that the average of the suite's full-direction spectra did not fall below 90% of the target elastic design spectrum for the 0.2T1–2T1 time range. According to the Turkish Earthquake Code, the target spectrum was established as the location's 5% damped elastic design spectrum. The first basic period of the bridge is denoted by T1. Simultaneously, in the longitudinal and transverse directions of the bridge, scaled acceleration data were enforced.

9.4 Result and Discussion

The DEM of the river basin was obtained through the SM-derived point clouds and top-view elevation model for the case study bridge by first using high-resolution UAV imageries and combining GCPs acquired along the river and the bridge. Between November 2016 and January 2021, 11 UAV flights were used to detect seasonal variations in scour depths around bridge piers. The examined bridge was photographed using seasonal UAV high-resolution images in Figure 9.6.

The analyzed bridge was exposed to ETHA following the nonlinear dead load scenario with the selected and scaled suite of ground motion records with the desired spectrum to assess the present performance of the bridge (Table 9.1 and Figure 9.6).

9.4.1 Scour depth and flood load calculations by hydraulic modeling

The Boaçay River basin border was recovered using TanDEM-X (TerraSAR-X add-on for Digital Elevation Measurement) digital elevation data with a

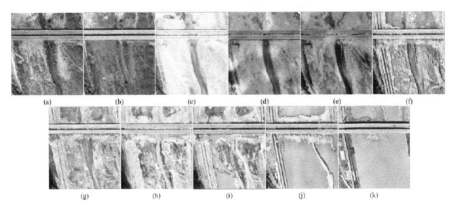

Figure 9.6 UAV images taken between the seasons (a)–(k) November 2016 and January 2021.

Table 9.1   Ground motion collection.

Earthquake	Station	M_w	R_{JB} km	V_{S30} m/s	Comp.	PGA g	PGV cm/s	PGD cm	Scale factor
Imp. Val. 06	Chihuahua	6.5	7.3	242	012	0.270	24.8	9.3	2.25
					282	0.254	29.9	7.7	
Imp. Val. 06	E1 Cent.Arr.#11	6.5	12.6	196	140	0.365	36.0	25.1	1.89
					230	0.380	44.6	21.3	
Imp. Val. 06	El Cent.Diff.Arr.	6.5	5.1	202	270	0.352	75.5	57.1	1.37
					360	0.481	40.9	16.4	
Superst.Hills 02	El Cent.Imp.Co.	6.5	18.2	192	000	0.357	48.0	19.3	1.90
					090	0.260	41.8	21.9	
Superst.Hills 02	Poe Road	6.5	11.2	317	270	0.475	41.2	7.7	1.96
					360	0.286	29.0	11.4	
Superst.Hills 02	Westm.Fire Sta.	6.5	13.0	194	090	0.173	23.5	15.0	2.33
					180	0.211	32.3	22.3	
Landers	Coolwater	7.3	19.7	353	000	0.283	27.6	18.2	1.73
					090	0.417	43.4	15.2	
Kobe	Amagasaki	6.9	11.3	256	000	0.276	33.6	26.6	1.38
					090	0.327	44.8	23.8	
Kobe	Tadoka	6.9	31.7	312	000	0.296	24.5	7.6	2.96
					090	0.194	14.7	10.3	
Kocaeli	Duzce	7.5	13.6	282	180	0.312	58.8	44.0	1.32
					270	0.364	56.6	25.0	
Duzce	Bolu	7.1	120	294	000	0.739	55.9	25.6	0.94
					090	0.806	65.9	13.1	

spatial resolution of 12 m before hydraulic modeling (Figure 9.7 (a)). The flow network, sub-basin boundaries, and adjoint basins by which the basin boundaries were obtained were disclosed by identifying flow directions and flow concentration zones (Figure 9.7 (b)). The day TRMM streamflow was defined with a spatial resolution of 0.25° (about 25 km) in latitude and longitude for each grid, and it was related to its corresponding region in the basin borders, which comprised the whole UAV measured part in the Boaçay River basin. Between 1998 and 2021, daily average rainfall time data were acquired from the TRMM satellite inside the TRMM grid, representing the study region for flood assessments.

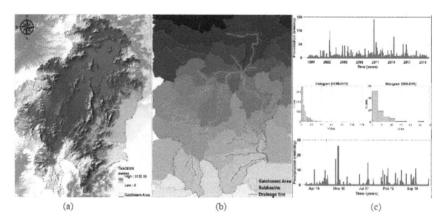

(a)   (b)   (c)

Figure 9.7   (a) Digital elevation data from TanDEM-X; (b) drainage lines with sub-basins.

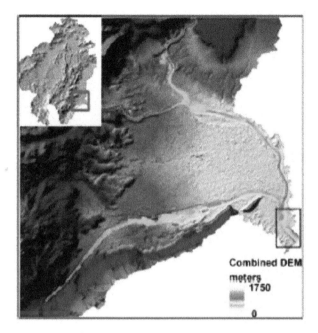

Figure 9.8 2D hydraulic model of the research area.

The UAV-derived surface models were coupled with a resampled DEM digital surface model to be utilized in HEC-RAS 2D hydraulic modeling to offer additional spatial information in the floodplain and to correctly represent all of the basin areas in the model Figure 9.8.

After considering the nonlinear loading history owing to later flood and dead load events, the bridge was subjected to ETHA for multi-hazard evaluation. The bridge FEM was created in this example using the maximum scour depth results from the HEC-RAS scour analysis.

Figure 9.9 shows the flood loading; the bridge members showed a linear elastic response. When comparing the existing condition of the bridge to the multi-hazard condition, the displacement demand (U_X and U_Y) rose in both directions. It nearly doubled in the transverse direction (y).

The flood-induced scour was demonstrated to have no impact on the internal forces of the pier columns (Figure 9.10 (a) and (b)). However, shear details in the transverse direction (V_y) were found to have increased somewhat from 1600 to 2200 kN, as illustrated in Figure 9.10. For the abutment shear walls, the moments along the longitudinal axis (i.e., strong axis) (Mx) were seen to almost quadruple from 7000 to 14,000 kNm.

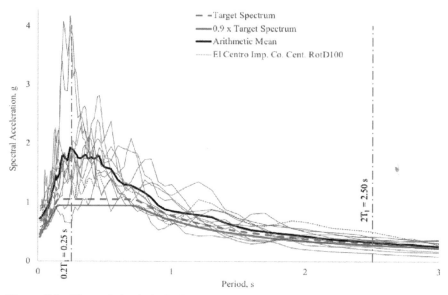

Figure 9.9   The scaled suite's RotD100 spectrum, the selected record, and the desired spectrum.

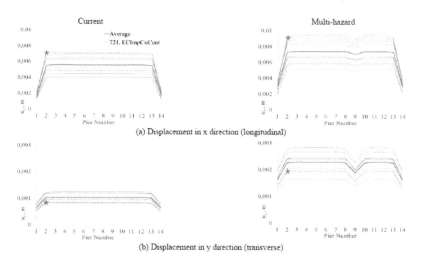

Figure 9.10   For current and multi-hazard circumstances, the maximum pier column displacement at the higher ends.

For the multi-hazard situation, a significant fluctuation in internal forces was seen concerning the rise in scour depth (Figure 9.11 (a) and (b)). Due to

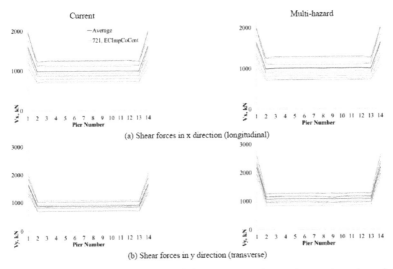

(a) Shear forces in x direction (longitudinal)

(b) Shear forces in y direction (transverse)

Figure 9.11 For current and multi-hazard circumstances, the maximum pier column internal forces.

the stiffness degradation in piles caused by the loss of the surrounding soil layers after scouring, the internal stresses increased by two to six times. This was especially true for shear forces in the bridge's longitudinal direction (V_x) (Figure 9.12). The lateral response of the bridge, considering plastic hinge locations and the hysteretic behavior of the selected bridge members, was monitored during seismic loading by ETHA using the El Centro Imp—Co. Cent. ground motion record, which was chosen at random from the ground motion suite.

The rotation performance levels of plastic hinges were tracked using ASCE/SEI 41-17, which considered rotation limits from A to E, with immediate occupancy (IO), life safety (LS), and collapse prevention (CP) limit states as acceptance criteria. All pier columns were monitored for rotation levels between IO and LS beyond yielding in the current state, although the abutments and piles were proven to respond elastically. In addition to the pier columns, several of the banks in the multi-hazard scenario showed inelastic reaction via plastic hinging with a lower rotation level across B and IO than the piers panels.

Between A and B, the abutment's lateral reaction remained elastic. The pier column and pile in Pier 2 were chosen for lateral response comparison in terms of hysteretic moment – rotation behavior under bi-directional lateral

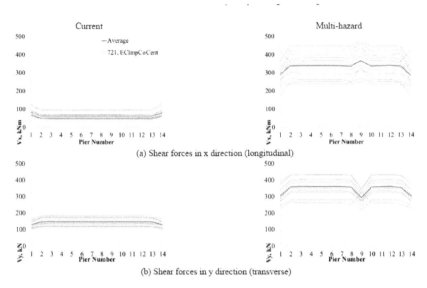

(a) Shear forces in x direction (longitudinal)

(b) Shear forces in y direction (transverse)

Figure 9.12   For current and multi-hazard scenarios, the maximum pile of internal forces.

cycles due to the selected record to track rotation levels. The chosen members' lateral displacement, pier column internal force, and pile internal force variations were shown (represented as the red star) with the selected ground motion record. Regarding the moments along the x-axis, which defined the bridge's transverse behavior, the pier column and pile were found to be in the elastic range for the present situation. However, minimal plastic hinging was detected for the bank under the multi-hazard situation. The pier column displayed inelastic behavior with a significant plastic rotation level in the longitudinal response (i.e., moments around the y-axis). Still, the pile exhibited elastic behavior in the current circumstances. The pier column, on the other hand, displayed an inelastic reaction with a lower plastic rotation level under the multi-hazard situation, as the piling was found to reach the inelastic range with modest plastic hinging.

As a result, the seismic load and displacement demands for the bridge with a more considerable scour depth were demonstrated to migrate from the pier columns to the piles after exploring in a multi-hazard scenario. This is because in the absence of soil after researching, the internal forces that were shared by the pile and the surrounding soil before grinding were alone resisted by the piles. As a result, it may be deduced that following scouring, the internal pressures previously resisted by the soil were transferred to the piles. This behavior resulted in a rising pile of internal forces (Figure 9.11 (a) and (b)) and, as a result, increased rotations and lateral displacements (Figure 9.9), whereas the pier column internal forces remained relatively constant (Figure 9.10). Furthermore, increased pile flexibility following the removal of adjacent soil layers resulted in increased lateral displacements. The lateral stresses operating in the longitudinal direction caused plastic hinging in the pier columns instead of the pile group in the examined bridge due to the arrangement of the columns such that their weak axis corresponded with the bridge's transverse axis.

Furthermore, the flood lateral forces were resisted by the pier columns' strong axis, and the scoured pile group opposed the flood loads after exploring, resulting in a linear elastic response because the flood loads were found insignificant in terms of the pier column and pile group's lateral load capacities. As a result, it was determined that scour significantly impacted the behavior of laterally laden piles and that the interaction of bridge components and soil includes multi-hazard performance evaluations of bridges.

9.5 Conclusion

This work proposed an automated UAV-based bridge multi-hazard assessment system for RC bridges crossing seasonal rivers under flood loading and seismic excitations, including the impacts of scouring. Because the UAV-based measuring approach proved unable to DEM buildings in submerged regions, the proposed method can only be used on bridges located on rivers with a dry riverbed for most of the year. The floodwater depths were determined after the HSC-RAS hydrodynamic assessments, and the consequent flood-induced scour depths were derived to forecast the multi-hazard performance. After that, the bridge FEM was created automatically. Finally, after flood loading, nonlinear ETHA was used to assess the bridge's multi-hazard performance with flood-induced scour depths, considering lateral displacements, internal forces, and plastic rotations. Furthermore, offering strong security to the WSN environment motivates the creation of security algorithms.

References

[1] Bhatt, Harshil, G. Pranesh, Samarth Shankar, and ShriyashHaralikar. "Wireless Sensor Networks for Optimisation of Search and Rescue Management in Floods." In *2021 IEEE International Conference*

on Electronics, Computing and Communication Technologies (CON-NECT), pp. 1-6. IEEE, 2021.

[2] Al-Mashhadani, Mohammad A., Mustafa MaadHamdi, and Ahmed Shamil Mustafa. "Role and challenges of using a UAV-aided WSN monitoring system in large-scale sectors." In *2021 3rd International Congress on Human-Computer Interaction, Optimization and Robotic Applications (HORA)*, pp. 1-5. IEEE, 2021.

[3] Prasad, Devendra, Afshan Hassan, Deepak Kumar Verma, PradeeptaSarangi, and Sunny Singh. "Disaster Management System using Wireless Sensor Network: A Review." In *2021 International Conference on Computational Intelligence and Computing Applications (ICCICA)*, pp. 1-6. IEEE, 2021.

[4] Kumar, P. Praveen, T. Ananth Kumar, Pavithra Muthu, Rajmohan Rajendirane, and R. Dinesh Jackson Samuel. "Security Analysis of UAV Communication Protocols: Solutions, Prospects, and Encounters." In The Internet Of Drones, pp. 167-190. Apple Academic Press, 2022.

[5] H. Mojaddadi, H. Pradhan Biswajeet Nampak, N. Ahmad, and A. H. b. Ghazali, "Ensemble machine learning- based geospatial approach for flood risk assessment using multi-sensor remote-sensing data and gis," Geomatics, Natural Hazards, and Risk, vol. 8, pp. 1080–1102, 2 2017. DOI 10.1080/19475705.2017.1294113.

[6] M. Sabet and H. R. Naji, "A decentralized energy efficient hierarchical cluster-based routing algorithm for wireless sensor networks," AEU - International Journal of Electronics and Communications, vol. 69, pp. 790–799, 2015. DOI: 10.1016/j.aeue.2015.01.002.

[7] Kumar, T. Ananth, S. Arunmozhi Selvi, R. S. Rajesh, and G. Glorindal. "Safety wing for industry (SWI 2020)–an advanced unmanned aerial vehicle design for safety and security facility management in industries." In Industry 4.0 Interoperability, Analytics, Security, and Case Studies, pp. 181-198. CRC Press, 2021.

[8] R. K. Kodali and N. K. Aravapalli, "Multi-level leach protocol using ns-3," 2014 International Conference on Circuits, Systems, Communication and Information Technology Applications, CSCITA 2014, pp. 132–137, 2014. DOI: 10.1109/CSCITA.2014.6839248.

[9] Avi, Alessandro, Matteo Zuccatti, Matteo Nardello, Nicola Conci, and DavideBrunelli. "Infrared dataset generation for people detection through the superimposition of different camera sensors." In *Proceedings of the IEEE/CVF International Conference on Computer Vision*, pp. 307-316. 2021.

[10] Daanoune, Ikram, Abdennaceur Baghdad, and AbdelhakimBallouk. "Improved LEACH protocol for increasing the lifetime of WSNs." *International Journal of Electrical & Computer Engineering (2088-8708)* 11, no. 4 (2021).

[11] E. Mykletun, J. Girao, and D. Westhoff, "Public key-based crypto schemes for data concealment in wireless sensor networks," IEEE Int. Conf. Commun., vol. 5, no. c, pp. 2288–2295, 2016, doi: 10.1109/ICC.2006.255111.

[12] Oliveria, L., A. Ferreira, M. A. Vilaca, H. Wong, M. Bern, R. Dahab, and A. A. F. Loureiro. "SecLEACH-On the security of clustered sensor network." Journal of Signal Processing 87, no. 12 (2007): 2882-2895.

[13] D. Wu, G. Hu, G. Ni, W. Li, and Z. Zhang, "Research on secure routing protocols in wireless sensor networks," Chinese J. Sensors Actuators, vol. 21, no. 7, pp. 1195–1201, 2018.

[14] Raj, E. D. (2012). An Efficient Cluster Head Selection Algorithm for Wireless Sensor Networks–Edrleach. IOSR Journal of Computer Engineering (IOSRJCE), 2(2), 39-44.

[15] Shankar, K., & Elhoseny, M. (2019). Secure Image Transmission in Wireless Sensor Network (WSN) Applications. Springer International Publishing.

[16] Sumalatha, M. S., Nandalal, V. An intelligent cross-layer security based fuzzy trust calculation mechanism (CLS-FTCM) for securing wireless sensor network (WSN). J Ambient Intell Human Comput (2020). https://doi.org/10.1007/s12652-020-01834-1

[17] C. T. Chen, C. C. Lee, and I. C. Lin, "Efficient and secure three-party mutual authentication key agreement protocol for WSNs in IoT environments," PLoS One, vol. 15, no. 4, pp. 1–28, 2020, doi: 10.1371/journal.pone.0232277.

[18] Elhoseny, M., Farouk, A., Batle, J., Shehab, A., & Hassanien, A. E. (2017). Secure image processing and transmission schema in a cluster-based wireless sensor network. In Handbook of research on machine learning innovations and trends (pp. 1022-1040). IGI Global.

[19] Q. Jiang, J. Ma, F. Wei, Y. Tian, J. Shen, and Y. Yang, "An untraceable temporal-credential-based two-factor authentication scheme using ECC for wireless sensor networks," J. Netw. Comput. Appl., vol. 76, pp. 37–48, 2016, doi: 10.1016/j.jnca.2016.10.001.

[20] A. Yavari, D. Georgakopoulos, P. R. Stoddart and M. Shafiei, "Internet of Things-based Hydrocarbon Sensing for Real-time Environmental Monitoring," 2019 IEEE 5th World Forum on Internet of Things (WF-IoT), 2019, pp. 729-732, doi: 10.1109/WFIoT. 2019.8767320.

[21] Rao, Meena, and Neeta Singh. "Energy efficient QoS aware hierarchical KF-MAC routing protocol in MANET." *Wireless Personal Communications* 101, no. 2 (2018): 635-648.

[22] Zhang, W., Liu, Y., Han, G., Feng, Y., & Zhao, Y. (2018). An energy-efficient and QoS-aware routing algorithm based on data classification for industrial wireless sensor networks. *IEEE Access*, 6, 46495-46504.

[23] Amjad, M., Afzal, M. K., Umer, T., & Kim, B. S. (2017). QoS-aware and heterogeneously clustered routing protocol for wireless sensor networks. *IEEE Access*, 5, 10250-10262.

[24] Yahiaoui, S., Omar, M., Bouabdallah, A., Natalizio, E., & Challal, Y. (2018). An energy-efficient and QoS-aware routing protocol for wireless sensor and actuator networks. *AEU-International Journal of Electronics and Communications*, 83, 193-203.

[25] Zhang, D. G., Gao, J. X., Liu, X. H., Zhang, T., & Zhao, D. X. (2019). A novel approach of distributed & adaptive trust metrics for MANET. *Wireless Networks*, 25(6), 3587-3603.

10

Air Quality Prediction using Machine Learning Techniques for Intelligent Monitoring Systems

Marimuthu Rajendran Ezhilkumar[1], Singaram Karthikeyan[2], Dimplekumar N. Chalishajar[3], and Rajappa Ramesh[4]

[1]Department of Civil Engineering,
Sri Krishna College of Engineering and Technology, India
[2]Centre for Environmental Studies, Anna University, India
[3]Department of Applied Mathematics,
Virginia Military Institute (VMI), USA
[4]Department of Science & Humanities,
Sri Krishna College of Engineering and Technology, India
E-mail: ezhil.1990.kumar@gmail.com; ksingaram @gmail.com;
dipu17370@gmail.com; rameshrajappa1982@gmail.com

Abstract

Real-time large data collection in air quality studies was found to be complicated. To overcome such scenarios, machine learning and IoT systems help researchers and regulatory systems to improve air quality and make decisions. This study has used the ANN approach to predict the air quality from the measured data for a street in Chennai, an urban metropolitan of Tamil Nadu. This study studied particulate pollutants of size 2.5 and 10 microns in street canyons at three different heights above ground level. Also, three different street canyons were chosen in this experimental investigation. Results showed that the concentration of the pollutants was not similar at all heights in all three streets. Seasonal changes were also analyzed as the monitoring period was one completed year. No similar profiles were identified among the seasons in all three street geometries. However, a minimum concentration load was observed during summer than other monitored seasons. Further, a back propagation neural network model was implemented in this study to predict the vertical concentration trend of $PM_{2.5}$ and PM_{10} pollutants. The results of the models showed good prediction and confirmed the suitability of the model to predict the vertical trend of PMs in any street canyon study. It also justifies the importance of street geometry, emission source, and meteorological factors in predicting the air quality of a typical street canyon. This mature field is being spun into commercial applications for developing intelligent air quality monitoring devices.

Keywords: particulate matter, street canyon, meteorological factor, neural network, ANN

10.1 Introduction

Machine learning and intelligent systems for air quality prediction play a major role in the current trend as they are found to be cost-effective and advanced techniques. Air quality in the present era is of serious concern, as they lead to significant health issues. Moreover, these issues are often reported in epidemic studies conducted in an urban environment due to urbanization and industrialization. Urbanization has brought a scarcity of construction space in the urban boundary and a new change in the building style to accommodate dense populations in small areas to satisfy the shelter needs of the migrants moving from rural to urban regions. The new change is the establishment of high-rise buildings, having more dwelling units constructed vertically one over the other in the defined plot area. Though it is a well-appreciated construction, there is a negative impact too, i.e., weakening the ventilation capacity inside the street, leading to pollution hotspots. Hence, researchers from various fields showed interest in understanding and improving the air quality in such environments.

"Street Canyon" (SC) refers to the continuous presence of buildings along either side of the road [1]. SCs are known to be hot-spots of the urban due to the confinement of traffic emissions and low ventilation inducing poor atmospheric dispersion [2]. Urban air quality studies have been conducted by many researchers and have reported that PM concentration seems to be higher in the urban environment compared to other environments. The sources of pollutant emission in this type of environment are road traffic. This again increases the health risk of occupants and pedestrians in the street environment. Hence, researchers from various fields show interest in understanding and improving the air quality in such environments.

Monitoring and modeling spatial air quality are standard and conventional research. Whereas changes in the building orientation, architectural aspects, and city infrastructure demand transformation in air quality studies. In this way, the concept of vertical air quality monitoring is performed by many researchers worldwide on a laboratory scale through field investigation and simulation models. The parameters that were taken into consideration in the street canyon air quality studies include the geometry of the street [3], emission sources [4, 5], meteorological parameters [6], and solar radiation [7]. More of these sectoral studies were carried out using simulation and prediction models. Artificial neural network (ANN) is a widely used prediction model for air quality prediction studies [8]. Compared to earlier statistical methods, ANN techniques can increase forecast accuracy. Back-propagation neural network (BPNN), multilayer perceptron (MLP), radial basis function (RBF), and adopted neuro-fuzzy inference system (ANFIS) are a few examples of ANN types.

Djebbri and Rouainia [8] performed a study using the ANN model to predict the importance of meteorological factors in deciding the ambient air pollutant concentration of the pollutants, i.e., NOx and CO, measured in the four major parts of Algeria. The model was trained for three different scenarios: in scenario 1, only meteorological variables were trained; in scenario 2, only pollutant concentrations were trained; and in scenario 3, both pollutant concentration and meteorological parameters. Model 3 performed well in the simulation, and predictions were significant compared to the other two scenarios. Kurt et al. [9] used a feedforward neural network (FNN) to predict the concentrations of SO_2, PM_{10}, and CO in the Greater Istanbul Area. The prediction was performed in two stages of data training. First, the data from day 1 to day 3 were trained and predicted. Secondly, the day 2 and day 3 concentration profiles were predicted using the first stage predicted dataset. Later the size of the dataset was optimized. Utilizing 3–15 historical days in the training dataset results in the most significant modeling performance with the lowest error rate. Authors see improved predictions with greater accuracy when the day of the week is included as an input parameter. Siwek et al. [10] conducted a forecasting study on PM_{10} pollutants using a neural network approach. In this study, various ANN models of a similar kind were used to identify the best prediction models. MLP produces better results, which were significant compared to the observed results.

Cortina-Januchs et al. [11] applied the ANN model to predict the concentration of SO_2 pollutants for an industrial zone in Salamanca, Mexico. The authors trained the model for two results: (1) to identify the dataset size for best prediction; (2) to establish the significant meteorological parameter influencing the pollutant concentration. The prediction accuracy of the trained models was validated using MAE and RMSE. The authors used FNN in the training model. The results showed that the most miniature dataset predicted better results and defined the importance of meteorological parameters in the model for the forecasting results. Arhami et al. [12] investigated the applicability of ANN and Monte Carlo simulations (MCSs) combination to predict the hourly concentration of air pollutants, i.e., nitrogen oxides (NOx), nitrogen dioxide (NO_2), nitrogen monoxide (NO), ozone (O_3), carbon monoxide (CO), and particulate matter of diameter of less than 10 μm (PM_{10}) for Tehran city. In addition, the major influencing meteorological parameters were also studied in the model. The trained cum optimized ANN model showed the best prediction results for the pollutants, i.e., CO, NOx, NO_2, NO, and PM_{10}, with R^2 of 0.82 – 0.92 between the observed and predicted values. While predictions show a poor correlation between O_3 pollutants with the observed values. The study concludes that ANN can be used as a good prediction model provided proper input, the architecture of the model, and the order of input variables play a significant role in making the model reliable.

ANN is a well-established model with high nonlinear relationships and can be trained precisely when new datasets are used for predictions. In this way, this paper discusses the use of ANN in predicting air quality concentration in three geometrically varying street geometries, which has a scope in intelligent monitoring systems used for air monitoring in industries.

10.2 Materials and Methods

The field-based investigation was conducted in Chennai, Tamil Nadu, India. The streets chosen in this region represent southern India's typical street models. Here, for the study, three street models were chosen. They are: (1) non-street canyon (NSC), (2) asymmetrical street canyon (ASC), and (3) symmetrical street canyon with viaduct (SSCV). The sampling locations are shown in Figure 10.1. The details of the street can be referred to in [12]. The parameters considered in this work are listed in Table 10.1.

Particulate matter (PM) was measured using ambient fine dust samplers (AFDSs). The vertical measurement of PM was done by placing three AFDSs

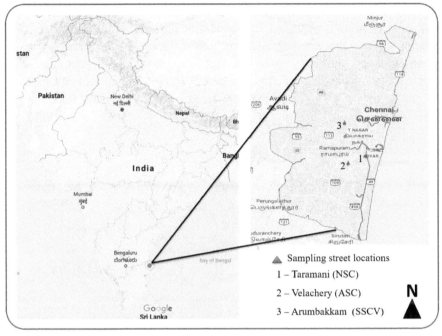

Figure 10.1 Map showing the sampling locations.

on the open terrace of the buildings at three different heights. The meteorological parameters were monitored using a portable weather monitoring station placed at the top of the building. The classified vehicle count study was performed by video surveying method.

Table 10.1 List of parameters measured and monitored in this study.

S.No.	Description	Parameters
1	Pollutants monitored	$PM_{2.5}$, PM_{10}
2	Meteorological factors	Wind speed, temperature, humidity, pressure
3	Other influencing factors	Vehicle traffic, street orientation
4	Frequency of monitoring of the above data (S.No. 1 to 3) except street orientation	Season: winter, summer, southwest monsoon, and northeast monsoon No of sampling days per season: 6 days per sampling location per season
5	Sampling height above street level	NSC: 3 m, 16 m, 37 m ASC: 3 m, 16 m, 38 m SSCV: 3 m, 17 m, 37 m

In the ANN model, a typical neural network type, i.e., feedforward neural network (FNN), was used. The model layer is shown in Figure 10.2. The input layers were categorized into three sectors: I 1 – pollutant type, concentration, and sampling height; I 2 – meteorological parameters; and I 3 – vehicle traffic and street geometry. The model was run in different phases to

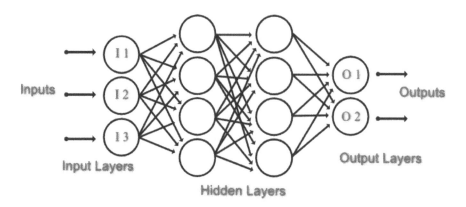

Figure 10.2   Neutral network architecture was developed for this study.

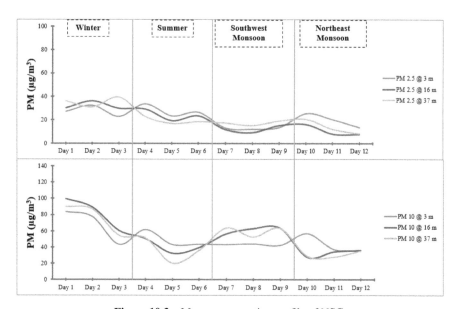

Figure 10.3   Mass concentration profile of NSC.

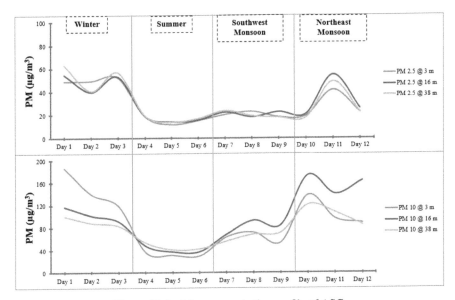

Figure 10.4   Mass concentration profile of ASC.

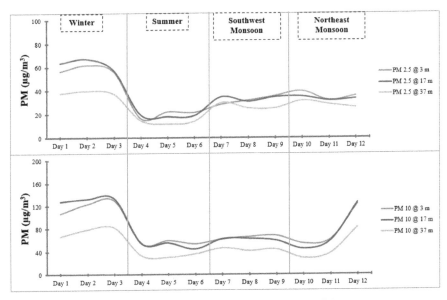

Figure 10.5   Mass concentration profile of SSCV.

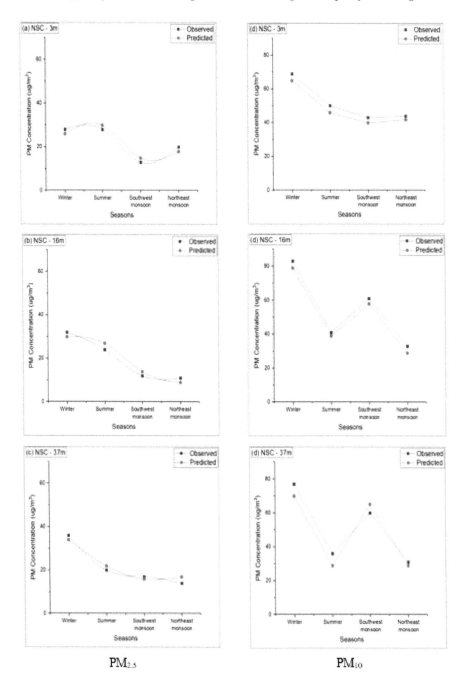

PM$_{2.5}$ PM$_{10}$

Figure 10.6   PM concentration prediction by ANN model for NSC.

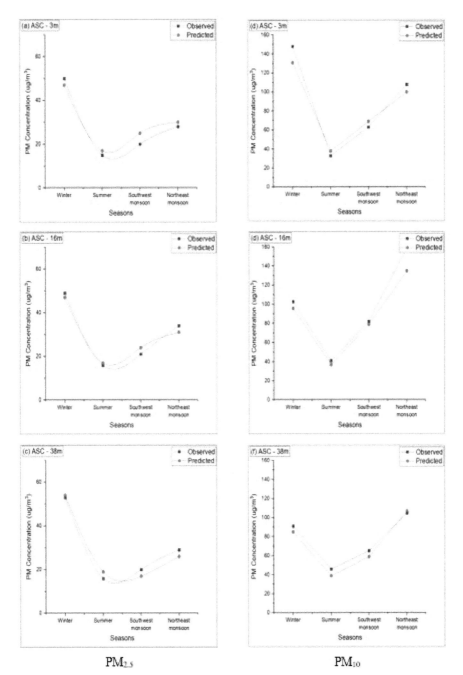

Figure 10.7 PM concentration prediction by ANN model for ASC.

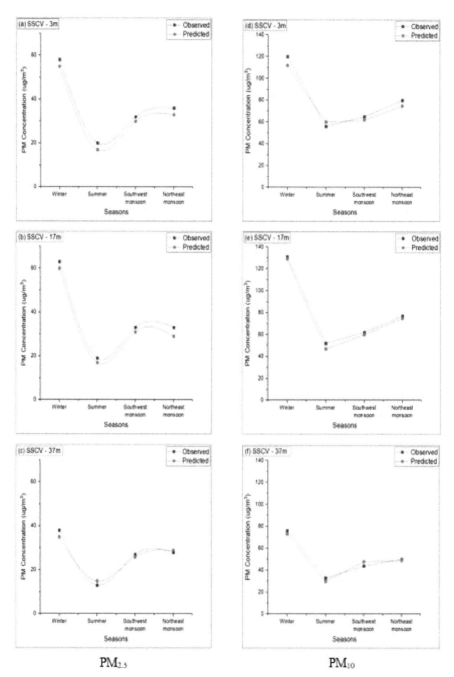

$PM_{2.5}$ PM_{10}

Figure 10.8   PM concentration prediction by ANN model for SSCV.

predict: (O 1) – pollutant concentration concerning each monitoring height; (O 2) – major factors influencing the pollutant fate inside the respective street canyons. The statistical methods that were used for the analysis were the root mean square error (RMSE) and the mean absolute error (MAE) to define the linear regression between observed and predicted values.

10.3 Results and Discussion

This section presents the report of the PM concentrations, ANN prediction of PM concentrations, and the major influencing factors in all three street geometries.

The mass concentration profiles (Figures 10.3–10.5) show that maximum concentrations were observed in winter for both pollutants in all three street geometries. Among the three sampling locations, $PM_{2.5}$ and PM_{10} were maximum at ASC. This could be due to various reasons, such as the street's geometry, local emission sources, and no better dispersion conditions.

The ANN model showed a good concentration prediction for the measured pollutants in all three street geometries (Figures 10.6–10.8). The prediction accuracy was about 94 percent from the overall observation, with an RMSE of 0.0114 for $PM_{2.5}$ and 0.0132 for PM_{10}. At the same time, MAE for $PM_{2.5}$ and PM_{10} were 0.0623 and 0.0498, respectively. The adequacy of the model with FNN showed 76 percent in the concentration prediction.

Similarly, the ANN prediction results of influencing factor showed significance for three parameters, i.e., street geometry, wind speed, and vehicle traffic.

10.4 Conclusion

This work investigated the applicability and efficiency of the ANN tool for predicting PM vertical concentration of size 2.5 and 10 in three varying street geometries. In addition, the factors influencing the pollutant profile inside the street geometries.

For the observed four seasons, the average correlation coefficient (R) between measured and predicted $PM_{2.5}$ and PM_{10} were 0.86 and 0.88, respectively. The accuracy of the ANN-developed model showed 94 percent for the prediction of PM concentrations in all three street geometries. Further, three significant factors were predicted to influence determining the PM pollutant concentration inside the street, i.e., street geometry, wind speed, and vehicle traffic.

Hence it is put forth to the research community that ANN models are a way forward tool in predicting air quality scenarios for street canyons. This model can be used in intelligent air monitoring devices to predict the quality of air using measured data. Further, the model can be trained with other environmental conditions and local geographical factors to make it more valid and reliable, which opens the scope for future work in this area.

References

[1] SJ. Jeong and MJ. Andrews, Application of the k–e turbulence model to the high Reynolds number skimming flow field of an urban street canyon, Atmospheric Environment, 2002.

[2] AT. Buckland, and DR. Middleton, Nomograms for calculating pollution within street canyons, Atmospheric Environment, 1999.

[3] MF. Yassin, and M. Ohba, Experimental simulation of air quality in street canyon under changes of building orientation and aspect ratio, Journal of Exposure Science and Environmental Epidemiology, 2012.

[4] Y. Zhou, and JI. Levy, The impact of urban street canyons on population exposure to traffic-related primary pollutants, Atmospheric Environment, 2008.

[5] T. Zheng, B. Li, X. Li, Z. Wang, S. Li, and Z. Peng, Vertical and horizontal distributions of traffic-related pollutants beside an urban arterial road based on unmanned aerial vehicle observations, Building and Environment, 2021.

[6] H. Zhang, T. Xu, Y. Zong, H. Tang, X. Liu, and Y. Wang, Influence of Meteorological Conditions on Pollutant Dispersion in Street Canyon, Procedia Engineering, 2015.

[7] J. Dong, Z. Tan, Y. Xiao, and J. Tu, Seasonal Changing Effect on Airflow and Pollutant Dispersion Characteristics in Urban Street Canyons, Atmosphere, 2017.

[8] N. Djebbri, and M. Rouainia, Artificial neural networks based air pollution monitoring in industrial sites, International Conference on Engineering and Technology (ICET), Turkey, 2017.

[9] A. Kurt, B. Gulbagci, F. Karaca, and O. Alaghab, An Online Air Pollution Forecasting System Using Neural Networks, Environment International, 2008.

[10] K. Siwek, S. Osowski and M. Sowinski, "Neural predictor ensemble for accurate forecasting of PM10 pollution," The 2010 International Joint Conference on Neural Networks (IJCNN), 2010.

[11] M. G. Cortina-Januchs, J. M. Barron-Adame, A. Vega-Corona and D. Andina, "Prevision of industrial SO2 pollutant concentration applying ANNs," 2009 7th IEEE International Conference on Industrial Informatics, 2009.

[12] Arhami, M., Kamali, N. & Rajabi, M. M. Predicting hourly air pollutant levels using artificial neural networks coupled with uncertainty analysis by Monte Carlo simulations. Environ Sci Pollut Res, 2013.

[13] M. R. Ezhilkumar, and S. Karthikeyan, Vertical Measurement of PM2.5 and PM10 in Street Canyons and Cohort Health Risk Estimation at Chennai, South India, Environmental Engineering Science, 2020.

11

Facial Emotion Classification for Industry Automation using Convolutional Neural Networks

R. Bharath Raam[1], Balaji Srinivasan[1], Prithiviraj Rajalingam[2], and Dinesh Jackson Samuel[3]

[1]Loyola-ICAM College of Engineering and Technology, India
[2]Assitant Professor, Department of Electronics & Communication Engineering, SRM Institute of Science & Technology, Kattankulathur, 603203
[3]Biomedical Engineering, University of California, USA

Abstract

In today's world, where businesses are constantly expanding and a need to transition to a virtual mode of operation exists, all sellers must have a direct line of sight into what their customers think about their idea, product, and the people associated with it. This is because moving to a purely digital infrastructure is necessary for modern business. The proposed solution analyzes the customer's macro expressions during a video call. We aim to utilize a convolutional neural network to classify the emotions expressed by the customer while on a video call. The proposed solution achieved an accuracy of 69.90 percent on the FER-2013 dataset and 73.24 percent on the JAFFE dataset. The proposed solution can achieve better results than the mini Xception architecture.

Keywords: convolutional neural network, emotion recognition, computer vision, business intelligence

11.1 Introduction

Emotion recognition is a subsidiary of artificial intelligence technology related to facial recognition, which aims to interpret the subject's emotional state purely based on facial expressions, physical cues, and body vital signals, such as heart rate and brain activity. But, in this project, we restrict ourselves to the least invasive and easily observable indicator of human emotion, the human face. This is a profitable avenue of research at the forefront of the development of service robots capable of being cognitive enough to understand human emotions and act accordingly.

The priority of affective computing is to remove the "robotic" feel for humans when interacting with computers. Today's systems are being bottle-necked by their inability to interpret and reciprocate emotions, which limits their intelligence and prevents them from interacting with the user, taking into account the user's emotional state. The system must be sensitive to human emotions to be more user-friendly and practical. In order to get an accurate interpretation of any given information, we need to consider both linguistic and nonverbal information. It is much needed to plan and build a system that can recognize a person's emotions using gestures, facial expressions, acoustic properties of speech, verbal information, and more, as it can help provide valuable business intelligence about how customers perceive the product. In reality, it is viable to detect predetermined emotions by measuring body signals and facial expressions recorded in real time by sensors and cameras. According to conventional wisdom, nonverbal communication accounts for 70–90 percent of human communication. Albert Mehrabian's study in 1967 established the "3V rule," which stated that verbal, vocal, and visual commu-nications constitute 7 percent, 38 percent, and 55 percent, respectively, in any interaction. This explains why nonverbal communication is so exciting and fortifies our approach to detecting emotions from facial expressions.

One possibility is to use a convolutional neural network (CNN) to investi-gate the facial expressions of human subjects while they are engaged in video calls to deduce how those individuals are feeling. In order to obtain more consistent results when locating the network's region of interest, the convo-lutional neural network uses the multi-task cascaded convolutional networks (MTCNN) framework. This framework was developed for both face detection and face alignment. We were able to create both a system for recognizing faces and a system for skeletonizing faces by using this framework.

11.2 Related Works

Understanding and detecting human emotions has been an enigma over the centuries and plays a significant role in human–human interaction. However, with the plethora of data and in a world of ever-evolving and increasing computing power, we are much closer than before to detecting and understanding the emotional response of humans. As stated concisely by Pantic et al. [1], the emotional intelligence of humans is integral for successful interaction rather than their IQ.

In a world progressing toward intelligent computers and AI, aiming toward emulating human intelligence, the ability to understand emotions is a non-negotiable trait it must possess. It goes beyond the fact that it would make computers human-like as there is significant evidence that the rational thinking of the homo sapiens is dependent on emotions [2]. Hence, affective computing is critical to advancing AI [3]. Affective computing is the study and development of systems and devices that can recognize, interpret, process, and simulate human effects, such as human emotions. Affective tries to extract ideas, sentiments, and emotions from people's behaviors, which can be collected automatically through their writings, facial expressions, speech, physiological signs, and movements.

Emotion, sentiment, and opinions are examples of affective data from the Web, which is the primary data source. Social signal processing (SSP) aims to analyze and model social interactions to provide computers with an emotional quotient [4]. The development of human–computer interfaces with an emotional quotient is the ultimate goal of SSP. Affective computing is a branch of SSP that combines artificial intelligence and cognitive technology to label the emotions of a human subject using data mined from their facial feature and body gesture [5]. Highly evolved humans can display their emotions through various means, from facial expressions to body movements, gestures, and micro-expressions. The tone, choice of words, and inflections in how people talk can also portray the underlying emotion of the conversation. Scientific studies show that it is possible to deduce the emotion experienced by a person by observing the electrical activity in their brain and heart via electroencephalography (EEG) and electrocardiography (ECG), respectively. We can also perceive the emotions detected through other physiological signals such as respiration rate analysis (RR), electromyogram (EMG), and galvanic skin response (GSR), to name a few [6]. In essence, visual, text, audio, and physiological signals can be processed and observed to understand human emotions.

The human face and eyes are the portals to understanding human emotions, as they are very responsive to humans' underlying emotions. A Simple video camera equipment is required to extract the emotion expressed by a person in real-time, and not much-specialized equipment is required [7].

The reactions to emotions are very much expressive and observable through human facial features and are the key to decoding the enigma of understanding emotions. Facial expressions provide a credible, non-invasive method for communicating with another person and comprehending their emotional state and the intentions they are trying to convey. The truthfulness of this cannot be called into question. The area of psychology known as emotion modeling sees a lot of research activity, and the methods that psychologists use to categorize and model emotions can vary significantly from one researcher to the next. Distinctive and dimensional emotion theories are the two main categories into which the study of emotions can be broken down. According to the discrete emotion theory, anger, disgust, fear, happiness, sadness, and surprise are the core categories of emotions. These discrete emotion models detect and categorize emotions by monitoring facial expressions like lip pursing, eyebrow raising, and eye blinking. The Ekman model [8] has shown the most promise among similar frameworks. Emotion recognition from facial expressions can be accomplished in several ways, from simple histogram of oriented gradient (HOG)-based methods to highly sophisticated convolutional neural networks (CNNs). Support vector machine (SVM) of HOG features and multilayer perceptron (MLP) artificial neural network (ANN) of HOG features are two examples of HOG-based methods that show promise but fall short when applied to real-world data [10]. Since our scenario takes place indoors, any of these solutions would work. As a result, researchers are looking into deep learning (DL) techniques to boost the generalization of different types of input data during deployment and to offer more accurate representations. Facial expression recognition is just one of many types of image recognition where DL methods like CNN have significantly improved results. The use of deep learning techniques yields more trustworthy and accurate results [11], according to a study that compared numerous approaches.

SVMs are among the most reliable classifiers available when the best possible kernel can be found. For facial emotion recognition, Ma Xiaoxi et al. [12] investigated the efficacy of an SVM-based fusion method. The authors have combined SVM with deep Boltzmann machine (DBM), a shallow model that can make accurate predictions and classifications based on data generated in a lab. Using the straightforward fusion approach proposed in [13], we combine the two models mentioned above. The models were trained using data from FERA 2015 (Second Facial Expression Recognition and Analysis Challenge) and tested using data from the SEMAINE database containing examples of emotional facial expressions. Although the SVM-DBM fusion model could achieve an accuracy of 91percent, this would not apply to our use case because it relied on static feature engineering. To solve computer vision problems, CNNs have surpassed physics-based models and other preprocessing techniques because they permit "end-to-end" learning directly from input images [14]. As a result, CNNs are now the go-to method for resolving computer vision issues. By analyzing the results of Breuer and Kimmel's [15] comprehensive study of CNN's performance across different FER datasets, we were able to zero in on the connection between the features generated by an unsupervised learning process and the Ekman model of labeling data. These facial expressions are among the most telling of inner thoughts.

Facial expression recognition can benefit significantly from access to the temporal context. However, developing helpful features manually is a time-consuming process. For the specified problem statement, two-stage convolutional neural network (CNN) models [16] were also considered as a possible means of relief. Images are used to extract temporal appearance features in the first stage. The second step involves extracting temporal geometry features from facial landmark points in the temporal domain. These two steps are necessary to address the issue at hand. They are combined using joint fine-tuning to improve the performance of the facial expression recognition system. The multiple-tier CNN model we proposed for incorporating temporal data into the learning process is computationally intensive because it necessitates fine-tuning the parameters of two separate CNNs. A hybrid approach [17] was developed to better account for time differences. To do so, this technique combines a convolutional neural network (CNN) for the spatial features of each frame with a long short-term memory (LSTM) for the temporal features of the following frames. This was done to expedite the process of making the necessary adjustments.

RNN-CNN [18] models, which combine data via simple temporal averaging, outperformed the baseline CNN model, which did not use RNNs. The 2015 dataset from the Emotion Recognition in the Wild Challenge was used for this analysis. The validation accuracy of the RNN-CNN hybrid model was 39 percent, which was higher than the accuracy of the CNN model alone (30%). The 3D Inception-ResNet architecture, proposed by Hasani and Mahoor [19], is followed by an LSTM unit. When coupled with the LSTM unit, this architecture can analyze the temporal and spatial relationships between faces in multiple video frames. It is worth noting that this network, too, takes facial features as inputs. As a result, the parts of the face that are more crucial to conveying emotion are highlighted, while the less crucial parts are downplayed.

11.3 Dataset Description

According to emotion theory, emotions can be treated categorically, which proposes only six basic, distinct, and universal emotions exist, or dimensionally, where we consider emotions to be a mixture of multiple factors. The categorical emotion model supports the proposed solution of using a convolutional neural network, as they provide hard and fast rules to classify emotions. The dimensional model of emotion is not widely used due to its innate complexity and the number of variables involved in classifying a single emotion.

Several datasets available can aid computer vision-based emotion recognition from facial expressions, but very few can be used to develop a generalized and robust model. The research analyzes and builds solutions using the FER 2013 and JAFFE datasets are shown in Figs. 11.1 and 11.2.

Pierre-Luc Carrier and Aaron Courville develop the FER-2013 as part of their ongoing project, and it is publicly available. This dataset used the Ekman model to label the images into seven distinct emotions following the discrete emotion theory. "Happy" has the highest frequency in the dataset. The baseline for random guessing is 24.4 percent across the dataset.

JAFFE – The Japanese Female Facial Expression dataset – is an image dataset that depicts facial expressions posed by Japanese women, accompanied by semantic ratings on nouns describing the expressions. The JAFFE dataset was developed by recording the facial expression of 10 different Japanese female subjects. The dataset has seven classes of emotions, six basic expressions, and neutral. Around 60 annotators labeled the images, and the semantic rating is the average rating of all the annotators. The dataset utilizes the Ekman model as a basis to label emotions.

11.4 Model Architecture

A succinct summary of the findings and an elucidation of this work's advancement or contribution to the field are included. MLP and SVM are machine learning techniques popularly used for emotion recognition but did not yield the desired results. Even with further research to improve feature extraction, these methods were not viable in real-time scenarios.

Deep learning (DL) approaches learn different levels of abstraction for input data representations, with higher representational levels providing more relevant features for differentiation and classification. This was the main driving force to look into using CNN for emotion recognition, as they gave better accuracy and generalizability.

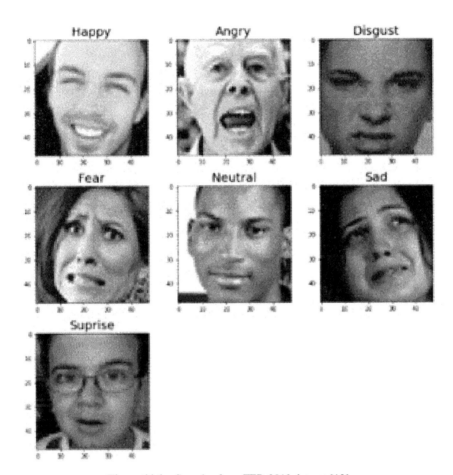

Figure 11.1 Samples from FER-2013 dataset [12].

Figure 11.2 Samples from JAFFE dataset [13].

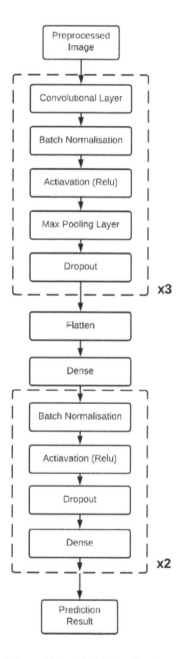

Figure 11.3   Model visualization.

Neural networks are not preprogrammed to function for the required task; they learn and adapt to do a specific task when they are being trained for the required task. An input layer will get the data that has to be fed to the CNN, whose dimension is determined by the dimensions of the input data. A deep neural network is a neural network composed of several hidden layers, where a few hidden layers will help the CNN to learn complex data interactions. An output layer that will give the final result, for instance, classification probabilities. The number of classes that the data is partitioned into determines the size of this layer in the hierarchy. The typical structure of a CNN consists of several layers, all of which are linked to one another. This indicates that all of the neurons in one layer are connected to all the neurons in the layer beneath it. We propose using a fully connected feedforward convolutional neural network for this problem. This has been proposed as a potential answer. This network has a $48 \times 48 \times 1$ input layer and a 7×1 output layer. The letterpress denotes the model's activation function, and the max pooling technique is used to sample the input more densely along its spatial dimensions. We prefer the "ReLu" activation function because it is sparse, which helps when dealing with dense representations, and because its gradient is less likely to vanish.

There are 1,328,167 parameters in the model, of which 1,325,991 can be trained and 2176 cannot. ADAM is the optimizer employed, with categorical cross-entropy as the loss function of choice. Dropout dilution, or DropConnect, is used at a rate of 0.2 in this context. Through preventing intricate co-adaptations on training data, this regularisation method is used to lessen the likelihood of overfitting in artificial neural networks. The dilution that occurs in a dropout layer is another name for it. This technique allows neural networks to perform model averaging efficiently.

11.5 Model Training

The model was trained using the train set of the FER-2013 dataset. The input data for training are grayscale images of 48×48 size, which are loaded as a array. Table 11.1 shows the pseudo code of the model training. . The input data's label is one-hot encoded to represent categorical data as binary vectors, as convolutional neural networks cannot work with data directly. The images and one-hot–encoded labels are then split into train and validation set in the ratio 80:20.

The model was supposed to be trained for 200 epochs but could be stopped early if the validation loss did not go down. With a learning rate of 0.001, if the validation loss stays the same for more than 12 iterations, the learning rate goes up by 0.1. It was found that the model was 69.60 percent right. The same setup was used to train on the JAFFE dataset, and the results showed that it was 73.24 Which is shown in Fig. 11.4.

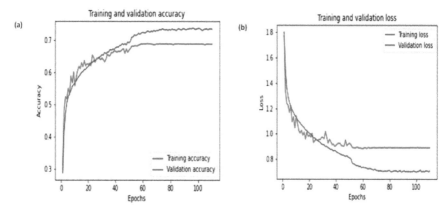

Figure 11.4   Model training and validation: (a) accuracy and (b) loss.

Table 11.1   Pseudocode for model training.

Pseudo code for training the model	
1	Import libraries
2	Load the dataset
3	Convert images to grayscale
4	Resize the image to size (48×48)
5	Split into test and train data
6	Build the model Initialize model.sequential() object • Add Conv2D, activation, MaxPooling2D layer, Batch normalization, flattened and dense layers as shown in Figure 11.3
7	Compile the model • Set the metrics as accuracy • Initialize ADAM optimizer with a learning rate of 0.001 • Monitor losses
6	Set hyperparameter: Batchsize, learning rate, early stopping criteria
7	Fit the model • If val_loss has no improvement over 12 epochs, reduce the learning rate by a factor of 0.1. • If val_accuracy has no improvement over 50 epochs, stop training.
8	Save the model weights : model.save('weights.h5')

11.6 Model Metrics

Analyzing a model's performance from a qualitative and quantitative perspective is required, and model metrics help us understand the strength and pitfalls of the model. Accuracy, precision, recall, and F1-score, to name a few metrics, were computed for the proposed solution across both datasets. Since the JAFFE dataset is of a smaller volume, there are high possibilities to overfit or underfit the model, contributing to the high-high and low-low values while metrics are computed. The proposed solution for the FER-2013 dataset achieved an F1-score in the range of .65–.8 over all the classes. The proposed model achieved an accuracy of 69.90 percent and 73.24 percent for the FER-2013 and the JAFFE datasets, respectively.

A table known as a confusion matrix can be used to provide a concise summary of the performance of your prediction model. A confusion matrix is a table where each cell reveals the percentage of times the model correctly identified the classes and the number of times it misidentified them. This matrix provides a graphical representation of true positive false negative network (TPFNN) representing true positives, false positives, and false negatives. Table 11.2 shows the different model metrics for different emotions.

- The rate at which a classifier successfully and accurately predicts a positive class is called the true positive (TP) rate.
- A classifier is said to have a "true negative" (TN) value if it can correctly predict a negative class by a certain percentage.
- "False positives," also known as FPs, are instances in which the classifier incorrectly predicts that the negative class belongs to the positive class.

Table 11.2 Model metrics.

Emotions	Recall		Precision		F1-score	
	JAFFE	FER-2013	JAFFE	FER-2013	JAFFE	FER-2013
Anger	67%	60%	80%	64%	0.73	0.62
Disgust	60%	71%	67%	78%	0.63	0.74
Fear	100%	44%	56%	60%	0.71	0.51
Happy	86%	90%	92%	88%	0.89	0.89
Sad	64%	54%	64%	56%	0.64	0.55
Surprise	64%	79%	100%	78%	0.78	0.79
Neutral	88%	78%	58%	61%	0.7	0.68
Macro avg	74%	69%	75%	68%	0.73	0.68
Weighted avg	77%	69%	73%	70%	.0.74	0.69

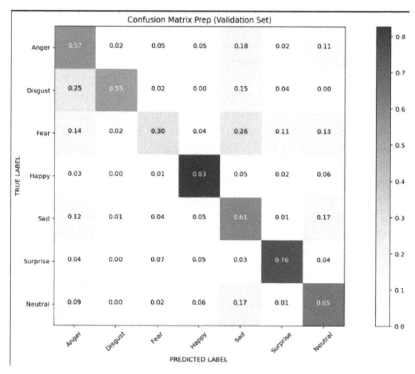

Figure 11.5   Confusion matrix.

- The frequency with which a classifier incorrectly identifies a positive class as a negative class is measured by a particular type of prediction error known as false negative (FN).

From the confusion matrix shown in Figure 11.5, we can observe the extent of misclassification. It gives a one-shot view of the classification and misclassification. This also helps us analyze the misclassification trends. We can see that the class happy is adequately classified about 83 percent of the time, and the classifier confuses the images labeled fear as sad for about 26 percent. This indicates that the features that distinguish fear and sadness are much correlated with each other.

11.7 Activation Maps

Activation maps are a qualitative method to observe the discriminative regions in an image utilized by CNN to distinguish among classes which is shown in Fig. 11.6.

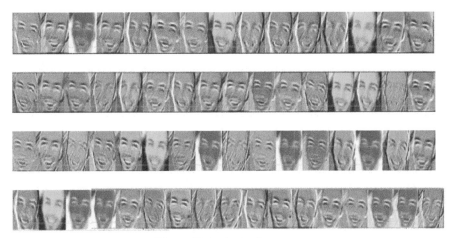

Figure 11.6 Activation maps.

This helps us observe the features the CNN considers to classify the input data. Activation maps illustrate that deep learning networks already have some built-in attention mechanisms. We can observe from the activation maps that the model also extracts facial features such as eyes and pursing of lips to classify emotions. This is similar to how the Ekman model uses facial features to classify emotions.

11.8 Implementation Workflow

The proposed solution can currently work with Google Meet, and the plan is to extend to other platforms. The entire application is cloud-hosted, alleviating any burden on the user hardware for processing the customer's emotions. The image is extracted from the video call and queued in the MongoDB database for further processing. The implementation workflow is represented in Figures 11.7 and 11.8. Multi-task cascaded convolutional network (MTCNN) is used for localization and extraction of region of interest (ROI), which is passed onto for preprocessing, whose output is to be fed into the model to classify emotions. MTCNN has better non-maximum suppression and consistency in localizing faces in an image than Haar cascade classifiers. Simply, it helps us give good-quality input data to receive good-quality output from the model.

The frames from the video feed of the live conferencing application such as Google Meet are extracted via a screenshot API provided by Google

Figure 11.7   Implementation workflow.

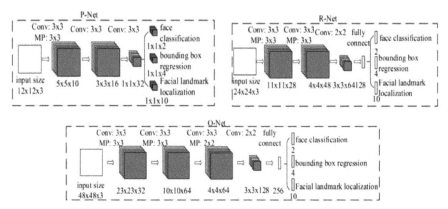

Figure 11.8   MTCNN architecture [22]: P-NET, R-NET, and O-NET.

Chrome. This video frame is then sent to a MongoDB database, which stores the image data for processing in the FER module. The data is stored in Base64 format in the database and converted back to a NumPy array, where each element represents the pixel intensity, to feed as an input to MTCNN. MTCNN extracts the ROI, which is essentially the region in the picture where the faces are present. The ROI is then further converted to the grayscale color space and resized to 48×48 before being fed to the CNN model as the input. The prediction of each emotion is displayed as probability scores, and the class of emotion which achieves the highest probability score is displayed as the module's output. The entire processing from the start to end is done in the cloud, using an AWS EC2 instance, alleviating the hardware dependency on the user end when deployed in real time.

The novelty of the proposed solution rests in its simplicity. The proposed solution can provide an instantaneous real-time response to the given input with high accuracy. It does not utilize complex architecture like the mini-Xception model but still significantly outperforms it. Using MTCNN in tandem with the CNN to extract ROI helps generate the ROI with high confidence, which improves the quality of input to the CNN model. The model performs well on a single dataset and retains the same performance across the JAFFE dataset. When talking about the real-world implementation of the solution, it is capable of handling real-world data and producing outputs instantaneously and is optimized for both cloud and edge-based deployment as it requires very minimal processing power to deploy a simple CNN as the one proposed in the paper.

11.9 Conclusion

The proposed solution aids in gaining insight into the customer's emotional response when interacting over a video call. It utilizes a convolutional neural network to classify emotions and show the emotions exhibited by the customer. The model achieved an accuracy of 69.90 percent while using the FER-2013 dataset and provides good scalability when in the future; the model is fitted to accommodate new data. This model outperforms the mini-Xception model, which achieved only 66 percent accuracy [11] on the FER-2013 dataset. With the growing online presence of shops and significant business meetings happening over video calls, the proposed system has the potential to become a ubiquitous part of companies' sales and CRM tools. Currently, the model can classify macro emotions only, in extension in the future; this can be extended to classify micro emotions too. If possible, we can generate a transcript of the meeting conversation and tag the emotions observed over each time stamp.

References

[1] Maja Pantic, Nicu Sebe, Jeffrey F. Cohn, and Thomas Huang. 2005. Affective multimodal human-computer interaction. In Proceedings of the 13th annual ACM international conference on Multimedia (MULTIMEDIA '05). Association for Computing Machinery, New York, NY, USA, 669–676.

[2] Picard, R. 1997. Affective computing. Boston: The MIT Press.

[3] Arumugam, Devi, Kavya Govindaraju, and Ananth Kumar Tamilarasan. "AIoT-Based Smart Framework for Screening Specific Learning Disabilities." In Machine Learning for Critical Internet of Medical Things: Applications and Use Cases, pp. 103-124. Cham: Springer International Publishing, 2022.

[4] Vinciarelli, Alessandro, and Maja Pantic. "Hervé Bourlard, 2009.'." Social Signal Processing: Survey of an Emerging Domain'in Image and Vision Computing 27: 1743-1759.

[5] Shoumy, Nusrat J., Li-Minn Ang, Kah Phooi Seng, DM Motiur Rahaman, and Tanveer Zia. "Multimodal big data affective analytics: A comprehensive survey using text, audio, visual and physiological signals." Journal of Network and Computer Applications 149 (2020): 102447.

[6] Joseph, Abin John, Nidhin Sani, K. Suresh Kumar, T. Ananth Kumar, and R. Nishanth. "Towards a Novel and Efficient Public Key Management for Peer-Peer Security in Wireless Ad-Hoc/Sensor Networks." In 2022 International Conference on Smart Technologies and Systems for Next Generation Computing (ICSTSN), pp. 1-4. IEEE, 2022.

[7] Marechal, C. et al. (2019). Survey on AI-Based Multimodal Methods for Emotion Detection. In: Kołodziej, J., González-Vélez, H. (eds) High-Performance Modelling and Simulation for Big Data Applications. Lecture Notes in Computer Science(), vol 11400. 307-324

[8] Tracy, J. L., & Randles, D. 2011. Four Models of Basic Emotions: A Review of Ekman and Cordaro, Izard, Levenson, and Panksepp and Watt. Emotion Review, 3, 397 - 405.

[9] Colombetti, Giovanna. "From affect programs to discrete dynamical emotions." Philosophical Psychology 22, no. 4 (2009): 407-425.

[10] C. Mayer, M. Eggers, and B. Radig, 2014. Cross-database evaluation for facial expression recognition, Pattern recognition, and image analysis, vol. 24, no. 1, 124–132.

[11] Kumar, Tamilarasan Ananth, Rajendrane Rajmohan, Muthu Pavithra, Sunday Adeola Ajagbe, Rania Hodhod, and Tarek Gaber. "Automatic face mask detection system in public transportation in smart cities using IoT and deep learning." Electronics 11, no. 6 (2022): 904.

[12] Xiaoxi, M., Weisi, L., Dongyan, H., Minghui, D., & Li, H. (2017). Facial emotion recognition. IEEE 2nd International Conference on Signal and Image Processing (ICSIP). doi:10.1109/siprocess.2017.8124509

[13] Pugazhendiran, P., Suresh Kumar, K., Ananth Kumar, T., & Sundaresan, S. (2022). An Advanced Revealing and Classification System for Plant Illnesses Using Unsupervised Bayesian-based SVM Classifier and Modified HOG-ROI Algorithm. In Contemporary Issues in Communication, Cloud and Big Data Analytics (pp. 259-269). Springer, Singapore.

[14] Walecki, R., Rudovic, O., Pavlovic, V. Schuller, B. Pantic, M (2017). Deep structured learning for facial action unit intensity estimation. In

Proceedings of the IEEE Conference on Computer Vision and Pattern Recognition, Honolulu, HI, USA; pp. 3405–3414.

[15] Breuer, R.; Kimmel, R. A deep learning perspective on the origin of facial expressions. (2017)arXiv.

[16] Jung, H.; Lee, S.; Yim, J.; Park, S.; Kim, J. (2015) Joint fine-tuning in deep neural networks for facial expression recognition. In Proceedings of the IEEE International Conference on Computer Vision, Santiago, Chile; pp. 2983–2991

[17] Ko, Byoung Chul. 2018. "A Brief Review of Facial Emotion Recognition Based on Visual Information" Sensors 18, no. 2: 401. https://doi.org/10.3390/s18020401

[18] Kahou, S. E., Michalski, V. , Konda, K.,(2015) Recurrent neural networks for emotion recognition in video. In Proceedings of the ACM on International Conference on Multimodal Interaction, Seattle, WA, USA, pp. 467–474.

[19] Hasani, B.; Mahoor, M. H. Facial expression recognition using enhanced deep 3D convolutional neural networks. In Proceedings of the IEEE Conference on Computer Vision and Pattern Recognition Workshops, Hawaii, HI, USA, 21–26 July 2017; pp. 1–11

[20] Goodfellow, I. J., Erhan, D., Carrier, P. L., Courville, A., Mirza, M., Hamner, B., Cukierski, W., Tang, Y., Thaler, D., Lee, D. H. and Zhou, Y., 2013, November. Challenges in representation learning: A report on three machine learning contests. In International conference on neural information processing, Springer, Berlin, Heidelberg 117-124.

[21] Lyons, Michael, Kamachi, Miyuki, & Gyoba, Jiro. (1998). The Japanese Female Facial Expression (JAFFE) Dataset

[22] Kaipeng Zhang and Zhanpeng Zhang and Zhifeng Li and Yu Qiao, (2016), Joint Face Detection and Alignment Using Multi-task Cascaded Convolutional Networks, IEEE Signal Processing Letters, 23, (1499-1503)

12

Automatic Hand Sanitizer Dispenser by Industrial Automation using Arduino and Photodiode

R. Kiruthika[1], T. Prabhu[2], and Naveenbalaji Gowthaman[3]

[1]Electronics and Communication Engineering,
SNS College of Technology, India
[2]Electronics and Communication Engineering, Presidency University, India
[3]Electronic Engineering, University of KwaZulu-Natal, South Africa
E-mail: kiruthika.r.ece.2020@snsct.org; prabhucbe1206@gmail.com;
dr.gnb@ieee.org

Abstract

The 21st century is evolving with the emergence of new diseases. In this pandemic Covid, we must protect ourselves from the harmful germs that mainly enter the human body through our skin, especially our hands. To be able to maintain hand hygiene, hand sanitizers provide an efficient way. The main problem with those hand sanitizer bottled containers is that they provide the chance to contaminate germs on their contact point. An efficient and elegant solution to this is given by the industrial automation of automatic hand sanitizer dispenser machines that are processed based on sensors, and it is wholly touchless such that infections and the spread of contagious diseases can be avoided. The problem with these automatic hand sanitizer dispensers is that the sensors fail in performance due to changes in atmospheric temperature, sunlight, humidity, and setup conditions. Most of the available brands of automatic hand sanitizer dispensers make use of ultrasonic and infrared sensors that are replaced by photodiode in our proposed design. The proposed design is based upon an Arduino circuit in which a signal from the microcontroller controls the reception of the signal from the user, also giving output by activating the motor. The photodiode proves to be worthy of selection by quickly detecting the user in a period that is very much less compared to that of the other sensors. The designed circuit was automated more than 25 times with varying parameters, and the results were discussed. The proposed design proved its worthiness in several experimental conductions. Designing an efficient system that meets all our needs and vision is essential, and we need to consider all the parameters that make necessary alterations in the existing system to help it function at its best. The main motive or aim of the designed performance is to empathize with the customers' needs. Hence this proposed system was found to be user-friendly and safe to use.

Keywords: pandemic, hand hygiene, automatic, automation, photodiode, Arduino, faster

12.1 Introduction

In December 2019, the pandemic outbreak was first identified in Wuhan, China. All the developing as well as the developed countries, were worst affected by this pandemic. India, which has the second largest population in the world, is suffering severely from COVID-19, and a substantial negative impact was observed on the economic growth of the country [1, 2]. The spread of COVID from an infected person to an average person was recorded mainly through the air molecules inhaled by them, and a considerable amount of viruses was found to be transmitted through the hands. Hence, hand hygiene behaviors were expected to be strictly followed in hospitals and public areas to prevent the pandemic from affecting the maximum number of people [3, 4]. Hand sanitizers were used to wash the hands frequently to kill the viruses on the hands, and they were also used to sanitize the surfaces suspected to be contaminated by germs [5]. Alcohol-based hand sanitizers were effective in inactivating more than 99 percent of the contaminated viruses when asked to rub both palms with the ABHS (alcohol-based hand sanitizer) [6]. There has been much work done by researchers from many fields to figure out how to make it easier to manufacture automatic hand sanitizer dispensers using state-of-the-art technologies. Automatic hand sanitizer dispensers have been developed and are currently available for purchase. Some notable characteristics of these dispensers include their ability to be wall-mounted and their incorporation of automatic sprayers. However, certain advancements have been made in the automation industry to ensure that users have access to high-quality products and are satisfied with those products. Automatic hand sanitizer dispensers [7–10] are triggered by an infrared obstacle detector and employ a simple monostable multivibrator. Some of the automatic hand sanitizer dispensers contained not only an automated dispensing mechanism but also temperature measurement, which initially used rechargeable batteries that were charged by solar panels and used two Arduino UNO boards with voltage regulators [11]. Several automatic hand sanitizer dispensers with sensor-imposed systems were developed and implemented for daily use in the market. The primary sensors used for this development were ultrasonic [13–17], but they did not match the expected results since their action was affected by the interference of temperature and environmental factors.

A deep study about the disadvantages faced by the existing system in industrial automation was made, and before producing an automatic hand sanitizer dispenser that meets all the consumer needs [21, 22], the sensor that is used to detect human hands [24] was changed in our study in a way that yields the best outcome. A photodiode was used to detect human hands faster, and the designed prototype also contains some of the added advantages, such as dispensing only once for the first detection and waiting for a few seconds for the subsequent detections to happen so that crowds can also be avoided. This system also proves to be cost effective and time efficient. The result of the comparative analysis of the existing systems with the proposed one proved successful.

12.2 Background

Arnes Sembiring et al. developed an automatic hand sanitizer dispenser using ultrasonic sensors and a mini DC water pump in which ultrasonic sensors prevented the people from directly touching the sanitizer container [23]. Although dispensers with an ultrasonic sensor proved efficient, they sometimes failed to provide a suitable industrially automated device due to damage, and their predetermined distance (3–5 cm) wasted the sanitizer liquid because of poor sensing and improper recognition of the user [25–28]. Automatic hand wash dispensers with battery-imposed systems and IR sensors for sensing were developed by MM Srihari. This contains an RC timer delay setup and a pipe to control the liquid flow, yet the consumer was inconvenient because of the additional expenses [29]. Since the impact, scientists and engineers have developed automatic hand sanitizers with advanced technological aspects. Innovative research has been done in this field, and effective outcomes have been recognized [30–34].

12.2.1 The goal

The prime aim of the proposed structure of automatic hand sanitizer dispensers is mainly to provide enhanced performance at an affordable cost. With more minor modifications that can bring a more significant advantage, the proposed work system is designed to meet the customer's needs and improve product quality. With the advent and the development of semiconductor technology, the efficiency and the time of operation of hand sanitizer dispensers have been widely improved

12.2.2 The extent of the sanitizer dispenser with photodiode

Every conventional system in the market uses either an ultrasonic sensor or an infrared sensor to detect the presence of human hands to dispense the sanitizer liquid. Nevertheless, no one can deny that the photodiode sensors that are the best results of developing semiconductor technologies are one of the perfect sensors for humans. They are capable of detecting the infrared radiations emitted by humans. All black bodies emit invisible IR radiation to human eyes, and the photodiodes can detect that radiation. The novel change of using photodiodes instead of ultrasonic sensors or infrared sensors can make the proposed work system stand as the best among other systems available in the market. The future-based novel design of the automatic hand sanitizer dispenser using Arduino and photodiode can be used as a hygienic way of cleaning the hands using the sanitizer liquid in schools, public areas where the crowd of people is above the desired rate, hospitals, public and private offices, for the usage of clinical persons and physicians, etc. This can also be used in place of the hand-pressed sanitizer machines as a means of improved health and hand hygiene.

12.3 Design of Extensive Hand Sanitizer

The automatic hand sanitizer dispenser circuit was designed to reduce the spread of COVID-19 and safeguard people from the pandemic. Various components and materials were selected with specific goals on the bucket list. The design was made such that it should be time-efficient, faster in action, and cost-effective. These prime aims were achieved and experimentally proved by simulating the designed circuit several times for precise action.

12.3.1 Requirements of the design

The Arduino UNO board is chosen as the main microcontroller, which controls the working of the whole circuit. The heart and soul of the embedded systems and the automated circuits are the microcontrollers that can function without needing additional external peripherals. The Arduino UNO consists of both analog and digital pins. This can take inputs from the analog pins for sensors and convert the analog voltage value with the help of an analog to digital converter. The Arduino board takes in the input from the photodiode sensor and gives its output through the LED and DC motor. The LED is used in the circuit to indicate the turning ON of the DC motor. A 12 V power supply is given as input to the DC motor. An NPN transistor is connected to the DC motor through a 1 KΩ resistor that amplifies the DC motor's power.

All the connections for the circuit of the automatic hand sanitizer dispenser have been made to the available components in the simulation software called Tinkercad, ensuring good internet connectivity. The tinkercad circuits can be stored and tinkered with or simulated for *n* number of times, and proper calculations can be made. The potentiometer, which is the variable resistance, contains three pins, out of which one is connected to the ground, the second is connected to the analog input pin of Arduino, and the other is the Vcc pin.

12.3.2 Development of the hand sanitizer dispenser framework

The photodiode inputs are given into the Arduino board's analog input pins A0 and A1, as shown in Figure 12.1, which converts the analog values into integer values. A red LED connected to the power pin through a resistor glows as an indication of when the system is ready to take up the sensor input. Another white LED glows when the photodiode gives the input to the microcontroller, and the DC motor turns on for a specific period specified by the resistance value in the potentiometer that can be tuned according to our needs.

12.3.3 Default pins and conditions associated with the sensor

Simply adjusting the potentiometer's knob allows the user to change the device's resistance, which is also known as the rotary potentiometer or pot. It typically has three pins: a GND pin connected to the GND potential, a Vcc pin connected to Vcc (5 V or 3.3 V), and an output pin connected to the analog input pin on the Arduino. The voltage is discharged through this pin.

The method that is used to calculate the voltage output that is provided by the potentiometer for the various turns of the knob is as follows:

$$\mathrm{Output\,Voltage} = \frac{\mathrm{angle}}{\mathrm{angle_{max}}}()_{cc}. \tag{12.1}$$

Arduino's analog inputs are pins A0 through A5, as indicated by their names. The analog input pin rounds the voltage up or down to an integer value (between 0 V and Vcc). The ADC value, also known as the analog value, is a positive integer between 0 and 1023. The Arduino's analog input can take on values between 0 and 1023, and the on/off delay can be adjusted from zero milliseconds to tens of seconds.

When the potentiometer is set at its maximum angle, it is expected to turn on the device for the maximum ADC value in the code and then turn it off automatically. This implies that if the potentiometer is at its maximum resistance by tuning it to the maximum angle, the output voltage will be equal to Vcc (i-e) 5 V, and the expected time is 10 s. Practically, results very close to the theoretical values are obtained by simulating the designed circuit with various potentiometer values.

12.3.4 Adjusting procedure of the potentiometer

One more additional work in the designed system is that by changing the value of resistance in the potentiometer, the amount of sanitizer liquid needed to be dispensed out can be customized according to our needs and places where we make use of the automatic hand sanitizer dispensers for maintaining good hand hygiene.

The potentiometer chosen here is of 60k resistance at its maximum range. By tuning it to different angles, different output voltages corresponding to the tuned angle are obtained and calculated as follows:

When the knob is set at $0°$ angle, which is the minimum angle and contains 0k, the expected output voltage is also zero.

$$\frac{\mathrm{angle}}{\mathrm{angle_{max}}}()_{cc}\frac{0°}{270°}. \tag{12.2}$$

As expected, when the knob was at 0 resistance, the pot gave no output voltage, and no sanitizer was dispensed.

This value can be seen clearly from the serial monitor when the knob of the potentiometer is kept at 0 resistance.

12.4 Theoretical and Mathematical Proofs

For a more detailed study and more substantial proof, the theoretical and the simulated values for the half-tuning of the potentiometer were studied. When the potentiometer is tuned to half of its maximum angle, it gives out half of its Vcc, giving out 2.5 V. Hence the device is expected to dispense for half of its maximum period i.e., for 5 seconds. This is proved as follows:

$$\frac{angle}{angle_{max}}()_{cc}\frac{half of the angle_{max}}{angle_{max}} * 5V = \frac{135°}{270°} * 5V = 2.5V\frac{V_{cc}}{2}. \quad (12.3)$$

Hence, the simulated result, which was observed in the serial monitor, shows a very close observation of the theoretical values. The maximum time for the tuning on of the device was set to be 10 seconds. When the angle is half in the potentiometer, it gives half of its maximum resistance, 60 KΩ, making the device turn on for 5 seconds and then turn off automatically.

Similar proofs and calculations were observed for tuning of the potentiometer to its maximum angle ($angle_{max}$). When the knob of the potentiometer is tuned to 270°, it is at its maximum resistance i.e., 60 KΩ. Hence it gives out the output voltage, which is equal to Vcc. It makes the on-off time reach its maximum value, and the device is on for 10 seconds.

$$\frac{angle}{angle_{max}}()_{cc}\frac{half of the angle_{max}}{angle_{max}} * 5V = \frac{270°}{270°} * 5V = 5V \ V_{cc}. \quad (12.4)$$

The potentiometer's ratio to control the sanitizer's volume to the on and off time should be 1000:10 at its maximum range. The simulated result was very close and precise to the expected values, i.e., the serial monitor shows 1000:9, which is much closer to the expected values. The closer value of the experimental result to the theoretical value suggests that the system works with incremental steps or procedures adapted to make the potentiometer function with different values of resistances at different working conditions.

The wastage of hand sanitizer or unwanted dispensing can be avoided with this action introduced in our proposed system. The amount of sanitizer that has to be dispensed out can also be decided by the customer according to their needs. A prescribed amount of hand sanitizer liquid is to be dispensed out, which varies with the age and conditions. Children need only a tiny amount of hand sanitizer, while doctors and clinical persons may require a large amount. By varying the resistance value in the potentiometer, the amount of hand sanitizer to be dispensed is varied, which accounts for an enhanced adaptation of the system. So, the proposed system of automatic hand sanitizer dispensers proved to be worthwhile in all situations. Adjusting the probe of the potentiometer can make desirable changes in the circuit, and even rural people can quickly learn how it works and customize the machines according to their needs and requirements.

12.5 Schematic Layout of the Proposed Work

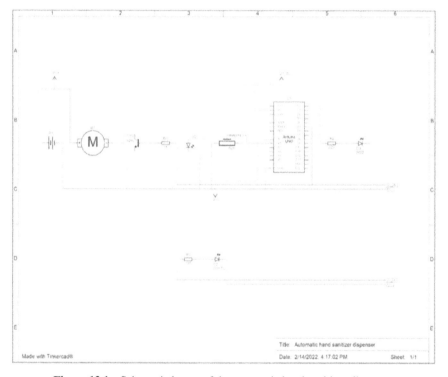

Figure 12.1   Schematic layout of the automatic hand sanitizer dispenser.

12.6 Examination of the Proposed Work

Every design of an engineer done in the lab with the help of tools and software has to be checked for performance and efficiency. The automatic sanitizer dispenser designed with the simulation software called Tinkercad must be checked and analyzed for its performance. Analyzing and experimenting with the proposed design system with different conditions and frequently changing specific parameters can be used to produce the required result of the experimental study. The main motive of the design was sensing the process that happens with photodiodes. Since the findings of the proposed system's operation are less distorted or impacted by the circumstances in the virtual environment, it is preferable to conduct precise experimental investigations in the virtual environment to produce more accurate results. There are also additional perks and advantages with the experiments that are done in the virtual environment using simulation software, like the presence of serial monitors that can be used to show the exact experimental readings. These readings can be used to compare the experimental values with the theoretically available values so that we can conclude that our system is working at its best. Usually, the conventional methods of checking a proposed work can be experimenting with all the designed systems after fabrication in real-time environments, calculating the recorded values, or taking the readings manually. However, the disadvantage of this system is that some of the fabricated machines can become waste when automated due to the faults caused by the conditions that affect their performance, so the designer may conclude that his design is a failure. However, there is no such chance with the experiments done through simulations, and they give the best results. Hence, the designed or proposed automatic hand sanitizer dispenser system can be tested, and the results are tabulated.

A comparative analysis is needed to prove that our system is the best compared to the existing ones in the industry. By comparing the results obtained from the experiment using software with the theoretically available readings, we stand strong and firm in proving that our idea is the best in comparison to the other machines available in the market. The working of the automatic hand sanitizer dispenser was analyzed by simulating the designed circuit using simulation software with different experimental conditions. On the whole, to showcase the working of the proposed system in varying conditions, the simulation was made at certain conditions of the potentiometer, and also, the simulation was done by varying the distance of the user from the sensor. The rpm of the DC motor was increased only when the distance between the sensor and the user was found to be higher than 78 mm. Hence the sanitizer liquid will not be dispensed if the distance of the human hand is less than the prescribed distance from the sanitizer machine. Additionally this could enhance the functionality of the automatic hand sanitizer dispenser and stop the sanitizer liquid from being wasted due to false sensing. Table 12.1 depicts the results of the comparative analysis made with the available machines in the market and the proposed system. Comparing various parameters of top brands of hand sanitizer dispensers available in the market and their performance with that of the proposed system shows that the proposed system is working at its best to satisfy all desirable conditions. With simple changes in the needed arena of the system, the best results can be obtained to meet the customer's needs and improve satisfaction.

Once the result values of the proposed system of automatic hand sanitizers are closer to the expected value, they can be fabricated and released into the market for use by the public. The designed circuit of the automatic hand sanitizer dispenser is so easy and compact, occupies significantly less space, and is even cost-effective to buy.

12.7 A Comparative Study with the Market Products

Table 12.1   A comparative study of the parameters of the designed prototype with the available dispensers in the market.

S.no	Name of the sanitizer machines	Price in ₹	Time consumption (sensor dispensing time)	Distance of sensing	Sensor used	Input power	Battery
1.	NETBOON automatic hand sanitizer dispenser	4491	1 second	12 inches	Ultra Sonic	90–270 V AC/50 Hz	1.5V AA
2.	KENT touchless automatic sanitizer dispenser	2490	3.25 seconds	10 cm	IR sensor	4.5 V (3 no's) (1.5 W)	4 C type batteries, 1.5V. Bt
3.	SVAVO automatic hand sanitizer dispenser	8316	0.38 seconds	2–12 cm	IR sensor	Power adaptor	4 AA batteries

Table 12.1 *Continued.*

S.no	Name of the sanitizer machines	Price in ₹	Time consumption (sensor dispensing time)	Distance of sensing	Sensor used	Input power	Battery
4.	Hi-genic automatic bulge sanitizer dispenser	1899	0.93 seconds	3–5 cm	IR sensor	110 V	6V/1A power adaptor
5.	BELTER automatic hand sanitizer dispenser	3199	Varies with conditions	2.4–4.5 inches	Motion sensors	110– 240 V DC 6V adaptor	4 C type batter- ies
6.	**Proposed design of automatic hand sanitizer dispenser using Arduino**	**900**	**0.32 milliseconds**	**78 mm**	**Photod iode**	**12 V power adap- tor/ 12 V from power gener- ator**	**Not needed**

12.8 Drawbacks of the Conventional System of Dispensers

The result of the literature review proved the worth of the proposed system. Most of the available dispensers in industrial automation were known to function with an ultrasonic or infrared sensor. The sensing time, or the time the sensors take, varies with the changing environmental setup conditions. The sensor action varies, and the efficiency of the sanitizer and machines decrease following the changes. Most of these devices in the market cost more than our proposed device, so our proposed system proves to be cost-efficient. The time taken by the photodiode to sense the user is just around 0.32 milliseconds which is much faster compared to that of other machines whose ultrasonic and infrared sensors are equipped with automatic hand sanitizers like NETBOON, HI-GENIC, and all others as compared in Table 12.1. Most of such identified devices work with AA batteries which have a faster discharging rate. Due to this faster discharging rate, the batteries need to be changed frequently, and they account for additional costs, including the maintenance charge. Another disadvantage of battery replacement is that rural people may need the help of educated ones as they might be unaware of the steps to follow during battery replacement. Since, this kind of hand sanitizer dispensers are available in the market, replacing conventional machines is the need of the hour.

12.9 Performance Comparison of Automatic Hand Sanitizer Dispensers

Batteries are required for the operation of the vast majority of self-service machines. Consequently, they need to have their batteries charged consistently and on time as part of their maintenance. If the batteries run out of juice, the consumer must make additional financial and time investments to replace them. Despite this, many Indian manufacturers of hand sanitizer dispensers have begun incorporating automated features in their products since the beginning of the pandemic. The customer's overall shopping experience should become more streamlined as a primary focus. Because contemporary hand sanitizer dispensers are powered by electricity, you will never need to worry about them running out of liquid. Because of this, the batteries in these sanitizer machines need to be replaced consistently, which can be an inconvenience and may increase the risk associated with device management.

12.10 The Desirable Properties of the Proposed Idea

The proposed system uses no battery and works wholly based on a 12 V power supply with a current of just 5 A. Hence, we can also use a 12 V supply from the power generator instead of preferring batteries that need additional expenses once discharged. The main microcontroller of the proposed system is the Arduino UNO. The maximum output capacity of the Arduino is 5 V. In addition to the output produced by the Arduino, we can make the system work with sufficient power by adding a simple 9 V battery. Even the amplification part in the proposed design that contains an NPN transistor with the resistor can contribute to power usage by amplifying it. Hence, no additional requirements are necessary here for power supply, and it makes the system run more efficiently than other machines in the market.

12.11 Additional Perks of the Industrial Automated System

Others disagree with the viewpoint held by some individuals who maintain that automatic dispensers always require human supervision. Because some areas become congested due to the automatic hand sanitizer dispenser, it is essential to maintain cleanliness in those areas. This is another reason why this place is so filthy and unclean. On the other hand, electric dispensers that spray a fine mist rarely require maintenance or repair. They are also very proud of how clean they are because this is the case. Even though you have to manually refill the hand sanitizer dispenser, doing so does not require much time or effort. There is also a time delay of 1000 milliseconds for the sanitizer machine to start for the next sensing as soon as it has dispensed the required amount of sanitizer for the previous sensing. This also ensures additional safety and hygiene in terms of avoiding crowding of people. The setting made in the software part of the microcontroller of the proposed system to make the sanitizer dispenser dispense the sanitizer liquid only for the determined distance is yet another added advantage of the system. It is determined and coded in the Arduino coding such that the sanitizer will be dispensed only when the distance of the human hand is more than 78 cm. This will add credit to your work because it prevents dispensing the hand sanitizer liquid for any fake sensing of the human hand when they are not sensed in the actual time.

12.12 Conclusion

The proposed system of automatic hand sanitizer dispensers will prove their efficiency in performance because of the novel change made in the existing system of dispensers. Replacing the batteries in the available machines in the market was difficult to replace and maintain the entire system. Hence the proposed system is designed in such a way as to overcome the disadvantage of many in which battery replacement is an essential one. The disadvantage can be overcome by using the output from the microcontroller and adding a battery of 9 V as an extra power supply. In the future, to expand this work, the addition of an amplifier stage can be used to amplify the power from the Arduino output. The amplifier circuit consists of the NPN transistor with a tank circuit that amplifies the voltage divider bias input. These are more straightforward and cost-effective machines that can be used for hand hygiene in various places, as discussed already, including homes, hospitals, and public places where the crowd of people is even slightly above the normal range. As the COVID precautions are increasing daily with the advent of new diseases like monkey fever, advanced COVID attacks, etc., in addition to the safety precautions declared by the health ministry, maintaining good hand hygiene is also very important. The proposed system of automatic hand sanitizer dispensers using Arduino and photodiode was expected to be an excellent way of preventing the spread of viruses through industrial automation. The research for adding an ESP8266 WiFi module and a temperature-sensing system is on hand. With the addition of the WiFi module, the amount of hand sanitizer dispensed out for each detector in the human hand and the temperature sensed by the temperature sensors can be recorded. In case of want of any temperature data regarding the person affected with COVID-19 or that of a person with the symptoms of the disease, the proposed system, with its extended additions of temperature sensors and WiFi modules, can help the health ministry a lot. These recorded data can also be used to further analyze persons with high temperatures and will also help check out frequently if the system is working with total efficiency. The recorded data by the microcontroller can be shared and processed from anywhere in the world through the WiFi module using the Internet of Things concept. The Internet of Things has an efficient way of adding performance efficiency to the systems by collecting data, storing data which is followed by the processing of data to make necessary modiïïñÄcations in the system or to process the stored data.

References

[1] Ghosh, A., Nundy, S., & Mallick, T. K. (2020). How India is dealing with the COVID-19 pandemic. Sensors

[2] Moore, L. D., Robbins, G., Quinn, J., & Arbogast, J. W. (2021). The impact of the COVID-19 pandemic on hand hygiene performance in hospitals. American Journal of infection control, 49(1), 30-33.

[3] Huang, F., Armando, M., Dufau, S., Florea, O., Brouqui, P., & Boudjema, S. (2021). COVID-19 outbreak and healthcare worker behavioral change toward hand hygiene practices. Journal of Hospital Infection, 111, 27-34.

[4] Ciotti, M., Ciccozzi, M., Terrinoni, A., Jiang, W. C., Wang, C. B., & Bernardini, S. (2020). The COVID-19 pandemic. Critical reviews in clinical laboratory sciences, 57(6), 365-388.

[5] Tamimi, A. H., Carlino, S., Edmonds, S., & Gerba, C. P. (2014). Impact of an alcohol-based hand sanitizer intervention on the spread of viruses in homes. Food and environmental virology, 6(2), 140-144.

[6] Santhosh, R., & Mahalakshmi, R. (2021, September). Low-cost automatic hand sanitizer dispenser for the Covid-19 pandemic period. In 2021 Third International Conference on Inventive Research in Computing Applications (ICIRCA) (pp. 534-538). IEEE.

[7] Das, A., Barua, A., Mohimin, M., Abedin, J., Khandaker, M. U., & Al-Mugren, K. S. (2021, April). Development of a Novel Design and

Subsequent Fabrication of an Automated Touchless Hand Sanitizer Dispenser to Reduce the Spread of Contagious Diseases. In Healthcare (Vol. 9, No. 4, p. 445). Multidisciplinary Digital Publishing Institute.

[8] Suryawanshi, V. R., Surani, H. C., & Yadav, H. R. (2021). Sensor-based automatic hand sanitizer dispenser. Medical Journal of Dr. DY Patil Vidyapeeth, 14(5), 543.

[9] Eddy, Y., Mohammed, M. N., Daoodd, I. I., Bahrain, S. H. K., Al-Zubaidi, S., Al-Sanjary, O. I., & Sairah, A. K. (2020). 2019 Novel Coronavirus Disease (Covid-19): Smart contactless hand sanitizer-dispensing system using IoT based robotics technology. Revista Argentina de Clínica Psicológica, 29(5), 215.

[10] Zainudin, Z. I. B., San, L. Y., & Abdulla, R. (2022). Smart hand sanitizer dispenser. Journal of Applied Technology and Innovation (e-ISSN: 2600-7304), 6(1), 10.

[11] Ciotti, M., Ciccozzi, M., Terrinoni, A., Jiang, W. C., Wang, C. B., & Bernardini, S. (2020). The COVID-19 pandemic. Critical reviews in clinical laboratory sciences, 57(6), 365-388.

[12] Boudjema, S., Dufour, J. C., Aladro, A. S., Desquerres, I., & Brouqui, P. (2014). MediHandTrace®: a tool for measuring and understanding hand hygiene adherence. Clinical Microbiology and Infection, 20(1), 22-28.

[13] Janga, P., Khan, M. S., Suneel, L., & Reddy, M. A. (2021, July). Design and implementation of automatic hand sanitization technique using Arduino and ultrasonic sensor. In AIP Conference Proceedings (Vol. 2358, No. 1, p. 050029). AIP Publishing LLC.

[14] Kumar, K. S., Mani, A. R., Sundaresan, S., Kumar, T. A., & Robinson, Y. H. (2021). Blockchain-based energy-efficient smart green city in IoT environments. In Blockchain for Smart Cities (pp. 81-103). Elsevier.

[15] Cure, L., & Van Enk, R. (2015). Effect of hand sanitizer location on hand hygiene compliance. American Journal of infection control, 43(9), 917-921.

[16] Sitorus, A., syahri Cebro, I., & Bulan, R. (2021). Experimental push and pull force data utilizing self-developed automatic liquid dispensers. Data in Brief, 38, 107308.

[17] Bördlein, C. (2020). Promoting hand sanitizer use in a University Cafeteria. Behavior and Social Issues, 1-9.

[18] Anderson, J. L., Warren, C. A., Perez, E., Louis, R. I., Phillips, S., Wheeler, J., ... & Misra, R. (2008). Gender and ethnic differences in hand hygiene practices among college students. American Journal of infection control, 36(5), 361-368.

[19] Iqbal, M. Z., & Campbell, A. G. (2021). From luxury to necessity: Progress of touchless interaction technology. Technology in Society, 67, 101796.

[20] Ward, M. A., Schweizer, M. L., Polgreen, P. M., Gupta, K., Reisinger, H. S., & Perencevich, E. N. (2014). Automated and electronically assisted hand hygiene monitoring systems: a systematic review. American Journal of infection control, 42(5), 472-478.

[21] Meng, M., Sorber, M., Herzog, A., Igel, C., & Kugler, C. (2019). Technological innovations in infection control: A rapid review of the acceptance of behavior monitoring systems and their contribution to improving hand hygiene. American Journal of infection control, 47(4), 439-447.

[22] Zeng, Z., Chen, P. J., & Lew, A. A. (2020). From high-touch to high-tech: COVID-19 drives robotics adoption. Tourism Geographies, 22(3), 724-734.

[23] Syahputra, M. I., Khair, U., & Sembiring, A. (2021). Automatic Hand Sanitizer Dispenser. ALGORITMA: JURNAL ILMU KOMPUTER DAN INFORMATIKA, 5(2)

[24] Gupta, a., Kumar, r., & Gupta, r. (2021). Novel design and performance analysis of automatic sanitizer dispenser machine based on the ultrasonic sensor. In recent trends in communication and electronics (pp. 320-325). CRC press.

[25] Deshpande, S., Aggarwal, A., Ponraj, A. S., & Jackson, J. C. IoT-Based Smart Hand Sanitizer Dispenser (COVID-19). In Smart Buildings Digitalization (pp. 281-302). CRC Press.

[26] Nof, S. Y. (2009). Automation: What it means to us around the world. In Springer handbook of automation (pp. 13-52). Springer, Berlin, Heidelberg.

[27] Kumar, B. K., Thanusha, N. J., Hiremath, S., Soujanya, K., Vanishree, B. C., & Navadeep, G. U. (2021, August). A Solar Powered Kiosk for Contactless Body Temperature Sensor and Hand Sanitizer Dispenser to Monitor and Control Covid-19 Disease. In 2021 International Conference on Recent Trends on Electronics, Information, Communication & Technology (RTEICT) (pp. 884-888). IEEE.

[28] Lastovicka-Medin, G., & Vanja, B. (2021, June). From Contactless Disinfection Intelligent Hand Sanitizer Dispenser for Public & Home towards IoT Based Assistive Technologies for Visually Impaired Users Institutional Responses to the COVID-19 Pandemic. In 2021 10th

Mediterranean Conference on Embedded Computing (MECO) (pp. 1-4). IEEE.

[29] Srihari, M. M. (2020, July). Self-activating sanitizer with the battery-imposed system for cleansing hands. In 2020 Second International Conference on Inventive Research in Computing Applications (ICIRCA) (pp. 1102-1105). IEEE.

[30] Ajayan, A. (2020, December). Automizer-An Automatic Sanitizer Dispenser. In 2020 IEEE International Women in Engineering (WIE) Conference on Electrical and Computer Engineering (WIECON-ECE) (pp. 153-156). IEEE.

[31] Bal, M., & Abrishambaf, R. (2017, March). A system for monitoring hand hygiene compliance based on Internet-of-Things. In 2017 IEEE International Conference on Industrial Technology (ICIT) (pp. 1348-1353). IEEE.

[32] Ganeshkumar, D. (2021, October). Design and Implementation of Hands-Free Electronic Sanitizer Dispenser. In 2021 Smart Technologies, Communication and Robotics (STCR) (pp. 1-4). IEEE.

[33] Nayana, D. K., Mallikarjun Patil, K. S., Manoj, A. M., Mallikarjun, G. N., & NS, S. (2021). AUTOMATIC HAND SANITIZER DISPENSER USING ARDUINO. NEW ARCH-INTERNATIONAL JOURNAL OF CONTEMPORARY ARCHITECTURE, 8(1s), 283-286.

[34] Syahputra, M. I., Khair, U., & Sembiring, A. (2021). Automatic Hand Sanitizer Dispenser. ALGORITMA: JURNAL ILMU KOMPUTER DAN INFORMATIKA, 5(2).

13

Energy Efficiency Investigation in Massive MIMO Communication for Industry Automation using Precoding Schemes

R. Surender[1], S. Sudharsan[2], S. Sundaresan[3], and Sunday Adeola Ajagbe[4]

[1]Department of ECE, Sathyabama Institute of Science and Technology, Chennai
[2]Department of ECE, Rajalakshmi Engineering College, India
[3]Department of Electronics & Communication, NIT Karaikal, India
[4]Department of Computer Engineering,
Ladoke Akintola University of Technology, LAUTECH, Nigeria
E-mail: surender.ragu@gmail.com; sudharsan.s@rajalakshmi.edu.in; sundaresanece91@gmail.com; saajagbe@psgchool.lautech.edu.ng

Abstract

Fifth-generation wireless access technology aims at consistent quality of everything (QoE), and this demand can be accomplished by enhancing the network throughput. Massive multiple input multiple output (mMIMO) system is a promising candidate that can be employed at the base station (BS) and afford high reliability and network sum rate, improving the network energy efficiency (EE). The network employing mMIMO system is analyzed in the presence of interference to attain better throughput and network energy efficiency. Different precoding schemes like maximal ratio combining (MRC), zero-forcing (ZF), and pilot zero-forcing (P-ZF) are employed in the network for mMIMO communication system analysis. Further, the work is analyzed by incorporating regular and superimposed pilot in the maximal ratio combining and zero-forcing precoding schemes. Performance attributes like average rate, BS energy efficiency, user equipment energy efficiency, and network power consumption are investigated for upgrading the mMIMO network performance in industrial automation.

Keywords: QoE, mMIMO, precoding schemes, superimposed pilot, industry automation.

13.1 Introduction

The tremendous growth in development of electronic gadgets and various emerging applications like artificial intelligence, augmented reality, big data analytics, virtual reality, ultra–high-definition transmission video, three-dimensional (3D) media, etc., have encapsulated the wireless communication field and created a substantial evolution in the wireless networks data volume. In the interim, mobile networks have become essential services for computing personal devices. As new technologies have emerged, the need for fast wireless services like switched traffic, multimedia, and IP data packets has grown. Without these services, there would be no way for mobile communication systems to work. On the other hand, the system's design should meet the customers' needs without making them pay extra. Balancing complexity, adaptability, data rate, quality-of-service (QoS), and cost is essential in commercial applications. Modern improvements in microelectronics, signal processing, mobile computing, and other related fields have enabled high spectral efficiency and high degrees of adaptability [1].

The conventional mobile system has difficulty fulfilling the traffic demand for data and spectral scarcity. The wireless system's spectral efficiency depends on attributes like signal-to-noise ratio and other attributes like spatial correlation, accuracy in channel estimation, hardware impairment, and signal processing resources. So, it is essential to enhance the spectral efficiency as it increases the demand for wireless services. Recently, advancements in the 5G systems have been exposed by deploying additional antennae at the transceiver. The capacity of the wireless system can be increased substantially without an increase in the bandwidth and transmission power. The design incorporating multiple antenna elements at uplink and downlink is a MIMO system [2].

In mobile communication [3], the signals transmitted are attenuated by fading and obstructed in between the transceiver by shadowing. This sequence yields a primary challenge for seamless communication, and the MIMO system can achieve it. The system uses spatial multiplexing to achieve multiplexing gain and improves the communication system's capacity. The effort to achieve the gain by spatial multiplexing has been lifted from MIMO to mMIMO. The base station serves several users simultaneously; even each user has a single antenna, which overcomes the limitation of propagation in the channel.

13.2 Evolution of Wireless Communication System

Wireless communication has become a vibrant part of the present communication system, transforming the present communication and living system. As the wireless system progress from one generation to other generation , there is upgradation in the system's data rate, mobility, coverage, and the operator's spectral capabilities. In the early 1980s, the 1G system was united with analog services with 2.4 Kbps which is more prone to noise and easily vulnerable [4]. The 2G system user digital services for voice communication uses 64 kbps data rate, whereas 2.5G systems like GPRS and EDGE have evolved with 144 kbps data rate.

In late 2000, the 3G wireless system imparted data rates up to 2 Mbps by merging mobile access with high-speed to IP-based services. This feature enhances the improvement in QoS and global roaming at more power consumption in the network. At the intermediate with an enhanced data rate of 5–30 Mbps, Universal Mobile Telecommunication System (UMTS) evolved [5, 6]. Later in 4G, to supplement the network capacity and to facilitate a more significant number of users with services like video on demand, file sharing, and Web services evolved to accomplish it. The 4G system is generally highlighted to be the inheritance of 2G & 3G standards, with a 3G partnership project (3GPP) standardizing the networks. The 4G wireless system improves the conventional approach by fully imparting an IP-based reliable solution. This makes ubiquitous communication a possible one when compared to traditional techniques of communication [7].

LTE enhances wireless systems' network capacity and mobility by using the core network and radio interface. LTE does not fulfill the service capacity of a 4G wireless. LTE-Advanced is an upgraded standard of the LTE, which delivers a high data rate, unlike current LTE networks, and is also known as True4G. LTE-A incorporates many hardware and software technologies to accomplish high network standards. They are:

i. *Increased uplink and downlink peak data rate*
ii. *Comparatively high spectral efficiency*

iii. *More number of active subscribers*
iv. *Improved performance at cell edges*
v. *Carrier aggregation*
vi. *Enhanced usage of multi-antenna techniques*
vii. *Relay nodes support*

The ubiquitous system exhibits an exponential increase in data traffic as it incorporates a more significant number of users. This data traffic makes the 4G system be replaced by a 5G system with beam division multiple access (BDMA) and filter bank multi-carrier (FBMC) . BDMA increases the system by allocating an orthogonal beam to each user; it will share the same shaft according to the location of MS. The 5G network with BDMA addresses the following challenge, which is not discussed by 4G [8]. They are high system capacity and data, latency reduction in end-to-end services, connectivity with massive device, and providing better quality of experience. To fulfill the user demands and to attain the challenges of the 5G system, a new network was designed for 5G wireless architecture. Here, the base station uses antennas on a large scale for network communication with users using BDMA technology, hence the name MIMO. Since conventional MIMO system has the constraint of using antenna terminals, it limits the attributes of improving the performance in the network. As MIMO uses an antenna on a large scale, the beneficial features obtained by the system are high in terms of capacity and gain in the network [9].

13.3 Challenges in the 5G Communication System

Fifth-generation cellular network demands high area throughput for the exponential evolution of wireless data traffic. To accompany the traffic growth in 5G technology, the system's throughput must be improved a thousand times. It can be enhanced by [10]

i. *providing a high user data rate;*
ii. *allocating more bandwidth to serve the 5G network;*
iii. *densifying the network with independent access points and small cell;*
iv. *improving the network efficiency.*

Various applications in wireless network may lead to many technical challenges for the users. To provide a reliable seamless service for these wireless applications and the requirements of 5G [11], the following components are involved:

With the advent of transmission waveforms, novel resource management methods, and multiple access control are developed.

To develop multi-hop technologies and advance inter-node coordination schemes, antennas in large-scale configurations are designed with multimode.

The design consideration of the network considers the data traffic, mobility handling capability, and novel and efficient way of interference management, which involves complexity in the integration of the network.

The usage of the spectrum includes a band of operation in the prolonged region of the spectrum. The process in this region forms a new set of concepts completely for the prolonged spectrum, and it must be prudently used in the system.

mMIMO is a multi-antenna technique to multiplex the user terminal over the entire bandwidth spatially and reduces the data traffic growth in the 5G cellular system. By reducing 5G network traffic, the system throughput can be significantly increased. It also provides other benefits, such as lower latency, cheaper parts, and robustness against intentional jamming.

13.4 Massive Multiple Input Multiple Output

mMIMO is the advanced and improved version of MIMO in which the antennas are grouped at the transceiver to enhance throughput and efficiency. It is a MIMO technology with a multiuser where a BS is deployed with antenna elements on a large scale. It employs these antenna elements to connect with single antenna UEs over a similar time and frequency band since it uses space division multiple access (SDMA). The SDMA makes the mMIMO into a scalable form that makes coherent signal processing over a large scale of antennas. In the downlink of the mMIMO system, transmit precoding is incorporated, and it is made to focus each signal to send at the intended terminal. In the uplink, receive combining is incorporated to eliminate the transmitted signals across various terminals [12]. The illustration of mMIMO transmission is shown in Figure 13.1.

Time duplexing mode is used in which the transmission of the signal occurs at identical frequencies but at different times. This condition highlights the responses of the channel are equal in both uplink and downlink directions. The system has many advantages to operate in time division duplexing (TDD) mode. First, the channel conditions must be known only to the base station for coherent processing using antenna elements. Second, overhead in the estimation of the uplink is proportional to the UE. Third, the approximation structure of channel responses will not degrade by using additional antennas

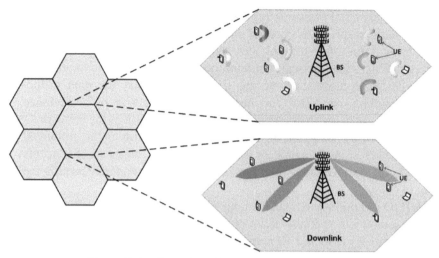

Figure 13.1 Illustration of transmission in an mMIMO.

at BS in TDD mode. It uses spatial multiplexing that depends on BS to estimate channels with proper information on the channel (CSI) in uplink and downlink. In downlink estimation, the pilots are placed orthogonal to one another, which varies the time and frequency of resources. The quality of the estimated channels might be reciprocated in TDD mode in the uplink, where it depends on the BS antennas [13]. The spatial multiplexing technique transmits the signal to the typical user and reduces the impact of interference on the other user. The intended signal quality is optimized by weighing and summing the antenna signals in the various antenna arrays.

The importance of multiple antenna systems is improvement in array gain, reduction in interference, and diversity gain. It provides a high multiplexing boost by exploiting both the transmit and receive antenna using a traditional MIMO system [14]. The improvement in array gain at the receiver is retrieved in the transceiver by coherent signal processing. The system gain is attained properly when the transmitter gains knowledge of the CSI and proper correlation with the received signals.

The concept of frequency reuse in wireless channels introduces network interference and degrades the performance of the wireless network. By using different spatial signatures and proper estimation of CSI, the interference in the network can be reduced. Diversity is another method to combat interference by reducing fading in the channels. The signal in deep fade for one user will not be the same for the other. The more independent the fading channel the higher the probability that the signal is not in the deep fade. The reason to use space diversity is that it shares the same frequency and time resource. To utilize this resource, the antennas must be appropriately spaced; otherwise, signals will correlate with interference and reduce the diversity gain.

To enhance the system performance, which is limited by interference, the transmitter has to be adopted a precoding scheme, as shown in Figure 13.2. A precoding scheme is a design process of the transmitting signal before transmission, making communication effective to the intended user in a multiuser MIMO system. Each antenna individually transmits a stream of data in a precoding scheme which is a linear combination of all data streams employed with beamforming weights which makes sharing a standard data DL at the transceiver and exploiting the DL reciprocity concept.

Wireless communication toward 5G makes energy efficiency an essential criterion for design in sustaining the evolution. The information and communication technology (ICT) sector focuses on rapid progress in evolving 5G, which expects to integrate at most everything across the world into the

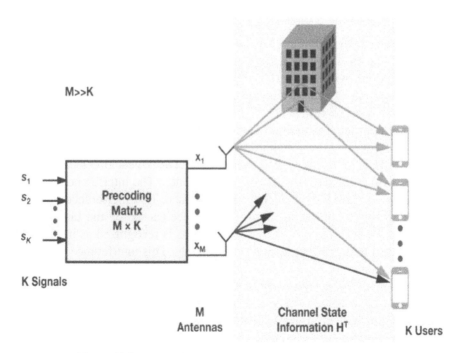

Figure 13.2 Illustration of precoding scheme at the transmitter.

Internet. The network has adequate access to power sources to serve several devices in an unprecedented manner, which is known as densification. The ultimate aim of densification is to provide capacity 1000 times than the conventional network. The 5G network operators spend more on network operation, emitting 2 percent of total carbon dioxide [16]. To overcome this constraint, the energy efficiency perspective is adopted, referred to as green communication.

mMIMO is a 5G technology that extracts energy and spectral efficiency over an LTE-A network with an extensive array of antennas. Energy-efficient communication has the advantage of exploiting the interference in co-channel. It also reduces the environmental effects like the dissipation of heat and electronic pollution. Compared to the conventional system, there are two ways to achieve energy efficiency on a large scale. First, to obtain the fixed throughput in a given system, the power transmission in the UE must be reduced by upgrading the transmitter side antennas. Second, more gain in the network can be achieved by incorporating more UEs in the system.

In the mMIMO system, an increase in BS and UEs does not guarantee energy efficiency improvement because circuit power consumption increases with the number of BS and UEs. Subsequently, an increase in BS can improve energy efficiency by reducing the UE's transmission power. Similarly, energy efficiency can be enhanced by incorporating more UEs at the dominance of power expenditure. As energy efficiency is inversely proportional to circuit power consumption, it can be attained by considerably diminishing overall network power consumption [17].

MIMO is a challenging multi-antenna technology to upgrade the data rate in a 5G system for seamless communication. As the mMIMO is characterized by the deployment of BS in large numbers, the network gets affected due to interference which reduces the network performance. The interference must be considerably reduced to enhance the performance. The interference in the system appears in the following ways: interference caused by the same UE in the same cells and UE formed in different cells is recognized as intercell interference and intracell interference, respectively. This interference can be moderated by using proper precoding schemes, which diminishes the interference and enhances the performance of MIMO. Another factor that degrades the mMIMO performance is pilot contamination which gets introduced due to the frequent use of pilot symbols and limitation in coherence block. By increasing the duration of the coherence block and proper channel estimation techniques, the system's performance can be upgraded by combating the interference that occurs due to pilot contamination.

Various studies have focused on maximizing the performance of the mMIMO communication system over the conventional MIMO system. However, most problems addressed in the published research papers are associated with traditional MIMO systems regarding the interference problem. Interestingly, such attempts have made a better pathway for other categories of research works toward different future advanced versions of MIMO networks. This section discusses the research contribution of interference reduction in the mMIMO network using a precoding scheme.

The first, LTE, was proposed by NTT DOCOMO of Japan, commercially launched by Sweden and Japan, and followed by the United States. More LTE networks were installed as GSM, UMTS, and CDMA 2000. Long-term evolution advanced is the enhancement of LTE, and it is used in 4G to support high-end applications [18, 19]. The essential characteristic is to improve the channel capacity and data rate in wireless application, and it can be attained by the MIMO system, which the idea was introduced by authors in [20]. As the conventional MIMO system is limited in base station antennas, the network's data rate is also limited. By deploying antennas on a large scale, the LTE-A network achieves the ability of a 5G network. The usage of the antenna on a large scale is said to be mMIMO which introduces interference from unintended users.

HQ Ngo et al. analyzed the uplink of the systems in perfect and imperfect CSI with precoding schemes like MRC, ZF, and minimum mean square error. The study of the proposed work demonstrated that moderate usage of the antenna on a large scale could considerably increase spectral efficiency [21]. Emil et al. [22] considered single-cell and multicell MU-MIMO networks to analyze the network's performance in perfect CSI and imperfect CSI using the precoding schemes ZF, MRC, and MMSE processing. The simulated result concluded that energy efficiency performance is preferable in the region of high SNR and can be attained by suppressing interference using the precoding scheme.

Wang et al. [23] demonstrated that ZF processing could seamlessly cancel the self-interference (SI) in a Rician fading, where the transceiver antennas are large. The study of the proposed work in the paper indicated that the SI could be canceled for short-range communications by using limited base station antennas. De Mi et al. [24], in the existence of reciprocity errors, deduced signal-to-interference noise ratio expressions (SINR) for ZF and MRT, and further investigation highlighted that effect of reciprocity errors could reduce the SNR. Lee et al. [25] investigated the mMIMO performance, and the numerical results proved that SE is reduced due to a high clipping ratio causing degradation in energy efficiency. The proposed iterative clipping and filtering technique gave better gain with the ZF precoding scheme.

Hoydis et al. [26] have presented a study on multicell mMIMO networks to analyze the performance of achievable rates in the uplink and downlink using different precoding schemes like regularized zero-forcing (RZF) and matched filter (MF). The authors have considered the work based on the imperfect CSI, path loss, and pilot contamination; and the outcome of the result proved that RZF preceding scheme can perform better than the MF preceding scheme with a limited number of BS antennas. Bjornson et al. [27] considered the scenario in the downlink of the single-cell system to analyze the energy efficiency in the cellular network with a modified form of precoding scheme known as multi-flow RZF with small cell access (SCA). The precoding scheme is introduced with a low-complexity algorithm that consumes static and hardware power in the network, improving the quality of everything (QoE).

Li et al. [28] investigated the performance in a cellular network with BS antennas on a large scale and analyzed the impact of both BS antennas and user equipment density in the network. The simulated outcome of the study highlighted that an increase in the thickness of BS would enhance the throughput linearly and then, in turn, increases the energy efficiency of the mMIMO network. Gao et al. [29] presented a study on performance measurement of massive antennas using ZF and MMSE processing in the downlink channel and compared it with dirty paper coding (DPC). The paper's outcome proved that using linear precoding schemes, 98 percent of the sum rate can be achieved compared to DPC with a limited number of antennas in BS.

Hu et al. [30] presented a study on the performance of SE in network MIMO compared to mMIMO architecture employing ZF precoding schemes. The web MIMO is operated by grouping the user equipment in the corresponding locations with time-frequency slots. The study's outcome proves that the proposed work achieves better users' spectral efficiency in different areas. The work in [31] analyzed the specific system sum rate with ZF and MRC precoding schemes. The outcome of the work proved the given data rate is achieved by minimizing the total power consumed at BS with optimal transmission power, BS antennas, and users in the network.

Hao et al. [32] proposed a framework to analyze the downlink of heterogeneous networks employing a low-complexity algorithm. The proposed work enhanced the tradeoff with optimal antennas in BS significantly. The authors in [33] presented the work on the downlink of mMIMO using MRC and ZF precoding schemes to study the problem of max-min fairness (MMF). The proposed work in multiantenna system incorporating multicasting, identified the optimal power for uplink pilots and downlink precoders which provided better spectral efficiency for modes of precoding schemes which can alter between them based on the system's parameters.

Hu et al. [34] incorporated the same set of pilot sequences in the mMIMO network and assumed it is reused in all cells. It mitigates the interference by exploiting covariance matrices. The proposed architecture in this paper is based on cooperative base stations and achieved a comparable spectral efficiency with the ZF precoding scheme. The authors in [35] used another method to combat interference, having longer pilot sequences than the users per cell using a similar set of pilots. This method reduced the impact of pilot contamination at the overhead estimation penalty, decreasing the data symbols incorporated in the coherence block.

Muller et al. [36, 37] proposed a method of subspace prediction to enhance channel estimation with power-controlled hand-off in multi-antenna systems. The proposed blind method does not need pilot data to identify the proper subspace, and it can mitigate interference without coordination between the cells. Yin et al. [38] presented a method of pilot allocation for desired and interfering UE in correlated channels. This novelty undertook the problem by allowing low-rate cell coordination in the channel estimation duration. It provided additional user channel information and proved a way to discriminate against interfering users even when pilot sequences correlate strongly. A pilot decontamination array processing method has been presented for the use of channels with discrete paths which is finite in number. This method improved the performance of the system compared to the existing approaches.

Takeuchi et al. [39] analyzed the large-scale antenna system using the replica method under the replica symmetry assumption. The study of the technique proved that pilot information is the finest in the condition of achievable data rates of successive decoding receivers for the antenna on a large scale. The study in the proposed results suggests that it can significantly gain the average SNR regimes. In [40], the authors proposed segregating method to improve the throughput. The simulation results depict that performance can be enhanced with reuse-1 architectures. Li et al. [41] considered an uplink system that uses pilot reuse to obtain the optimum pilots reuse factor between the cells using the MRC precoding scheme. The numerical results proved that pilot reuse could achieve high throughput in cellular networks, in which the traditional interference term controls the pilot contamination term. Noh et al.

[42] proposed an algorithm for pilots to exploit the interference that degrades the network's performance. The resulting low-complexity design generates optimal pilot sequence beam patterns for the given parameters and proves the importance of the proposed algorithm.

Upadya et al. [43] investigated the DL performance of a network that uses SP to estimate the channel to reduce pilot contamination. The authors used a normalized mean-squared error channel estimate for matched filter and compared it with Bayesian Cramer-Rao lower bound. The former channel estimation proved that the system's throughput decreases with an increase in antenna number. It further improved the DL throughput using SP than the regular pilots. Jing et al. [44,45] stated that contamination of the pilot and interference in the data are two essential features that reduce the SP-based channel estimation accuracy. The authors proposed an approach to improve the interference and proved that the proposed method mitigates the interference and improves the channel estimation and SE.

Zhang et al. [46] presented an SP method for the estimation of channel schemes and studied the outcome of SP on a very large-scale antenna. This method established that the SP scheme's outcome results could improve pilot contamination. It is proficient in increasing the frame size and enhancing the spectral efficiency. Li et al. [47] used SP to estimate channels in the mMIMO system using simple linear detection like MRC and ZF. The proposed scheme yielded a superior performance over the conventional method. Upadhya et al. [48] proposed a scheme for uplink channel estimation based on SP employing matched filter precoding scheme for channel estimate. This precoding scheme utilized reduced the overall interference. The study of the simulation proved the effectiveness of the proposed schemes. Li et al. [49] proposed a superimposed pilot in the mMIMO system using MRC and ZF precoding schemes. The study of the proposed work demonstrated that channel estimation with SP yielded a better result by maximizing the network performance. Verenzuela et al. [50] evaluated the network performance with MRC estimated with different methods. They proved that the proposed SP work outperforms the other estimated methods by reducing interference and enhancing energy efficiency.

Tominaga et al. [51] investigated the performance of mMIMO and revealed that NOMA-based mMIMO provides significant gain compared with different precoding schemes. David et al. [52] enabled the usage of critical technologies with mMIMO, like the carrier design, advanced sleep mode, and machine learning, and highlighted the need for QoS demands for end-users. The authors also stated that MRC, characterized by lower complexity, achieves higher energy efficiency than ZF. But ZF having the ability to combat inter-cell interference outperforms MRC in terms of average sum-rate EE.

This work aims to investigate the 5G network performance by implementing mMIMO communication. This will allow seamless communication between industrial automation systems. Further, the work contributes to achieving seamless communication by incorporating different precoding schemes with regular and superimposed pilots considering the interferences in the network. The work in this chapter is advanced to implement a reduced interference network for a compatible real-time application for 5G IoT-based industry automation.

13.5 Precoding Schemes

To simplify the receiver's structure and reduce the receiver's consumable power, the precoding process is used at transmit side instead of receive side. Precoding is a linear processing technique that exploits convey diversity, i.e., the source transmits the coded information of the transmitted signal to the receiver to realize the CSI. Therefore, the precoding technique is employed at the transmit signal before transmission, which reduces the performance degradation caused by the interference and channel fading [53].

In the mMIMO LTE-A network, each BS is employed with an M array of antennas to communicate simultaneously to K single antenna UEs. To recover the signal from a noisy channel, coherent processing is accomplished by employing transmit precoding and receive combining in the downlink and uplink, respectively.

13.5.1 Maximal ratio combining

In MRC, signal amplification process is carried out by adding coherent components to the receiver. This process is called array gain, which is proportional to number of M antennas in the BS. Typically, the transmit signal vector is given by $x = \sqrt{\rho}W s$,

where s is the transmitted signal before precoding
ρ is average BS transmit power
W is the precoding matrix.

The downlink's conjugate transpose matrix is used to represent the matched filter (MF) precoder and it is represented as $W = \sqrt{\alpha}H^*$. Therefore, the received signal vector (y_{MR}) of an MRC is given by

$$y_{MR} = \sqrt{\rho \alpha}\ s\ H^T H^* + n_0, \qquad (13.1)$$

where α is the scaling factor to normalize signal power
 H^T is of downlink channel matrix transpose
 H^* is of downlink channel matrix conjugate
 n_0 is the noise matrix.

The conjugate transpose of the channel matrix is the downlink precoder. When the BS is large in number compared to UEs in the network, the optimal solution is attained by the diagonal matrix of the term $H^T H^*$ [54].

13.5.2 Zero forcing

It is a precoding scheme that considers inter-user interference, irrespective of noise. By sending the signal in the direction of the desired user ZF cancels out the interference of other users. An array gain that is proportionate to the (M-K) antennas in BS is produced by the signal amplification in ZF and is given by

$$y_{ZF} = \sqrt{\rho \alpha}\ s\ H^T H^* \left(H^T H^* \right)^{-1} + n_0 \qquad (13.2)$$

The $H^T H^*$ matrix's diagonal elements represent the channels' relative power imbalance, while the off-diagonal elements reflect the channels' interdependence. When additive noise is absent, ZF is an optimal precoding scheme; otherwise, it is not optimal [55, 56]. Eqn (13.1) and (13.2) are the general form of the received signal vector of MRC precoding and ZF precoding, respectively.

13.5.3 Pilot zero-forcing (P-ZF) precoding scheme

Intercell interference is mitigated across K channels in a conventional ZF precoding scheme. P-ZF combining proposed in [57] mitigates intercell and intracell interference. Channel directions that are estimated are orthogonalized to combat interference that is known at the BS by synchronizing combinations across B cells. Hence,

P-ZF precoding scheme will combat both interferences and enhances the network performance.

The P-ZF channel matrix is given by

$$y_{P-ZF} = H_{\gamma j} (H_{\gamma j}^H H_{\gamma j})^{-1}, \qquad (13.3)$$

where all channel users are represented $H = [H_1, H_2 \cdots H_K]$. Here ξ are the pilot signals that originated from the code book and it is provided by

$$\xi = \{\nu_1, \cdots \nu_B\}, \text{ where } \nu_{b1}^H \nu_{b2} = \left\{ \begin{array}{ll} B, & b_1 = b_2 \\ 0, & b_1 \neq b_2 \end{array} \right\}, \tag{13.4}$$

with B signals of the pilot to form orthogonality in BS on the constraint of $1 \leq B \leq C_B$.

The network coherence block has a limited size where the channel is assumed as static and frequency flat. The channels are estimated using orthogonal pilot sequences in finite numbers. As the pilot sequences used are the same used in multicell mMIMO system, coherence interference is generated known as pilot contamination between UEs. This pilot contamination reduces the channel estimation and mMIMO spectral efficiency. To minimize interference in the conventional or regular pilot (RP), the pilot and data transmission are accompanied individually within the coherence block.

13.6 Superimposed Pilots

A superimposed pilot is one in which the data symbols and transmission pilot both take place concurrently within a coherence block. The idea behind superimposed pilots is to aggregate the data samples and the pilot samples into a single total, rather than separating them based on time and/or frequency. The UE broadcast signal can be employed to estimate data or pilots or to superimpose the two, depending on the methodology.

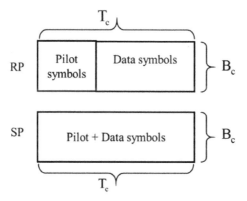

Figure 13.3 Regular and superimposed pilot protocol.

Figure 13.3 [58] illustrates the regular and superimposed pilots' respective coherence frame formats, which can be used to gain an understanding of the regular and superimposed pilot concepts. The pilot contamination has been decreased as a result of using the complete coherence block of SP pilots, which has improved the channel estimate. Additionally, there is no penalty incurred in the pre-log factor.

13.7 System Model

The multicell mMIMO network for the uplink model is considered here in which each base station with M antennas serves K user equipment. The number of channels obtained by dividing the network bandwidth B_W by the coherence bandwidth B_C is $\frac{B_W}{B_C}$. The time duration of every coherence block T_C contains $\tau_C = T_C B_C$ complex samples. Because they provide an acceptable data rate, the uncorrelated Rayleigh fading channels are used in multicell mMIMO systems.

The channel between the $UE_{l'i}$ and M antennas BS_l is modeled as $h_{ll'i}$ a small-scale fading condition $c_{ll'i} \sim CN(0, \zeta_{ll'i}I_M) \forall l, l' \in \phi_\lambda$ with $\zeta_{ll'i} \geq 0$ large-scale fading condition. For instance, the distance between K single antennas and BS antennas is considered to be significant in number for studying large-scale fading. The condition also represents the received signal y_0 from the base station BS_0 [58].

$$y_0 = \sum_{l' \in \phi_\lambda} \sum_{i=1}^{K} h_{0l'i} X_{l'i} + n_0, \qquad (13.5)$$

where $h_{0l'i}$ is the channel vector, $x_{l'i}$ is the transmitted signal, and n_0 is the noise vector

13.8 Regular Pilots

In each regular pilot coherence block, τ_p samples are used for pilot, and a fraction $\left(\frac{\tau_c - \tau_p}{\tau_c}\right)$ of samples are used for data. Each base station allocates $\tau_p(\tau_p \geq K)$ pilot sequences to UEs in its cell given as $\Phi_{l'i}$. It is given as to recognize the users sharing the same pilot UE_{0k} in different cells $P_{0k}^{RP} = \{\{l', i\} : \varphi_{0k}^* \varphi_{l',i} \neq 0\}$. The UE_{0k} sends pilot Φ_{0k}^T with other users for τ_p

instances of eqn (13.5), and the signal Z_{0k}^{RP} received at BS$_0$ is [58]

$$Z_{0k}^{RP} = \sum_{l' \in \phi_\lambda} \sum_{i=1}^{K} \sqrt{q_{l'i}} \, h_{0l'i} \, \varphi_{l'i}^T + \bar{N}_0, \tag{13.6}$$

where $q_{l'i}$ is the transmission power of $UE_{l'i}$, the pilot symbol and noise matrix, $\bar{N}_0$ Now the received signal sequence Z_{0k}^{RP} (eqn (13.6)) grew $\frac{\Phi_{0k}^*}{\sqrt{\tau_p}}$ to correlate pilot signals with equivalentUE_{0k} pilot sequences. The despread received signal is given by [58]

$$z_{0k}^{RP} = \sum_{\{l',i\} \in P_{0k}^R} \sqrt{q_{l'i}\tau_p} \, h_{0l'i} + \bar{n}_0, \tag{13.7}$$

where $\bar{n}_0 = \frac{\bar{N}_0 \Phi_{0k}^*}{\sqrt{\tau_p}}$ is a noise represented as $\bar{n}_0 \sim CN\left(0, \sigma^2 I_M\right)$ with no information vanished in the despreading process.

13.9 Superimposed Pilot

Coherence block samples are used in this transmission to send the pilot and data symbols. Each BS assigns $\tau_c (\tau_c \geq K)$ pilot sequence to its UE in its cell and represents $\psi_{l'i}$ to identify the different cell users sharing similar pilot UE_{0k}s. The UE_{0k} sends pilot sequence ψ_{0k}^T for other users and it is given by [58]

$$Z_{0k}^{SP} = \sum_{l' \in \phi_\lambda} \sum_{i=1}^{K} \sqrt{q_{l'i}} \, h_{0l'i} \psi^T \, _{l'i} + \sum_{l' \in \phi_\lambda} \sum_{i=1}^{K} \sqrt{p_{l'i}} \, h_{0l'i} s_{l'i}^T + n_0, \tag{13.8}$$

where $p_{l'i}$ is data symbol power, $s_{l'i}$ is a vector that encapsulates the transmission data symbols. n_0 is the noise vector represented by $n_0 = [n_{01}, \ldots, n_{0\tau_c}]$, whereas $n_{0j} \sim CN\left(0, \sigma^2 I_M\right)$. The SP signal Z_0^{SP} (eqn (13.8)) grew $\frac{\psi_{0k}^*}{\sqrt{\tau_c}}$ to correlate the pilot signals with respect pilot sequenceUE_{0k}, and it produces

$$z_{0k}^{SP} = \sum_{\{l',i\} \in P_{0k}^S} \sqrt{q_{l'i}\tau_c} \, h_{0l'i} + \sum_{l' \in \phi_\lambda} \sum_{i=1}^{K} \sqrt{\frac{p_{l'i}}{\tau_c}} \, h_{0l'i} s_{l'i}^T \psi_{0k}^* + \sum_{j=1}^{\tau_c} n_{0j} \frac{[\psi_{0k}]_j^*}{\sqrt{\tau_c}}. \tag{13.9}$$

13.10 Energy Efficiency for Different Precoding Schemes

The average sum rate per unit area to the ratio of the average power consumption per unit area can be used to calculate the EE in multicell mMIMO systems [67]. It is represented as

$$\text{Energy Efficiency (EE)}$$
$$= \frac{\text{Average sum rate per UE } (R_{0k})}{\text{Average power consumption per BS}(P_{BS})}$$

13.11 Average Rate per Unit Area

The channel for both conventional precoding scheme and precoding with SP has been LMMSE estimated using eqn (13.7) and (13.9) is computed between the BS and UE, respectively [58].

The achievable rate for UE_{0k} with P-ZF precoding scheme and conventional or RP is given by [58]

$$R_{0k}^{RP} = \left(1 - \frac{\tau_p}{\tau_c}\right) B_w \log_2 \left(1 + \gamma_{0k}^{RP}\right), \tag{13.10}$$

where γ_{0k}^{RP} is the SINR of the regular pilot and is provided by

$$\gamma_{0k}^{RP} = \frac{G_f p_{0k} \zeta_{00k}}{\frac{G_f}{\tau_p} \sum_{l' \in \phi_\lambda} \sum_{i=1}^{K} \frac{p_{l'i} \, q_{l'i}}{q_{0k}} \frac{\zeta_{0l'i}^2}{\zeta_{00k}} + \frac{1}{\varphi_{0k}^{RP}} \left(\sum_{l' \in \phi_\lambda} \sum_{i=1}^{K} p_{l'i} \, \zeta_{0l'i} + \sigma^2\right)}. \tag{13.11}$$

φ_{0k}^{RP} is the channel estimate quality of RP and is provided by

$$\varphi_{0k}^{RP} = \frac{q_{0k} \tau_p \zeta_{00k}}{q_{0k} \tau_p \zeta_{00k} + \sum_{l' \in \phi_\lambda} \sum_{i=1}^{K} p_{l'i} \, \zeta_{0l'i}^2 + \sigma^2}. \tag{13.12}$$

G_f is a factor scale caused by array gain from a different precoding strategy as

$G_f = M$ for MRC

$G_f = M - K$ for ZF

$G_f = M - B$ for P-ZF.

The achievable rate for UE_{0k} incorporating SP precoding schemes is given by

$$R_{0k}^{SP} = B_w \log_2 \left(1 + \gamma_{0k}^{SP}\right), \tag{13.13}$$

where γ_{0k}^{SP} is the SINR of superimposed pilot and is given by

$$\gamma_{0k}^{SP}$$
$$= \frac{G_f p_{0k} \zeta_{00k}}{\frac{G_f}{\tau_c} \sum_{l' \in \phi_\lambda} \sum_{i=1}^{K} \frac{p_{l'i} q_{l'i}}{q_{0k}} \frac{\zeta_{0l'i}^2}{\zeta_{00k}} + \frac{G_f}{\tau_c} \sum_{l' \in \phi_\lambda} \sum_{i=1}^{K} \frac{p_{l'i}^2 q_{l'i}}{q_{0k}} \frac{\zeta_{0l'i}^2}{\zeta_{00k}} + \frac{1}{\tau_c^2} \sum_{l' \in \phi_\lambda} \sum_{i=1}^{K} \frac{p_{l'i}^2}{q_{0k}}}$$
$$\frac{\zeta_{0l'i}^2}{\zeta_{00k}} + \frac{1}{\varphi_{0k}^{SP}} \left(\sum_{l' \in \phi_\lambda} \sum_{i=1}^{K} p_{l'i} \zeta_{0l'i} + \sigma^2 \right),$$

$$(13.14)$$

where φ_{0k}^{SP} is the channel estimate quality of SP and is given by

$$\varphi_{0k}^{SP} = \frac{q_{0k} \tau_c \zeta_{00k}}{q_{0k} \tau_c \zeta_{00k} + \sum_{l' \in \phi_\lambda} \sum_{i=1}^{K} q_{l'i} \zeta_{0l'i} + \sum_{l' \in \phi_\lambda} \sum_{i=1}^{K} p_{l'i} \zeta_{0l'i} + \sigma^2}$$

$$(13.15)$$

13.12 Average Power Consumption

The power consumption per unit area (P_{BS}) is computed by considering the network transmit and circuit power requirements. The power combination in linear processing P_{LP} and channel estimation P_{CE} studies the system power consumption. The linear power consumption consumes two times of power for SP, and it is given by [58]

$$P_{LP} + P_{CE} = \begin{cases} \frac{B_w}{L} MK & for\ RP - ZF \\ \frac{2B_w}{L} MK & for\ SP - ZF \end{cases},$$

where L is the processor's computational efficiency.

The EE of the network using different precoding schemes with SP is given by

$$EE = \frac{R_{0k} K}{P_{TX} + C_0 + C_1 K + D_0 (M - K) + P_{LP} + P_{CE} + A (R_{0k}) K},$$

$$(13.16)$$

where $P_{TX} = \frac{\rho \Upsilon}{\eta} \frac{\Gamma(\alpha/2)+1}{(\pi \lambda)^{\alpha/2}}$ is the average transmit power for UE and η is the overall power amplifier efficiency. Here C_0 is the static power consumed at the BS, D_0 which is the power consumed by the base station transceiver chains, which scales with M base station antennas, and $C_1 K$ is the power consumed by the user equipment at the base station during signal processing. A is the proportionality constant for coding and decoding.

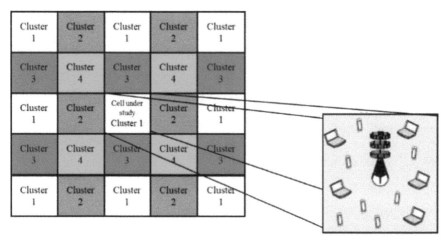

Figure 13.4   Cell under investigation surrounded by a cluster.

13.13 Results and Discussion

A multicell scenario of each 500 m ×500 m cell size is employed for simulation using the latest MATLAB software version, which can be used for developing a real-time 5G network, as shown in Figure 13.4 [22]. The users are dispersed evenly throughout the network, and the Monte-Carlo simulation was used to simulate the scenario, which is likely to experience user interference in all directions. An energy efficiency investigation in a 5G network using different precoding schemes and the superimposed pilot has been performed. The simulation is carried out using a propagation model based on the 3GPP standard [59] listed in Table 13.1.

13.13.1 Performance of various precoding schemes

Figure 13.5 highlights the energy efficiency of different precoding schemes under different ranges of BS antennae for mMIMO communication. The P-ZF energy efficiency increases to 16.32 Mbit/J until $M = 210$ and becomes steady with increased BS antennas.

This is because P-ZF mitigates intercell and intracell interference and enhances the performance associated with that of another precoding scheme. However, SP-ZF energy efficiency increases to 12.89 Mbit/J till $M = 180$, and ZF energy efficiency increases to 9.72 Mbit/J till $M = 140$, decreasing gradually as the ZF precoding scheme mitigates only intercell interference. The SP-MRC energy efficiency rises to 7.44 Mbit/J at $M = 155$, and MRC

Table 13.1 Simulation parameters.

Parameter	Value
Number of BS antennas, (M)	300
Number of UEs, (K)	120
Transmission bandwidth, (B_w)	20 MHz
Coherence block length	400
Propagation loss (Υ)	120 dB
The efficiency of power amplifier, (η)	0.40
Symbol time, (τ)	$0.5 \times 10^7 \ (s/symbol)$
Static power consumption, (C_0)	$10 \ W \times \tau \ (J/symbol)$
UEs circuit power (C_1)	$0.1W \times \tau \ (J/symbol)$
BS antenna circuit power (D_0)	$0.2W \times \tau \ (J/symbol)$
Signal processing coefficient, (D_1)	$1.56 \times 10^{-10}(J/symbol)$
Coding/decoding/backhaul power, (A)	$1.15 \times 10^{-9}(J/bit)$
Noise variance, (σ^2)	$10^{-20} \ (J/symbol)$

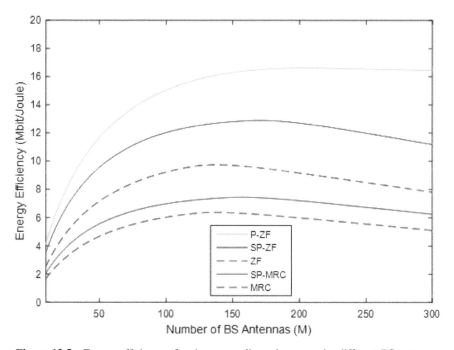

Figure 13.5 Energy efficiency of various precoding schemes under different BS antennas.

energy efficiency rises to 6.36 Mbit/J at $M = 140$ and then reduces gradually as the MRC precoding scheme mitigates only intracell interference.

13.14 Power Amplifier Power of Different Precoding Schemes

Figure 13.6 impacts the network's power consumption effects for various precoding schemes under different BS antennas. The power utilized by the precoding scheme incorporating superimposed pilots is comparatively high than that of the precoding scheme incorporating regular pilots. Since a superimposed pilot employs twice the power of a traditional pilot for channel estimation and signal processing. The RF power consumed by the P-ZF precoding scheme is considerable because it estimates the channel with B pilot signals and utilizes the ability to mitigate intercell and intracell interference.

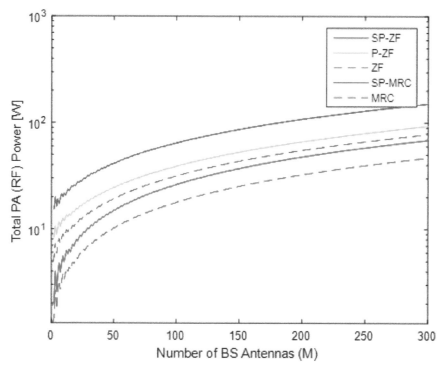

Figure 13.6 Total power amplifier power of various precoding schemes under different BS antennas.

13.14.1 Average sum rate of various precoding schemes under different BS antennas

The average rate per UE under various precoding schemes is shown in Figure 13.7. The P-ZF precoding scheme estimates the channels with pilot signals across different B cells with the BS antenna and transmits data streams in the network. Hence, it achieves a comparatively higher sum rate than other precoding schemes. A precoding scheme employing a superimposed pilot accommodates pilot sequences in large numbers for channel estimation and allows more data streams for transmission across different BS stations. The ZF precoding scheme uses τ_p coherence block samples, reducing the channel estimate quality and achieving a relatively low average sum rate per UE.

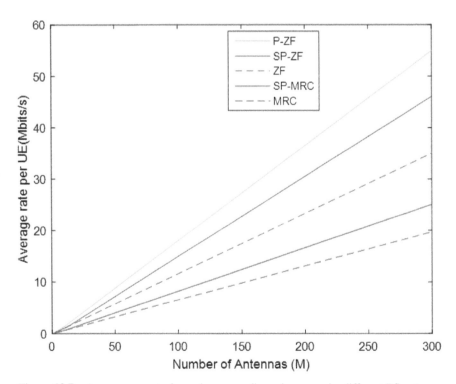

Figure 13.7 Average sum rate for various precoding schemes under different BS antennas.

13.14.2 Performance of various precoding schemes for different UEs

Figure 13.8 portrays the performance of various ranges of UEs in the network. When $K = 47$, the UEs EE incorporating the P-ZF scheme rises up to 19.6 Mbit/J and decreases. As the P-ZF precoding scheme estimates more cells, it includes more UEs and improves the performance than other precoding schemes. When $K = 48$, the energy efficiency of UEs employing SP-ZF increases to 15.53 Mbit/J, and when $K= 42$, ZF, energy efficiency rises to 12.13 Mbit/J and then decreases gradually. The SP-MRC EE rises to 7.44 Mbit/J at $K = 22$, and MRC energy efficiency upsurges to 6.36 Mbit/J at $K = 20$ and then drops. Superimposed pilot incorporates more pilot samples for channel estimation, employs more UE, and comparatively enhances energy efficiency than regular pilots in the network.

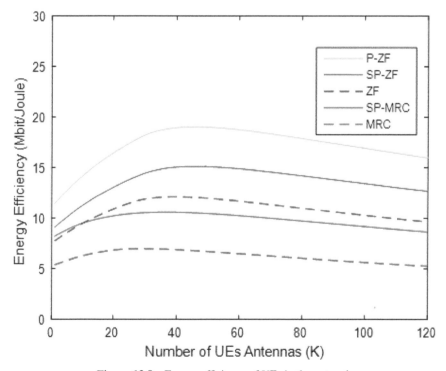

Figure 13.8   Energy efficiency of UEs in the network.

13.14.3 Average rate per UEs using different precoding schemes for various coherence block length

Figure 13.9 investigates UEs average rate for different precoding at various coherence block lengths. The result infers that the average sum rate per UE increases gradually with coherence block length increase. Precoding scheme incorporating SP uses entire τ_c coherence block samples for both data and pilot transmission, which remains static for the whole duration and comparatively achieves a high sum rate per UE. The P-ZF and ZF precoding schemes use τ_p and τ_c samples for transmission, which limit the range in the coherence block. This makes the pilots to be reused in the conventional precoding scheme, which is defined in the precoding scheme using SP. Thus, the SP precoding scheme outperforms the traditional precoding scheme regarding the average rate per UE. But P-ZF mitigates both the interferences and achieves an equivalent sum rate than that of the SP precoding scheme.

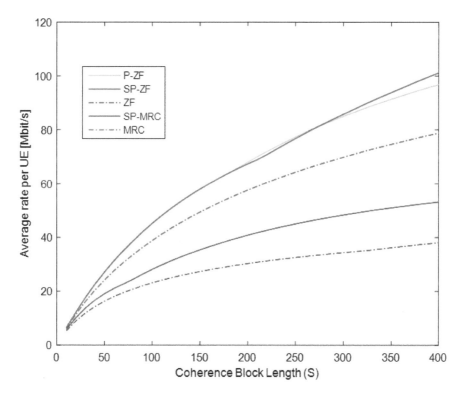

Figure 13.9 Energy efficiency of the network for different coherence block length.

13.14.4 Energy efficiency for various levels of SNR

Figure 13.10 implicits the sum rate per UE of different precoding for various SNRs in mMIMO network. Average sum rate per UE is obtained using the term SINR. When the network interference vanishes, the performance of the 5G network improves gradually. The P-ZF precoding scheme can mitigate both the interference and achieves high SNR compared to other precoding schemes. The average sum rate per UE for precoding scheme using SP increases with increased SNR. The precoding scheme using SP utilizes the τ_c samples of coherence block length for data transmission, achieving high SNR. The conventional precoding scheme operates the uses τ_p out of τ_c symbols for data transmission, and hence it achieves a relatively low SNR.

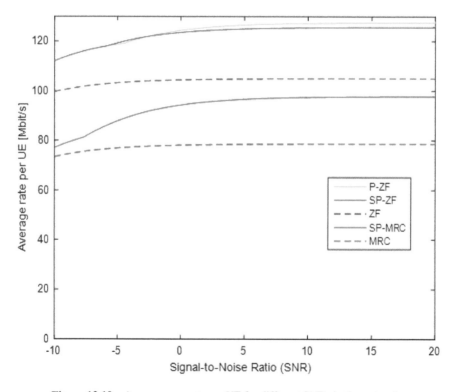

Figure 13.10   Average sum rate per UE for different SNRs in the network.

13.15 Conclusion and Future Scope

This chapter examines how precoding schemes can improve 5G network energy efficiency by reducing network interference. The 5G Internet of Things industry automation-based network uses several precoding strategies to test its performance. P-ZF, along with other precoding schemes, saves more energy when a large number of BS antennas are used, according to the research. It reduces interference and improves mMIMO network performance compared to other precoding strategies. A precoding scheme that superimposed multiple pilots investigated 5G network interference caused by pilot contamination. SP in precoding schemes with longer coherence blocks can reduce network interference. It improves communication channel estimation methods and reduces pilot interference, reducing pilot contamination. P-ZF reduces both types of network interference and achieves high energy efficiency for 5G IoT industry automation. SP-ZF only reduces intercell interference. The following potential areas that might be interesting for researchers to pursue and explore in the future are efforts that can be made to use MMSE precoding in 5G system-based IoT industry automation and interference reduction with a power control technique. Further, industry automation performance can be improved by employing energy-efficient algorithms and better decoding algorithms. Further, 5G network-based energy efficiency investigation would be necessary considering hardware impairment techniques that are not utilized as system parameter optimization.

References

[1] C. J. Anumba, X. Wang, Mobile and Pervasive Computing in Construction, John Wiley & Sons, Technology & Engineering, 2012

[2] D. Tse and P. Viswanath, "Fundamentals of Wireless Communication," Cambridge University Press, Cambridge, UK, 2005.

[3] D.Gesbert, M. Kountouris, R. W. Heath Jr., C. B. Chae, and T. Sälzer, "Shifting the MIMO paradigm," IEEE Signal Processing Magazine,vol.24,no.5,pp.36-46, Sep.2007

[4] T. Rappaport, Wireless Communications: Principles and Practice, Prentice-Hall, Englewood Cliffs, NJ, 1996.

[5] T.alonen, J. Romero, and J.Melero, GSM, GPRS, and EDGE Performance: Evolution Towards 3G/UMTS. New York, Wiley, 2003.

[6] K. R. Santhi, V. K. Srivastava, G. Senthil Kumaran, and A. Butare, "Goals of true broad band's wireless next wave (4G-5G)," in

Proceedings of IEEE 58th Vehicular Technology Conference, Orlando, FL, USA, vol. 4., pp. 2317–2321, Oct. 2003.

[7] B. Furht and S. A. Ahson, Long Term Evolution: 3GPP LTE Radio and Cellular Technology. Boca Raton, CRC Press, 2009.

[8] S. Sesia, I. Toufik, and M. Baker, Eds., LTE: The UMTS Long Term Evolution. John Wiley and Sons, 2009.

[9] C.-X. Wang, F. Haider, X. Gao, X.-H. You, Y. Yang, D. Yuan, H. Aggoune, H. Haas, S. Fletcher, and E. Hepsaydir, "Cellular architecture and key technologies for 5G wireless communication networks," IEEE Communication Magazine., vol. 52, no. 2, pp. 122–130, Feb. 2014.

[10] T. V. Chien, and E. Bjornson, "MMIMO Communications," in 5G Mobile Communications, pp. 77-116, Springer, 2017.

[11] A. Osseiran, F. Boccardi, V. Braun, K. Kusume, P. Marsch, M. Maternia, O. Queseth, M. Schellmann, H. Schotten, H. Taoka, H. Tullberg, M. A. Uusitalo, B. Timus, and M. Fallgren, "Scenarios for 5G mobile and wireless communications: the vision of the METIS project," IEEE Communications Magazine, Vol. 52 , Issue 5, pp. 26 – 35, May 2014.

[12] T. L. Marzetta, "Non-cooperative cellular wireless with unlimited numbers of base station antennas," IEEE Transactions on Wireless Communications, Vol. 9, Issue 11, pp. 3590–3600, November 2010.

[13] T. L. Marzetta, E. G. Larsson, H. Yang, and H. Q. Ngo, Fundamentals of MMIMO. Cambridge Press, 2016.

[14] Tamilarasan, Ananth Kumar, Suresh Kumar Krishnadhas, Sundaresan Sabapathy, and Arun Samuel Thankamony Sarasam. "A novel design of Rogers RT/droid 5880 material based two turn antenna for intracranial pressure monitoring." Microsystem Technologies 27, no. 9 (2021): 3579-3588.

[15] Rajesh, R. S., G. Tamilselvia, and P. Sivananainthaperumala. "A New PAPR reduction Technique based on Precoding and Gamma Companding Technique for OFDM system." Scientific Journal of PPI-UKM 3, no. 4 (2016): 182-186.

[16] A. Yazdan, J. Park, S. Park, T. A. Khan, R. W. Heath, "Energy-Efficient MMIMO: Wireless-Powered Communication, Multiuser MIMO with Hybrid Precoding, and Cloud Radio Access Network with Variable-Resolution ADCs," IEEE Microwave Magazine, Vol. 18, Issue 5, pp. 18-30, August 2017.

[17] K. N. R. S. V. Prasad, E. Hossain, and V. K. Bhargava, "Energy Efficiency in MMIMO-Based 5G Networks: Opportunities and Challenges," IEEE Wireless Communications, Vol. 24, Issue 3, pp. 86-94, June 2017.

[18] Harri Holma, Antti Toskala, LTE for UMTS - OFDMA and SC-FDMA Based Radio Access, John Wiley & Sons 2009.

[19] Moray Rumney, LTE and the Evolution to 4G Wireless: Design and Measurement Challenges, Agilent Technologies Publication 2009.

[20] A. Paulraj, R. Nabar & D. Gore, Introduction to Space-time Communications. Cambridge University Press, 2003.

[21] H. Ngo, E. Larsson, and T. Marzetta, "Energy and spectral efficiency of very large multiuser MIMO systems," IEEE Transactions on Wireless Communications, vol. 61, no. 4, pp. 1436–1449, February 2013.

[22] E. Bjornson, L. Sanguinetti, J. Hoydis, M. Debbah, "Optimal Design of Energy-Efficient Multiuser MIMO Systems: Is MMIMO the Answer?" IEEE Transactions on Wireless Communications, vol. 14, no. 6, pp. 3059-3075, June 2015.

[23] S. Wang, Y. Liu, W. Zhang, and H. Zhang, "Achievable Rates of Full-Duplex MMIMO Relay Systems Over Rician Fading Channels," in IEEE Transactions on Vehicular Technology, vol. 66, no. 11, pp. 9825-9837, Nov. 2017.

[24] D. Mi, M. Dianati, L. Zhang, S. Muhaidat, and R. Tafazolli. "MMIMO performance with imperfect channel reciprocity and channel estimation error," IEEE Transactions on Communications, Vol. 65, no. 9, pp. 3734-3749, March 2018.

[25] B. M. Lee, "Improved Energy Efficiency of MMIMO-OFDM in Battery-Limited IoT Networks," in IEEE Access, vol. 6, pp. 38147-38160, 2018.

[26] J. Hoydis, S. ten Brink, and M. Debbah, "MMIMO in the UL/DL of cellular networks: How many antennas do we need?" IEEE J. Sel.Areas Commun., vol. 31, no. 2, pp. 160–171, February 2013.

[27] E. Björnson, M. Kountouris, M. Debbah, "MMIMO and Small Cells: Improving Energy Efficiency by Optimal Soft-Cell Coordination," Proceedings of International Conference on Telecommunications (ICT), Casablanca, Morocco, May 2013.

[28] C. Li, J. Zhang, and K. B. Letaief, "Throughput and Energy Efficiency Analysis of small Cell Networks with Multi-antenna Base Stations," IEEE Transactions on Wireless Communications, Vol. 13 , Issue 5, pp. 2505-2517, May 2014.

[29] X. Gao, O. Edfors, F. Rusek, and F. Tufvesson, "MMIMO performance evaluation based on measured propagation data," IEEE Trans. Wireless Commun., vol. 14, no. 7, pp. 3899–3911, July 2015.

[30] H. Huh, G. Caire, H. C. Papadopoulos, and S. A. Ramprashad, "Achieving mMIMO" spectral efficiency with a not-so-large number of

antennas," IEEE Trans. Wireless Commun., vol. 11, no. 9, pp. 3226–3239, September 2012.

[31] . V. Cheng, D. Persson, E. Björnson and E. G. Larsson, "MMIMO at night: On the operation of mMIMO in low traffic scenarios," IEEE International Conference on Communications, pp. 1697-1702, London, UK, June 2015.

[32] Y. Hao, Q. Ni, H. Li, S. Hou, "On the Energy and Spectral Efficiency Tradeoff in MMIMO-Enabled HetNets with Capacity-Constrained Backhaul Links," IEEE Transactions on Communications, Vol. 65, Issue 11, pp. 4720 – 4733, November 2017

[33] H. Huh, G. Caire, H. C. Papadopoulos, and S. A. Ramprashad, "Achieving mMIMO" spectral efficiency with a not-so-large number of antennas," IEEE Trans. Wireless Commun., vol. 11, no. 9, pp. 3226– 3239, September 2012.

[34] H. Yin, D. Gesbert, M. Filippou, and Y. Liu, "A coordinated approach to channel estimation in large-scale multiple-antenna systems," IEEE J.Sel. Areas Commun., vol. 31, no. 2, pp. 264–273, February 2013.

[35] J. Vinogradova, E. Bjornson, and E. G. Larsson, "On the separability of signal and interference-plus-noise subspaces in blind pilot decontamination," in Proc. IEEE ICASSP, pp. 3421–3425, March 2016.

[36] H. Q. Ngo and E. Larsson, "EVD-based channel estimation in multicell multiuser MIMO systems with very large antenna arrays," in Proc. IEEE Int. Conf. on Acoustics, Speech and Signal Processing (ICASSP), Kyoto, pp. 3249–3252, March 2012.

[37] R. R. Muller, L. Cottatellucci, and M. Vehkaperĺa, "Blind pilot decontamination," IEEE J. Sel. Topics Signal Process., vol. 8, no. 5, pp. 773–786, Oct 2014.

[38] H. Yin, D. Gesbert, M. Filippou, and Y. Liu, "A coordinated approach to channel estimation in large-scale multiple-antenna systems," IEEE J. Sel. Areas Commun., vol. 31, no. 2, pp. 264–273, Feb. 2013.

[39] K. Takeuchi, R. R. Muller, M.Vehkaperĺa, and T. Tanaka, "On an achievable rate of large rayleigh block-fading MIMO channels with no CSI," IEEE Trans. Inf. Theory, vol. 59, no. 10, pp. 6517–6541, Oct. 2013.

[40] H. Papadopoulos, G. Caire, and S. Ramprashad, "Achieving large spectral efficiencies from MU-MIMO with tens of antennas: Location-adaptive TDD MU-MIMO design and user scheduling," in Proc. IEEE ASILOMAR, Nov. 2010, pp. 636–643.

[41] Y. Li, Y. H. Nam, B. L. Ng, and J. Z. Zhang, "A non-asymptotic throughput for mMIMO cellular uplink with pilot reuse," in Proc. IEEE

Globalcom, Anaheim, CA, USA, pp. 4500–4504, Dec. 2012.

[42] S. Noh, M. D. Zoltowski, Y. Sung, and D. J. Love, "Pilot beam pattern design for channel estimation in mMIMO systems," J. Sel. Topics Signal Process., vol. 8, no. 5, pp. 787–801, Oct. 2014.

[43] K. Upadhya and S. A. Vorobyov, "An array processing approach to pilot decontamination for mMIMO," in Proc. IEEE 6th Int. Workshop on Computational Advances in Multi-Sensor Adaptive Processing (CAMSAP), Cancun, pp. 453–456, Dec. 2015.

[44] X. Jing, M. Li, H. Liu, S. Li, and G. Pan, "Superimposed Pilot Optimization Design and Channel Estimation for Multiuser MMIMO Systems," in IEEE Transactions on Vehicular Technology, vol. 67, no. 12, pp. 11818-11832, Dec. 2018.

[45] J. Ma, C. Liang, C. Xu and L. Ping, "On Orthogonal and Superimposed Pilot Schemes in MMIMO NOMA Systems," in IEEE Journal on Selected Areas in Communications, vol. 35, no. 12, pp. 2696-2707, Dec. 2017.

[46] J. Zhang, Y. Wei, E. Björnson, Y. Han and S. Jin, "Performance Analysis and Power Control of Cell-Free MMIMO Systems with Hardware Impairments," in IEEE Access, vol. 6, pp. 55302-55314, 2018.

[47] J. Li, H. Zhang, D. Li and H. Chen, "On the Performance of Wireless-Energy-Transfer-Enabled MMIMO Systems with Superimposed Pilot-Aided Channel Estimation" IEEE Journals and Magazines, vol. 3, pp, 2014 - 2027, October 2015

[48] K. Upadhya, S. A. Vorobyov, and M. Vehkapera, "Superimposed pilots are superior for mitigating pilot contamination in mMIMO," IEEE Trans. Signal Process., vol. 65, no. 11, pp. 2917–2932, June 2017.

[49] J. Li, H. Zhang, D. Li and H. Chen, "On the Performance of Wireless-Energy-Transfer-Enabled MMIMO Systems with Superimposed Pilot-Aided Channel Estimation" IEEE Journals and Magazines, vol. 3, pp, 2014 - 2027, October 2015.

[50] D. Verenzuela; E Björnson; and L. Sanguinetti, "Spectral and Energy Efficiency of Superimposed Pilots in Uplink MMIMO" IEEE Transactions on Wireless Communications, Volume: 17, no. 11, Pages: 7099 - 7115, August 2018 (23)

[51] Eduardo n. Tominaga, Onel l. A. López, Hirley Alves, Richard Demo Souza, and João Luiz Rebelatto, " Performance Analysis of MIMO-NOMA Iterative Receivers for Massive Connectivity," IEEE Access, Volume: 10, pp: 46808 – 46822, April 2022

[52] David López-Pérez, Antonio De Domenico, Nicola Piovesan, Geng Xinli, Harvey Bao, Song Qitao, and Mérouane Debbah,"A Survey on 5G Radio Access Network Energy Efficiency: MMIMO, Lean Carrier Design, Sleep Modes, and Machine Learning" IEEE Communications Surveys & Tutorials, Vol: 24, Issue: 1, pp:653 - 697, January 2022

[53] N. Fatema, G. Hua, Y. Xiang, D. Peng, and I. Natgunanathan, "MMIMO Linear Precoding: A Survey," IEEE Systems Journal, Vol. 12, Iss. 4, pp: 3920–3931, Dec. 2018

[54] J. Zhu, R. Schober, and V. K. Bhargava, "Secure downlink transmission in mMIMO system with zero-forcing precoding," in *Proc. 20th Eur. Wireless Conf.*, Barcelona, Spain, pp. 1–6, January 2014.

[55] X. Gao, O. Edfors, F. Rusek, and F. Tufvesson, "Linear precoding performance in measured very-large MIMO channels," in Proc, of IEEE Veh. Technol. Conf., San Francisco, CA, USA, pp. 1–5, April 2011.

[56] T. Parfait, Y. Kuang, and K. Jerry, "Performance analysis and comparison of ZF and MRT based downlink mMIMO systems," in Proc. 6th Int. Conf. Ubiquitous Future Network, Shanghai, China, pp. 383–388, June 2014.

[57] E. Bjornson, E. G. Larsson and M. Debbah, "MMIMO for Maximal Spectral Efficiency: How Many Users and Pilots Should Be Allocated?" IEEE Transactions on Wireless Communications, vol. 15, no. 2, pp. 1293-1308, February 2016.

[58] D. Verenzuela; E Björnson; and L. Sanguinetti, "Spectral and Energy Efficiency of Superimposed Pilots in Uplink MMIMO" IEEE Transactions on Wireless Communications, Volume: 17, no. 11, Pages: 7099 - 7115, August 2018

[59] A. Mezghani and J. A. Nossek, "Power efficiency in communication systems from a circuit perspective," in Proc. IEEE Int. Symp. Circuits and Systems (ISCAS), pp. 1896–1899, March 2011

14

Internet of Things and Cybersecurity Mechanism for Industrial Automation Systems

Shitharth Selvarajan[1], Gouse Baig Mohammed[2], Mohamed Sirajudeen Yoosuf[3], D. Shivaprasad[3], Mustapha Hedabou[4], and C. K. Yogesh[5]

[1]Cyber Security & Digital Forensics, School of Built, Environment, Engineering and Computing, Leeds Beckett University, LS1 3HE Leeds, U.K.
[2]Department of Computer Science & Engineering, Vardhaman College of Engineering, India
[3]School of Computer Science and Engineering, VIT-AP University, Andhra Pradesh, India
[4]School of Computer Science, University Mohammed VI Polytechnic, Morocco
[5]School of Computer Science and Engineering, VIT Chennai Campus
Email: s.selvarajan@leedsbeckett.ac.uk; gousebaig@vardhaman.org; md.sirajudeen@vitap.ac.in; siva.22phd7130@vitap.ac.in; mustapha.hedabou@um6p.ma; yogesh.c@vit.ac.in

Abstract

Cyberattack on our country's infrastructure could be easily prevented if we had access to our personal information or the information of our own business network communities. IT professionals and networked businesses face an infinite number of cyberattacks. Machine-to-machine (M2M) communication, used to link and transport data from one computer to the other, is a common use of the Internet of Things (IoT). However, cybersecurity threats are also being communicated so an attacker can access and follow the data. Manufacturing processes and efficiency can be improved by implementing the Industrial Internet of Things (IIoT) idea. Existing hierarchical models must be converted to a fully connected vertical model to accomplish this. IIoT is a novel method, and as such, the ecosystem is vulnerable to cyberthreat vectors and challenges with standardization and interoperability. New communication models and technologies are required to accomplish the needed levels of data security in the IIoT M2M. These include 5G, TSN ethernet, self-driving networks, etc. Malicious actors may take advantage of system flaws caused by the faulty implementation of security standards if no measures are in place to assess the risks and vulnerabilities. A cybersecurity project for Industry 4.0 is presently underway, and the findings in this report are based on that work. Converged/hybrid cybersecurity standards are explained in this research, and best practices are reviewed. A roadmap for identifying, aligning, and implementing the correct cybersecurity standards and tactics for protecting M2M communications in the IIoT is also provided.

Keywords: cybersecurity, IoT/M2M, Industry 4.0, Industrial IoT, threats

14.1 Introduction

Cybersecurity has been a significant subject for as long as the Internet has existed, and its relevance has only grown in recent years due to a greater reliance on IT infrastructure for telecommuting, online entertainment, and online business, to mention a few significant areas. In recent years, the amount of data transmitted over networks has increased dramatically due to faster internet connections, increased users, and increased number of devices [1]. Businesses and society might lose much money if there are interruptions in data flow. Organizations are under constant threat from increasingly sophisticated and complex security threats and assaults, many of which make use of automation. For security specialists, the time-consuming task of patching and analyzing systems and identifying dangers can be automated in order to make systems more secure against a wide range of threats. There is much space for progress in the automation of complicated security jobs. Automating security operations ranges from simple scripts to more complicated methods, such as incorporating machine learning and artificial intelligence into the software [2].

The privacy of IoT users has also been a hot topic in related industries. Recent studies have focused on web technologies, big data analytics systems, NoSQL data storage, data stream management, and RFID technologies (e.g., [3]). For example, [4]. These approaches, however, fall short of solving the new dilemma that IoT ecosystems face. The complexity of data flows between

IoT devices and back-end systems makes it easy for consumers to lose control of how their data are transported and handled. The lack of control over how multiple IoT devices' data are combined to generate new information about individuals further worsens this situation. On the other hand, we believe that giving users more control over IoT platform data management is critical.

In response to this problem, we have developed an essential framework to give users more say over how IoT systems use their personal data. We offer a unique approach to facilitate the specification of privacy choices governing data analysis in IoT environments and associated enforcement methods [5]. It is hoped that the suggested framework will help prevent the inference of sensitive and confidential user information from the aggregation of data provided by numerous IoT devices belonging to the user. It is vital, in terms of data management, to let customers specify their privacy choices for how their personal information is used, which they may do by utilizing well-established privacy management principles like "purpose," "duration," and "disclosure to third parties." Because of this, various IoT systems have created a common IoT platform framework that can be used. By way of illustration, it restricts, among other things: (1) access to and the aggregation of personal user data; (2) what analytics algorithms cannot deduce from user data. Because of this, it is easy for users to create new privacy settings that regulate the processing of new data acquired via analytics activities. Because of a lack of technical skills and competence, the ordinary user of an IoT device may not be able to set their privacy choices. To make the framework even more user-friendly, we want to add tools that aid users in customizing privacy settings in the future. Although the Internet of Things has provided numerous benefits, it has also created problems for those using it [6].

Data security and privacy concerns are front of mind for the researchers and security professionals interviewed for this article. Two issues have many companies and government entities perplexed. Cyberattacks on the Internet of Things (IoT) have been demonstrated to be susceptible. There is a vulnerability in the Internet of Things that needs the implementation of additional security measures [7]. Security and privacy are the most significant impediments to the widespread use of the Internet of Things. Unfortunately, most customers are unaware of the security concerns until there has been a breach, resulting in huge losses like the theft of sensitive data. Services that do not sufficiently secure client information have seen a reduction in customer interest. In a recent study on privacy and security, the Internet of Things made for consumers did not do well. The safety features of cars today are not as reliable as they could be. Industry 4.0/Industrial Internet of Things (IIoT) is a concept for a smart and innovative factory that uses disruptive technologies

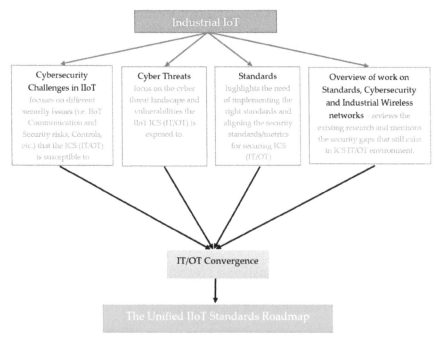

Figure 14.1   The study's scope, structure, and objectives.

(like IoT and cloud computing) and innovative solutions (like IIoT and automation) to improve the production environment in terms of reduced costs, increased agility, increased efficiency, remote operations, etc. Data and network security are critical when operating in a completely autonomous system. Security threats to IIoT applications and services have widened in scope, necessitating the development of new controls and safeguards [2–4].

During the pandemic, Internet threats and breaches must not be overlooked. A breach would be critical in the Industrial Internet of Things (IoT) arena because of exposures connected to M2M communication and surroundings [8]. Connected factories rely significantly on 5G and time-sensitive networking for their communication networks. The linked factory's infrastructure is built around self-auto-mating, self-guiding, and self-learning networks. Future M2M gadgets will incorporate artificial intelligence and machine learning algorithms to operate autonomously and make decisions. Because of the potential for disruptive risks, operational security is necessary for certain sorts of equipment. The IIoT environment is more exposed than ever to existing security risks because of the significant gap between current

IT and operational technology (IT/OT) domains. Hackers could exploit many points of entry created by industrial IoT/M2M devices, resulting in the loss of valuable assets and confidential data. Without sufficient standards and security measures, it will be difficult to detect the cyberthreat impact and the information that has been modified. The entire environment [5] is at risk if the breach is not noticed in time. Data analysis and cybersecurity are required for advanced use cases such as smart industrial robots and digital twins to safeguard vertical industries. It is possible to reduce the risk of Industry 4.0 (I4.0) and industrial control system (ICS) incidents by bridging the security metrics gap. This will help ensure end-to-end (E2E) security in ICS. The study's distinctive features include a thorough examination of cybersecurity standards, recommendations for designing/converging IT/OT security architectures, an emphasis on the need to implement interoperable and hybrid standards connecting various complex interfaces, the bridging of the IT/OT divide, and a strategic alignment to mitigate IT/OT cyberrisks in the IIoT. The National Institute of Standards and Technology conducted the research (NIST). All these elements work together to help readers fully grasp the topic.

14.1.1 IoT security

This is understandable in light of the growing popularity of the Internet of Things (IoT). Hackers will soon gain access to your entire network by breaking into your coffee machine. Businesses worldwide are more vulnerable to cyberattacks because of the Internet of Things. The Internet of Things also raises concerns about data sharing and privacy. When billions of gadgets are networked, think about the issues that will arise in the future. Businesses will have to deal with the enormous volumes of data that these gadgets will generate. Keeping the massive volumes of data collected while allowing easy access, tracking, and analysis will be a significant challenge. Security and risk management should not be taken for granted when developing new Internet of Things applications.

14.1.2 IoT and cloud computing

The Internet of Things encompasses all the devices and services we use daily linked to the Internet (IoT). Cloud computing, which acts as a front end for IoT, will also help it succeed. One way cloud computing can help with IoT is by allowing users to perform normal computer activities using services made available through the Internet. Because of memory or space limits on their

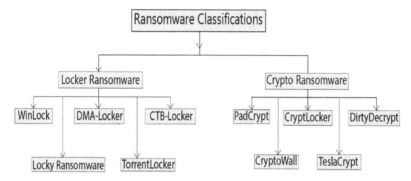

Figure 14.2   Hierarchy of ransomware families.

computer, an employee may be forced to abandon a large project that needs to be submitted to their management. If a program is hosted on the Internet, memory and storage limits can be reduced. Workers can use cloud computing services to complete their tasks because the data is stored elsewhere. You may also need to reinstall or reformat your mobile device's operating system if it has a problem. Google Photos allows you to share your images online. After the reformatting or reinstalling process, you may move your photographs back to your device or access them online at any time [9]. Figure 14.2 present the ransomware classifications.

Because of this, personal information like the user's location, contact information, accounts, and photographs are in danger. Antivirus and malware detection apps are also missing from most Android smartphones [4, 6]. Sandboxes, access controls, and a signature and authorization mechanism have been offered. API calls are used to deliver M0Droid's signatures to client devices for hazard identification [9]. The author in [10] has developed a new malware detection method based on application data consumption. Also, [16] built a system for monitoring the frequency of Dalvik activity codes on Android, which might be used to detect malicious programs. The author in [11], introduced Crowdroid framework out of the box for client and server components [12]. The client uses the Linux trace function for Android system calls. According to [13], Copper Droid is a framework for detecting and executing Java code. Previous Android malware detection research has relied heavily on a small number of features to identify malware [5, 6, 14, 18, 20].

The combination of blockchain and machine learning for intelligent model training and safe information sharing is gaining traction in the fight against this dilemma. Because of its high credibility and efficiency, blockchain technology is more famous for exchanging IoT data because it is more secure and reliable.

The remaining paper is structured as follows: Literature Survey in Section 14.2, security requirements are the focus of Section 14.3, detailed methodology and proposed research model discussed in Section 14.4, while the breadth of cyberthreats attached for IoT are discussed in Section 14.5. For the sake of this research, Section 14.6 includes data security attacks. Section 14.6 includes cybersecurity challenges in IIoT, followed by Section 14.7, results and discussion, and Section 14.8, which gives detailed information on challenges in IIoT, a roadmap to a unified standard framework for minimizing cyberthreats and standardization challenges that develop in the I4.0/IIoT environment as a result of IT/OT convergence gaps in Section 14.9 followed by conclusion and future scope in Section 14.10.

14.2 Literature Survey

Technologies like cloud computing and the Internet of Things should make it possible to analyze and store data so it can be shared worldwide. Cloud solutions like Microsoft Azure, Amazon Web Services (AWS), and Google Docs are expected to provide standard gateways for integrating physical objects with computing and communication capabilities across various applications, services, and technologies. There are a number of interesting new technologies that could change the way ubicomp infrastructure is built shortly (IoT). Most people think that cloud computing will have something to do with this [4]. Using big data analytics and cloud computing, the data from IoT devices will be looked at and figured out.

Also, more and more cloud-based services are adding web-based interfaces that make it easier for users to talk to each other and work together. According to [14], traditional computing and Internet connectivity platforms must be expanded beyond the typical mobile communication that connects people. This is necessary for the Internet of Things to work (IoT). This framework can be used to make connections that are smart and aware of their surroundings. People think that the Internet of Things will create many data that will need to be stored, processed, and shown in a way that is easy to understand. This is because billions of devices are expected to be connected to the ecosystem. Cloud computing is a must for Internet of Things services to work with a virtual infrastructure [15]. Data can be tracked and stored, computations (and analytics) can be done, data can be visualized, and services can be offered to customers [2]. Gubbi and his coworkers say that the IoT's vision is clear when seen from the point of view of both a "Thing" and the "Internet." Because it is built around the Internet, the Internet of Things has changed its focus from Internet-as-a-services to device data. IoT services and apps that use a thing-centric architecture [16] focus on the connected things rather than the network that links them.

Many experts agree that networked "smart environment" devices will be the next big technological step [2]. As we move from www (online static pages) to www2 (web of social networking) to web3 (web of things), there will be much demand for data-on-demand searches that are both smart and easy to use (ubiquitous computing, also known as the web of things). The post-PC era has begun, and smartphones and other forms of technology have significantly changed our surroundings and how we talk to each other. The situation is improving because the format has changed to be more about teaching and getting people involved. Mark Weiser says that a "new ecosystem" refers to a "smart environment" that has "sensors, actuators, displays, and computational elements seamlessly integrated into everyday things" [8].

Pervasive computing is growing because of cloud computing and the Internet of Things. In his article [18], Kevin Ashton says that putting RFID and other sensors into everyday objects would lead to a new era of machine awareness and help set up the Internet of Things. Since then, there has been a lot going on around this idea. Burhan et al. [10] describes the Internet of Things (IoT) as a group of parts that can be found, addressed, and read by any other part. This means that services can be sent and received instantly from anywhere and on any device. Because of this, people, pets, computers, books, cars, appliances, and even food will all be connected to the Internet of Everything (Figure 14.3).

The term "Internet of Things" was initially introduced in the annual ITU Network Reports of 2005 [19]. In the study, the Internet of Things is described as a scenario where various devices interact intelligently. For instance, a car alarm can notify drivers of errors, a briefcase can remind its carrier of forgotten items, and clothing can transmit preferences for colors and temperatures to a washing machine, among other capabilities. (Figure 14.4)

The European Research Cluster on the Internet of Things (IERC) defines IoT as an integral aspect of the future Internet with the following features (Figure 14.5).

The Internet of Things (IoT) has been the subject of numerous studies since then. Using distributed systems as an example, [20] examined Internet of Things features and security problems. Issues ranging from identification and authentication to access control and protocol were covered.

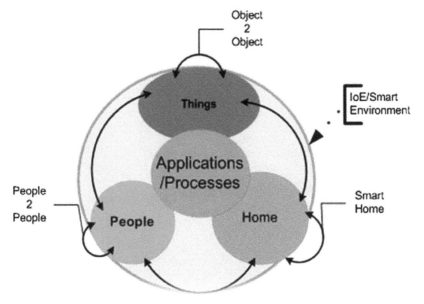

Figure 14.3 Futuristic Internet of Everything (IoE) ecosystem [10].

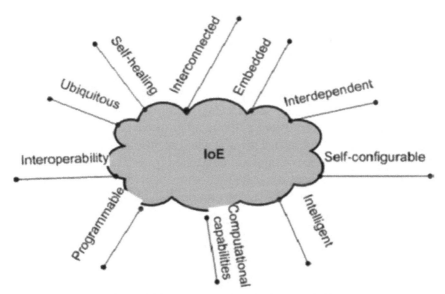

Figure 14.4 Characteristics of a future IoE [21].

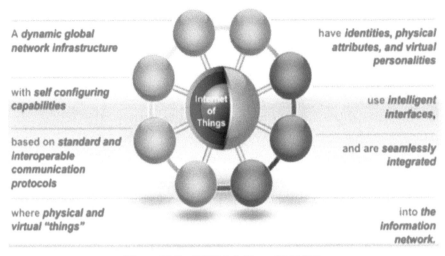

A *dynamic global network infrastructure*

with *self configuring capabilities*

based on *standard and interoperable communication protocols*

where *physical and virtual "things"*

have *identities, physical attributes, and virtual personalities*

use *intelligent interfaces,*

and are *seamlessly integrated*

into *the information network.*

Figure 14.5 IERC definition of IoT [22].

14.3 Security Requirements

In this section, I will review the previously discussed layers of vulnerability for the major Internet of Things technologies. In addition, I examine the most typical IoT scenarios and the issues they raise regarding ensuring user data privacy in these settings. In order to address some of these concerns, I then look at some of the most significant security measures that other academics have recommended. Finally, I discuss how blockchain technology might be used to safeguard IoT data. All of these ideas are broken down into four primary categories: securing IoT using blockchain, IoT vulnerabilities, IoT security measures, and more [6, 21, 23, 24]. There has been a tremendous increase in assaults in recent years as the number of connected devices has increased. We need to protect our privacy when we use electronic devices, such as smart locks and security systems controlled by the Internet of Things (IoT). If two or more devices are linked via wireless networks, it makes no difference how secure the network is. The proliferation of protocols and interfaces within the same ecosystem, which makes it impossible to manage them all, is another difficulty with today's sensor and connected device ecosystem. We are likelier to use separate applications to operate many devices if they are connected. Web, cloud, and mobile interfaces are all part of the problem. Physical access is the most straightforward method of attacking a gadget. It is critical to be aware that multiple persons may be using the same device and to use all available safeguards. Many types of cyberattacks can target Internet of Things (IoT) devices. There are a few things to want to have a safe Internet of Things:

a. **Authentication:** It is the procedure used to verify that a person truly is who they say they are. It is one of the most pressing issues in the Internet of Things because of the sheer volume of connected devices. Figuring out if someone or something is who or what they claim to be. When it comes to IoT, many entities must be authenticated for these interactions (such as service providers, devices, people, and processing units). In order to keep corporate networks safe, all devices must be authenticated. Authorization is the act of enabling someone else to do or have something that they want. Based on the user's unique identification, it grants them access to specific resources within the system. In most security systems, the first step is to authenticate the user, and the second is to authorize them.

b. **Integrity:** Techniques for limiting access to data modification to those granted permission. Because the Internet of Things relies on many connected devices sharing data, the data must be kept secure. Protection of integrity also includes safeguarding against sabotage. The IoT system's fault tolerance and resilience are essential determinants of data integrity. Password-protected systems keep your data safe.

c. **Availability:** Internet of Things (IoT) users should have access to all data at all times and from any location. IoT systems must maintain their desired levels of availability and meet their applications' performance requirements.

d. **Privacy:** Maintaining the information in secure locations and employing effective security measures is the goal of this requirement. Many privacy concerns have surfaced in the IoT's rapid expansion over the last year, as well as the fact that many products now fail to provide all of the warranties users expect.

e. **Confidentiality:** It is critical that the data is only accessible to those granted permission to use it. These users may include equipment, services, people, and other items within the system. Encryption techniques provide privacy protection.

f. **Non-repudiation:** An entity's involvement can be proven through a variety of methods. It is frequently used for digital signatures, contracts, and e-mails. Digital signatures, confirmation services, and timestamps can all be used to ensure non-repudiation.

g. **Lightweight solutions** are a new type of security measure offered by IoT devices because of their limited power and processing capabilities. Communication protocols on a local or vast area network that are simpler, faster, and easier to maintain is called simplified protocols.

h. **Heterogeneity:** A wide range of devices and systems can be connected to the Internet of Things (IoT). Because of this, protocols must be developed to work in various settings and on a wide range of devices. The Internet of Things (IoT) intends to connect different networks and devices. In comparison to other devices, each one works and communicates differently. Other factors like privacy, integration, and identity may be hampered due to this problem.

The security of devices in the perception layer is critical since these devices typically lack the memory required for full security technology. At the nodes where data is transferred to the transport layer, these assaults occur from external sources. One of the main goals of assaults on this layer is to disrupt the ability of sensor nodes to identify objects accurately. Intrusion detection and wireless encryption are two countermeasures that can be found in this layer. The primary technologies utilized at the perception layer, such as RFID(Radio-Frequency IDentification), WSN (Wireless Sensor Network), and NFC(Near Field Communication) are examined for security vulnerabilities.

14.4 Methodology

The Internet of Things (IoT) is becoming a powerful amplifier for cyber-attacks as it gains popularity [7]. Their vulnerability is the weakest link in today's computer networks' security chain. According to an HP poll, IoT gadgets are vulnerable to hackers and identity thieves because they have simple or no passwords and use unencrypted network services. Malicious software (malware) and private information can easily be installed on unprotected IoT devices in a vulnerable environment [12]. Malicious botnets significantly threaten the IoT (Internet of Things). Botnets are compromised computers exploited by cybercriminals for malicious purposes on the Internet [13]. Malware known as Mirai [8] was responsible for Distributed Denial of Service(DDoS) attacks against Krebs on Security and Dyn provider, which generated more than 1 Tbps of network traffic. AutoBotCatcher uses dynamic analysis based on network traffic flow to detect botnets in IoT device communities. Agents and block generators are crucial players in a P2P

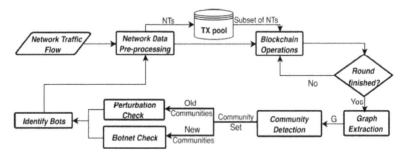

Figure 14.6 AutoBot Catcher system flow.

botnet detection approach for the blockchain-based Internet of Things (IoT). (Figure 14.6)

14.4.1 Privacy and technology knowledge in IoT

As part of a person's right to privacy, they can choose who can see their personal information [9]. Identity privacy, data privacy, attribute privacy, and task privacy are some of the many things that privacy can cover [10, 11]. When dealing with data that can be changed, deleted, or added to, there are worries about the security of information that can be used to identify a person. "Privacy" includes more than just user-initiated actions and data. It also includes technologies like crowd-sensing, which uses devices to collect location data without the user's permission [12], and the unexpected use of

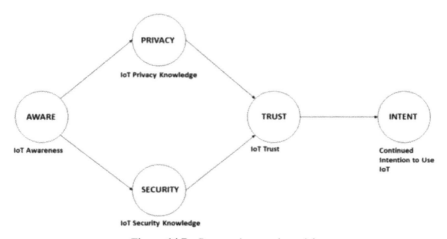

Figure 14.7 Proposed research model.

personal data [13]. As people learn more about privacy and security issues, they are putting more pressure on device makers to fix those [14]. Privacy-protecting and pseudonymous authorization frameworks that allow people to own and govern their data are decentralized. A lack of security can jeopardize an IoT application's integrity and existence. By their very nature, Internet of Things (IoT) devices are delicate. Many products and gadgets in an IoT ecosystem are connected and share sensitive data. Sensitive data and device communication must be safeguarded in such a setting. More than one million devices are evaluated for compliance with necessary digital certificates in the IoT. Devices can be identified digitally, making it impossible to manipulate the blocking. It is also possible to increase scalability by dynamically updating device information. Incorporating blockchain technology can make distributed data exchanges more secure [4]. Regarding privacy and security, research shows that blockchain technology can connect IoT devices.

In order to ensure the security of the new technology, companies must first check and comprehend it, thoroughly examine the security risks involved, and devise strategies for resolving them. The author addresses cloud computing security challenges and hazards in this paper and outlines methods an organization may take to mitigate these risks and protect its resources. Cloud computing has its strengths and limitations, as well as its applications in risk management [58].

14.5 Cyberthreats on IoT

In recent years, there has been an increase in malicious software such as malware, spyware, phishing attacks, ransomware, and zero-day attacks. Because of this, the influence of these threats and risks on new communication models and standards needs to be evaluated. M2M communication in IIoT/I4.0 depends on particular specifications such as URLLC(Ultra Reliable Low Latency Communications), mMTC (Massive Machine-Type Communications), and eMBB (Enhanced Mobile Broadband) [25], which provide real-time data with low latency and good reachability in a low-latency fashion [1]. Guidelines for cybersecurity should be thoroughly comprehended and implemented to lessen the impact of these dangers [27, 28]. However, only a few industries have been able to implement them successfully, and even fewer are aware of their company's level of security maturity concerning the risks currently facing their industry. All three aspects of improved ICS(Integrated Communications System) cybersecurity—detection, prediction, and prevention—depend on these actions. ENISA(European Union

Agency for Network and Information Security) threat landscapes [2] evaluate the risks and vulnerabilities associated with IIoT across 5G networks. This assessment also considers the network resources and the sensitivity of the IIoT. When you use this model, you are provided with a more in-depth technical view of the 5G architecture, sensitive assets, cyberthreats that influence those assets, and threat agents. The information used to create the threat environment came from sources open to the public. These sources included 5G standardization groups and bodies (such as ETSI(European Telecommunications Standards Institute (ETSI)) and 3GPP) [26] and 5G investors such as mobile carriers, technology providers, and national and international organizations.

14.5.1 Device attack

Hacking the Internet of Things devices is possible with this method of attack. Its primary purpose is to make the system's architecture more vulnerable (depending on the devices involved). If an attacker successfully compromises the base device, they can take down the entire RFID-powered inventory control system (e.g., the server is the target). As a result of a device attack, disruptions to the neighborhood area network (NAN) of an electrical grid could lead to distributed denial-of-service attacks on the entire grid. Device attacks can be caused by various malfunctions at the middleware layer of the operating system, including IP configuration errors, memory corruption, and incorrectly executed code, to name a few.

14.5.2 Network attack

In this assault, messages are either delayed or lost, compromising inter-device communication. Network assaults have the potential to devastate IoT configuration systems' computational activities. Attacks like these are aimed at disrupting the functionality of home network equipment, such as cameras and routers (Home Area Network). Similarly, a similar assault might prohibit linked devices from accessing important information from other devices in nearby networks (NANs). SQL injection, denial-of-service assaults, and code execution are all examples of this type of attack. Table 14.1 shows the vulnerabilities in Wireless Sensor Network; Table 14.2 shows the vulnerabilities in RFID and Table 14.3 shows the vulnerabilities in WiFi.

"Cyber threats" come in many forms, but the most common ones involve stealing, changing, or destroying data in cyberspace (exploiting data confidentiality, integrity, and availability). Criminals commit these crimes

Table 14.1 WSN vulnerabilities (main threats and countermeasures).

WSN vulnerabilities	
Main threats	Countermeasures
Wormhole	Synchronized clocks are used. A combination of directional antennas and multidimensional scaling is required.
Sybil	Verification of location and economic incentives are all part of a trusted certification. Random essential dispersal and testing of resources.
Spoofing	A WSN authentication protocol and data encryption should be implemented.
Ping flood	Perimeter adjustments to a firewall detection of IDS are required (Intrusion detection system).

Table 14.2 RFID vulnerabilities (main threats and countermeasures).

RFID vulnerabilities	
Main threats	Countermeasures
DoS attacks	Incorporate a tighter mechanical link between tags and merchandise. Assign an alarm function to tags that are in use.
Eavesdropping	Encryption of the tag-reader communication.
Skimming	Incorporation of blockchain-based monetary instruments.
Replay attack	Schemes that are countered schemes based on the passage of time.
Side channel attack	Reduce the amount of data that is made public. Remove the connection between the information that's been released and the information that's been kept concealed.

Table 14.3 Wi-Fi vulnerabilities (main threats and countermeasures).

Wi-Fi vulnerabilities
Main threats Countermeasures
Wi-Fi password cracking, malware installation, WPA2, and web content screening should be introduced. Data Thieves and Bad Neighbours.

using many different methods, such as eavesdropping, denial of service (DoS) attacks, viruses and other types of malware, and denial of service attacks (i.e., hacktivists, state-sponsored, knowledgeable insider, organized crime, hackers, amateur, etc.). Direct or indirect cyberattacks can threaten industrial control systems (ICS). However, passive attacks are harder to spot, putting systems at risk by letting hackers listen in on conversations. This could put both security and reliability at risk.

14.6 Data Security Attacks

Keeping up with current threats and attacks is a significant challenge for data security. Public cloud services may require different privacy, security, and confidentiality standards for processing information. In order to develop better security methods to secure data in a cloud computing environment, it is required to identify potential security threats and assaults. We are simply thinking about web application data security attacks when it comes to cloud data security threats and attacks. Using Web 2.0 (the leading technology for using SaaS in cloud computing) vulnerabilities, attacks are launched against Web 2.0 sites. Many attacks on cloud data security have been reported. However, only malware injection attacks on cloud web applications have been included in this study. In order to cause harm or obtain access to data, malware injection attacks target cloud systems by injecting a malicious service or virtual machine into the system. Malicious code is injected into the web application as a new instance of service implementation and begins redirecting legitimate services to the attacker's instance, allowing the attacker to steal private session information. In our study of Malware injection attacks on cloud computing web applications, we primarily focused on the most frequent attacks, such as SQL injection and XSS(Cross Site Scripting) assaults.

14.6.1 SQL injection attack

In order to perform a SQL injection, security flaws in the software must be exploited. Attackers take advantage of the vulnerabilities in web servers and inject malicious code to avoid authentication and obtain access to the database without authorization. Botnets (private networked computers infected with malicious software) are commonly used to launch this attack, also known as a zombie army. If the attacker is successful, he/she can remotely execute system instructions, retrieve confidential data, change database contents, and seize control of the web server. This attack is carried out by thousands of bots equipped with a SQL injection kit, which can be seen in the botnets. Botnets have infected millions of URLs at various websites throughout the world using SQL injections. Merchants use SaaS (Software as a Service) applications to host and sell their products online in the cloud computing environment. SQL injection can be divided into three different types.

14.6.2 Attack by cross-site scripting

Phishing attacks (fraudulent attempts) are used to obtain data this way. To carry out this attack, a malicious hyperlink is typically used to acquire data. An output page appears to be a legitimate piece of content on the website, but it contains the malicious data initially given to the web application [7]. It is the most prevalent method of leaking information contained in user cookies, which can lead to a breach in security. The attacker receives access to the session information, such as the user's ID, password, credit card information, etc. With this attack, an attacker can alter the user's preferences and take control of their account, steal cookies, or allow intrusive advertising. It is possible to run arbitrary code on a victim's computer if cross-site scripting is used with other flaws [8]. Malicious pages or parameter values can be the source of a cross-site scripting attack. It is possible to accurately detect cross-site scripting assaults by knowing the attack's source, time, and signatures [9]. A cross-site scripting attack uses a weakness in cross-site scripting to bypass the system's access controls. Many intrusion prevention systems miss cross-site scripting, even though it is a simple assault to detect. Many security experts believe it poses a minor risk [8].

14.7 Results and Discussion

Cyberattack has long relied solely on the work of Yandex, Google, and other counterparts to blacklist fraudulent sites. Machine learning and artificial intelligence techniques and methods are employed in modern anti-phishing defences and various other techniques and methods. A wide variety of algorithms are constantly being created and refined in order to identify phishing sites. In most anti-phishing algorithms, sites are searched and compared to the original, such as by comparing how the site's name is written and displayed in the address bar and the content on the site itself. Thanks to such algorithms, it is possible to develop browser extensions that alert users to the unreliability of a site and the likelihood of phishing, as well as spam filters in e-mail accounts. Users' credentials are protected by storing their hashes rather than their passwords to prevent phishing. However, despite tremendous investment in research and development, no technologies can guarantee 100 percent protection from phishing attempts, regardless of how much money is spent on this research and development. Phishing assaults typically involve the victim in some way, which is why most anti-phishing defences include technical and social engineering capabilities.

14.7.1 Cyberattack in Industrial IoT devices

Using the experimental data, the significance of the extracted components of the proposed framework's suggested framework is proven. Clustering findings for a noisy and high-dimensional dataset are shown in Figure 14.8. The red color indicates dangerous samples, and the blue color represents benign samples over two axes in clustered data after feature reduction.

Table 14.4 Methods of prevention.

Scheme	Type	Solution	
Social engineering phishing	Fake ICO	Prevent dangerous financial investments by thoroughly inspecting project paperwork and site traffic.	using bookmarks instead of links; installing anti-phishing extensions on browsers; not clicking on links or downloading suspicious attachments; verifying the SSL certificate before using services; educating users about phishing; launching offline copies of crypto wallets; using two-factor authentication; using complex passwords (at least 14 symbols); avoiding public Wi-Fi; and using.
	Bloating		
	Pyramids, ponzi		
	Clones	Secure mail servers and databases for employees, customers, and investors; monitoring activities on corporate and community web pages.	
	Aimed phishing		
	Social networking		
	Fake cryptowallets		
Technical phishing	DNS based	Create an alternative to DNS, such as ENS (the Ethereum name service).	
	Hijacking	Ensure that the sender and receiver addresses are correct.	
	Malware	Attachments should not be opened or installed.	

Table 14.4 (Continued.)

Scheme	Type	Solution
	Key loggers	Keep an eye on processes in the device's task management, verify signatures, use on-screen keyboards, and keep a password wallet handy.

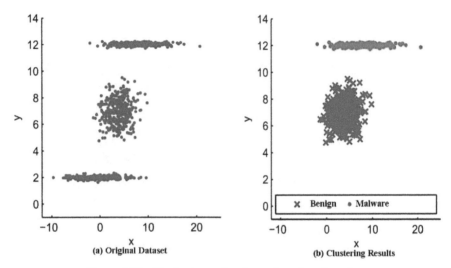

(a) Original Dataset

(b) Clustering Results

Figure 14.8 The benign and malware detection clustering.

The depiction of two distinct clusters is clearly dominated by smoothing over the subspace region of the feature. On the other hand, it is difficult to tell the two groups apart because of the point distribution representation. Hyperplane placement can be seen more clearly when two clusters of data points are projected onto each other. It is difficult to draw such data projections since it necessitates an in-depth investigation of each data point throughout the separation process. Examples of the outcomes of several sample data projections are shown in Figures 14.9 and 14.10, illustrating that the technique we recommend effectively distinguishes between benign and malicious samples.

Malware data was extracted from the blockchain using machine learning techniques such as clustering and classification. The history of all malware information can be communicated through the blockchain, allowing for excellent detection of new viruses. The clustering technique determines

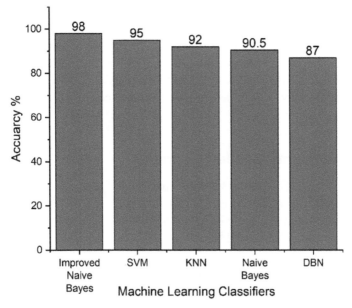

Figure 14.9 Accuracy of classifiers based on machine learning.

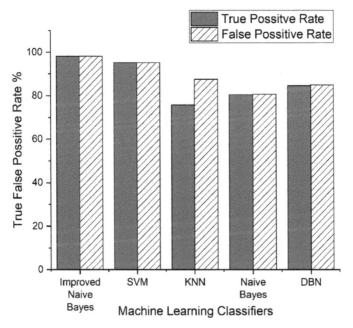

Figure 14.10 Comparing false-positive and true-positive rates.

the weights of each feature set and repeatedly removes the unnecessary features that can be highly efficient in discriminating between malware and non-malicious programs. In order to attain high classification accuracy and robustness, the Bayes classifier, which uses a decision tree to deal with multi-feature problems, is also used. Our system's permissioned blockchain-based malware database allows us to detect malware more accurately and precisely in real time.

14.8 Cybersecurity Challenges in IIoT

This section discusses several security challenges (such as denial of service, data theft, manipulation, eavesdropping, etc.) [8–11]. As a result of unresolved vulnerabilities in the IIoT/I4.0 sector, industrial environments are vulnerable to security breaches [12, 13].

14.8.1 IT/OT (Data security issues)

Over the past few years, there has been a dramatic rise in the number of attacks on operational technology (OT) [14, 15]. This is most likely attributable to the increased flexibility and remote access afforded to new and old OT systems (such as SCADA, PLCs, etc.) by new interfaces (such as IT systems, the cloud, etc.). Researchers and policymakers have become interested in this field of study due to the alarming increase in cyberattacks against ICS. One example of this increase is the most significant fuel-pipeline ransomware attack in the United States [16]. Because the IIoT relies on innovative forms of communication, there is cause for concern regarding the confidentiality of trade secrets in the manufacturing industry [3]. Whereas operational technology (OT) is more concerned with the security of industrial control systems (ICS), information technology (IT) is more concerned with the security of applications and supporting technologies. Because operational technology (OT) and information technology (IT) systems do not communicate with one another, targeted cyberattacks are possible [17].

14.8.2 Cybersecurity threats to the Industrial Internet of Things

Machine-to-machine (M2M) communications rely on cutting-edge networks like 5G, Wi-Fi 6, and time-sensitive networking (TSN) to realize their high throughput and low latency goals. Due to the unique communication types and devices used in IIoT environments, these spaces are open to

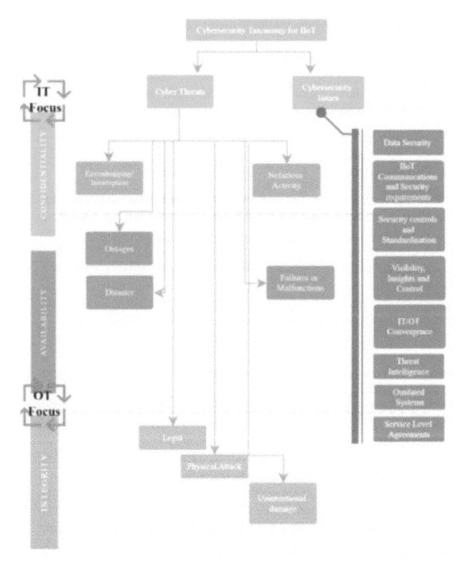

Figure 14.11 Cybersecurity taxonomy for IIoT.

various cyberthreats. IoT device endpoints present several security challenges, including assessment, monitoring, and security (e.g., lack of standard regulations for all IoT devices from different vendors [9, 10], and trusting third-party cloud vendors). It is essential to consider a variety of potential dangers when securing the M2M communication ecosystem. Lack of

M2M communication standardization, malicious IoT nodes, and improperly configured devices are some dangers (IoT, cloud, edge, etc.). The severity of the damage caused by compromised M2M devices can be gauged using a combination of impact type (a threat materializes, compromising confidentiality, availability, and/or network integrity) and impact factor/scale (the total number of users, the duration of downtime, the number of cells affected, and the information altered or accessed).

14.9 The Roadmap for Unifying IIoT Standards

A unified approach is required to protect and standardize the fully connected and intelligent industrial environment. In the Industrial Internet of Things (IIoT), vulnerabilities can originate from sources other than IT and OT, such as a lack of essential skill sets, inefficient processes, etc. A unified strategy developed by the author helps bridge the gaps between various communication standards and security objectives and other areas that impact the whole cybersecurity domain. Figure 14.12 presents the interoperability roadmap that has been developed for I4.0's unified standards. In order to have an environment that is both autonomous and interoperable, there needs to be compliance with a number of different standards (hybrid standards). The same method is applied to analyzing common metrics used in hybrid standards. This causes gaps and vulnerabilities to transition from unknown (reactive) to known (proactive). Heterogeneous network architecture is essential to the Internet of Things (IoT) and Industry 4.0 (I4.0). A sector's expansion prospects and performance indicators could be hampered if forced to rely exclusively on a single communication network. BP1-CPNI [109], IEC 62351 [12], and NIST 800-82 [10, 11] are three methods that can be utilized to segment a network successfully. You can anticipate receiving direction from them when implementing security standards such as NIST 800-53 or ISO 27001. Since standards can only be practical if they are selected and evaluated following a company's particular goals and objectives, the authors of I4.0 strongly advise production environment designers to do so for the time being. This recommendation is based on the fact that standards can only be effective if they are done so. The level of security that ICS/SCADA and IoT devices provide should be considered when determining the order of priority for these types of devices. The traffic flow should be organized according to which lanes serve the most important functions, and then it should be redirected to other areas. Cyberattacks that are successful at this layer can result in denial of service (DoS) and financial and asset losses, but they can also alter

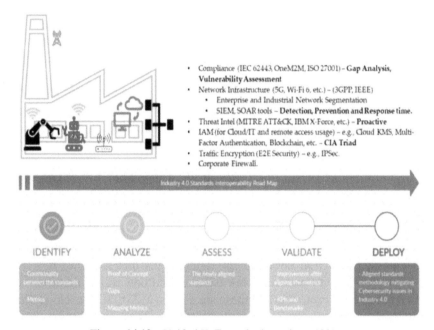

Figure 14.12 Unified IIoT standards roadmap [23].

the quality of the product or produce defective items that threaten public safety. Implementing SIEM and SOAR tools at this layer will help you better understand the reactive strategy for detecting, preventing, and quickly recovering from attacks or failures involving ICS. [8] Extending or modifying the table's dimensions is possible depending on the operational and functional capacities of the production environment.

The importance of the data and other factors can be considered when establishing security goals with the help of the unified roadmap for IIoT standards. Is there a cap on how far the information can travel? To what extent are your options limited? etc. If the user is familiar with ICS/SCADA and all it can do, a comprehensive gap analysis encompassing security standards, communication protocols, and threat intelligence frameworks can be carried out. Users can accomplish this by using this procedure from beginning to end.

14.10 Conclusion and Future Scope

Even though many cybersecurity standards and protocols have been put in place, the IIoT/I4.0 is still vulnerable to a wide range of cyberthreats and dangers, as mentioned in the studies above. For an IIoT/I4.0 fully connected, autonomous factory to be built, there needs to be a set of universal standards that all vendors can use. At the same time, it is essential to fix the fact that the different control systems and standards do not work well together regarding security. One way to reach this goal is by making rules that apply everywhere. To meet each smart factory's unique service and security needs, it is essential to create a comprehensive security strategy that considers the many different cyber standards already in place while also making the threat landscape less dangerous. A unified roadmap has many benefits, such as providing a framework for implementing different levels of protection, (ii) providing alignment between IT and OT, and (iii) providing guidelines for risk assessment and mitigation of new cybersecurity-based threats in a heterogeneous production environment. This means that it shows how to make a lot of different standards work together and how to use them in the IIoT/I4.0 ecosystem. Protocols like these are used in M2M, 5G, the cloud, the edge, and many other places.

References

[1] Gouse baig Mohammad and Dr. Prabhakar Kandukuri, "Detection of Position Falsification Attack in VANETs using ACO," in the Journal of International Journal of Control and Automation. 2019; Vol 12, No 6:715-724,

[2] Sicari, S., Rizzardi, A., Grieco, L. A., & Coen-Porisini, A. Security, privacy and trust in Internet of Things: The road ahead. Computer Network. 2015; 76: 146–164.

[3] S. Karnouskos, A. W. Colombo, T. Bangemann, "Trends and Challenges for Cloud-Based Industrial Cyber-Physical Systems," in Industrial Cloud-Based Cyber-Physical Systems. 2014; 231-240.

[4] S. L. P. Yasakethu, J. Jiang, "Intrusion Detection via Machine Learning for SCADA System Protection," in Proceedings of the 1st International Symposium on ICS & SCADA Cyber Security Research. 2013;101-105.

[5] L. A. Maglaras, J. Jiang, "Intrusion Detection in SCADA Systems Using Machine Learning Techniques," Science and Information Conference (SAI), London. 2014; 626-631.

[6] Gouse Baig Mohammad, S.Shitharth, Puranam Revanth Kumar' Integrated Machine Learning Model for an URL Phishing Detection', International Journal of Grid and Distributed Computing, vol. 14, Issue 1, pp. 513-529, 2021.

[7] Joseph, A. J., Sani, N., Kumar, K. S., Kumar, T. A., & Nishanth, R. (2022, March). Towards a Novel and Efficient Public Key Management for Peer-Peer Security in Wireless Ad-Hoc/sensor Networks. In 2022 International Conference on Smart Technologies and Systems for Next Generation Computing (ICSTSN) (pp. 1-4). IEEE.

[8] R. C. B. Hink, J. M. Beaver, M. A. Buckner, T. Morris, U. Adhikari, S. Pan, "Machine Learning for Power System Disturbance and Cyber-Attack Discrimination," in Proceedings of the 7th International Symposium on Resilient Control Systems (ISRCS). 2014; 1-8.

[9] S.Shitharth, Sangeetha, Praveen Kumar, 'Integrated Probability relevancy classification (IPRC) for IDS in SCADA,' Design Framework for a wireless network, Lecture notes in network and systems, Springer , vol. 82, Issue 1, 2019, pp. 41-64

[10] Burhan, M., Rehman, R. A., Khan, B., & Byung-Seo, K. IoT elements, layered architectures and security issues: A comprehensive survey. Sensors. 2018; 18(9),

[11] Chatterjee, S., Kar, A. K., & Dwivedi, Y. K. Intention to use IoT by aged Indian consumers. Journal of Computer Information Systems. 2018; 1–12.

[12] Carrion, G., Nitzl, C., & Rold'an, J. Mediation analyses in partial least squares structural equation modeling: Guidelines and empirical examples. Partial least squares path modeling. 2017; 173–195.

[13] B. Thirumaleshwari Devi, S.Shitharth, 'An Appraisal over Intrusion Detection systems in cloud computing security attacks', 2nd International Conference on Innovative Mechanisms for Industry Applications, IEEE Explore, ICIMIA -2020, pp. 122 , DOI: 10.1109/ICIMIA48430.2020.9074924

[14] Krishna Keerthi Chennam, Rajinikanth Aluvalu and S.Shitharth,' An Authentication Model with High Security for Cloud Database', Architectural Wireless Networks Solutions and Security Issues, Lecture notes in network and systems, Springer , vol. 196, Issue 1, 2021, pp. 13-26.

[15] Duan, R., & Guo, L. Application of blockchain for internet of things: A bibliometric analysis. Mathematical Problems in Engineering. 2021; 1–16.

[16] J. M. Beaver, R. C. Borges-Hink, M. A. Buckner, "An Evaluation of Machine Learning Methods to Detect Malicious SCADA Communications," in 12th International Conference on Machine Learning and Applications (ICMLA), 2013; vol. 2: 54-59.

[17] N. Erez, A. Wool, "Control Variable Classification, Modeling and Anomaly Detection in Modbus/TCP SCADA Systems," International Journal of Critical Infrastructure Protection. 2015; vol. 10: 59-70.

[18] M.Padmaja, S.Shitharth, K.Prasuna, Abhay Chaturvedi, Pravin R. Kshirsagar, A.Vani, 'Grow of Artificial Intelligence to Challenge Security in IoT Application,' wireless personal communication, Springer, https://doi.org/10.1007/s11277-021-08725-4

[19] M. Hedabou. A Frobenius Map Approach for an Efficient and Secure Multiplication on Koblitz curves. International Journal of Network Security, Vol. 3, N. 2, PP.233-237. 2006. (+4)

[20] K. Stefanidis, A. G. Voyiatzis, "An HMM-Based Anomaly Detection Approach for SCADA Systems," in IFIP International Conference on Information Security Theory and Practice. 2016; 85-99.

[21] E. Byres, J. Lowe, "The Myths and Facts Behind Cyber Security Risks for Industrial Control Systems," in Proceedings of the VDE Kongress, vol. 116, 2004.

[22] S. Shitharth, K. M. Prasad, K. Sangeetha, P. R. Kshirsagar, T. S. Babu and H. H. Alhelou, "An Enriched RPCO-BCNN Mechanisms for Attack Detection and Classification in SCADA Systems," in IEEE Access, vol. 9, pp.156297-156312, 2021, doi: 10.1109/ACCESS.2021.3129053.

[23] Sanfilippo, M. R., Shvartzshnaider, Y., Reyes, I., Nissenbaum, H., & Egelman, S. Disaster privacy/privacy disaster. Journal of the Association for Information Science & Technology. 2020; 71(9): 1002–1014.

[24] Schneier, B. BOTNETS of things. Most Technology Review. 2017; 120(2): 88–91.

[25] Sharma, M., Joshi, S., Kannan, D., Govindan, K., Singh, R., & Purohit, H. C. (2020).

[26] Internet of Things (IoT) adoption barriers of smart cities' waste management: An Indian context. Journal of Cleaner Production, 270, Article 122047.

[27] Gouse baig Mohammad and Dr. Uppu Ravibabu, "RCAC: A Secure and Privacy-Preserving RFID based Cloud-Assisted Access Control to IoT Integrated Smart Home, "in the International Journal of

Innovative Technology and Exploring Engineering (IJITEE). 2019; 8(4): 1-8.

[28] M. Hedabou. Cryptography for addressing Cloud Computing Security, Privacy and Trust Issues. Book on Computer and Cyber Security : Principles, Algorithm, Applications and Perspective. CRC Press, Francis, and Taylor Publisher. USA, 2018

15

Illustrating the Mesmerizing Edge AI Journey for Industry Automation

Pethuru Raj[1] and Chellammal Surianarayanan[2]

[1]Edge AI Division, Reliance Jio Platforms Ltd., India
[2]Centre for Distance and Online Education, Bharathidasan University, India
E-mail: peterindia@gmail.com; chellammals@bdu.ac.in

Abstract

Edge AI is emerging and evolving fast to be a promising and potential paradigm for envisaging and implementing scores of real-time and intelligent applications and services for businesses and people. Edge AI is the cutest and cognitive combination of two hugely popular domains of edge computing and artificial intelligence. Edge AI represents the next and new version of edge data analytics. All kinds of the Internet of Things (IoT) edge devices interact with one another. This purposeful interaction results in a massive amount of multi-structured data. It is therefore essential to collect, cleanse, and crunch edge data in order to extract actionable insights in time. Thus, the aspect of edge analytics has become an indispensable tool for bringing forth context-aware, real-time, and people-centric services and applications.

Going forward, the traditional data analytics methods are being advanced through the surging popularity of AI algorithms (machine and deep learning (ML/DL)) and models. Highly optimized AI models are being produced through the training of ML/DL algorithms on datasets (training, validation, and testing) for automating and accelerating a variety of professional and personal tasks. So, it is not an exaggeration to state that the AI domain is being seen as a paradigm shift in the business world. With the accumulation of IoT edge devices in our mission-critical environments (homes, hotels, hospitals, etc.), computing, which generally happens in nearby and faraway cloud server clusters, moves over to IoT edge devices, which are called networked embedded systems. This fusion of AI and edge computing is being proclaimed as the most inspiring venture in the ensuing knowledge era.

Keywords: Edge AI, Edge computing, Artificial intelligence, IoT edge devices, Data analytics, Industry automation

15.1 Delineating the Paradigm of Cloud Computing

There are predominantly two types of IoT edge devices and sensors (resource-intensive and resource-constrained). Typically, resource-intensive IoT devices are termed IoT servers/fog devices. There are plentiful IoT middleware solutions (IoT gateways/hubs/buses/brokers), which are resource-intensive and hence contribute as IoT edge servers. That is, these IoT edge devices are primarily for real-time data aggregation, enrichment, encryption, processing, and storage. On the other hand, there are resource-constrained IoT sensors, which primarily are leveraged for data capturing from their environments and from the assets on which those sensors are embedded internally and externally. Further on, these IoT sensors transmit the captured data to a nearby IoT middleware solution to be stocked and analyzed. Thus, the idea of on-device data processing for generating real-time edge intelligence is gaining the attention of many these days. The much-discussed concept of real-time and intelligent computing is gathering momentum with the arrival and convergence of several cutting-edge technologies and tools. There are integrated platforms for performing edge data analytics through the leverage of traditional streaming analytics methods.

In the recent past, the phenomenon of running well-defined machine and deep learning (ML/DL) models directly on IoT edge servers is attracting the attention of technical experts. Businesses are also excited about this transition. It is expected that there will be scores of fresh possibilities and opportunities. This chapter is fully dedicated to explaining the expanding scope of edge AI. Before understanding edge AI, it is ideal to have some details about the currently popular cloud AI.

15.2 Enterprises Embrace the Cloud-first Strategy

There are many state-of-the-art digitization and digitalization technologies dramatically and distinctively empowering the digital era. The Internet of Things (IoT) and communication technologies such as 5G fuse well for producing connected digitized entities out of all kinds of physical, mechanical, electrical, and electronic systems. When these digitized elements interact with one another purposefully, a humongous amount of digital data gets generated. With a multitude of pioneering integration technologies such as middleware solutions (message brokers, hubs, buses, gateways, adaptors, queues, etc.) emerging and evolving fast, all kinds of business workloads and information technology (IT) services are being linked up to give integrated information and applications.

Clouds represent the highly organized and optimized IT infrastructure. Further on, clouds are consolidated, centralized/federated, and shared IT environments with a host of automated tools for meticulously monitoring, measuring, managing, and maintaining cloud operations. In short, the cloud idea guarantees much-insisted IT affordability, agility, and adaptivity. The cloudification aspect supports and sustains the IT phenomenon. The hard-to-solve challenges and concerns such as IT elasticity, application scalability, continuous availability, high reliability, heightened security, easy maneuverability, etc., are being simplified and speeded up through the fast-growing cloud paradigm.

15.3 Tending Toward Cloud-native Computing

Due to the inherent and sustainable strength of the cloud phenomenon, there are noteworthy evolutions and revolutions being unearthed and rolled out in the cloud space. Firstly, the wider adoption of microservices architecture (MSA) and event-driven architecture (EDA) has resulted in event-driven microservices, which turn out to be the optimal software building block. Microservices are front-ended with application programming interfaces (APIs) thereby microservices are self-contained to be autonomous, business-centric, and technology-agnostic. Microservices are interoperable, portable, independently deployable, horizontally scalable, publicly discoverable, network-accessible, shareable, and composable. Enterprise-class software applications are being built and upgraded through a collection of different microservices. In a nutshell, the microservices architecture has laid down a stimulating foundation for visualizing and realizing state-of-the-art software products, solutions, and services. The ready availability of no-code and low-code application development platforms fast tracks software production. The service composition platforms further accelerate the realization of composite services, which are business-critical, process-aware, and adaptive. Service mesh is an important module in linking up microservices toward accomplishing bigger and better tasks in a deterministic fashion.

Secondly, the tenet of containerization has permeated into the cloud world. With the surging popularity of containers as the next-generation runtime environment for software services, applications, platforms, middleware, and databases, the containerization era has dawned. Especially, containers are being projected as the most optimal solution for hosting, running, and managing microservices. The combination of microservices and containerization is being seen as a win-win situation for business enterprises and IT service providers. Containers guarantee the most important aspect of portability for software applications. Due to their low memory footprint, microservices-hosted containers ensure real-time scalability as they can be provisioned in a matter of seconds. Both stateless and stateful microservices can be run in containers comfortably. With a deeper understanding, container images are being formed and deposited in public as well as private image repositories. Such centralized stores facilitate quick discovery and smart leverage. There are container-enablement platform solutions to make containerization penetrative, pervasive, and persuasive.

Thirdly, there is widespread adoption of DevOps practices and tools to simplify and speed up the challenging task of taking your software services and applications to production environments. Gradually it has become the norm for Web-scale companies to deploy their applications several times per day. Thus, with the growing frequency, the role and responsibility of DevOps solutions go up sharply. DevOps techniques and tools contribute immensely to fulfilling the varying requirements for continuous integration, delivery, deployment, feedback, and improvement. There are optimized processes and products toward agile programming. We need agile techniques to easily and swiftly take developed software to its runtime environment. Highly competent DevOps toolkits are emerging and evolving to automate and accelerate the process of deployment and management of containerized microservices. The critical need of incorporating the security feature into the DevOps process gets fulfilled through the advanced paradigm of DevSecOps. Thus the end-to-end software lifecycle management gets accelerated through agile software production, deployment, and management methods.

Fourthly, the arrival of Kubernetes platform solutions is being seen as a boon for business houses and IT service providers. Kubernetes is the leading container orchestration platform. Self-scaling, healing, and other complex cloud operations are being automated through the power of Kubernetes. The container lifecycle management tasks are being simplified through Kubernetes. In short, the faster maturity and stability of Kubernetes platform solutions are being seen as a boon in the cloud era. The strategically sound combination of microservices, containers, container orchestration platforms, and DevOps toolsets is to shape up the software engineering field.

In the realm of microservices, leveraging a service mesh enhances companies by amalgamating security and operations into a unified infrastructure layer situated between the containerized application and the network, effectively mitigating risks such as service impersonation, unauthorized access, and data exfiltration attacks. A service mesh can help manage encryption, authentication, authorization, policy control, and configuration. And with role-based access control (RBAC), service mesh supports the zero-trust philosophy of "trust no one, authenticate everyone."

The other prominent advancements include site reliability engineering (SRE) and value stream management (VSM). The operational aspects of business workloads and IT infrastructure and platform services are very vital for the ensuing knowledge era. Sometime back, someone predicted that software eats the world. The continuous availability, high reliability, unbreakable security, portability, easy findability, accessibility, manageability and maneuverability of software solutions are being termed as the most significant factors for ensuring real business transformation. The above-mentioned technologies, tools, and processes come in handy in envisaging and realizing state-of-the-art software applications, which turn out to be very critical and crucial for solid and sustainable business empowerment. The non-functional and tough-to-implement characteristics (portability, interoperability, composability, scalability, shareability, reliability, and availability) are being hugely simplified through the adoption of the mesmerizing cloud idea. That is, cloud applications are being innately provided with such qualities without much sweat. With this powerful motivation, enterprising businesses, independent software vendors, and IT service organizations ensure that enterprise-grade applications are natively built with cloud distinctions. Having understood the impending needs of business organizations, massive and monolithic applications are being methodically dismantled and modernized as cloud-native applications, which are then migrated to cloud environments to reap all the originally expressed cloud benefits.

15.4 The Edge AI Enablers

The device ecosystem is growing rapidly. There are purpose-specific and agnostic devices. Devices are becoming miniaturized and multi-faceted. There are wearables, handhelds, hearables, portables, mobiles, and nomadic, implantable, fixed, and wireless devices being manufactured in plenty to meet up the growing needs of people and businesses. Devices interact with one another in the vicinity. Also, they get hooked on the Internet and are also integrated with cloud-based software services, platforms, middleware, and databases. For every complex and mission-critical device on the ground, a corresponding digital twin is running in cloud environments. Thus, connected devices (networked embedded systems) are pervasive and persuasive too. Through a host of innovations in the information and communication technologies (ICT) space, connected devices (also termed IoT devices) can be emboldened to offer pioneering capabilities. This is the first and foremost step toward the era of edge AI.

Secondly, the deployment of cellular and low-range communication networks across the globe has set in motion for everyday devices to provide low-latency applications to their users. Especially, 5G is regarded as the one for enabling edge devices to be powerful and path-breaking in their operations, offerings, and outputs.

Thirdly, the chip industry has gone through a lot of mesmerizing transformations. We have been fiddling with CPUs for a long time. Now we have high-performance chips to tackle specific requirements. We have graphics processing units (GPUs), vision processing units (VPUs), tensor processing units (TPUs), neural processing units (NPUs), etc. These are application-specific and AI-centric processors. Such hardware accelerators go a long way in adequately facilitating edge processing and analytics.

Finally, the techniques and tools for producing highly optimized AI models are fast maturing and stabilizing. Pruning, quantization, federated learning, knowledge distillation, online learning, etc., are some of the promising methods for creating and running highly advanced yet lightweight AI models for tackling various problems such as machine vision and intelligence, natural language processing, streaming analytics, etc.

A flurry of distinct developments happens in the edge space so that we will be surrounded by autonomous edge devices. Our places (working, walking, and wandering) will be decisively stuffed and saturated with AI-enabled devices, which are self-, surroundings-, and situation-aware. In short, with the fusion of many cutting-edge technologies, the much-expected paradigm of edge AI is going to be ubiquitous and a utility.

The recent phenomenon of cloud-native computing is being replicated in edge devices. Edge devices are typically distributed and heterogeneous. They follow different data formats and data transmission protocols. Also, different operating systems are being installed on different devices. To fulfill the long-pending demand for service and application portability and interoperability, the aspect of containerization is being replicated in edge devices. By incorporating a container engine, a layer of abstraction is being incorporated to fulfill the portability need. With more resources being stuffed in edge devices, multiple containers are being created and run in an edge device.

Now containers are found to be a highly optimal runtime for microservices. Therefore, microservices are containerized and container images are being stocked in image repositories so that software developers can use those containerized microservices. Further on, multiple microservices can be composed to create process-aware and business-critical applications. For ensuring high availability and reliability, there can be multiple containers hosting and running the same microservice. For creating and managing multi-container composite services, the arrival of container orchestration platforms for taking care of the end-to-end container lifecycle management activities is being seen as a positive omen.

DevOps toolkits are emerging and evolving fast to simplify and streamline service flows. Data pipelines are also being built to smoothen data flow from a source to its corresponding sink. Thus, containerization, orchestration, microservices and event-driven architectural styles, DevOps, value stream management (VSM), and other technological paradigms immensely contribute to elevating edge computing to be an enterprise transformation method. Edge-native applications are being constructed and released to sharply enable the penetration of the edge phenomenon.

Going forward, many edge devices can be clustered to form device clusters or clouds. Kubernetes, a market-leading container orchestration platform, is enabling the setting up and sustenance of edge device clouds, which are gaining popularity for performing bigger and better tasks. Thus, with the arrival and accumulation of a myriad of competent and cognitive technologies, the edge computing model is gathering momentum across industry verticals.

15.5 Machine and Deep Learning (ML/DL) Algorithms on Edge Devices

Several years back, we could deploy Apache Edgent, which is an open-source programming model and runtime for analytics, in edge devices.

eKuiper (https://www.lfedge.org/projects/ekuiper/) is a lightweight IoT data analytics/streaming software to be run on edge devices. This streaming analytics solution can be run on all kinds of resource-constrained edge devices. It can migrate cloud-based real-time streaming analytics frameworks such as Apache Spark, Apache Storm, and Apache Flink to run on edge devices to facilitate edge analytics. Thus, the shrunken version of data analytics platforms is being installed in edge devices to extract actionable insights in time. Now with the surging popularity of AI algorithms (ML and DL), the data analytics scene is changing forever. That is, ML and DL models are generated, downsized, and deployed in edge devices to empower edge devices with all kinds of right and timely insights.

Machine learning algorithms are comparatively smaller in size and hence running their models in edge devices is quite straightforward. However, that is not the case with deep learning (DL) models, which are naturally bulky. Deep learning teaches computers to learn by example.

Deep learning models can achieve state-of-the-art accuracy and even surpass human-level performance. DL models are typically trained on big data and the neural network (NN) architectures may contain several hidden layers. Computer vision (CV) and natural language processing (NLP) applications are being enabled through deep learning algorithms. In certain scenarios, there is an insistence on real-time detection, recognition, notification, and action. Data security and privacy besides the need for affordability have been mandated for running lightweight DL models on edge devices. The current operating model is to train DL models in cloud servers and take them to edge devices for inferencing. There are research works initiated and implemented to perform model training, retraining, and refinement in edge devices. In the next section, we talk about cloud AI and how edge AI can solve some of the toughest problems of cloud AI. The widely used ML use cases include malware detection, business process optimization and automation, predictive maintenance, spam filtering, etc.

15.6 The Emergence of TinyML

Considering the resource constrictions at the edge, tiny ML models are being insisted upon. TinyML is all about arriving at lightweight or downsized ML models. We all know about the budding concept of frugal ML. ML model optimization, hardware accelerators, architectural styles, energy efficiency, and other methods are being used to arrive at efficient ML models that can run comfortably on IoT edge devices. TinyML can perform on-device sensor data analytics.

With the massive increase in data generation and storage, data processing at the edge is gathering speed. Edge AI is being touted as the most promising digital transformation technology for enterprising businesses across the world. There will be fresh edge AI use cases and there will be more investments in this space by technology giants and pioneers. With edge device clusters and clouds, bulkier AI workloads can be handled.

15.7 The Significance of Edge Security

For the concept of edge AI to thrive, edge security is extremely important. With connected devices flourishing in important junctions, the quality and quantity of cyberattacks vary greatly. The connectivity enlarges the attack surface. For securely accomplishing data analytics through AI models, edge security turns out to be an important factor and facet.

Edge security is for ensuring unbreakable and impenetrable security for edge data. Similarly, the security and safety of edge devices are also equally important. Additional measures are being taken to boost edge security. These key security measures include the creation of a secure perimeter for tightening access to edge devices and their resources through encrypted tunnels, firewalls, and access control. Secondly, edge-native applications have to be comprehensively secured beyond the network layer. Security analytics has to be consciously performed to predict any impending threats and to identify breaches proactively. With security insights in hand, it is possible to eliminate any security implications proactively and pre-emptively. Edge devices have to be empowered through automated patching to surmount any security attacks and minimize the attack surface. Vulnerability management is very important toward edge security. When edge device data gets compromised, then the decision and conclusion being arrived may go wrong.

15.8 Cloud AI vs. Edge AI

This is an interesting topic to be deliberated deeply and decisively. We have been running AI models on cloud servers to crunch all kinds of log, operational, performance/throughput, health condition, security, transactional, and analytical data. Further on, business, machine, device, sensor, people, IT application and service, and IT infrastructure data are also being meticulously gathered, cleaned, stocked, processed, and mined to emit useful information and insights through the power of AI models. Thus, cloud environments play a stellar and sparkling role in transitioning data to information and to knowledge. Cloud environments are stuffed with a lot of powerful yet affordable server machines, storage appliances, and network components to AI-powered data analytics. Clouds store and process big data. Databases, data warehouses, and lakes are being run on cloud environments to store and facilitate AI-backed data analytics. Thus, clouds are being positioned as the next-generation one-stop solution for all kinds of analytics on big and streaming data. Clouds have both the hardware and software capacities and capabilities to ensure high-quality data analytics. But there is a problem. Cloud environments typically fall short and fail/fumble on fulfilling the goal of real-time data analytics because the network latency is being seen as the main culprit. In other words, both public and private clouds, which are situated far away from the place, wherein all eventful things happen, cannot guarantee producing and supplying real-time insights out of event data.

Here comes the mesmerizing idea of edge AI. That is, engineering, evaluating, optimizing, and deploying AI models directly on IoT edge devices is being presented as the workable idea for achieving real-time insights. That is, the much-celebrated computing moves over to the places wherein all things happen. In other words, the processing logic reaches to where the data resides. Previously data moves whereas logic stays. But in the big data era, data stays whereas logic traverses. AI models are optimized and compressed through a host of powerful methods such as pruning, quantization, knowledge distillation, federated learning, transfer learning, etc., and then the models are migrated to edge devices to empower the aspect of local data analytics. That is, on-device processing for proximate analytics is termed as the future of knowledge discovery and dissemination. Several breakthroughs are being unearthed and rolled out in order to empower edge devices to participate in data storage and processing. AI-centric processing units are plentifully produced and marketed. AI model optimization techniques and tools are flourishing with consistent nourishment from AI researchers and IT professionals spread across the globe. Edge devices are being stuffed with more memory, storage, and processing power to contribute for the much-insisted edge analytics. With the dramatic power of 5G communication, edge computing and analytics have become the new normal. Slowly yet steadily, the hybrid version of cloud and edge computing paradigms takes over. There are containerization and serverless technologies and platforms for simplifying and speeding up the setting up and sustenance of edge device clusters/clouds. Thus, the faster maturity and stability of multiple path-breaking digitization and digitalization technologies has come in handy in fulfilling the edge AI ideals.

15.9 The Key Motivations of Edge AI

The flourishing field of edge computing brings data storage and processing to the place wherein data gets generated and gathered. This technology-backed transition paves the way for real-time data capture and crunching. Low-latency services can be realized through edge processing. The expensive network bandwidth is being saved. Newer services can be envisaged and elegantly fulfilled. Computing happens in a distributed and decentralized manner. There are many digitization and digitalization technologies and tools such as containerization for ensuring application portability. Microservices architecture (MSA) orchestrates enterprise-scale applications through the assembly of decentralized, self-contained, and configurable elements. Further on, the lightweight versions of the Kubernetes platform are emerging and evolving fast to speed up the process of setting edge device clouds, which are famous for ingeniously tackling big data and tasks.

The other noteworthy instigation is the steady generation of massive amounts of multi-structured digital data. With edge analytics through traditional analytics platforms and AI algorithms, the aspect of real-time edge intelligence has been gaining the attention of many in the recent past. As the quantity of operational, transactional, and analytical data is going up exponentially, business houses must make use of them for squeezing out actionable insights in time to produce real-time competencies. Every bit of data has to be meticulously collected, cleansed, and analyzed to emit viable intelligence. The data value is great and appreciable if it is subjected to a variety of deeper and more decisive investigations immediately. The value of data is bound to go down if it is not processed immediately. Thus, for the widespread acceptance and adoption of the edge AI paradigm, the ready availability of data plays a very vital role.

With the mammoth surge in devices (purpose-specific and agnostic), the quantity of edge data is bound to grow exponentially in the days ahead. There are multi-faceted edge devices, machinery, drones, robots, medical instruments, equipment, appliances, wares, utensils, etc., being stuffed in many of our everyday assets and environments such as manufacturing floors, warehouses, ports, railway stations, eating joints, entertainment plazas, hypermarkets, vehicles, crowded locations, tunnels, expressways, defense areas, aircraft, auditoriums, and other sensitive and secure places. Further on, purpose-specific and agnostic IoT sensors are being embedded in all kinds of tangible artifacts in our personal and professional places. Thus, there are wearables, handhelds, hearables, mobiles, portables, and nomadic, wireless, and implantable devices to assist us in our typical assignments and engagements. When these entities find, bind, and interact with one another purposefully, a tremendous amount of useful data gets generated and stocked. Thus, for the paradigm of edge AI to arrive and thrive, the role of edge data is undoubtedly paramount.

Thus, the vital ingredients empowering the edge AI concept are the growing device ecosystem, the exponential growth of edge data, the maturity and stability of data analytics platforms, data stores, knowledge visualization dashboards, etc.

In a nutshell, the edge AI conundrum carries several business and technical advantages. The local storage and proximate processing enabled through edge computing and analytics can take pressure off centralized cloud servers. Edge data goes through filtering locally so that the repetitive and irrelevant data gets eliminated at the source. Such a shift has led to saving network bandwidth. With edge computing in place, data security and privacy along with the huge savings of network bandwidths are being achieved.

By utilizing AI chips, Edge AI is capable of guaranteeing superior performance. As we all know, AI is destined to empower ordinary systems to be extraordinary in their actions and reactions. In short, intelligent machines, devices, and things will flourish everywhere with the clever usage of AI.

15.10 The Edge AI Implications

Edge AI can unlock several benefits for businesses and common people in the long run. A growing number of hitherto unheard innovations and disruptions are being unearthed and rolled out for the benefit of end-users, employees, and executives. Industries are looking out to visualize and realize fresh possibilities and opportunities with the evolutionary and revolutionary characteristics of edge AI. The much-anticipated real business transformations can be availed and fulfilled through the smart leverage of edge AI. The distinct advancements in machine and deep learning (ML/DL) are directly and indirectly contributing to the unprecedented success of the edge AI paradigm.

Experts have pointed out that tactic and strategic benefits are being accrued out of the fledgling domain of edge AI. Multiple industry verticals are keenly exploring and experimenting with the power of edge AI. Manufacturing, healthcare, telecom, retail, inland security, supply chain, agriculture, and other verticals are seriously working toward offering edge AI-inspired premium and breakthrough services to their consumers and customers. Digitally transformed homes, hotels, hospitals, warehouses, airports, cities, etc., are being realized through edge AI.

15.11 The edge AI advantages

The aspect of edge AI is emerging as a new frontier through the seamless and spontaneous combination of edge computing and artificial intelligence. All the local and real-time computing capabilities are being fluidly extended to AI. The prominent advantages of edge AI are as follows

15.11.1 Enabling real-time data capture and analytics

Edge devices can gather their environments' data and make sense of edge data quickly. Thus, the long-standing goal of real-time analytics is to emit real-time insights. With edge AI, there is no need for transmitting edge data to faraway cloud platforms for storage and processing. Edge AI astutely contributes to a myriad of tasks such as prediction, classification, association, clustering, regression, recognition, detection, tracking and tracing, translation, summarization, captioning, etc.

15.11.2 Edge AI supplements with cloud AI

Edge AI takes some of the loads off the cloud platform. Thereby the precious and expensive network resources get saved. The network-induced latency comes to nil. The cybersecurity attacks on confidential and personal data are getting nullified. Edge devices are stuffed with additional modules to be computational, communicative, and vision-enabled to be sensitive and perceptive, AI-powered to be decision-making, articulative, and active. In-memory database systems are being embedded to store a lot of sensitive and temporal data. With the fast proliferation of heterogeneous, connected edge devices in our daily environments, it is possible to add additional devices on demand to fulfill fresh resource requirements. That is, the much-discussed horizontal scalability is being achieved in the device world also.

Thus, with more resources ingrained into new-generation devices, edge computing is to become a utility. Edge computing and analytics will become ubiquitous. Devices join with one another in the vicinity and with remote devices through networking. It is anticipated that edge devices emerge as the new IT powerhouse for the ensuing digital era. The scalability and versatility of edge devices are being seen as a good omen for the future. With the voluminous production and deployment of multi-faceted edge devices, there will be a multitude of edge-native applications to delight users in the days to unfurl. There are integrated development, deployment, and management platforms being made available by product, platform, and tool vendors to take the edge concept to the next level. The promising cloud-native principles are being replicated in the edge environment to produce edge-native services, which, in turn, can be composed to realize and deliver process-aware, business-critical, people-centric, and context-sensitive applications in real time. It is a fact that machines generate more data than men.

15.11.3 Transitioning to intelligent machinery and devices

In a nutshell, with the accumulation of high-end and resources-intensive devices embedded with state-of-the-art machine and deep learning (ML/DL) models in our working, walking, and wandering places, individuals and inno-vators can embark on envisaging ground-breaking use cases. Newer services and applications can be visualized and realized toward business and people empowerment. Precisely speaking, machines, robots, drones, equipment, and instruments are all set to be cognitive in their decisions, deals, and deeds. The edge AI conundrum has the wherewithal to grow and glow across industry verticals. Establishing and sustaining intelligent and real-time enterprises will see the reality sooner than later. Further on, smarter homes, offices, stores, warehouses, clinics, and cities will be quickly set up and sustained. The ingenuity factor of edge AI is to transform the entire world substantially. Researchers have proclaimed extensively about the plausible use cases of edge AI through a bevy of peer-reviewed articles. There are case studies, well-written blogs, white papers, e-books, webinars, and podcasts explaining the growing power and promise of the edge AI paradigm.

The edge AI power is being attached in multiple systems, solutions, and services these days with the sole aim of empowering them adequately to be deft and decisive in their operations, offerings, and outputs. The renowned examples include autonomous vehicles, traffic control systems, voice assis-tant apps, home security products, secure banking services, edutainment games, metaverse environments, smart manufacturing facilities, humanoid robots, cognitive drones, etc. Airport security is ensured through edge AI, which is getting widespread recognition and reward for automating many manual activities with ingenuity and alacrity.

15.12 Edge AI – Individual and Industrial Use Cases

With a greater and deeper understanding by business executives and IT pundits, there comes a slew of fresh use cases for individuals, institutions, and innovators. This new and next-generation paradigm has all the ingredients and wherewithal to create a lasting impact on many industry verticals. In this section, we are to focus on a few domains and use cases to convey the point clearly. Every worthwhile domain is keenly strategizing and planning to embrace this pioneering paradigm to deliver premium services to their consumers and customers.

15.12.1 Speech recognition

This is one of the finest use cases of edge AI. Edge devices can recognize human voices and act upon them with clarity and alacrity. The latest innovations and disruptions in the field of deep learning (DL) have raised a glimpse of empowering edge devices to recognize human communication. The recognition accuracy is going up steadily. There are automated speech recognition tools and libraries gathering attention lately. Today we have highly advanced speech recognition systems guaranteeing the feature of speech-to-text transcription going beyond the basic feature of speech-to-text transcription. Experts have pointed out that this functionality (7 AI features changing speech recognition I Enable Architect (redhat.com)) results in a few interesting use cases.

1. Sentiment analysis – This is to extract and elegantly articulate the emotions and sentiments in a speaker's speech.
2. Entity detection – This feature is to identify and categorize noteworthy entities in a language text.
3. Speaker identification – This capability identifies different speakers in an audio or video file.
4. Content safety detection – This is for checking content if there is any hate and harmful information in the content.
5. Personal information removal – This is to identify and remove personally identifiable information (PII).
6. Summarization – This generates a summary of a speech.

There arise several real-world use cases. Voice commands are being recognized by edge devices and such an emerging capability is being widely used for making online purchases. Emails are being dictated through voice instructions. Meeting discussions and court arguments are being noted down.

Resource-intensive smartphones and digital assistants are empowered with such unique capabilities. Voice-activated payment systems are getting a lot of adoption. Voice has become important biometry for security enablement. AI models are being prepared and deployed in edge devices to receive and recognize voice commands. Several allied tasks such as background noise cancellation and speech enrichment are also being addressed through edge AI.

Speech processing needs high-performing, energy-efficient, and highly affordable chips. Fortunately, there are AI-specific chips such as GPUs, VPUs, NPUs, TPUs, etc. Precisely speaking, with the immense contributions of the state-of-the-art chips and compressed AI models, speech recognition and synthesis at the edge get accomplished elegantly.

15.12.2 Smart healthcare

Elegant edge devices such as sensors and actuators are being attached to patients to minutely monitor and measure various body parameters. There are miniaturized and multi-faceted wearables, hearables, and implantable devices being built and manufactured in large quantities nowadays. These aid in precisely tracking the intended patients' progress. Various decision-enabling details are continuously captured and cognitively crunched to understand the factual condition of the patients. Such empowerment helps doctors, specialists, surgeons, nurses, and other caregivers to correctly diagnose and to recommend expert medication.

15.12.3 Ambient assisted living (AAL)

This is another formidable requirement for people who are diseased, disabled, and debilitated. Edge devices empowered with AI capability are being proclaimed as the prominent contributors to ambient assisted living. Patient monitoring, management, and maintenance are being facilitated through the edge AI phenomenon. There are several other possibilities being enabled through the distinct power of edge AI.

15.12.4 Intelligent robots and drones

Increasingly all kinds of mission-critical environments are being stuffed with robots and drones to automate a variety of repetitive tasks. Robots and drones are being advanced through software enablement. By running AI models on these devices, it is possible to have intelligent robots and drones to accomplish bigger and better things. There is no need for any manual intervention, instruction, or interpretation to activate AI-enabled drones and robots. Warehouses, retail stores, healthcare facilities, defense zones, manufacturing floors, oil rigs and fields, tunnel and expressway-building, and other vital junctions are to benefit immensely through AI-powered drones and robots. All the noteworthy advancements being realized in the domains of computer vision (CV) and natural language processing (NLP) are being embedded in robots and drones to excel in their operations, offerings, and outputs. In a nutshell, everyday robots and drones are becoming connected, competitive, and cognitive by expertly leveraging the growing power of edge AI. So there is no doubt that edge AI is penetrating every sunshine domain.

15.12.5 Predictive maintenance

This is a well-known use case of edge AI. Machinery, equipment, appliances, utensils, flight engines, IT hardware, and other business-critical instruments ought to be monitored to ensure their continuous functioning. Any slowdown or breakdown is to impact business operations and the brand value of service providers. Thus, the tenet of predictive maintenance has acquired special attention. Edge AI has the wherewithal to provide such a facility to elongate the lifeline of all kinds of critical infrastructures.

15.12.6 Edge AI in retail industry

There are online as well as offline stores for retailing and merchandizing. Edge AI is to bring in a series of automation for retail service providers. Customer management, inventory management, and replenishment management activities are dramatically enhanced through edge AI. Customer delight will be fulfilled through the smart leverage of the distinct improvisations being achieved in the edge AI space.

15.12.7 Edge AI for video surveillance system

Real-time detection and counteractions are important for ensuring the tightest security and safety for properties and people in crowded places. The delectable innovations accomplished in computer vision have brought in a series of advancements. Edge devices are being vision-enabled to see and understand what is happening around them. Cameras are being stuffed with CNN and RNN models to gain vision capability and to interact with nearby machines and men naturally. Thus, the concept of on-device data processing to emit edge intelligence has laid down a sophisticated foundation to envisage and build ground-breaking use cases for business behemoths and start-ups. Machine vision and intelligence provided by edge AI are to empower airports, railway stations, nuclear installations, bus bays, warehouses, tunnels, oil wells, refineries, pipelines, etc. Smart traffic cameras automatically adjust light timings to nullify traffic snarls and congestion. Autonomous vehicles facilitate the automated platooning of truck convoys. This is to allow drivers to be removed from all trucks except the one in front.

15.12.8 Edge AI in smart homes

As we all know, smart homes provide several exciting features and facilities to homeowners and occupants. Energy management, home security, and asset management are well-known use cases. Security cameras, video doorbells, and alarms emit a lot of security-related data, which gets locally collected and crunched to empower security-enablement systems to act quickly so that any kind of security breaches can be nipped in the bud. There are competent AI models for extracting security insights in time. Edge devices hosting such lightweight AI models guarantee the utmost security for people and properties. Similarly, entertainment, education, water, garbage, drainage, and gardening management activities are made smart through edge AI. A security camera recognizes your face as you walk into your house and it then automatically adjusts the room temperature, lights, and music as per your previously set preferences.

With CNN models embedded inside security cameras, familiar faces are recognized. Otherwise, cameras send an alert message to the concerned if an unknown person comes in.

15.12.9 Edge AI for banking and financial services

Customer management becomes highly personalized by promoting the right financial products and services. For example, SoftBank's Robotic Pepper is a robot designed for people. It connects with, assists, and shares knowledge with customers. This robot is friendly and engaging and capable of creating unique experiences to form real relationships. Pepper interprets and responds to client information requests using natural language processing, and it can even detect and respond to basic human emotions. This can process massive amounts of data in real-time. Thus, edge devices stuffed with competent AI solutions can be a game-changing affair for service providers and consumers. Edge AI enhances customer satisfaction.

15.12.10 Edge AI in automobile: Enhancing real-time capabilities

Edge AI is increasingly prominent in autonomous vehicles, smart cities, process-centric manufacturing, healthcare, and improving monitoring and management of product assembly lines, etc. Its scope continuously enlarges across multiple industry verticals. Image, audio, and video analytics happen at edge devices directly thereby real-time actions can be guaranteed. AI workloads are getting moved to edge devices from cloud servers. AI-assisted edge devices can showcase greater power and efficiency. Low-latency applications are being attempted through edge AI.

15.12.11 Edge AI is transforming Enterprises

Business operations are being meticulously automated and accelerated through the leverage of information and communication technologies. With the wider acceptance and adoption of AI and edge computing technologies, enterprising businesses are bound to achieve extreme automation. As we discussed above, every worthwhile industry vertical is methodically exploring and experimenting to know how edge AI is tactically and strategically beneficial.

As businesses keenly embrace digitization and digitalization aspects to journey in the right direction toward the designated destination, many praiseworthy digital innovations and disruptions are being experienced. The idea of digital intelligence is also acquiring special significance with the solid improvements in the data analytics space. Therefore, the mission of digital transformation gets activated and accomplished across several business domains with all the alacrity and clarity. Edge AI, a breakthrough digital technology, is getting increased attention as it has the wherewithal to succulently transform worldwide enterprises in a risk-free and rewarding manner.

15.12.12 Edge AI impacts the IoT

Every commonly found and cheap thing in our personal, social, and professional environments is being digitized through a host of digitization and edge technologies (sensors, actuators, microcontrollers, RFID tags, barcodes, stickers, beacons, LED lights, smart dust, specks, etc.). With a host of connectivity technologies, local and global networks are being formed out of all kinds of digitized entities. Such a network of digitized entities turns out to be game-changing for business houses to dream and deliver big things for their clients, employees, and end-users. Besides digitizing ordinary objects, IoT technologies (a combination of digitization and connectivity technologies) enable digitized elements to interact with one another in the vicinity and with remotely held software applications and data stores through networks such as the Internet. Such purposeful connectivity, collaboration, and correlation can generate a lot of digital data, which has to be cleanly gleaned and subjected to a variety of deeper investigations to squeeze out viable and venerable information. Conventionally, digital data thus produced is taken to cloud storage and processing systems to produce digital intelligence.

Now with the ready availability of the fabulous edge AI capability, edge data is being locally collected and subjected to proximate processing to instantaneously discover hidden patterns in data mountains. Knowledge, thus discovered, goes a long way in empowering business and IT systems in many ways. That is, traditional systems are systematically emboldened to exhibit adaptive behavior in their service deliveries. The bewildering edge AI is being pronounced as the silver bullet for industrial automation.

15.12.13 Edge AI for smarter homes

Our living spaces are adorned with different kinds of sensors and actuators. Energy management, security enablement, device management, provisioning of choice, convenience, care, and comfort for the owners and occupants, etc., are being accomplished through edge AI. Homes need such breakthrough technologies.

15.12.14 Edge AI for smart cities

Cities across the globe are bubbling with population. Drainage, water, garbage, and utility management ought to be technologically enabled to smoothen city life for the people. Traffic congestion avoidance is a big need for city people. Apartments, hospitals, IT company premises, hotels, and other prominent locations in any city have to be carefully monitored and managed. Herein, the role and responsibility of edge AI are definitely vital.

15.12.15 Edge AI for smart manufacturing

A variety of manufacturing activities are precisely accelerated and automated through AI-enabled machines, assembly lines, and industrial assets. Intelligent asset management becomes critical for industry automation. Real-time edge intelligence elevates factories to a greater height. Business partners, employees, and customers all will be succulently provided with a bevy of real-time services.

15.12.16 Surveillance

Continuous monitoring and real-time decision-making are essential for deriving and delivering a number of fresh capabilities. Edge AI opens up new possibilities and opportunities across industry verticals. This is one of the well-known use cases for the runaway success of edge computing. Surveillance, proximate data processing, real-time knowledge discovery, and dissemination go a long way in safeguarding expensive properties and ensuring people's security. AI-enabled CCTV cameras are being liberally used these days in important junctions, eating joints, entertainment plazas, stadiums, auditoriums, retail malls, educational campuses, tunnels and expressways, nuclear installations, etc., to accurately pinpoint problems and activate the concerned ones to plunge into appropriate countermeasures in time. Any kind of deviation and deficiency can be detected proactively and proper solutions can be articulated by predictive and prescriptive AI models.

15.12.17 Mining, oil, and gas and industrial automation

The business value of edge-based ML models (increasingly enabled through TinyML frameworks) becomes obvious in the oil, gas, and mining industries. Employees are supposed to work in remote and rough environments. This is full of risks. Herein, AI-powered robots and machinery come in handy. These empowered systems capture a variety of decision-enabling data and make accurate decisions by analyzing the captured and cleaned data instantaneously. That is, they work autonomously. For complicated decisions, the control goes to people put up at remote control centers. Such an arrangement goes a long way in ensuring the safety and security of people and properties. Critical assets across industry verticals are being technologically monitored so that any kind of deviation and disturbance can be pre-emptively pinpointed and suitable countermeasures can be considered and activated to nullify any incoming disasters.

15.13 The Distinctions of Edge AI

With the flourishing of IoT edge devices in our everyday environments such as homes, hotels, hospitals, etc., the data processing steadily moves over to edge devices. That means edge devices join mainstream computing. Increasingly edge devices are being embedded with more memory, storage, and processing power. Analytics platforms are installed in resource-intensive edge devices to do proximate data analytics. Especially streaming analytics is surging in the edge world.

Edge streaming analytics platforms can collect and analyze edge device data to find useful findings with minimal latency. Herein, there is no need to transmit edge data to nearby or faraway cloud environments to perform data analytics. Instead, edge devices with sufficient computing and storage resources can host a streaming analytics platform to receive and crunch edge data quickly to emit real-time insights. Thus, the long-standing goal of data-driven insights and insights-driven decisions is getting fulfilled.

The much-celebrated centralized and shared cloud environments across the globe are enabling this expectation. Now with edge devices individually and collectively emerging as the new IT powerhouse, the aspect of data analytics moves over to high-end edge devices. This shift is capable of bringing in advanced use cases for people as well as enterprising businesses. Several start-ups have emerged in the recent past to make use of this strategically sound phenomenon. In short, any bit of data getting generated is meticulously gathered and analyzed immediately to create full and long-lasting value out of data. Due to edge analytics, the data processing happens in real-time thereby real-time insights are produced and shared to empower the process of building real-time services and applications. Precisely speaking, edge analytics through traditional analytical methods and the latest AI algorithms have laid down a stimulating and sparkling foundation for real-time enterprises. Thus, running highly optimized and purpose-specific AI models getting installed in edge devices is to fulfill a dazzling array of real-time and intelligent products, solutions, and services.

There are several advantages to on-device data processing. Real-time analytics results in timely insights, which can be fed to actuation systems to embark on counteractions immediately with all clarity and confidence. Thus, edge AI stands in contrast to the proven paradigm of cloud AI, in which AI models are being developed and run entirely on cloud platforms. Cloud AI enjoys all the originally expressed benefits of the indomitable cloud paradigm.

15.14 Conclusion

Edge AI is going to be a sophisticated combination of edge computing and artificial intelligence. The real digital transformation initiatives by business houses and government organizations are being hugely simplified and spearheaded through the methodical usage of edge AI. The enabling technologies and tools of edge AI are simply mesmerizing. Product vendors, research labs, IT companies, and academic institutions are striving hard and stretching further to make edge AI pervasive and persuasive. Edge devices are being stuffed with more memory and storage capacities and processing capabilities. Edge devices emerge as data-processing entities. With edge devices increasingly getting ordained with AI capabilities, it is possible to visualize a dazzling array of next-generation services through edge devices. Edge devices can form clusters to tackle bigger problems. That is, device clusters/clouds will become the new normal in the days to come. There are competent technologies such as lightweight versions of Kubernetes for forming and managing edge clouds to do edge data analytics. Especially, the prospect of performing edge analytics by leveraging AI models brightens. Thus, the journey humbly started with edge computing for on-device data processing. Then came the transition toward forming and firming up edge clouds for doing complicated tasks. Edge analytics is one of the crucial requirements for extracting actionable insights out of edge data in real-time. Now we are heading toward the idea of edge AI, which is for accomplishing AI-powered analytics on edge device data.

Thus technological evolutions and revolutions have vividly led to the realization of applying highly optimized AI models on edge data to unravel the useful patterns hidden in data heaps.

15.15 The Glossary of Terms

1. **Artificial intelligence (AI)** refers to a collection of technologies and tools to analyze (through batch or stream processing) a huge amount of data to emit actionable insights, which comes in handy in automating and accelerating business processes. That is, data becomes information and knowledge. By receiving any discovered knowledge, our everyday devices including computers, communicators, robots, drones, and other digital assistants can exhibit adaptivity and ingenuity in their operations, outputs, and offerings.

2. **AI Chips** – These refer to high-performing processing units such as GPUs, VPUs, TPUs, NPUs, etc., to handle AI workloads efficiently. The usage of general-purpose chips like CPUs can go down in the AI era. AI chips can complete large-scale computing through parallelization.

3. **Bandwidth** refers to the amount of information that can be sent over a connection in a measurable amount of time. This is generally

measured in kilobits, megabits, gigabits, etc. In the forthcoming 6G communication, it may reach terabits per second.

4. **Cloud environments** represent highly optimized and organized IT environments comprising hundreds of thousands of IT infrastructure modules such as computing machines, storage appliances, network solutions, and security devices. Development, deployment, delivery, orchestration, integration, security, government, and management platforms are being installed on cloud infrastructures. Analytical, operational, and transactional applications are being run on these platforms.

5. **Cloud AI** is to leverage cloud platforms, databases, middleware, etc., to train and run AI workloads.

6. A convolutional neural network (CNN) is a type of artificial neural network (ANN) for computer vision (CV) tasks, which include the extraction of useful and usable information from images, videos, and other visual data.

7. **Edge computing** – Data gets collected and processed at the source of the data. Instead of sharing the data through risky Internet infrastructure, edge or local devices embark on data storage and processing. Such a transition facilitates real-time data capture, analytics, and knowledge discovery. This empowerment results in the formation of real-time services and applications

8. **Edge AI** combines AI and edge computing. With AI at the edge, doing real-time analytics of edge data gets strengthened to provide real-time insights.

9. **Machine learning** – There are powerful algorithms for empowering machines to learn automatically from input data. These algorithms pinpoint useful patterns in the dataset.

10. **On-device learning** – IoT devices are empowered with memory, processing, and storage power. Further on, there are additional modules such as sensing, actuation, communication, etc., being attached to IoT devices. By deploying AI models, devices are empowered to learn from data. Such on-device learning yearns for a lot of technical and business benefits. Devices can continuously learn from data streams to exhibit intelligent behavior.

11. **Few-shot learning** is the ability to empower AI models to learn and adapt to a few labeled data samples. Consider keyword spotting, where the task is to identify when a keyword is spoken, such as "Hey Snapdragon," using always-on machine learning.

12. **Continuous learning** is to empower AI models to continue learning on new data even after their deployment.

References

[1] Edge computing: 4 use cases for the industrial sector | The Enterprisers Project
[2] Applied Edge AI: Concepts, Platforms, and Industry Use Cases - 1st Edi (routledge.com)
[3] What Is Edge AI and How Does It Work? | NVIDIA Blog
[4] Exploring the edge AI space: Industry use cases - ScienceDirect
[5] Edge AI | Industrial Use Cases 2023 (xenonstack.com)

16

Edge Computing and Analytics: A New Computing Paradigm for Better User Experience

Santosh Das[1,2] and Pethuru Raj[3]

[1]SWAN Lab, Indian Institute of Technology, Kharagpur
[2]Department of Computer Science & Engineering,
OmDayal Group of Institutions, India
[3]Edge AI Division, Reliance Jio Platforms Ltd., India
E-mail: santoshdascse@ieee.org; peterindia@gmail.com

Abstract

The term "edge computing" refers to the compute power and infrastructure offered by devices located closer to the network's periphery. Considering that the number of sensors and devices deployed at the network's periphery is expected to reach the billions in the next years, the volume of data being produced by these devices is staggering. Edge data processing is becoming more popular as it is realized that all edge data contains some actionable insight. The timely discovery of useful information in massive datasets depends on it. Since the value of data decreases over time, processing data as soon as possible is essential for extracting time-sensitive business value. The distributed architecture at the edge of the network is tried and true. Edge computing is a decentralized approach, while cloud computing is very centralized. When it comes to gathering and processing data at the network's edge, several heterogeneous devices freely work together. Containerization addresses the issue of device heterogeneity. Additionally, container lifecycle management technologies like Kubernetes make it possible for a wide variety of devices to contribute to business computing.

Keywords: EDGEAI, IIoT, Digital Twin, Edge Computing, Blockchain, Edge computing

16.1 Introduction

With edge computing, data from various clients is processed at the network's edge, as near to its point of origin as possible. Business intelligence and the ability to monitor and manage mission-critical functions in real time are only two examples of the many uses for data in today's businesses. Huge volumes of data may be routinely acquired from sensors and IoT devices running in real time from remote places and harsh working environments practically anywhere in the world, leaving modern organizations adrift in a sea of data. But this digital deluge is also altering how organizations approach computing. Moving ever-increasing rivers of real-world data presents significant challenges for the old computer paradigm based on a centralized data center and the everyday Internet. Such efforts can be hampered by a confluence of factors, including low bandwidth, high latency, and random network outages. Companies are using edge computing architecture to address these data issues. In its simplest form, edge computing involves relocating some amount of data storage and processing capacity away from a centralized data center and closer to the location where the data was originally generated. Data processing and analysis are carried out at the point of origin, be it a storefront, a manufacturing facility, a utility's vast service territory, or an entire smart city. Only the results of this computing effort at the edge, such as real-time business insights, predictions for equipment repair, or other actionable solutions, are sent back to the central data center for review and other human interactions. As a result, edge computing is influencing profound changes in the IT and business computing sectors. Explore the definition, operation, cloud's impact, edge use cases, trade-offs, and implementation of edge computing.

16.1.1 Edge devices

We already use devices that do edge computing every day – like smart speakers, watches, and phones – devices which are locally collecting and processing data while touching the physical world. Internet of Things (IoT) devices, point of sales (POS) systems, robots, vehicles and sensors can all be edge devices – if they compute locally and talk to the cloud.

16.1.2 Network edge

It is not necessary to set up a special "edge network" in order to do edge computing (it could be located on individual edge devices or a router, for example). Since this is just another node on the road between users and the cloud, 5G can be useful in this scenario when a different network is in play. With 5G's low latency and high cellular bandwidth, edge computing may now support intriguing new uses, such as autonomous drones, remote telesurgery, smart city projects, and more. When high responsiveness is needed yet it would be too expensive and inconvenient to place computation on premises, the network's edge can be a great resource (meaning the cloud is too distant).

16.1.3 On-premises infrastructure

These are for managing local systems and connecting to the network and could be servers, routers, containers, hubs, or bridges.

16.2 Importance of Edge Computing

The majority of computing is now performed at the edge, in areas like hospitals, factories, and stores, where the most sensitive data and powering of key equipment must occur reliably and safely. Solutions for these areas should have minimal latency and function without a network. Edge's promise lies in its ability to revolutionize enterprise processes everywhere they are applied, from front-facing customer interactions to back-end manufacturing. Edge computing enhances proactive and adaptable business activities, frequently in real time, resulting in novel and improved user experiences.

With edge, companies can bridge the gap between the digital and the real world. The incorporation of digital resources, such as databases and recommendation engines, into traditional storefronts making it possible for machines to teach themselves and for humans to learn from machines constructing protective and comfortable habitats. What all of them have in common is the use of edge computing, which is allowing businesses to locally execute mission-critical applications with stringent time-to-market, data-volume, and reliability requirements. In the end, this paves the way for increased speed of innovation, the launch of brand-new items and services, and the development of fresh income channels. Edge's potential to revolutionize companies across the board is what makes it so intriguing. This includes front-and back-office activities, as well as front- and back-facing interactions with customers.

16.3 The Recent Technological Fusion

At the edge, centralized and decentralized systems coexist. The edge and the cloud both contribute to the creation of novel user experiences. Data is created or collected in a variety of places, but once in the cloud, where computation is centralized, it can be processed efficiently and cheaply at scale. Edge computing employs locally generated data to offer real-time responsiveness, allowing for the creation of novel experiences in a secure and cost-effective manner. By completing tasks closer to their points of origin rather than in the faraway cloud and waiting for a response, edge computing reduces latency.

- *5G* guarantees the transfer of crucial control messages that allow devices to make autonomous decisions, making edge deployments seamless. By bridging the gap between the edge and the Internet's backhaul, this solution guarantees that edge devices are properly configured with the appropriate software-defined network settings.

  The *Internet of Things (IoT)* and other linked devices are valuable resources that must be protected and properly identified in the cloud. The "Edge" is located close to or even on these data stores.

- *Containers* give programmers a uniform setting in which to construct and distribute their applications. Containers are designed to be portable, so they can be run on any computer system, regardless of the hardware's specifications or software.

  Data and services that are stored in different containers and databases at the edge can be deployed and queried via a service and data mesh. These meshes provide a unified front end that automatically manages and routes data and services. This crucial enabler allows for queries to be performed in bulk for vast populations within the edge, rather than on each individual device.

  Users are able to set up their own overlay networks with the help of software-defined networking. It also simplifies the process of configuring routing and bandwidth for inter-edge device and cloud connectivity.

- The *digital twin* facilitates the integration of the physical and digital, as well as the cloud and the edge. The twin eliminates the need to manually configure data and applications based on database tables and message streams, and instead allows them to be set up in terms of assets and production lines. Domain experts (as opposed to software engineers) can use digital twins to set up applications for edge sensing, reasoning, and action.

Edge is strengthened by other technologies, such as *artificial intelligence* and *blockchain*. When AI processes data at the edge, for instance, less processing power is required at the data center. Furthermore, edge enhances blockchain by reducing the potential for human error and increasing confidence in the system as a whole. Through the rising usage of sensors and cameras on the edge, more and richer data will become available for analysis and action in real time, and machines can gather and send this data directly. When it comes to automation, edge is at the forefront of a revolution that is shifting the focus from systematic procedures in regulated settings like factories to intricate shows in more natural settings like farms.

16.4 Edge Computing Benefits and Application

When combined with the cloud, edge will provide companies the ability to completely rethink customer experiences. Edge computing now has potential uses outside of traditional manufacturing and the Internet of Things. Edge can be used to increase relevance at each touch point, allowing for faster decision-making and better user experiences. Now, with the support of the cloud as a backbone, edge is crucial in the generation of novel insights and user experiences.

Some benefits of edge computing include:

Rapid response: Transmitting data requires time. There isn't enough time for data to travel to the cloud and back in some applications, such as self-driving cars or remote surgery. When response speed is of the essence, edge computing makes perfect sense.

High data volume: Although large amounts of data can be stored on the cloud, there is still the matter of transmission costs and the inherent limits of network capacity to consider. It may make more sense to process the data at the edge in some circumstances.

Privacy: Sometimes, users need to keep private information off of the cloud for legal or ethical reasons.

Remote areas: Both physically distant uses (like an offshore oil drilling platform) and functionally distant uses (like some home automation systems) fall under the category of "remote" (involving mobile or transportation-related scenarios using edge).

Cost sensitivity: Various locations on the cloud continuum have different costs associated with processing data, which can be adjusted to reduce overall system costs.

Autonomous operations: Where connectivity to the cloud is not possible – or likely to be intermittent or unreliable – users may need end-to-end processing within the local environment to keep operations up and running.

The prime advantage of edge computing is clear: User experience improves because relevance increases with edge. Additionally, edge unlocks valuable data to shape new opportunities and innovation for the future. More sensors generate more data, and there is more processing at the location where the data is created – which is faster, more reliable, and safer. Integrated with knowledge from the cloud, the system yields better predictions and more relevant information, repeating in a cycle of continuous improvement. Other characteristics of edge use cases include:

Intelligent machines and real-time productivity: Edge let users process data with velocity, enabling robots and sensors to make split-second decisions and complete tasks in smarter, faster, and safer ways. This is revolutionizing everything from smart signage to assembly-line quality assurance.

Optimized close to consumption: Using the Internet of Things, real-time data, and AI makes the creation and use of digital products better and faster.

Experience with extended reality: These use cases can incorporate digital twins and optimize rich experiences in healthcare, the workforce, and entertainment, from smart health to mixed-reality gaming.

Privacy and security by default: By processing sensitive data on the edge, these use cases improve reliability and protect privacy. Examples include wearable health devices and the processing of regulated data.

Always-on and untethered: Edge allows for decision-making and processing independent of connectivity for mission-critical and remote applications, like POS or autonomous operations.

16.5 Edge Computing Examples

Edge, in conjunction with cloud computing, will allow businesses to reimagine the customer service they give. This opens up new possibilities for edge computing beyond IoT and conventional manufacturing. Through the usage of edge, we can improve the quality of our interactions with users at every stage of the user journey, leading to quicker decision-making and more satisfying interactions overall. Now that the cloud is acting as a foundation, edge is essential for creating new insights and user experiences.

Below are just a few of the many advantages of edge computing:

Instinctive reaction: Data transmission is a slow process. Some applications, like self-driving cars or remote surgery, don't have time to wait for data to go to and from the cloud. Edge computing is ideally suited for use in situations where a quick response time is crucial.

Heavy data loads: While it's true that massive volumes of data can be kept in the cloud, it's also important to keep in mind the costs of data transfer and the constraints imposed by any given network. In some cases, it could be preferable to perform data processing at the periphery.

Users may want to avoid storing sensitive data in the cloud for legal or ethical reasons requiring anonymity.

Remote regions include both those that are physically removed (such as an offshore oil drilling platform) and those that are merely functionally removed (such as some home automation systems) (involving mobile or transportation-related scenarios using edge).

Sensitivity to cost: The total system cost can be lowered by shifting data processing to a cheaper point on the cloud continuum.

Autonomous operations: Users may require end-to-end processing within the local environment to keep operations up and running where access to the cloud is not possible or is likely to be intermittent or unreliable.

The primary benefit of edge computing is obvious: better user experience due to increased relevance. Furthermore, edge provides access to vital data that can be used to mould future possibilities and innovations. Faster, more reliable, and safer data processing can be achieved by increasing the number of sensors and bringing that processing closer to the point of data creation. The system improves with each iteration, thanks to the incorporation of cloud-based knowledge, which allows for more accurate forecasting and more pertinent analysis. Some further features of edge applications are:

Edge allows users to digest data quickly, allowing robots and sensors to make split-second judgments and carry out operations in a more efficient, timely, and secure manner. This has far-reaching implications, improving processes from digital signage to quality control on the production line.

Edge computing, used in contexts such as content delivery or on offshore oil wells, is an example of digital production and consumption being optimized for the best experience and lowest cost close to the point of consumption.

These applications of extended reality, from smart health to mixed-reality games, can optimize immersive experiences in fields as diverse as healthcare, the workplace, and entertainment.

These use cases boost dependability and protect privacy by processing sensitive data at the edge. Wearable medical gadgets and the handling of restricted data are two such examples.

Edge computing enables always-on, decentralized decision-making and processing for crucial, off-network applications like point-of-sale systems and autonomous vehicles.

16.6 Case Studies in Edge Computing

Let's examine a couple of current edge use cases that are only going to get better when 5G expands and new advancements are made.

Store of Tomorrow is a new integrated vision for the near future of commerce that centers on a flexible, customer-centered experience. A crucial enabler for the human-centered experiences at the model's core is edge technology, which will soon become a central retail competency. The checkout process at stores can be made easier with the help of edge. Stores lose an estimated $37.7 billion in revenue every year in the United States due to customers abandoning their purchases due to long waits.

Customers can avoid standing in line by leaving the store past a self-service kiosk that appropriately charges their accounts using data acquired by in-store cameras and artificial intelligence (AI) that has been trained to recognize inventory items. It helps stores deliver better customer service, reduce instances of shoplifting, and optimize their supply chains.

In the medical field, robots have made surgery more manageable for doctors and shorter, less traumatic, and more efficient for patients. As a result of using edge computing, the incisions can be smaller, the surgeon can sit down and have a better view of the location, and the controls can be more natural and intuitive.

16.7 Challenges and Opportunities in Edge Computing

When businesses try to reap the rewards of edge computing, they sometimes run across resistance. Finding the optimal plan for your company's competitive advantage might be challenging, but trial and error is essential for making progress. Typically, we encounter these sorts of problems:

The necessary infrastructure (cloud provider(s), network, and devices) is needed to get started with edge; however, there is a lack of standard and integrated architectures. It is common for businesses to employ a variety of incompatible technology stacks, all of which must be synchronized for edge to function properly.

In a rapidly evolving ecosystem with a wide variety of technological options, it is essential to make informed choices quickly. The situation is made more complicated by the ongoing development of new network capabilities, such as MEC and 5G.

Value for business not yet realized at the edge: It might be challenging for businesses to fully appreciate the value that can be unleashed by edge solutions. For edge computing to provide a sustainable return on investment, businesses must look beyond simple use cases that generate short-term profits and instead invest in experiences that customers will find appealing, practical, and viable.

Unfortunately, many businesses aren't built to quickly adapt and scale beyond the proof of concept stage, leading to innovation fatigue and pilot purgatory.

Edge isn't about retooling, especially for firms that are already embracing the cloud, and there is a lack of cloud professionals who understand what belongs at the edge, why, and when. The goal is to bring those capabilities to the periphery. Deploying at the edge requires only a basic hardware connection, so you can take advantage of your current cloud expertise.

The edge presents its own unique security concerns, as security must be maintained in all potential edge instances, from the cloud on out, but IoT and edge security is significantly different from IT security. Time-critical, secure, and self-driving tasks abound in the periphery. Security models account for the long product lifecycle and existing base of edge devices. Production and security can be jeopardized with each reboot, and they become comparatively antiquated quickly. Devices may also be deployed in untrusted or far-flung locations, necessitating a multi-layered approach to security that incorporates both cyber and physical measures. The distribution of security patches is made more difficult by heterogeneous hardware, software, and network configurations.

16.8 Next-generation Analytics on the Cutting Edge

By bringing cloud resources (such as computing, storage, and network) closer to the edge devices (smart devices where the data are produced and consumed), edge technology can improve performance and efficiency. Two new concepts in edge technology – edge computing and edge analytics – have emerged as a result of the incorporation of processing and application into edge devices. Data from edge devices can be analyzed with the help of various methods and algorithms used in edge analytics. Edge devices are now fully functional thanks to the development of edge analytics. The analytical

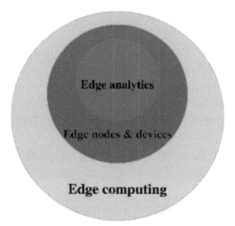

Figure 16.1   Venn diagram showing the overlap between edge devices, edge computing, and edge analytics.

methodologies are not fully supported by edge analytics at the moment. Due to limitations in power, memory, resources, etc., edge devices are unable to run complex analytics.

16.9 The Urgent Requirement for Edge Analytics

IoT's meteoric rise around the world has prompted researchers and businesses alike to focus on edge analytics. Significant work has gone into the development of efficient and effective frameworks for carrying out edge analytics for the various scenarios that can arise in practice. In order to facilitate the linking of devices and the processing of data streams from devices, numerous IoT platforms have been developed and put into operation. Popular services include Arkessa, ThingSquare, and Thing Worx. Previous work by us also offered a cloud-based solution for processing of actionable analytic events in real time. Typically, data from IoT devices is collected and processed using the Platform as a Service (PaaS) cloud service architecture and lightweight messaging protocols like Messaging Queue Telemetry Transport (MQTT) and Constrained Application Protocol (CAP) (CoAP).

Stream processing must be relocated closer to or onto the edge, and this has given rise to the concepts of edge computing and fog computing, as the computational power of the edge has increased significantly in recent years and cloud IoT analytic services incur high latency and unstable networking to edges. Still, they haven't figured out how to define and deploy processing closer to or onto the edge in a flexible manner. By reducing the time and effort required to build and deploy changes to the processing logic on the fog node, real-world IoT applications would benefit from a more flexible fog node. To limit the amount of data devices send to the cloud from the edge, but keep the essential events of users' interest, researchers are focusing on the heterogeneity of device data in order to execute flexible data processing on the edge. Edge-based IoT data reduction can make use of a variety of strategies, the most prominent of which being time series compression and aggregation and event or rule-based data filtering. Edge-based IoT data reduction can make use of a variety of strategies: time series compression and aggregation, and event or rule-based data filtering. These strategies are predicated on locating "critical points", whereas piecewise approximation, another technique for data reduction, is used for fitting curves to the data. However, these solutions tend to be application-oriented, leaving users with less leeway when it comes to using them in their own IoT context. Such solutions, however, tend to be application-oriented, leaving users with less leeway when it comes to using the aforementioned methodologies in their own IoT context.

In contrast, rule-based data filtering streamlines IoT information in accordance with industry-specific policies rather than time series features. As an illustration, Cisco's open-source project Krickitt is working on defining a data format and mechanism for "telling the network-edge devices" which data to forward and in what manner. These methods still rely on edge developers to implement data reduction logic, but go no farther than building rule engines and policy languages for expressing data reduction. To attract the growing market, cloud service providers are looking for ways to simplify the management of edge analytics by making it possible for users of Internet of Things (IoT) applications to create and deploy their analytic logic on the edge in a manner that allows for maximum flexibility. So, the three largest cloud service providers in the world – Microsoft Azure, Amazon Web Services (AWS), and IBM Watson – are all pushing their edge analytic services – Azure IoT, AWS Greengrass, and IBM Watson IoT Platform, respectively.

All have a generally similar architecture, with a microservice on the edge managing the connectivity of edge analytics and device data, a cloud-based messaging service, and a cloud-based service managing the operation of devices and analytics. They also offer a standard method for defining analytical logic for the edge in the cloud, making that logic available for use in edge microservices. While Azure IoT and IBM Watson IoT Platforms give programming-free "task" and "rules-based analytic model" approaches to edge analytic logic and RESTful APIs for service composition, AWS Greengrass offers local lambda programming capability in Python to increase analytic flexibility. Our proposed analytic model for the IBM Watson Platform is able to access any local services via an edge resident broker, whereas AWS Greengrass core, which is responsible for local lambda function execution, has restrictions on accessing external services (such as local file systems or local 3rd party service). In contrast to the AWS Greengrass core and the Azure IoT edge SDK, which use multi-threaded runtime to handle many analytic processes in parallel, our single-threaded edge engine can process rule-based analytic with minimal overhead.

16.10 Definitions of Edge Analytics

Data gathered by edge devices might be either visual or textual, and this distinction informs how edge analytics are applied. There are two main types of edge analytics – image analytics and video analytics – depending on the type of media being processed. Again, there are two distinct kinds of edge analytics based on textual data: descriptive analytics and regression/predictive analytics. Analyses performed at the edge of the network can be further categorized using sound samples. There have been no proposals for edge analytics; hence we have not included them in the taxonomy. The field of edge analytics is broken down into two distinct subfields, image edge analytics and video edge analytics, depending on whether the underlying data source is images or videos. Video is used as the foundation for picture edge analytics. A video is an animated series of still images called frames. Accordingly, a frame is the starting point for picture edge analytics. A video is used as the input in video edge analytics. In order to process videos with limited computing power and resources, videos are broken down into groups of video frames before being processed.

GigaSight is a VM-based cloud with a distributed hybrid architecture that allows for video edge analytics. Cloudlets are edge nodes in the architecture that execute video analytics, modify video streams to safeguard privacy, and retain films for finite amounts of time in accordance with pricing regulations. Each video is altered in a separate virtual machine (VM) within the cloudlet, with the level of denaturation being automatically decreased based on the fidelity of the video stream the user selects. To avoid overwhelming the computer with too much work, the denaturing procedure is done to a small subset of the video at a time. When a video is denaturated, two files are generated: a thumbnail and an encrypted version of the video that is saved to a different cloud service; the thumbnail video serves as an outline of the video's content for indexing and query purposes. Video frames are passed unaltered through a binary filtering process based on metadata (such as location and time). The computational complexity of this filtering is low, and it filters based on the content. The indexing operation's throughput is proportional to the number of objects requiring detection. For efficiency's sake, indexing is handled in a separate VM while the classifier is applied to the database's most vital objects.

To find videos that are relevant to a given user, we first conduct a standard SQL search using metadata and tags obtained from the index, and then we conduct a second, more computationally intensive search on the actual content to provide users with more relevant videos. Also, GigaSight can conduct time-sensitive video searches. Video processing output and metadata are stored in the cloud. Because of its reliance on virtual machines, GigaSight is limited in the number of queries it can handle at once. Since edge devices have fewer resources, a smaller number of efficient virtual machines is possible. The number of concurrent requests is further reduced because indexing occurs in a separate virtual machine.

16.11 ML and Near-real-time Analytics on the Periphery

Edge technology is an opportunity for researchers to develop machine learning algorithms with reduced computational requirements. Edge nodes can generate actions for events without the need for programming by incorporating AI and machine learning algorithms into edge devices. For new data, inference requires less computing power to run and produce results. Therefore, inference helps provide a low-latency response to the user's request when executed at edge nodes. Microsoft's Azure IoT edge allowed for the integration of machine learning and edge computing. Using models stored in the cloud, AWS Greengrass performs machine learning inference locally on edge devices. The edge nodes have a lot of issues because of machine learning techniques. Some of the issues are as follows.

- An edge node only receives a fraction of the whole data. Consequently, the performance of the machine learning algorithm when deployed to edge devices is inadequate.
- The information in real time is always changing. Therefore, the training that the machine learning algorithm does becomes obsolete after some time has passed.
- Every single machine learning method has the same requirement: a lot of computer processing time. Thus, such algorithms cannot be supported by edge nodes due to their limited resources, power, processing, etc.

In what follows, we'll take a look at some of the methods that have been proposed to bring together machine learning and edge analytics. The edge-deployed convolution neural network (ECNN) is a distributed data analytics architecture that enhances the efficacy of data gathering and analytics in smart grids. Many of the first layers are convolutional or filtering or pooling or fully connected (FC) or use the Softmax function to classify data. On both the cloud and edge devices, you'll find a plethora of convolution and pooling layers. Further, classification is performed by FC layers at the edge nodes. These nodes' local data generates local inference, while more data-intensive inference is generated in the cloud. Since local inference is conducted on a small scale, transmission costs are reduced. ECNN is used to aggregate data, which helps in cross-regional inference and decision-making. An examination of federated learning could be undertaken to develop data-intensive inferences without resorting to the cloud. Sarabia-Jacome et al. developed a proposal for an edge gateway with a predictive analytics module that makes use of deep learning models.

The system is private, secure, and compatible with other systems. Container-based virtualization is used for managing scarce resources. Predictive analytics uses cloud-based services based on a deep learning model to discover and predict trends in data collected from edge devices. An enormous amount of time and energy is needed to create an inference system for a deep neural network. That's why we draw conclusions about the world from data stored online. The results are then transmitted to the edge nodes. Edge devices with three-axis accelerometers can collect user feedback in the form of textual information. In their proposal for a data analysis framework, Moon et al. proposed delegating specific analysis tasks to various edge nodes. With this architecture, you can leverage the power of the cloud and the speed of the edge nodes. Edge nodes collect data while also monitoring and operating the actuators in real time. Edge analytics uses machine learning algorithms in the cloud to create models based on information acquired by edge devices.

Not all information gets uploaded to the cloud, however, to protect users' privacy. Since then, the cloud has been limited to using only publicly available information. The cloud houses the modules responsible for managing IoT data and machine learning models, while edge nodes host the IoT interaction module. Module 1 is where we collect and process training data. In the second part, the data is trained. The IoT interaction module makes forecasts according to the user profile. The models employed in edge analytics eventually become obsolete, leading to subpar output. The system is more reliant on the cloud because the edge analytics necessitate constantly refreshed forecasts. Restricting some data owing to privacy concerns reduces the accuracy of the forecast. Dey and Mukherjee developed a deep learning-based architecture for analytics at the network's periphery. Based on a deep convolutional neural network model, the framework provides procedures for dividing up resources between edge devices (DCNN). However, tuning the DCNN's hyperparameters consumes a lot of computing power. There are three phases of edge analytics' resource management: intermediate resource standardization, intermediate resource supply, and offloading execution to serve small devices. Standardized resources have many advantages, including low latency and data management.

In addition to increasing customer confidence and facilitating magnetization, these features also facilitate the commercialization of services created by third parties and analytics designers. Intermediate resource provisioning is utilized for efficient load balancing. Different configurations of control unit, graphics processing unit (GPU), and random access memory (RAM) are used to test out the performance of a deep learning model. They are profiled and used as data in the form of training exercises. In order to offload the processing of the analytics tasks associated with deep learning, they are split up and sent to the many external devices that are connected to the local network. The optimal offload implementation makes use of a simple capacity-based segmentation method. It is not possible to separate the processing of each layer for parallel processing due to the coarse granularity of the partitioning used in the architecture. Since deep learning is a computationally intensive process, it is possible to complete the operation without the cloud by distributing it among a number of edge devices. Also, if you divide the work up according to the available resources, you should be able to finish it much more rapidly.

16.12 Edge and Big Data Analytics

Data analysis is performed in two ways by the many edge devices that are linked to the edge gateway: via edge analytics and via big data analytics. Analytics for massive amounts of data can be done on the cloud. When large amounts of data are collected that lack clarity, exhibit unusual patterns, or yield unpredictable outcomes, this is when big data analytics comes into play. Big data analytics necessitates a robust cloud environment. One of the main challenges of big data analytics at the edge is ensuring data quality and consistency - especially when dealing with heterogeneous and distributed data sources . We can see a connection between big data analytics and analytics at the edge. scale, or the number of computers, networks, storage devices, etc., that are spread out across a large area. Supporting these complicated and cutting-edge technologies that need to calculate the data also necessitates powerful analytics and large-scale computing systems. The cloud is home to big data analytics because it is capable of accommodating the humongous amounts of storage, computing power, and network bandwidth required by these applications.

Integrating data analytics into edge devices is a primary focus of edge computing. Because it's possible that the analysis will be performed by the data source itself in that case. Meanwhile, the development of edge analytics has just begun. Edge computing allows for the compact storage and processing of massive datasets (i.e., router). It will decrease both transmission costs and bandwidth utilization, among other benefits. However, the edge analytics applications are not yet highly developed or sophisticated. Getting the kind of power source that can support such high-tech applications has become an issue. Therefore, in the event of a request needing robust compute, edge analytics must rely on the cloud.

16.13 Applications

Several sectors make use of edge analytics, such as the energy sector, the logistics sector, the manufacturing sector, and the retail sector. Edge analytics can be used for a wide variety of purposes, such as analyzing client behavior in retail settings, keeping tabs on industrial and logistics equipment, keeping an eye on energy usage remotely, and detecting fraud in financial institutions (ATMs). This section discusses how edge analytics can be applied to address problems in a variety of disciplines. Edge devices such as Wi-Fi networks, sensors, and CCTV are widely used by the retail industry to collect raw data. The number of customers at different times of day, the frequency with which discounts were used, and the quantity of images and videos taken are all examples of the information that was collected. By analyzing the raw data, businesses may better anticipate consumer behavior and tailor promotions to entice repeat business. Transferring data to the cloud for processing, however, will cause a delay in getting the results back. Thus, timely analysis is required to entice shoppers before they leave the business. Edge analytics are useful in these kinds of circumstances.

Sony et al. provided a service-oriented framework for personalized and real-time suggestion based on an interactive screen-based edge analytics system. Edge information and social media profile data are matched using matching algorithms based on common criteria like name and address. This ensures that analytics are consistently applied across all client channels inside the edge analytics framework. Social media engagement is a leading indicator of consumer intent to buy. As an example, edge analytics just needs to consider a customer's recent purchases and a small portion of their social media activity to provide them with real-time, customized suggestion services. It can be difficult to properly connect two entities, a social media entity and a business entity, because a single client may have many accounts on social media with different or similar names, as well as multiple bank accounts. Privacy should be prioritized in the edge analytics since some customers may want to use the service while keeping some purchases or items private.

The use of sensors to track which animals enter fields of crops, automated irrigation systems, real-time weather updates, and other forms of smart technology are all helping to elevate the agricultural sector. However, a human presence is still required round-the-clock, in case the owner needs to be notified to move the animals away from the crop field, for example. The use of edge analytics can help cut down on manual processes. We can keep an eye on the animals owing to video edge analytics. The alarm will ring if the animals go too close to the crop fields, and scare them away if they do. In the event that any livestock grazes outside of the designated area, or if another animal or unauthorized person enters the area, the owner is notified immediately. A weather report is essential for preserving the quality of the harvest. Say it's late in the day, and there's a probability of rain. After that point, morning irrigation of crops is no longer performed. In a similar vein, if the temperature is high, more crops will need to be watered. Bhargava et al. have proposed using edge analytics as a useful strategy for achieving precision in the dairy industry. The data is gathered by collars, in-field sensor nodes, and edge gateways. Monitoring the environment and the weather, the infield nodes are essential to any modern farm. Dairy cows are equipped with collar technology that monitors their vital signs and movement. These gadgets feed information into edge gateways, which subsequently forward it to the cloud. Due to the typically poor Internet connectivity present in a farm setting, the solution employs a delay-tolerant application. Because of this, it's possible to seamlessly move information between edge gateways and the cloud.

The GPS data is analyzed to get an idea of where the cow is. Because of storage constraints, the GPS data is now only sampled once every 15 minutes. By setting it up in this way, the device will last, on average, longer while consuming less power. The technology encrypts and compresses the raw data collected by the collar devices. Linear-SIP data compression is used to expand storage while decreasing processing time. The edge analysis helps keep an eye on the cows without the need for human intervention.

16.14 Transportation

A smart city's intelligent mobility system (ITS) allows for convenient and safe transportation via a network of sensors, wireless connections, and autonomous vehicles. Smart sensors installed in automobiles pave the way for ITS. These edge devices collect a plethora of disparate information about the passengers, the immediate environment, the car itself, and other nearby vehicles, all of which must be processed in real time. For efficient transportation, the vehicle, rather than the driver, must make a number of crucial decisions. Having these data transported to the cloud, analyzed, and then delivered back so that action may be taken; however, has a major impact on quality of service. As an added downside, postponing decisions can cause disastrous results like traffic bottlenecks and accidents. Because of this, ITS requires efficient edge analytics to facilitate timely decision-making based on real-time data.

There are a variety of sensors built into the automobile that keep tabs on things like speed, gas mileage, and driver fatigue. As storage on edge devices is sometimes meager and data overflows can lead to the loss of critical information, it is essential that unneeded data be purged. The amount of data that needs to be processed is still immense, even after filtering; therefore edge analytics must be efficient to quickly calculate such a vast quantity of real-time data. When an edge device can swiftly calculate to identify the optimal path, ITS's quality of service improves. A self-driving automobile must make its own decisions about how quickly to accelerate, where to go, and how to turn. These factors are, however, affected by the presence of nearby vehicles, people, and traffic signals. Congestion has a major impact on the route taken. Traffic congestion and delays can occasionally be caused by unforeseen circumstances, such as accidents. Rapid computation of real-time data is required to suggest a quick course correction to the driver in order to avert the driver from traveling such a road. The cars can be driven either manually by the driver or automatically. Mode switching in these automobiles is lightning fast. When the driver is in charge, the car is constantly giving them suggestions, such as when they are too near to another car or the best route to go.

However, it is difficult to provide such guidance since human drivers frequently make unanticipated decisions. The stakes are high if an attacker can trick an edge analytics machine into drawing the erroneous conclusions, therefore the technology must be solid. When a car is in self-driving mode, the human driver may not be able to take over the wheel immediately, making the situation extremely dangerous. Edge analytics can occasionally employ erroneous data, leading to poor conclusions, thus it's important to think about the safety of edge devices. To improve ITS, Jiang et al. presented a blockchain-based video edge analytics system. A vehicle and a node known as a road side unit (RSU) make up its two edge devices. Edge analytics are located in the road side unit, whereas the camera is located in the automobile node. The vehicle extracts individual frames from a video and sends them via vehicular networks to edge analytics, where they are processed. Blockchain technology allows for the secure storage of video in the RSU node and the exchange of data between several vehicles. The process of video edge analytics is broken down into sub-steps due to a lack of resources. The video decoding module is responsible for real-time decoding and decompression of the encoded video. The video is broken down into individual frames by the protocols used for real-time streaming. The preprocessing module makes adjustments to the brightness, contrast, and color temperature to fix problems caused by uneven lighting.

Semantic objects of a certain class can be located using the object detection feature. It is essential for the progress of driverless cars. The use of deep learning techniques to improve object recognition has led to significant advances in computer vision applications. The object tracking component determines where the object or objects have been at various periods. It's also used to make educated guesses about how busy the roads will be along the path the car takes. The path's environment can be better understood with the help of the semantic segmentation module, which can then be used to decide whether to make a course correction. A label is assigned to each pixel in a photograph, and that label is then assigned to one of several categories. The stereo module is responsible for transforming the camera's 2D images into 3D data. The optical flow component provides data for use in other programs as well as doing its own motion estimation and tracking. Through the use of the suggested edge analytics, the video offloading and resource allocation problem is converted into a discrete Markov decision process in which the reward is optimized. We apply deep reinforcement learning methods to solve the discrete Markov decision problem. Due to the unpredictability of traffic conditions, object detection processes need to be sped up. The computational demands of deep learning make it inappropriate for use in object detection.

The program should also perform well with dim or fuzzy videos (e.g., the video takes at a rainy season or during rain).

At busy intersections and elsewhere, the INcreasing TRAffic SAFety with EDge and 5G (InTraSafEd5G) system will detect bikes and pedestrians in the blind spots of cars and issue alerts. Computing and communication are the system's two primary components. The calculation is a joint effort of the hardware and the software. Installing edge devices, calculating space requirements, and placing cameras in optimal locations are all part of the hardware setup for ensuring constant surveillance of key intersections and walkways. The software part is known as edge analytics. Edge analytics receives footage from edge devices and then processes it with deep learning object detection techniques. The communication module relays user messages sent by the edge analytics in real time. An integral part of every communication system is the network and the applications that use it. The network piece is responsible for transmitting the data to the many drivers who are approaching the crossroads in a timely manner. The application's job is to keep tabs on the car's whereabouts and notify the driver of any problems via the app's user interface. TraSafEd5G facilitates communication via 5G networks. 5G is essential for instantly notifying motorists. To do this, TraSafEd5G uses cameras installed at busy junctions and pedestrian crossings. The videos are captured and sent to the camera's in-house edge analytics. Edge analytics are constantly processing the videos to identify people on foot and cyclists. When a vehicle is approaching the area, the edge analytics sends a notification with details on the number of items and a picture of each item detected. The driver's mobile device runs an app that can display and play audible alerts.

Information and videos are not stored for privacy concerns. If object detection is always active, it could take more time to process the video frames containing the item. The camera also requires constant power in order to function. There's a chance that the gadget can also gauge how fast the approaching vehicles are moving. Then, a special color on the traffic lights can alert pedestrians and cyclists. The (SCADA) infrastructure requires a connection to pre-existing remote telemetry units (RTUs). The inference feedback from the edge gateway to the RTU is handled independently. When the edge gateway uploads the latest data to the cloud, MLM(Masked Language Modelling) is refreshed to reflect the changes. Rod pumps and artificial lift systems are used to boost hydrocarbon production in producing wells. The effectiveness of rod pumps is measured by the use of dynagraph cards (i.e., position vs. load graphs). Generating a dynagraph card is a quick and simple process that requires no more than a few seconds. As a result, there is an issue with the storage of these cards. Data file management and archiving on a local level are employed for this purpose. The information is gathered by the RTU and sent to the SCADA host. It takes time for a specialist to spot any mechanical or manufacturing flaws. There is a window of time between gathering data and the risk of losing it. For this reason, these tasks are typically executed by means of machine learning algorithms. A supervised learning approach is utilized for cloud training.

To train a generic model with machine learning methods, historical dynagraph cards are digitized and then pixelized. The ability to foresee manufacturing issues is honed using a historical database of 6000 dynagraph cards. Subject matter experts label and categorize the cards prior to being used by operators or rod pumps. The assembling method combines MLM's prediction, giving more weight to the model that performed best for a given class of problems. The model is trained multiple times to get the desired level of precision. Once the MLM has reached the required accuracy, it is sent to the edge gateways. These inferences can make predictions in a matter of seconds while requiring fewer resources in practice. The training dynagraph cards require expert labeling. However, the constant generation of dynagraph after small intervals is the cause of the frequent modification of interference. As a result, edge analytics rely heavily on involvement from humans. Boguslawski et al. proposed an edge analytics strategy for rod pump monitoring. It makes use of ML approaches.

At the cutting edge, analytics may take the form of either assembly or generalization. The assembled technique develops a meta-model from the learned models. Data is trained on the edge devices. The failure of a machine or process can be more easily pinpointed with the help of the meta-model. Those inferences allow for the usage of less expensive hardware. The edge devices save the data to disc on a regular basis. The edge analytics continue to work even if there is no Internet connection. Disconnection in the cloud may lead to less precise inferences due to the small training dataset. Once the connection is established, the training model and the conclusions it generates are sent to the cloud. In cases where the user values secrecy, they can employ this technique. Machine learning methods that necessitate a lot of compute can't be run on edge devices because of the amount of effort required to assemble the techniques. Therefore, edge devices cannot support the implementation of a wide variety of machine learning methods. Edge analytics can deliver inferences without the cloud, albeit with reduced precision. A diagram showing how federated learning works. There are multiple devices, such as smartphones and laptops, that have local data and models. They communicate with a central server that aggregates the local models and updates the global model. Federated learning allows the devices to learn from each other without sharing their data, thus preserving privacy and reducing communication costs.

Edge analytics for end-to-end water leak localization and burst detection scheme proposed by Kartakis et al. takes advantage of the difference in arrival time of changes measured at the sensor location, as opposed to the traditional scenario of periodic reporting between backend servers and sensor devices. The event's timestamp is relayed to the backend, allowing for precise localization of the water explosion while simultaneously reducing communication costs. The decision control procedure decides how the pipe network will be modified using remotely controllable valves. The timestamp of the data is an input for edge analytics, which uses it to identify occurrences. The data from the sensor node pair is analyzed iteratively using edge analytics to spot outliers. Edge analytics can take compressed data as input, although the compression method is inefficient and has a limited storage capacity (10,000 rows maximum). Instability of the data can be influenced by the efficiency of the compression process. The system could use more memory-efficient data compression methods and more edge devices to lessen data volatility. The degree of data volatility changes according to the topology's edge nodes.

16.15 Hopes and Plans for the Future

In the near future, edge analytics will likely replace other technologies as the industry standard, creating new opportunities. The most promising avenue is the development of miniaturized hardware with enhanced processing power and storage capacity. Algorithms/techniques must be highly efficient and accurate while utilizing as few system resources as possible, according to software engineers. The backbone of edge analytics is information derived from either textual sources or images/videos. Music, like other forms of media, conveys information. The good news is that we can strengthen national security without punishing law-abiding citizens. Voice calls and the telephone can facilitate both domestic violence (including stalking) and international terrorist plots. A warrant and supporting proof are typically required before authorities can access a person's phone records in many countries. As a means of thwarting terrorist plans and other criminal enterprises, the government is lobbying for the ability to track the whereabouts and phone histories of its citizens. A common counterargument is that such widespread surveillance violates individual rights.

Edge analytics is the solution to this problem. At the edge, analytics can examine each call for context. Phone numbers and other identifying information are passed along to the proper authorities whenever a call involves potentially dangerous language, such as threats or harassment. To ensure the privacy of both parties, the system will delete any and all data associated with a regular or encrypted call. To this end, scientists are focusing on cutting-edge technologies with the help of federated learning (FL). For the purposes of federated learning, which is a type of machine learning, an algorithm is trained in a decentralized manner, meaning that it is learned by a network of devices. Edge analytics greatly benefits from federated learning due to the latter's ability to make the most of the limited resources available. A machine learning algorithm's training request from the edge analytics is often referred to as a "FL server." The FL server selects several edge devices from which to collect data for model training. From time to time, edge devices will update the FL server with new model data, which may include revised weights and parameters. In order to get the appropriate level of accuracy, this process is done as many times as necessary. There are numerous issues that need to be resolved, despite the fact that federated learning is a fantastic technique to employ machine learning algorithms in data analytics.

It's possible that not all edge devices utilized for federated learning have access to the same dataset. This increases the cost of communications as the dataset must be distributed over multiple edge devices. The trained model's performance may suffer if there is an unbalanced distribution of classes. In such a case, an additional rebalancing step is carried out. The selected edge devices have their data for the subclasses enhanced during pretraining. The cost of both sending and receiving texts is a major issue as well. Throughout each training session, there is a great deal of back-and-forth communication between edge devices and FL servers. In addition, a high-dimensional dataset necessitates additional rounds of transmission. Choosing which edge devices will take part in the network without using a load balancing mechanism is another difficulty. In any case, a staggered node will cause a delay in the training process. In light of the importance of achieving true cloud independence for edge analytics, FL is a viable option worth examining. In the sixth generation of communication networks, edge devices will be essential (6G). One of the most important specifications for 6G is a latency of less than 1 millisecond, and edge devices play a crucial role in achieving this.

The 6G network will rely heavily on edge devices to guarantee global coverage, high network node density, privacy, secrets, and security. Edge computing is one of the technologies that enables sixth-generation mobile networks. Edge devices will enable 6G and provide high-speed Internet with fewer interruptions. There will be real-time analysis of data. Edge devices (like drones) will act as key network nodes in times of crisis. At this time, the network's nodes are unable to communicate with one another. Wireless networking will be utilized to connect the edge devices that will be put throughout the network at crucial spots. Having a way to stay in touch with the rest of the world is made much easier by having access to a network like this. The timely distribution of food, medicine, and medical care is hampered by inadequate communication.

Edge devices will manage cutting-edge technology like holographic in addition to the home, traffic, grid, and environment. Augmented and virtual reality, telesurgery, tactile web browsing, and other similar technologies are all in the works.

16.16 Extreme 5G Networking

The market has recently been flooded with 5G advertisements from various telecommunications companies and service providers. Indeed, why not? Edge computing's advent and widespread use has spurred innovation in AI applications, while 5G has altered the landscape of edge computing significantly. It is fueling and hastening the adoption of cutting-edge and AI technology. In the contemporary epidemiological setting, there are numerous examples of 5G in usage. These are promoted as having high bandwidth and low latency, and they can be used for a broad variety of purposes, from distance education and gaming to watching live sports. There is potential to improve performance, strengthen data security, and elevate digital experiences by combining edge computing with 5G technologies. This essay will provide an introduction to 5G from an edge computing perspective.

16.16.1 A vocabulary for the 5G frontier

As we have seen in prior blog posts, edge computing provides new opportunities for businesses across many different industries. In order to fully grasp what or how 5G enhances various use cases, it is helpful to first become familiar with basic 5G-related terminology.

The 5G base station, or gNodeB, is in charge of transmitting and receiving data from and to UEs on the mobile network. Novel radio, a novel radio access method, is used (NR).

mmWave is a common kind of transmission for 5G networks. Due to the shorter range and the possibility of interference from building walls, the cells can only be as large as microwaves. Millimeter wave networks can employ much smaller antennas than older cellular networks did.

MEC: In a multi-access edge computing network architecture, supplementary processing is stored on the network's periphery, where it may be accessed quickly by users running latency-sensitive applications.

Virtualization, also known as network function virtualization (NFV), is an approach to network design that makes use of IT virtualization technologies to implement full virtualization of entire classes of network node operations.

Users' devices are linked to the rest of the mobile network by a radio connection at the RAN. 5G is able to accommodate both virtual radio access networks and the more traditional, physical aspects of a network (vRAN).

Software-defined networking (SDN) is an approach to managing network devices like routers and switches via a network using standard protocols for configuration and management.

In the 5G era, the packet gateway is known as user plane function (UPF). The parts in this set facilitate packet forwarding and routing, network connectivity, and policy enforcement. UPF is sometimes referred to as the data plane.

The 5G design has integrated network function virtualization (NFV) with native cloud standards/technologies to simplify network and service deployment, operations, and management.

16.17 Edge Data Classification and Storage Analysis

When using edge computing to assess IoT data at the edge, we are met with a deluge of information. The vast majority of the data that is generated every second by all devices—whether it be audio, video, sensory, or telemetry—is never stored locally, analyzed, or transmitted north to enterprise data centers or public clouds. Business organizations do not have the resources to store and handle all of this information. So now what are we supposed to do with all of this information? It is possible for businesses to properly classify edge data by adhering to a few criteria that will help them determine which data is essential and which can be safely discarded.

It's common to classify information according to the context in which it was gathered, be it a certain discipline or method. Statistics makes use of both quantitative and qualitative information. Data science takes it a step further by classifying data as nominal, ordinal, discrete, or continuous. In the world of database management systems, there are three types of information: transient, persistent, and useless. In order to better manage security and compliance, firms can classify data as either public, internal-only, confidential, or restricted. Additionally, there are methods for automatically classifying data based on its context and content. However, the data industry relies on three distinct classification methods: content analysis, context analysis, and user analysis.

16.17.1 Classifying information for a cutting-edge approach

There are two types of data that can be used in an edge solution:

Information about the end-user generated by the solution's devices, as well as information about the solution itself that is required for configuration and operation.

16.18 Edge-clustering Phenomenon

In many cases, the restricted resources of IoT devices and the high computational power required for processing and storing data render it impossible to run applications that rely heavily on IoT devices. Companies can use edge clusters to give their operations teams the adaptable, dependable environments they require to handle their data's storage, compute, low latency, high performance, and high bandwidth demands. In addition, the scalability that Kubernetes clusters are meant to provide can be required by some highly accessible on-premises shared services, such as edge cloud deployments.

An organization's use of an edge cluster as a logical resource barrier is common. The cutting-edge technologies are expensive for businesses to purchase. A large number of older, specialized devices with fixed functionality may have previously been installed and paid for. As a means to improve and secure their applications for the future, businesses can leverage edge cluster technology. An IoT platform or device management solution connects these devices via a small-footprint edge cluster. A previous blog entry titled "Policies at the Edge" demonstrated how to manage and run an edge cluster like an edge device.

16.18.1 The primary benefits of edge clusters are as follows

Make it easy and possible for users to increase the cluster's capacity as needed, a feature known as "scalability." The system may be set up to scale automatically, which reduces the workload on the operations staff.

Because the edge cluster processes and analyzes more data, you gain insights and can take action more quickly without spending as much time or money transmitting data to the cloud.

In addition to meeting data residency and isolation needs, processing data at the edge cluster also aids in meeting regulatory compliance needs. Highly available: The failback options on the cluster and the flexibility to add new nodes as needed ensure that the application will continue to run smoothly even if some nodes fail. Safe: No unsecured data transfers between the cluster's various app servers.

16.19 Safety on the Fringe

The large number and dispersed location of these devices makes their management a nightmare from a security perspective. Now that I think about it, the centralized nature of the solution and cloud-based control systems have caused problems with the IoT method in that very case. Prospective buyers are naturally interested in knowing how the benefit will be safeguarded. What are the best practices for shielding data and workloads at the edge against intrusion attempts? Can a modified device be detected and rendered ineffective? Can problem edge nodes be dealt with? Customers want to know whether there are any special precautions or new processes they should learn before venturing to the edge.

In an effort to answer these questions, this blog has evolved into a two-part story, with a high-level overview in the first part and more specifics in the second. Like this, IT safety is achieved.

Due to the nature of an edge solution, complete stack solutions are uncommon. The typical infrastructure includes hardware from a server provider, software from an IT technology supplier, sensors and devices from a wide variety of manufacturers, and (perhaps) the network from a telecom provider. It makes sense to rethink how we protect our IT networks now that they are largely hosted in data centers and the cloud.

All the equipment in a factory, for instance, is usually hermetically sealed so that no contaminating air may get in. In response, those who make industrial machinery have come up with highly specialized software for monitoring and controlling devices. We had to make those environments more open to give people more options, and it left them more vulnerable to attacks from hackers. Both Industry 4.0 and the Internet of Things played a role in this.

16.20 Alternatives in Edge Architecture

16.20.1 A boundary architectural choice

There is a wide variety of novel solution architectures at the periphery. Differences emerge as a natural consequence of the heterogeneity of edge topologies' many constituent parts, which might range from edge devices and compute servers to networks and clouds.

The key design concerns and the reasoning behind the chosen solutions are documented in well-known IT architectural decisions. In most cases, they are deliberate choices made throughout the design process that affect either the entire software system or one or more of its fundamental components and connectors. The same is true for developing cutting-edge answers. Solution architects are frequently put in the position of deciding which protocol, 5G vs. Private 5G, or edge server is best suited to receive data from a certain device. These, along with a great many other architectural details, require careful thought and decision-making.

Every AD, along with its justification, ramifications, and any rebuttals, needs to be recorded for future reference. In this article, we'll discuss some of the most frequently overlooked considerations while planning an edge architecture. To restate, edge includes everything from devices at the far edge to cloud-based processing and storage.

16.21 A Peripheral Approach to Automation

There are two ways to interpret the article's title. For those in the telecom industry, it's analogous to edge automation of networks. In the enterprise IoT/edge computing space, it evokes images of autonomous robots and other gadgets. Both statements are correct and relevant since network automation at the network edge is required to enable the autonomous devices at the network's very tip (i.e., the device edge). Network automation in the telecom business is enabled by 5G and software-defined networks (SDNs), while automation at the enterprise edge is enabled by smart devices, app auto-deployment, and AI/ML inferencing.

As mentioned in a previous article titled "5G at the Edge," edge computing and 5G connection offer near real-time automation, unlocking opportunities to enhance digital experiences and performance at the edge. The topology diagram in Figure 16.1 should help you recall this. The challenge is in determining which part to automate first and how to do it in a way that causes minimal disturbance.

16.22 The Edge and Data Sovereignty

Data sovereignty and sovereign clouds may seem at odds with edge computing and distributed clouds; however, this is not the case. The location of the command and control plane under administration appears to be the top priority. The cloud control aircraft is often asked to operate under strict limits set by customers. So long as the edge sites don't leave the country's borders, they can take part in the distributed cloud model while still meeting the sovereignty condition. Some examples will help:

- An international, remotely managed control plane flies beyond national airspace.
- Both remote-controlled and management-controlled aircraft are permitted within the territorial airspace of a nation.

16.23 Problems and Obstacles

The following are some of the most pressing concerns and difficulties associated with edge analytics:

Workload optimization involves taking into account energy consumption, latency, bandwidth, and construction and maintenance costs in order to determine how best to optimize the workload. Since edge devices are compact, their resources, battery, etc., are also compact. The complexity of the optimization problem increases as a result of the additional constraints placed on the four parameters.

Edge devices have limited memory because of their small form factor, which prevents them from processing or generating large files. This is problematic for both the input and the output, as data training for predictive edge analytics requires a large number of datasets, but edge analytics can only use a subset of these data for training.

Edge devices' limited storage space means that any data created by their sensors must be filtered and sent to the cloud for safekeeping; otherwise, the data will be destroyed from the edge devices to avoid memory overflow and to protect users' anonymity.

Powered by its own energy supply, computation and data analytics at the edge can function independently of a central data center. The small size of edge devices precludes the installation of large-sized batteries; hence, batteries used in edge analytics must be compact, secure, long-lasting, and rechargeable. One option is to use energy harvesting. The energy harvesting system includes the energy harvester, a power regulator, and a storage capacitor. Nonetheless, the output power is typically low and erratic, which is a major drawback. Because of this, there are constant blackouts. Due to a loss of power, the current execution has been aborted. Non-volatile memory is the answer to this problem. Process state and the currently used stack can be saved in non-volatile memory thanks to non-volatile processors (NVM). Checkpointing is the term for this process. Power management presents another challenge, as does balancing hardware and software needs. The majority of the time and energy spent while writing to NVM is caused by software. In hardware, the capacitor is used to hold the charge while waiting for the power supply to be restored. Another source of energy waste is the capacitor. More energy is consumed during charging if the capacitor's desired charging voltage is high.

Edge devices receive raw data, most of which is redundant. As a result, edge analytics requires the use of data-filtering techniques. In addition, the raw data needs to be transformed in some way before it can be used by the analytics program.

Powerful computational applications, such as deep learning, are being implemented by edge analytics. These highly computational apps cannot be deployed on edge devices because they lack the necessary infrastructure. As an added bonus, edge analytics allows for the use of numerous computationally-intensive algorithms in a single edge device. Therefore, it is challenging to schedule and manage resources for these algorithms.

In the case of computational offloading, the most crucial task is the construction of an optimal decision engine. The decision engine evaluates each task and decides whether or not to parallel split the computation and offload it to a remote server or the cloud. Due to the complexity of the decision-making process, offloading adds cost (e.g., offload time, latency, computation time).

16.24 Conclusion

When considering the speed at which the globe and its data are expanding, it becomes clear just how sluggish the cloud may be. To address this issue, a new type of technology called "edge computing" is being developed to place users' devices in physical proximity to cloud servers. In this work, we demonstrate how edge devices can perform analytics with the help of edge analytics. Several edge applications that can process text, images, and videos are also discussed. Using data filtering performed at the edge, cloud storage and bandwidth are conserved. In addition, it explains how machine learning and AI algorithms may make edge analytics smarter, allowing them to function autonomously (as in industry) while still aiding healthcare and smart devices. But edge analytics is just getting started; it faces several obstacles in its infancy. The phrase "need to be addressed" implies that the challenges are urgent or important and cannot be ignored or postponed.

Index

About the Editors

Pethuru Raj PhD works as a chief architect at Reliance Jio Platforms Ltd. (JPL) Bangalore. Previously, he worked as cloud architect in the IBM global Cloud Center of Excellence (CoE), an enterprise architect in Wipro consulting services (WCS), and software architect in Robert Bosch Corporate Research (CR). In total, he has gained more than 22 years of IT industry experience and 8 years of research experience. He finished his CSIR-sponsored Ph.D. degree at Anna University, Chennai and continued with UGC-sponsored postdoctoral research in the Department of Computer Science and Automation, Indian Institute of Science (IISc), Bangalore. Thereafter, he was granted a couple of international research fellowships (JSPS and JST) to work as a research scientist for 3.5 years in two leading Japanese universities.

Dr. Abhishek Kumar is currently working as an Assistant Director/Associate Professor in the Computer science & Engineering Department in Chandigarh University, Punjab, India. He has a doctorate in computer science from University of Madras and is post-doctoral fellow in Ingenium Research Group Ingenium Research Group Lab, Universidad De Castilla-La Mancha, Ciudad Real, and Ciudad Real Spain. He has total of more than 11 years of academic teaching experience along with 2 years of teaching assistantship. He has more than 100 publications in reputed, peer reviewed national and international journals, books & conferences. He has guided more than 30 M.Tech and M.S. Projects at national and international level and guided 6 Ph.D. Scholars at national and international Level. He is acting as Series Editor for three books series, Quantum Computing with Degruyter Germany, Intelligent Energy System with Elsevier, and Sustainable Energy with Nova, USA.

Dr. T. Ananth Kumar works as Associate Professor and R & D head in IFET college of Engineering (Autonomous) affiliated to Anna University, Chennai. He received his Ph.D. degree in VLSI Design from Manonmaniam

Sundaranar University, Tirunelveli. He received his master's degree in VLSI design from Anna University, Chennai and bachelor's degree in electronics and communication engineering from Anna University, Chennai. He has presented papers in various national and international conferences and journals. His fields of interest are networks on chips, computer architecture and ASIC design. He has received awards such as Young Innovator Award, Young Researcher Award, Class A Award – IIT Bombay and Best Paper Award at INCODS 2017. He is the life member of ISTE, IEEE and few membership bodies. He has many patents in various domains. He has edited four books and has written many book chapters for Springer, IET Press, and Taylor & Francis press.

Dr. Neha Singhal has about 13 plus years of experience in teaching. She is presently working as an Assistant Professor, Dept. of Computer Science at Christ University, Central Campus, Bangalore, India. She obtained her Ph.D. Degree from VTU, Belgaum and M. Tech in Computer Science degree from Banasthali University, Rajasthan. Her teaching and research interests are in the field of web services, AI,ML and IoT. She is a professional member of ISTE and IEEE society. Dr. Singhal has published research papers and book chapters in various Scopus-indexed and ESCI indexed journals. She has delivered technical talks and has been invited as a resource person to several colleges in Bangalore and India. She received four government funded projects from various funding agencies during 2018 to 2020. She has received an "Appreciation Award" for her exemplary services at RRCE.

For Product Safety Concerns and Information please contact our EU
representative GPSR@taylorandfrancis.com
Taylor & Francis Verlag GmbH, Kaufingerstraße 24, 80331 München, Germany

www.ingramcontent.com/pod-product-compliance
Ingram Content Group UK Ltd.
Pitfield, Milton Keynes, MK11 3LW, UK
UKHW021111180425
457613UK00001B/23